# Fragile Lives

## Violence, Power and Solidarity in Eighteenth-Century Paris

Arlette Farge

Translated by Carol Shelton

Polity Press

This English translation © Polity Press 1993
First published in France as *La vie fragile* © Hachette 1986

First published in 1993 by Polity Press in association with Blackwell Publishers

Published with the assistance of the French Ministry of Culture.

Editorial office:
Polity Press
65 Bridge Street
Cambridge CB2 1UR, UK

Marketing and production:
Blackwell Publishers
108 Cowley Road
Oxford OX4 1JF, UK

ISBN 0 7456 0643 1

ISBN 0 7456 1243 1 (pbk.)

A CIP catalogue record for this book is available from the British Library.

Typeset in 10 on 12 pt Sabon
by Best-set Typesetter Ltd., Hong Kong
Printed in Great Britain by TJ Press (Padstow) Ltd., Padstow, Cornwall

This book is printed on acid-free paper.

# Contents

# Introduction

---

This book was born out of the archives – not from a set of documents, nor from chronicles, memoirs, novels or treatises of a judicial, administrative or literary nature. No, none of these.

It came quite simply from the judicial archives – the odd scrap, snatch of a phrase, fragments of lives from that vast repository of once-pronounced words that constitute the archives – words emerging from the darkness and depths of three successive night-times: of time and oblivion; of the wretched and unfortunate; and last (and most impenetrable for our own stubborn minds), the night of guilt and its grip. Such are the archives, or as Michel Foucault has put it: 'Lives of a few brief lines or pages; misfortunes and mishaps without number, all bundled together in a handful of words ... Inglorious lives put to rest in the few brief lines that brought them down.'[1]

Historians who find themselves caught up with original sources become so fascinated by the archives that involvement with them makes it almost impossible to avoid self-justification through them or to resist the temptation to suppress any doubts these might cast on their own perceptions and systems of rationality or those of others. The impact the archives have on the historian (scarcely ever recognized explicitly) sometimes has the effect of actually denying their value. Fine though they might be, they are nonetheless full of pitfalls, and the corollary of their beauty is their deceptiveness. Any historian taking them on board cannot but be wary of the improbable outlines of the images they conceal.

This ambiguous relationship with the archives, resulting from various movements and ideological trends, has marked the course and development of historical writing over a long period. That is to say, one could, if one so chose, study recent trends in historical writing by means of an analysis of the successive tensions that history has created between itself and the archives. It was, for instance, in the hope of breaking free from the imperialism of a certain type of social and economic history, as well as from the somewhat tedious history of ideas, that the history of 'mentalities' came into being.

Fundamental to this approach was the conviction that the 'everyday' could be discovered in whatever one happened to glean from the individual subjects of history; that priority should be given to sources which hitherto had not been considered as such; and that one should no longer work on the 'great' figures and 'grand' events of history, but with 'the odd word here and there'.[2] Beliefs, emotions, the irrational and the marginal came along to lend colour to a view of the world which had hitherto been portrayed solely through the ideas of the great and mighty. An average man was constructed who was supposedly representative of a certain type of society; and the metaphors used for this discovery were those of the apparent and the visible, of light and dark. The archives reigned supreme.

But then our sight became blurred and our spirits recoiled before this over-generalized elaboration of the ordinary, everyday man as the typical portrait of a nation or epoch, and hence the arrival on the scene of the extreme, the atypical and the extraordinary which became in their turn some of the standards by which social complexities might be assessed. And once again in order that the historian's irrepressible urge to avoid wandering too far afield from the paths of explanation might be respected, there arose the notion of the 'exceptional normal',[3] which is so admirably illustrated by the Italian school of *microstoria*. Parallel with this development came the rise of 'case-studies', under the growing influence of anthropology and its particular ability to let the detail speak.

To provide a fuller account of the many and various inflexions of history would obviously require a much more detailed explanation; at the present time there seems to be a certain weariness with detail, perhaps from fear of losing the thread of the great historical adventure as a result of the tenacious pursuit of it or of losing sight of the solid bones of a past which must be retained at all costs, lest by some misfortune the future should slip through one's fingers (which would be quite unreasonable).

There is, therefore, a steady if barely perceptible return to what one might call more structured horizons, where once again the important task is the creation of grand theses and syntheses and the attribution of global explanations to a past which one would dearly love to see firmly within the grasp of one's senses. It is as though one needed to rediscover some previous history of ideas with a reassuring profile but with its features all fresh and rejuvenated thanks to all the recent 'minimal' and 'minuscule' work that has been carried out. And thus those sites which had barely been opened up a few years ago are being closed, and rumour has it that history is elsewhere and that work on them is no longer fashionable.

In the course of these developments, however, two questions concerning the connections with the archives remain unanswered.

First, does the seductive influence of the archives risk falsifying or distorting the object being studied; and might not the emotional and aesthetic link with these once buried words be itself a handicap or a rejection of reality, or prove too facile and ambiguous a means of entering into a discourse with history?

Second, is there a tendency to attribute overmuch meaning to these archives, emerging as they do from silence; and rather than a reflection of the real, might they not in fact be the oasis for satisfying our own thirst to see the poor and wretched spring to life? And might not one particular or exceptional document risk ruining the source work by earning the label of *misérabilisme*?

I have been in constant dialogue with these two questions (archives as seductress and archives as deceptive mirror of reality) for several years. I have chosen to work only from judicial archives, and my reading of popular Parisian society in the eighteenth century is based on these. The archives are the motivation for my practice and work as a historian. They are the grain which I sift for form and meaning. It is through them that I have met Robert Mandrou, Philippe Ariès and Michel Foucault, and it is thanks to them that I can today attempt a reply to the two questions formulated above.[4]

In the discipline of history, anything in the way of feeling or emotion is suspect; and in all fairness it is a mistrust that is well founded, for to it we owe the avoidance of many a deadend, particularly when identification and personal projection lead to embarrassing anachronisms.

Yet it is impossible to avoid entering the realm of aesthetics and emotion, given the kind of documents which have been discovered. The fine sand of history is made up of poor and lowly lives, impoverished and tragic existences, and of mean, contemptible and lacklustre personalities; they constitute its fragile yet essential thread. Surfacing as they do from oblivion, they remain at a distance from literature because they are stuck awkwardly in the cramped forms of the judicial apparatus. They are fragmentary lives because they were broken, or quite simply interrupted one day under interrogation. Coming into contact with them arouses emotion although it is not quite clear why. Perhaps it is because they failed in this way that these lives give the impression of possibilities or perhaps it is because they are so strange and distant that they can seem so close.

Emotion. The word is out! It is a word which is almost taboo for anyone who professes to be a student of social matters. But as I understand it, emotion is not, as is commonly believed, an exclusion of reason nor a kind of sugary sentimentality to be used for coating over whatever sections of reality it encounters with a uniform gloss. On the contrary it is one of the main supports for the process of research and understanding; and it is through the breach opened up between oneself and the object under consideration that enquiry enters in. Emotion does not necessarily engender contemplation nor oblation; it is also the ardour and assiduity required for understanding the violence and weakness of things and the mediocrity and extraordinariness of situations; it is also an encounter with the unfamiliar as well as a means of allowing oneself to be affected by what one already knew.

Thus if we can agree that emotion requires our acknowledgement (itself an achievement) then the emotional and the aesthetic can be seen differently, and are no longer what historians, quite rightly, prefer they should *not* be. For emotion is not fusion between oneself and the archives or the annihilation of all capacity to think in concrete terms, but rather the development of a reciprocity with the object, by which access is given to meaning. Emotion opens up into an attitude which is proactive rather than passive, allowing one to lay hold of the written word in order to take it, not as the result of research, but as a means of apprehending social life and thought. It can project the receptive person beyond his or her own preferences and ideologies, received thinking and stereotypes, and its surprises can be disturbing (surprise or fright, disgust or fear always take one outside oneself). We might find some of our usual habits coming unstuck as we encounter some of the rather strange characters reconstituted from the archives. The emotions which arise from such discoveries might lead us along uncertain paths which call on an unknown part of ourselves, which is a far cry from the 'mollification' which is so often described and decried. Emotion is, in fact, animating!

The archives are not precise, in the sense that one would understand the science of mathematics, for example; nor do they reveal the secret source where the organization of the truth might reside. Nor are they any more attractive for being tragic (evoking as they do, those chaotic lives in which frenzy, wickedness and cunning combine with the pitiful, to reveal more often than not, incompetence, insignificance and petty malice rather than solemn heroism). There is nothing sublime about the archives, or if there is, then it is only in the sense that each one of us is no more nor less sublime (no more than Christine V and no less than Cartouche).

Putting on stage a few poor bit players might upset some of our emotions; for it means dwelling a while on what is small or modest, imperfect or vile, in order to consider its meaning and make sense of it.

Nor does the meaning deliver itself up immediately. The judicial archives, for example, are entirely bound up within the judicial and police systems of the eighteenth century which produced and managed them. What they put on view results from their origins and they exist only because a certain exercise of power brought them into being. They thus allow us to see the manner in which personal and collective behaviour overlapped and interlocked for better or for worse in the very conditions formulated by the authorities themselves. They are not 'reality', but at every step of the way, they demonstrate a particular type of adjustment to certain forms of coercion or to norms which were either imposed or internalized. This adjustment, consisting of words, deeds and cries of hope or defiance, is the motive force of historical reflection and the instrument for considering the period and its social groups. This obligatory coexistence between the State and private lives conceals shattered figures whose outlines we may be able to perceive.

In fact, one may go even further: a single isolated document from the archives has all the beauty of rarity – so rare in fact that there is a tendency to attribute overmuch meaning to it. But it is not, in fact, *the* word of the people nor of the poor. It defies and flies in the face of scholarly argument and discourse and, should one read it thoroughly, it shatters received opinion. Here, in support of my case, I take up once again one of the approaches of J. Rancière in his book *La Nuit des prolétaires* which sees more 'sophistication' in the archives than is customarily admitted.

The argument is that what is portrayed in the archives is in itself evidence of an entrenched 'need for the real'; (and there is certainly no shortage of concerned prose on the subject offering us a picture of popular misery and naivety which in itself contains traces of an imaginary or perceived landscape and thus a rejection of the everyday). These traces are worth pursuing and considering if we ourselves are to avoid becoming stuck in well-worn paths or predetermined schemas.

It is possible that the archives may be a rejection of the meaning we seek to attribute in advance to events and a shift away from any attempts at global theorizing. For me, they are the emergence of existences which offer our knowledge an extra bonus in as much as one is prepared to admit the possibility of transforming the accepted rules of social evolution. The archives are always explosive, and their meaning is never grasped once and for all. In this case, they are neither faithful to reality nor totally representative of it; but they play their part in this reality, offering differences and alternatives to other possible statements. They are not the truth but the beginnings of a truth and an eruption of meaning maintaining the greatest possible number of connections with reality. The archives present the exceptional and never the normal; in an excess of normality or lack of it we may discover bits of reality which otherwise might be lost to us in the overworked terrain of our knowledge.

I also like to think of the archives as an eruption; because eruption suggests an attack, an incursion, or a sudden and unexpected entry or invasion; for it is in this way that the archives come into their own. They burst bounds, break out, overflow. They are caprice, whim, tragedy – neither endorsing nor affirming. They neither summarize nor smoothe over conflict or tension. They ruffle the feathers of the real with their inopportune sorties and sallies. From this the historian must tease both sense and nonsense and, from all these loose ends, contradictions and observations, knit together a text – a rugged text – in which each incident is presented in its own terms.

In my study of popular Parisian behaviour in the eighteenth century, I am reconstituting shapes and forms and sketching outlines from minute accounts or forgotten conflicts. I am putting on view pictures from the past not for the love of drawing (or the picture itself) nor for the sake of the description, but because it is through these that one is able to follow men and women as they grapple with the whole of the social scene. We see them face to face with each other – choosing or encountering one another; meeting and parting; living with their children and their neighbourhood. And then, faced with work in the workshop or factory, we see them forming themselves into associations in order to improve their lot or finding themselves controlled and dominated by the utopian thinking of the authorities and the police, who were themselves also known to entertain conflicting dreams and aspirations in which individuality and awareness of self played their part. And finally, we see them in the face of collective events – the street spectacles and displays of power by the authorities of either a festive or a repressive nature, revealing beneath their apparent impulsiveness and impetuosity, the rules of their rationality or modes of thought.

From these sketches there emerges a picture of precariousness and strength along with a determination not to allow oneself to be abused or sold short. In Paris everything lived, moved and died in endless succession before the eyes of everyone else in an open space where one's neighbour, whether friend or foe, was the permanent witness to oneself. Emerging from the physical promiscuity, the inevitable sharing of fear and want, the difficult separation between public and private life, there is a profile of men and women stubbornly pursuing their way.

In these fragments clipped from their lives, disruption scarcely conceals their wrath and determination; and behind the written words – sometimes false, unjust or outrageous – there are traces of decisive encounters: those between men and women according to the roles assigned them by their sex; those made to accommodate the social and economic conditions imposed on them; and those gatherings together as a crowd, when in their own way they sought the greatest possible proximity with the justice of things.

It is of these encounters that I have attempted a considered account.

# Part I
# Feelings and Metamorphoses

---

# 1

# Space and Ways of Life

———————————

The apartment building in the Quinze-Vingts market, parish of Saint-Roch, looks like every other apartment building in Paris – a profusion of shops and workrooms intersected by passages and alley-ways and packed to the roof with lodgings and dormitories.[1] Laying bare its secret places and displaying its wounds, it offers scant refuge but none the less affords some sleep and rest of a kind, albeit without comfort and with practically no privacy.[2]

This damp anthill of a place is populated from top to bottom, not even the smallest space remaining unused. On the ground floor Widow Cochard has a struggle to keep her cod dry on account of the water dripping down the walls; but this has allowed the old Rambure woman to set up trade in herbs and chicory. What surplus there is can be sold each morning on the market square; and in the butcher's shop the stalls hardly leave enough room for the boys and journeymen who sleep on the wooden trestles once their day's work is over.

In the back room of a poultry shop overlooking the courtyard, there are turkeys roasting until dawn, ready for sale the next morning; and through the open windows of the carpenter's workshop come the sounds of the master joiner encouraging his two apprentices to get on with their planing instead of waving to customers and calling to the lads across the way. The flat above them belongs to Mme Simonne. She sells cooked meats made from scraps left over from the plates of the rich which she keeps in huge earthenware bowls prior to selling them off on her market stall. This she guards jealously, as it is in such an enviable position; she has even been known to resort to blows to defend it from street sellers who had risen early and beaten her to it.

Her bedroom door opens onto the unlit hovel which is the home of a coachman and his wife, a washerwoman. There are a lot of washerwomen living in this building, where the smell of dirty washing is barely distinguishable from the river water brought up from the Seine each morning by watercarriers, who keep the butts on each floor well filled. Through two half-open doors, trails of washing ignore the damp and steal onto the landing in a bid to get dry. Down below in the passageway, next to the herbalist, bundles of linen await delivery that same evening. Windows steam up, the stairs are slippery and the damp gets into everything. On the landing, the aroma of roast turkey mingles with the stench of filthy water, if not with the more pungent reek of dried cod.

On the quarry balcony – a type of verandah running around the inner courtyard of the building[3] – three little boys play quoits in between errands for their parents. They hardly notice one of the herb-grower's servants pestering a little girl who has come up to the pinmaker's on the third floor to collect her supply of pins for sale in the street.[4] Noise! Noise everywhere – and eyes – following you from window to door, landing to passageway. The dressmaker from the fourth floor decides to take advantage of the better light in the courtyard and do some finishing-off on the pavement. The journeymen joiners give her the usual chat but she's neither young nor old enough to mind.

Suddenly, everything stops. Between door and landing of the third floor an argument breaks out involving the seamstress and the men billeted beneath the roof. It's the fourth time in two days that they've bawled insults and abuse at one another.[5] Three gent's handkerchieves have apparently gone missing and the seamstress seems in a peculiar hurry to embroider some rather similar-looking items. Sitting in front of her door, she discreetly smuggles the linen between her legs and gathers it up under her apron. Her neighbour from the room opposite comes to her rescue; she is a fishwife, hot-tempered and loud-mouthed.

Everyone has stopped work. Axes stand ready, needles poised mid-air, wash dollies in hand. Everyone is waiting to see what will happen. The racket grows louder – the joiner's wife dashes upstairs four at a time, hurriedly unfastening her apron, which she brandishes at the men. They can't make out whether she is angry or joking, which annoys them even more. The youngest one grabs hold of the seamstress by her lawn bonnet. She loses her balance, trips on the stairs and falls flat in the middle of the children's game. Then all at once, for whatever reason – fear of going too far, or having to summon help yet again, or of being hauled up once more before the police commissioner whose premises are close by,[6] everything calms down. Everyone carries on as before, coming and going as normal. It was just another one of those unfortunate incidents.

The evening is drawing in now and is only likely to be disturbed by the nightly flight of young Gervais, a slender young lad of 11, employed in the master locksmith's shop nearby. Every single night the locksmith's wife and the most senior journeyman chase after him to get him to clear up the workshop, and every single night he clears off, as crafty as a cat, cutting across lodgings and passageways in one bound, knowing the building inside out, as he does. He finally comes to a halt at the top of the loft, where he presses his nose to the window and pronounces on all and sundry, lord of all he surveys.

Dark silhouettes and everyday scenes. The customary restless activity of a building which combined within its walls the hours of work and time at home, daily contact and petty squabbles, chit-chat and callousness. What it amounted to was having to live in full view of someone else's gaze, that ever-present visitor whose intervention shaped lives and transformed them. One life interfered with another, and at times the two became merged. The apartment building was a living person and, along with all the others, it made up the district.

There were 20 districts in Paris and 48 commissioners to keep an eye on them, closely monitored and under the strict supervision of the Lieutenant-General of Police. They were all different and, as Lenoir wrote in his 'Mémoires': 'In each part of this city, there was a marked difference in the customs and way of life.'[7] Each district afforded an informed dialogue with the police and provided an invaluable frame of reference for its inhabitants.

The police commissioner, who was regularly in receipt of complaints, advice, letters and requests, tested its pulse from day to day, and as agent of calm, moderation, provocation and consolidation, he lived within the rhythm of its minor hiccups or its serious traumas. It was his job to keep it informed, running smoothly and in decent shape. He talked and wrote about it as he would a person, and whenever the Lieutenant of Police consulted him on a serious matter affecting the district, he used a vocabulary which could equally well have applied to a harmless, yet uncontrollable animal. The commissioner's infinite capacity to 'hear' the district was, without doubt, an altogether indispensable yardstick for the Lieutenant-General of Police.

The district was a well-defined territory in which everyone found his or her place in relation to a neighbour or to someone else – someone in such and such a trade, for instance, or serving in this or that shop, or standing anxiously at a certain place in the main concourse to be sure of keeping a 'business' pitch which was, in effect, a livelihood. The channels of information traceable from housemaid to journeyman, from servant to street seller, were fluid and imprecise – having all the hallmarks, in a word, of hearsay.

As well as an area, the district was a sounding board, a kind of living entity reacting to events and to the good and bad fortune of its people, a background presence throughout testimonies and interrogations. It was always a good sign to be known in one's area, but on the other hand it did no good to be seen as a bit of an oddity or a layabout, and worse still, to upset the community. It received both people and their situations, weighed up reputations and transmitted them. It was the director of a complicated game with serious consequences for those who lost their way. An actor of exemplary ability, it was at once faceless and multiform, and while lacking any consistency other than geographic, it nevertheless extended its influence daily. It held no civil or judicial authority, yet at the same time possessed both. It was also an impressive transmitter, imparting its wisdom at the point between action and assimilation – incidents later diagnosed by the police and the State as feverish or mad, docile or passive, innocent or loyal.

Nothing of what happened here was insignificant, either for the police or for its inhabitants. If we take a closer look at some of these incidents we shall hopefully gain a better understanding of the position it held, and of the methods used to interpret and ultimately contain it.

All the basic aspects of life were under police supervision. Traffic and commerce, amongst other things, had to flow freely, the collection of refuse needed monitoring, and the rules applying to *cabarets*[8] and proprietors of furnished lettings had to be respected. The list was obviously endless, but the chief fear of the Lieutenant-General of Police never varied: should he do his utmost (or do nothing) to prevent the spread of rumours in the various districts?

The whole subject of 'weight', for instance, was a notorious sore point which could quite often lead to litigation, as it was here that fraud, trafficking and injustice kept constant company, bringing in their wake the wrath of the public who were naturally concerned about their food supplies.[9]

In 1766 the Lieutenant-General of Police, Sartine, wrote hastily to his commissioners that there had been a wave of public discontent over meat which had been badly bled, as well as inaccurate measures and the resulting unfair prices. He wrote:

> On my instructions police inspectors are to monitor the purveyance of meat in their districts. However, this precautionary measure is not sufficient in itself, and I would be most obliged to Your Good Selves if you could occasionally look into the matter by checking with your police courts that weights and measures are accurate and that there are no monopolies which I ought to clamp down on.[10]

But in spite of these precautions the price of meat continued to rise at an alarming rate and two years later complaints were clearly audible. This time Sartine wanted everything under control, not just the complaints, but also the comments on everyone's lips which were lending a worrying tone to the district. He exclaims:

> The price of meat is going up and they have the audacity to inform the public that it is with my approval. As this is most certainly not the case, I would be most grateful if you would keep me informed of any complaints which might be referred to you concerning this matter of price rises as well as any mistaken assumptions held by the butchers, their stallholders or their errand boys.[11]

The hunt for loose talk, comment and rumour was one of the essential preoccupations of the government of the capital. The attachment of so much importance to this activity, as in the planting of *mouches*[12] and official observers whose job it was to 'seize' anything said in public places,[13] shows well enough how useful a tool the spoken word was for the police. It was in fact a tide to be harnessed and stemmed. Such an attitude to what one might call gossip is hardly surprising when one considers that its importance in the eyes of those responsible for its circulation was enhanced in proportion to the vigour of the police in pursuing it. This interaction resulted in a never-ending game of elaboration and embellishment between the 'talking' public on the one hand, whose verbal communication was considered a highly prized instrument, and the police on the other hand, whose responsibility it was to gather the gossip, the more effectively to contain it. Neighbourhood gossip was not just a product of the district, it was also the fruit of whatever the circumstances, the inhabitants or the police chose to make it. It was a sophisticated product which cannot be attributed entirely to the people, as though they alone were responsible for secreting, nurturing and manipulating it, for by gathering the gossip, the police were actively involved in its generation, a parameter well worth remembering.

This constant ebb and flow of words affected everyone in the neighbourhood but they knew how to deal with it. There was nothing more powerful, for instance, than those exchanges of words between neighbours, which could sometimes be taken as veritable declarations of war, and where even a loose word might result in an arrest or a summons to appear before the commissioner.

Martin Triollet (a humorous man as his cross-examination indicates), knew this only too well. In 1750 he was accused of saying to a neighbour who was out of work and bemoaning his lot, 'Go and beat up the Provost or, better still, grab hold of some children. You should be able to make a living then.' He was referring to the abduction of children in the very middle of Paris. He chose his words badly, however, and was immediately suspected of abducting children himself; his sarcastic comments and witty remarks were quickly taken as proof of his own illicit activity. Under interrogation, he reacted strongly to the distortion of his words and pointed out that 'he knew very well that he had enemies who wanted him out of the way';[14] but he added that 'as the Good Lord had also had them, he knew he must be patient'.

There is no doubt that patience in the face of the rapid spread of gossip is wisdom of a kind. Some words are akin to waves. They swell, unfurl, then break and die, leaving in their wake a brief moment of respite.

The district did not live by words alone, however. It lived to the rhythm of its own internal events, which held it in their sway and affected it more or less seriously. These ranged all the way from schoolboy japes to serious scandal, by way of insulting behaviour towards prostitutes. Whatever it might be, it was all an integral part of the 'décor' which lent each district its own particular features.

Causing a scandal was good enough reason for the police to intervene and was the motive usually cited for putting a stop to situations deemed potentially harmful to the social climate. The 'care'[15] of the district required the commissioners to deal with any problems in danger of stirring up public opinion. Subsequently a part of their time was devoted to 'the friendly resolution of quarrels and disputes within the walls of their *hôtels*'.[16] If this should fail, the parties concerned were to be 'forbidden from further insulting and abusing one another and then sent back to settle things as best they might'.[17]

The task was of the essence – scandal and public order were mutual enemies! 'Whether scandal is the result of fact or fabrication, it stirs up such ferment amongst citizens as to be detrimental to their peace of mind.'[18] It couldn't be clearer. If anyone was petitioning for the imprisonment of someone whose behaviour was thought to be outrageous and unacceptable, the commissioner would summon that person to his *hôtel*; and he would talk with the complainant. Occasionally he would summon whoever was at the root of the scandal, attempt to hear one or two witnesses and test the pulse of the neighbourhood with the help of a few observers. Then he would calm things down, discuss, moderate, chide and scold and finally send off a report to the Lieutenant-General of Police.[19] In this, he would state quite clearly which of the parties, if any, he thought enjoyed a good reputation, which would obviously influence the decision. The important thing about this endearing little procedure was basically the reputation of the district, which brought it either peace and stability or ferment. Nor was the parish priest inactive in such matters. It was not uncommon for him to alert the commissioner to facts which he considered intolerable and which were thus ruining good relations within his district.

In 1777 the priest of the Ile Saint-Louis wrote to Commissioner Thierry urging him to take a firm hand in the following matter:

Sir: Marie Anne Bassin, fruiterer, Rue des Deux Ponts, Ile Saint-Louis, is the wife of Marie Marc Plombier who lives some 20 leagues from Paris as the result of a banishment order carrying the death penalty to which he was condemned ten or twelve years ago for stealing lead. From the moment her husband left, this brazen woman has lived openly in the most shocking state of moral dereliction, and in particular for the last five years, with Etienne Chair. He is a Protestant and former wine merchant's assistant. Now married and an established wine vendor himself, he has premises next to the aforementioned fruiterer. By their mutual consent, she has had three children by him in three years, in full public light and knowledge. First, a boy, 24 January 1770, another boy 22 November 1771 and a girl 30 June 1773. She has two others by one or two different fathers and one of these children is at La Pitié.[20] The commissioners' registers are full of such children, as we know. Moreover, her house is used as an address for prostitutes and her behaviour is upsetting everyone in her district and the rest of the 'Ile' on account of the widespread publicity given to her disorderly conduct. You must impose your authority.[21]

The 'Ile', it would appear, was in disarray and her disorderly behaviour was attracting widespread publicity. What was more, the man was a Protestant and the children were born and bred 'in full public light and knowledge'. The community was outraged, things had come to a head and everyone was of the same mind – it was time to intervene! But it was the commissioner who had the final say and Thierry seemed not to share the view that the Ile Saint-Louis was at boiling point. He replied laconically, 'Give her a month to mend her ways for she has a business to conduct and besides, she is the main tenant in the building where she lives.' (Being in charge of a block of flats was no mean thing, of course, and in any case, most things work out in time . . .).

Although it was primarily an 'oral' society, the spread of scandal was not always restricted to word of mouth and it did sometimes arise in written form as in the case of defamatory posters, for instance, which were another source of anger and indignation. Usually written in an unpractised hand and more often than not phonetically, they were glued hastily to the doors of houses. Here are two such anonymous and defamatory posters, placed on the walls of the Ile Saint-Louis in 1763 (the second in February):

Monsieur Barbot, Deliverer of Infants, Rue Gratier has got Peras the young surgeon's apprentice living round his place and this lousy debaucher has been living for some time with the wife of Cayou the master mason's son in the same street and they're always together night and day and Jannot Cayou puts up with it and one of them ought to be put away and the other one sent off to the workhouse but what else can you expect from a rascal like this who has seen both his parents on the gallows at the Place de Grève, and the rest of them on the run for the same thing.[22]

Lamare, joiner, Rue St Louis, is a whoremonger and he's had the pox three times. He's got the wife of a poor serving man for his tart and he's given her the clap and her husband as well. The husband caught them both at it and got the guard to take them up before a commissioner. Now that the woman's at the workhouse, he's got some other woman in to have some fun with. He's got Julienne Rousselot acting as his Madam. It's my pleasure to inform the public so that they may know that the women and girls going into that house are low-life.[23]

Posters and comments. All part of neighbourhood life, that intimidating shadow, crossroads of reputations, and manufacturer of honour or disgrace, which reared itself up like a person to be reckoned with. It was called as witness, defied or ignored, but in a serious conflict such as stoppage of work or a skirmish on the arrest of a beggar, for example, it would be sought after and would emerge in great numbers and in full cry. In a punch-up it would have already sorted out the rights and wrongs of the matter well before the arrival of the guard; it would also have separated the combatants, assessed the blame or further inflamed the fighting. The noise of the crowd would determine the attitude of the police, who themselves were torn between the need to make concessions or to reprimand what they referred to as 'la canaille'.[24]

Observed and captured in its secret moods and moments, spied on when angry, the district was also invited by order of police to rejoice, dance and pray to the rhythm of a specific sequence of events. Every year, for instance, the commissioners were obliged to pay particular attention in their districts to the celebrations associated with the festivals of Lent and Corpus Christi. As Berryer, Lieutenant-General of Police, wrote on 1 June 1757:

Commissioners must see that booths and stalls are inspected and make sure that any that are unsafe are taken down. There is to be appropriate policing of all streets in the district where the procession of the Blessed Sacrament is to pass. In the event of any resistance to your instructions, the offenders are to be referred to me for dealing with in accordance with your recommendations. Would you also inform me of any gaps in the cobbles so that I can have them repaired. With regard to the temporary altars in each district, I have instructed the police architect to examine them. As far as the ambassadors of Protestant states are concerned, the police will patrol the forecourt of their residences and notify them in advance.[25]

The regulations relating to the Lent period were renewed each year to make sure that the use of fat in each inn and *cabaret* was respected and police inspectors were instructed to pass the names of offenders to the commissioners for immediate entry on their records; from there they would be reported to the Lieutenant-General of Police.

The festivals of patron saints, such as Sainte Geneviève, also gave rise to the same punctilious regimentation; and there were also other occasions when the participation of each district was requisitioned. These were the royal victories, those happiest of occasions for the King's troops. During the period July 1756 to March 1763, for example, Commissioner Thierry was called upon seven times to organize illuminations and the singing of the *Te Deum* on the occasion of military exploits:

24 July 1756. Monsieur is instructed to organize illuminations for tomorrow when the *Te Deum* will be sung in acts of thanksgiving for the capture of the island of Minorca and Fort Saint-Philippe. I enclose copies of my instructions which are to be posted throughout Paris.[26]

France was at war. England, fearing that France might bring down the House of Austria, thus allowing her to turn her sights on the colonial interest, was attempting a series of alliances in Europe. Although France naturally wanted to prevent this, it would have meant the surrender of her own hegemony in Europe. However, the anti-Austrian faction at court, manipulated by the military interests of the nobility, plunged France into a series of harmful wars. Beaten in Europe and outclassed by a superior British navy, France lost Canada in 1760 and England went on snatching the principal colonial possessions of both France and Spain up until 1763. A peace treaty was signed in 1763 and England, now mistress of the seas, kept control of Canada but handed back other territories.

This period of military setbacks was thus punctuated by the occasional French victory which the monarchy obviously wanted to make a great show of. On 13 August 1757 it was a victory obtained with the troops of the Empress of Hungary and then on 27 September 1758, Commissioner Thierry was instructed to arrange celebrations in his district in honour of victories in Canada and a month later for the triumph at Lutzerberg and then another on 28 April 1759 at Bergen. For the ratification of the peace treaty on 12 March 1763, the preparations were to be on an even grander scale. It would be announced by cannon and rocket fire and there were to be food distributions in each district in anticipation of the full-scale festivities on the publication of the peace treaty, so that on this occasion, it was not necessary to organize illuminations.

Royal occasions, whether sad or happy, were also celebrated and each district was cordially expected to participate. Thus, on 10 October 1757, it was: Rejoice! The birth of a son to the Dauphine! And then later on there was the recovery of the King from illness. In 1757 regular prayers were requested for the exorcism of the evil incurred by Damiens's assassination attempt against Louis XV. The preparations for the execution of the regicide were on a scale hitherto unprecedented. Then, in June 1763, no doubt on account of the signing of the peace treaty, a statue erected to Louis XV had to be inaugurated. Thierry received a long list containing advice on procedure and protocol from Sartine, the then Lieutenant of Police: bread and meat were to be distributed on every square and the state of the streets was to be inspected; arrangements were to be made for firework displays; bands were to play on the public squares (with a particularly impressive one at the Place de Grève); shops were to close; the pavement outside each house was to be hosed down the night before; and most important, 'no one is to be sent to jail unless the offence is particularly serious'. In short, no effort to be spared. Every stick, stone and inhabitant to be attended to in minute detail!

> Let all the world
> In every district sing,
> The Glory of the King...

These frequent appeals to the population to merge themselves as one in acts of collective rejoicing or shared grief gave shape and rhythm to the days. There was a regular celebration of all aspects of the King's life and times in respect of his person as well as his achievements. Whether it be his health, his grief, happy occasions for members of his family or minor victories, it was immaterial. What really mattered was Him – His Royal Self, His Essential Kingliness. Consequently the whole district was required to beat time in unison with the rhythm of the royal days and to harmonize with the body Physical, Spiritual and Martial of God's own Prince. Each royal occasion and occurrence was to be an opportunity for celebrating the marriage of the King with His people. The 'people's king' and the 'king's people' were called to embrace each other in a collective celebration where 'wrong' was no more and where bread and meat abounded beneath the flash of lights and fireworks. This was the time of Bounty, a carefully marked time which, for the poor, meant the suspension of poverty and deprivation. It was a time prepared in minute detail by police commissioners and inspectors who would make reports to their Lieutenant and hence, ultimately, to the King.

However, the gift to the inhabitants of the district carried with it the obligation to give of themselves in return and to ensure that no trace of the difficulties normally experienced in the course of their days and hours should be apparent. The entire district, without exception, was invited to live whilst barely existing. Tomorrow would be time enough for it to resume its normal modes of thought and being, self-expression and communication, but until then, today was elsewhere, caught up and confused with Royal Time.

The bearing of the district upon its inhabitants had a double effect – whilst seriously limiting personal life and privacy it nevertheless insisted that one's reputation remain unsullied. Over and above the clearly felt need of the people to be part of the crowd or undifferentiated mass, and an object of the King's power, there did, in fact, exist another level of consciousness concerned with creating a space for oneself, or with possessing a name, rank and place by which one might be recognized in the eyes of the neighbourhood as well as distinguishing oneself from everyone else. For it was here, in this space, so barely protected from the public eyes, that honour resided.

But according to the memoirs and chronicles of the day, the people were hardly likely to have any 'honour' because it was precisely on the subjugation of the people that the honour of the great and mighty was founded. By refusing the people their own individuality and considering them incapable of their own thoughts, they thereby deprived them of their honour. But the reality was in fact very different. There were so many subtle hierarchies within the lowest social classes that they inevitably gave rise to all kinds of factions, connivances and conflicts where honour and reputation were often the most vital stakes at play.

Paris was certainly a case in point for here, year after year, the city swelled to the successive uprootings of the peasant population. For many of the migrants, Paris was a daunting place because it was unknown. It was the centre at some time of numerous comings and goings; some returning to the country in the summer and coming back to the city in the winter. Then there were those who would decide to return to their families at least once or perhaps bring back the rest of their relatives who had stayed behind in the provinces. The most unstable of the lower social groups, the unskilled tradesmen, made up a kind of microcosm where the customs and ways of life were completely different from those of the master craftsmen or well-heeled traders with a stake in the town.

Social instability, economic uncertainty and housing problems undoubtedly provoked a climate of extremes. One had to hold one's own in such shifting conditions that violence and conflict were the inevitable companions of uncertainty or the need to protect oneself against the unknown. To all of that, one must also add the confusion existing between public and private space and the impossibility of distinguishing between 'open' and 'closed' in a situation where each space communicated with the next, opened out onto another, or overlooked and was overlooked by everyone else, offering no protection at all.

In this context where it was essential to maintain a decent level of economic survival at all costs, honour and reputation were absolutely indispensable, for without them the possibility of ruin was never very far away. The defence of one's honour against someone else's injurious comments was a common motive behind many conflicts, a fact well known in law where it has always been customary to rank honour very high on the scale of values (admittedly with the aristocracy and elites in mind rather than the simple journeyman). 'The loss of goods or an inheritance is always reparable by one means or another, but loss of honour or one's life – never!'[27] So wrote the Provost of Paris, Jean de Mille, at the beginning of the seventeenth century. For the least privileged, the loss of one's honour had serious economic consequences which was all the more worrying in an oral society, as Beccaria underlined in his treatise *Des délits et des peines*, which appeared in 1764: 'It is often public opinion which is the scourge of crude and wise alike.' Where public opinion reigns, the approval of others is not only useful, it is indispensable to anyone seeking to maintain equal status with his fellow citizens.[28] As for the Lieutenants of Police, they were well aware of the extent to which their legal proceedings were encumbered by insults and slander, as Lenoir explains in his 'Mémoires': 'Complaints about verbal abuse and defamation of character were common in Paris. Some sought restitution before the lower courts but by far the greater number of Parisians beset the police with their domestic quarrels and their points of honour.'[29] Could there be a better example of the sealing together of public and private life than by this honour,[30] that most inner and private of possessions which is ours alone yet which rests in the hands of everyone else. That men and women should also quarrel on this matter serves as further evidence.

In such a climate of insecurity, the union between a man and a woman was necessary for survival. It was the minimal relationship allowing for hope and the building of a relative degree of stability. The conditions of the union (courtship, seduction, living together, worsening relationship, marriage, legitimate or illegitimate pregnancy) contained within themselves some of the conflicts and strategies employed in the defence of honour. The space created or destroyed between a man and a woman was also the place where self-esteem was built. The conflicts which arose, as detailed in cross-examinations and witnesses' accounts, reveal the ways in which both men and women perceived the nature of existence, their concern for self and other and their perceptions of normality in male–female relationships. In short, one finds in such encounters and disputes the explanation of a code of existence which is possibly the fruit of collective representation, a product of individual creation, or both.[31]

# 2

# Girls for the Marrying

Whether one was Parisian or a fresh, young country girl, it was essential to get established. The city positively encouraged contact and kindled hopes of marriage whilst the ways of life across the Parisian space also provided men and women with ample opportunities for meeting and greeting, picking and choosing, and seducing one another.[1] There was the promiscuous closeness of the lodgings for instance, or walks and strolls in the street or public gardens, or perhaps a stop at one of the *cabarets*.

The poor girl earned her living and went about town just as much as the man, not at all the prisoner of convention and matrimonial strategy as was the young bourgeoise. Her open charm and vivacity, as well as a capacity to earn her own living, were a constant source of admiration for one of her contemporaries, Louis-Sébastien Mercier, who was without doubt one of the few writers of his time to be so preoccupied by her. We are indebted to him for numerous close observations of the various behaviours of women according to social class which he differentiated and categorized in minute detail.

His concern at the growing number of bachelors in Paris and at the number of girls awaiting marriage had led him to write at length about the daughters of the poor. His thesis was quite simply this: that 'the number of girls beyond a marriageable age was past counting' and that there were umpteen others living alone.[2] The truth was that marriage was being viewed increasingly as a burdensome institution, preferably to be avoided in favour of an infinitely calmer and more peaceful celibacy. 'Men do not marry any more, or do so with regret. What a turnabout in the social order!'[3] However, Mercier went on to argue that the current state of affairs did not in any way affect society as a whole but that the disorder was rather a peculiar phenomenon. 'It is,' he says, 'only the poor people who are getting married',[4] and this unbalanced situation, he felt, exacerbated the whole question of poverty:

The well-to-do, who don't marry, or who marry late, usually have very few children, whereas the poor, who go straight into marriage, far too early, have a lot. The effect of all this is that wealth is being concentrated increasingly in fewer and fewer hands and that the social group who needs most receives least.[5]

What was causing this disruption of the social order? For Mercier, everything stemmed from the abuses of wealth and luxury and the frantic passion for money. The appetite for riches was ruining everything and turning marriage into a business 'deal'. Therefore it was hardly surprising that the resulting marriages were poor, since economic considerations took precedence over natural inclination and affection, and in this respect the author echoes the themes of social satire of the period; namely, the lack of affection between husband and wife; the rivalry that existed between them; and the extravagance of each.

It was essential, therefore, to root out the evil which Mercier had no compunction in identifying; he centred all his criticism on one institution in particular, which he held responsible for a good many ills, and that was the dowry. It deterred people from entering into marriage, distorted relationships within the marriage and always ended up by ruining the widower; its surreptitious intervention at each stage of married life was a constant source of difficulty and failure. Where families provided dowries for their daughters, they looked for the maximum number of economic guarantees from the families of the young men, hoping to avoid a bad match at all costs. This was certainly true of the middle classes, who were fanatical in their attempts to calculate the social and economic viability of the marriage. 'It is as difficult to arrange the marriage of the stationer's daughter as that of a king. . . . I think there will always be an eternal divide between the goldsmith and the locksmith, the grease-lined grocer and the candle-maker.'[6] Other families had great difficulty in finding a dowry: 'There is nothing so difficult as a marriage. It is not tying the eternal knot that is the problem, but the obligatory visit to the lawyer to pledge the dowry. There is no shortage of plain nubile girls, it is the pretty ones who are the problem.'

In the end, the people were probably better off as a result of not even being able to contemplate a dowry. 'The young milliner is happier in her poverty than the young bourgeoise.'[7] So says Mercier. It was probably not so simple. Nevertheless the choice of spouse in the case of the former was obviously very different. Even if an economic alliance were necessary, the absence of material possessions or of a dowry meant adopting a more complicated strategy which might eventually lead to other forms of association. Marriage was to be seen as a later stage consecrating the possibility of setting up home together. In the meantime, concubinage or living together seemed a perfectly 'natural' state from which one might one day envisage an official union which might possibly be the guarantee of economic stability, precarious though that might be.

Once the marriage had been contracted, the dowry immediately became a source of friction and here Mercier again picks up another well-worn theme of satirical writers, namely, the woman's so-called privileged position vis-à-vis the finances. We are assured that she was the one who had a taste for luxury and possessions; that it was she who squandered the domestic purse and who threw money around on numerous frivolities. Coquettish and extravagant, she brought ruin on her husband and created economic havoc wherever she passed. The dowry could not help but reinforce this state of affairs, particularly in Paris where custom had invested the woman with widespread powers, making it necessary to consult her on all financial matters. Domineering at the outset, she became more and more demanding and interfering. 'The dowry ineluctably results in female domination and that means mollycoddling which is an affliction to the spirit of man and to his ability and character.'[8]

In Paris the situation was proving to be untenable even up to the death of the wife; bereavement meant ruin for the man for, as we know, he had to hand back the dowry. Mercier's opinion on the matter was quite clear; for him the dowry was a deterrent to marriage as it increased the number of bachelors and it therefore had to be stopped.

He was sufficiently observant and realistic, moreover, to stress the need for the finances to be equally balanced between both partners. Of the wives of artisans and small traders he wrote: 'They work in partnership with their men and do very well as a result. They are used to handling small amounts of money and there is a perfectly equal sharing of responsibility for which the household is all the better.'

These suggestions are quite modern. Mercier was acutely aware of the importance of the financial side of married life and the need for real equality in the distribution of money. In the case already mentioned there was no real difficulty in achieving this balance since both partners had to work together of necessity and a considerable part of their relationship was bound up in their mutual commitment to their economic survival. It was the bourgeoise, whether girl or married woman, who was the target of his attack, whereas the wives and women of the people were objects of his esteem. But for all that, he did not lose sight of their harsh and often wretched living conditions, which aroused his indignation:

What is distressing to behold are those unfortunate women who go about the streets well before dawn. Their eyes are bloodshot, their faces red and their backs bent beneath the weight of their heavy baskets.... One suffers on their behalf.... But even so, their weatherbeaten skin, their daily drudgery, their toughness and their calloused hands have still not turned them into men and for the discerning eye, their sexuality is still apparent.[9]

It is worth underlining the originality of the thought for, as we know, the authors of the eighteenth century preferred to describe the women of the people as not much more than animals who had lost all trace of humanity and had become, at best, manly and haggard. This type of description died hard and in the nineteenth century we see the Goncourt brothers adopting the same attitudes in their book *La Femme au XVIII*<sup>e</sup> *siècle*. The poor and the loose woman are placed together in the same chapter (ch. 7) and the ensuing portrait is bland and featureless:

> A creature appeared whose only claim to womanhood was her gender and who was more 'people' than 'woman'. In his *Cris de Paris*, Bouchardon has captured the strong profile and the manly carriage. His powerful drawings reveal the heavy masculinity and virility that lie beneath the thick layers of woollens and rough homespun of all such labouring women.[10]

The same thinking is apparent in the Goncourts' description of even the very youngest girls who were supposed to be dim and vacant right from childhood and destined for an inevitable state of idiocy, unlikely to know anything other than wickedness and brutality:

> The girls of the people are destined for seduction from early childhood. They grow up in an atmosphere of cynicism, surrounded by ignoble sentiment and crude language as their sole examples. They are defenceless and unable to protect themselves, and there is nothing and no one to help them develop and retain a sense of honour, so that their judgement is violated whilst barely formed. Of religion they retain only a few superstitious practices, such as the saying of mass for the Virgin each Saturday, a custom still secretly cherished in the very depths of their decadence. Any idea of duty or womanly virtue is likely to be as a result of disapproval by the neighbours or of being the butt of jokes and mockery such as the horns made in the street at young girls who behaved badly who, as the people used to say, 'must be at the widow's game, you know'. The picture of marriage she is offered is one of marriage at its most repugnant, with the household reverberating to the sound of insults and blows.[11]

But Mercier's approach was altogether more subtle and sensitive and he did not fall into the traditional traps so common to his own contemporaries. Arthur Young, for instance, in his *Travels in France* (1792), described the serving girls and country women as a bunch of walking dung heaps whom the locals only referred to as women out of politeness; but Mercier's attitude was entirely different. For him the poor girl was rich in character, concealing within herself a wealth of freedom and imagination even though she might display the damaging effects of hard work. Removed from the restrictions of an overly narrow education, she was free to give and receive love as she chose.

> Only the daughters of the petty bourgeois, the humble artisan and the people are completely free to come and go as they please and to make love as they choose [even though their forwardness might sometimes alarm their suitors, causing] many a bachelor upon seeing their hair-do's and all the fineries and fripperies of which these dedicated fashion followers are so fond, to stop and think, do his sums – and stay celibate.[12]

The weddings of simple folk were living proof of the very real joy which was their characteristic. 'They dance long and hard, being the last to abandon their joyful traditions even though their pastimes are being denigrated on all sides.'[13]

The underlying idea was quite simply that although poverty and hardship might foster cunning and sharp practice financially, they left the heart innocent and fresh. The poor girl was the embodiment of the 'real' woman. Available and artless, she was there for the taking, a point of view confirmed by other writings on rustic encounters. Happy the man who had a country girl for his mistress, through whose good offices he might discover all!

> The rich, who spend so much money on unappreciative women, have no idea of the charm inspired by the surprised smile of a tender young mistress as she casts her eyes over all these things that are new to her, and then turns her gaze towards you, amazed at every word you utter.[14]

Mercier's portrait of the ordinary young girl was always very sexual. For him she was 'charming' and 'appealing' and his defence of her is a perfect illustration of his own fondness for both Rousseau and Diderot. Whilst he elevates female freedom, he preaches the benefits of a liaison with a young girl from the country who, being that much closer to nature, was all the more likely to be impressed by masculine *savoir-faire*.

# 3

# 'Seduced and Abandoned'

---

In that interim period when the young woman of the people was attempting to establish herself in marriage, it was not uncommon for her to find instead either breakdown or desertion, which left her alone and defenceless and very often burdened with the fruits of her encounter – a child – either on the way or newly born.

Girls like these, who had been 'seduced and abandoned', lodged their complaints with the police commissioner in the hope of receiving some form of material compensation in the face of this male desertion which would drag them into poverty and despair. Their complaints tell the story of a trust given and then betrayed and of a private conflict which swelled out onto the judicial stage thence to be heard and labelled in the hope thereby of avoiding the rumours and recriminations which could only harm their honour and reputation.

These statements, which recur so often in the police commissioners' archives provide us with a chronicle of discord and disruption just when everything seemed on course for a marriage and when a pregnancy occurred which provided obvious proof of the union. The contest that then followed on the desertion of the woman was a strange affair owing to the absence of one of the protagonists, and herein lay the crux of the drama. In such cases there was no direct confrontation between the man and the woman; the woman, who was usually about to give birth, would provide a statement about her encounter and name the father. Witnesses were called to support her claim, and in the majority of cases the presumed father was brought before the court to reply to the charges made against him. If he admitted to being the father he would be asked to pay a fine to cover the cost of the confinement and a few months' nursing. As far as the woman was concerned, the most important thing for her was to convince the police commissioner that marriage had always been intended as the natural outcome of the encounter and that the fact that it had been imminent justified sexual relations having taken place in the course of their meetings together.

This account would be opposed by the man who gave his own version of events. He argued that the liaison (should he actually admit to it) had meant nothing and that there had never been any question of their coming together in marriage. What was more, the pregnancy itself was ample proof of the wiles and loose ways of women.

There is a consistency in the composition and structure of the records – female account, witnesses' evidence, man's reply – which first of all makes it possible to analyse the conditions conducive to a marriage. Next, we have the event of desertion itself and then the obligatory confession of sexual relations which inevitably sharpened the tone of the narrative.

The woman described what had happened to her in two parts: first, that the courtship of which she was the object could have meant only one thing – and that was marriage; and second, that the sexual act which she had agreed to undertake had taken place in all innocence.

The man naturally denied this version of events. He attributed a much more instinctive, impulsive and almost animal-like character to the liaison. Thus, we see the real blending with and sustained by the imaginery as well as the merging of factual situations with the perceptions attributed to them by each protagonist. And from these one is able to make out the roles of each as well as the means by which both the man and the woman attempted to portray their respective actions as perfectly normal, for they both had to persuade the commissioner that no offence had actually taken place. Certainly, the girl was abused – but her friend had given her every reason to trust him and every indication that this was a legitimate courtship. The man for his part felt perfectly justified in behaving as he did, and summoned as evidence one of the best-known of traditional male roles, that of the conqueror commanding female submission to the innate impulsiveness of the male.

It should be understood that it is not our purpose here to sort out the true from the false in all that was said to convince the commissioner, but rather to uncover the woman's hopes for marriage and how she might have anticipated this from her interpretation of the telling signs in the attitude of her partner. What she has to say about the marks of attention of which she had been the object reflects what she might, by rights, have expected. She is making a statement about what she considered to be the norm and is speaking out for what she understood by intimacy. In so doing, the declaration she makes is a testimonial to her social and emotional existence. As for the man, his choice lay between recognizing the facts or translating them in terms of pleasure which he believed he had every right to look for in a woman. From such conflicts and their ultimate derisory material resolution, there emerges an order of things which was likely to be perceived very differently by the man and the woman.

In the course of a survey in the archives of Le Châtelet, a hundred or so petitions for seduction and abandon were unearthed, which constitute a homogeneous whole.[1] The information relating to age, domicile, socio-professional status, meeting place and form of seduction have allowed consideration of the conditions conducive to a matrimonial alliance between a man and woman of the people, thus helping us towards a better understanding of who meets whom and how. From these indications, we begin to get an idea of the encounter as it really was – or was dreamt to be – it does not really matter; for what one needs to see, perhaps, is an outline of certain possibilities within which commonly held schemes and plans might be entertained, or even found to be satisfactory. The records are sufficiently detailed for us to demolish a long-held stereotype, namely the belief that in the city, where the lives of men and women were thought to be promiscuous, sexual attraction had no regard for either form or ritual and that Paris was still sufficiently rural to allow for the odd tumble in the hay. This is a somewhat oversimplified view and the petitions show the importance of the forms and conventions within which the seduction and hopes of marriage were almost certainly inscribed.

## Necessary pre-eminence

It certainly came as no surprise to find that there was a distinct age difference between the man and the young woman; it was certainly true of half the cases and no one seemed to find it unusual. On the contrary, it would appear that such an age difference was likely to make a young woman feel more confident.

Jeanne Benoist was cook for Lépine, clockmaker to the King. In 1775, she met Georges Neveux, a baker, who proposed marriage to her on several occasions. She finally succumbed and when she was later abandoned she explained that 'the fact that the aforesaid Neveux was more than 32 years old had made her more inclined to accept his proposals as she felt that there was every reason to trust his promises.' Thirty-two was not considered to be too old, and sometimes the gap between the partners was even greater, as much as 10 or even 30 years. Age was a sign of maturity and also a guarantee that one would be marrying into an already well established professional situation. In two-thirds of the cases, moreover, the girls were very young indeed, aged between 15 and 22, with no secure professional future ahead of them.

It is also interesting to note that of the women who were abandoned in the course of their pregnancy, more than half were servants – kitchen girls, shop hands or chambermaids at best. The others helped their parents, who were probably shop-owners or lodging-house keepers. Only a minority were employees in the female trades such as worker in the fashion-trade or in quilted petticoats, washerwoman, wardrobe apprentice or perhaps lacemaker's assistant. These young serving girls rarely went far afield to find a partner and their encounter took broadly two forms: half of them allowed themselves to be seduced by another servant, either from the same establishment or one nearby; and for the rest, it was the lot of the 'other' lover that fell to them.[2] It was usually their master or the shopkeeper who would enjoy their favours, so at this price, marriage could never be anything but an illusion. If one looks at the body of evidence as a whole, it is clear that the most common type of encounter (roughly two-thirds) was between a man and woman of the same socio-professional level, apart from the fact that the woman was nearly always much younger and thus less secure economically, although her family background was the same as that of her seducer. The milliner was attracted to the journeyman clockmaker; the daughter of a journeyman gardener might aspire to live with a postman working at one of the branches of the Parisian postal service, whilst a kitchen girl might receive the attentions of the baker who came to deliver the daily bread.

The other significant cases (approximately one-third of the total) were those where the woman was seduced by a man of higher professional status than herself; her master, for instance, or an already well-established artisan, and even, on occasion, a solicitor or lawyer visiting Paris. There were also a few surprise encounters that are worth noting. There was the case of the wealthy merchant's daughter who fell in love with a marquis; and then there was the exceptional case (the only one in the entire survey, in fact) of the wigmaker's assistant who fell in love with his master's daughter, which obviously incurred a somewhat vigorous family reaction. He was accused of having ambitions to better his station rather than seeking a genuine marriage of the heart. The police commissioner asked him sternly, 'How could he possibly have allowed himself to abuse the daughter of the master in whose employ he was? He surely could not be ignorant of the severity of the Law on this point?' The boy replied that it was solely because he wanted to marry her; but his audacity was to result in a prison sentence and it was only a plea for clemency on the part of the parents of the seduced girl that finally led to his release.[3] One need not labour the point; we know that if the positions had been reversed – a shop girl seduced by her master, for instance – there would have been no prison for the master, nor any such fuss; that is the way it was.

Of course, data such as age, trade, professional status etc. go some way towards explaining how a man and a woman might select each other; but the complaints made by the women following their desertion also have something else to say. They are the narrative of a personal adventure which was theirs and theirs alone. Admittedly, it was an adventure that turned out badly, but not before it had first assumed all the colours of pleasure, attachment and hope. These statements can be read at two levels: firstly, as the coverage of a sequence of events and a period of waiting; and then as the depiction of feelings and disappointments which were at the same time both the history of a reality and an illusion. From the narrative of this intimate affair that had been found to be so badly wanting and which was about to be so brutally exposed, one sees emerging, not only a number of precise events, but also a mental horizon whose contours are complex. The first frame of the story, the meeting, is taken amidst a clutch of contending realities and images which outline the way in which marriage might have been contemplated. As well as portraying a particular situation, it is also a means of expressing a philosophy of the self and other, without which existence is nothing. The women are saying why they were entitled to experience pleasure and seduction; how they arrived at this recognition and the extent to which they considered it legitimate. And even if things had not quite happened in this way, what of it? That is how it should have been, and it was necessary for the court to be of the same mind if it were to be convinced that the man was to blame for the misfortune that then ensued. The account of the meeting, the evidence brought to bear and the witnesses' statements open onto a secret place in the woman's private space where self and definition of self had their existence. By means of the words and the actions of another, from the time of the first approach to the stage of trust and confidence, she is making a statement about what it was that determined her choice. These were the times in life when nothing was obligatory but everything happened because it corresponded to a scheme or dream and thus to a satisfactory image of one's existence, an equation between self and concept of self. What is undoubtedly interesting here is that these statements touch on an area that is both little known and always called into question when one is dealing with the popular classes, namely, the capacity for self-awareness and the ability to determine for oneself a code of ethics. These are matters about which historians have been quite prolific where elites have been concerned, with the result that disparities in social competence and ability are all too well documented. Furthermore, the generally accepted gap between the brutishness of the people and bourgeois civility[4] has made it practically impossible to imagine the formation of concepts of taste, beauty and harmony amongst the classes for whom, it would appear, the only route was that of necessity.

## Time, words and gestures

A fondness for the other person grew with time, whilst words, both spoken and written, and gestures also had their part to play in creating a climate which allowed trust and affection to become established. It was a landscape described in detail by the deserted woman. For if feeling and desire were to grow, it was essential to take time over lovemaking and almost all the women refer to this initial period when the courtship game began, as a privileged period in the middle of their ordinary lives when reality was suspended. Getting to know each other took time – and take it they did. In this way they distinguished themselves from the brute beasts, the common soldier or the street girl.

Denise Richard, a 21-year-old chambermaid, said of her lover who had come to see her every day for a year that 'he had crept his way into her affections with fine words and attractive promises'.[5] And not only did it take time, the time had to be taken from the other in such a way as to interrupt the normal course of things by capturing her attention and inserting oneself into her personal space. For two-thirds of the couples, one or two years went by before they made up their minds and there were rarely any who 'got involved' within less than six months; a quarter of the couples had waited anything from two to seven years, during which time they were still busy trying to win each other over. When things seemed to have been going on for far too long and there was still no decision to marry, the man always seemed to have a perfectly plausible answer: 'He kept telling her father that he had every intention of marrying her but that he just needed to wait until he was paid back the five hundred pounds he was owed.' 'To be sought in marriage', as they nearly all said, did indeed open up onto a secret path and a personal journey. There was no doubt that there was mutual attraction at the beginning ('he caught her eye immediately'; 'he captured her heart and soul'; 'he won her heart at once'), but there was still a long way to go before a marriage seemed likely, making it possible to envisage sexual relations before the wedding ceremony, a course which in the end varied greatly.

One woman based her decision on the mature years of her partner and another woman reached her decision because of his comfortable situation; alternatively, the decision might be made because of the rather subtle but dependent relationship the woman had with him on account of the domestic service she provided. There were also some rather unusual grounds for confidence, as in the case of Jeanne Benoist who allowed herself to be seduced by the baker, Neveux:

> She first got to know him about two and a half years ago because at the time he was courting her cousin, Jeanne Bouquain, a kitchen maid for an attorney at La Huchette. As this girl had been dead these last three years, this same Neveux had been coming to see her at the mercer's shop where she was in service and he had proposed to her on a number of occasions. There was no reason not to trust his promises because she knew that he would have married her cousin had she been alive.

The death of her cousin did not cast its shadow over Jeanne; on the contrary, it brought the two destinies together, and was proof for her that Georges Neveux had every intention of linking himself with the Benoist family. One died, the other didn't. Therein lay a concept of marriage and death and a personal construction of the family and the world which was quite serene and in whose wisdom the life of Jeanne Benoist was gently inscribed.

For other women, their trust was born of a feeling of self-worth as perceived through the eyes of the other, something which could not be discounted if one were just a simple chambermaid to the widow of a gentleman farmer, for instance. Monique Félix, aged 23, met a bourgeois by the name of Cogny who 'gave her every reason to trust him. He said how sensible she was and regarded her as being well born. And so he proposed to marry her – but not straight away.'[6] The kindness and consideration she saw in him, combined with the fact that he was taking his time so as not to rush into anything, not only corresponded with the image Monique Félix had of herself, but also with her idea of good manners. She therefore gave in to Cogny. On the other hand, a young girl like the laundress Marie-Jeanne Dubuisson aged 17, was led to think that marriage with Jean-Jacques Toussaint was a distinct possibility 'because the two young people were of equal birth and status'.[7] This perfectly reasonable equation was enough to allow her plans to take shape and substantiate the subsequent actions.

Their explanations of all these choices is punctuated throughout with a sense of what is just, beautiful and wise. Even if things did not quite happen in this way (one should not forget that these statements were intended to convince the commissioner of their innocence on becoming the mistresses of men who had left them), the statements made concern an ideal of the Self, of Good and of the Justice of things.

As well as the basic merits of the situation, the majority of the women also had a good deal to say about all the other signs and signals there had been, including words and actions, which had all contributed to the construction of those brief moments of happiness and 'the intensely devoted courtship' to which they nearly all made some claim; and here the accounts are embellished with quite a richness of vocabulary: 'He always used to "flirt" with her on the stairs'; then there was the fellow who brought her material for under-garments who kept on laughing and 'teasing' her. He made her 'a million promises' a day or even 'used every conceivable protestation of love' or 'did everything possible to seduce her'. The most commonly used expression, which in fact sums it all up, was: 'he did everything he could to seduce her' or 'have his way with her'. It was usually something amusing, a piece of flattery or an expression of tenderness which did the trick that helped start the acquaintance and establish trust. All it took from the man were a few kind and well-chosen words to convince her that she was indispensable to his happiness; but, for these words to register and implant themselves in her life, it required time. And so the daily routine came to a halt, during which the talk was all to do with oneself, which was obviously an essential prerequisite for any prospect of a marital bond. The appropriate gestures were also required apparently: 'he liked to kiss her when their master was away'; 'he spent a lot of time with her, playing her music and talking to her and kissing her'; 'he went to a lot of trouble for her'. Madeleine Cogny, a kitchen maid, had the following to say about all her lover's efforts:

> He kept on telling her that she was the one he wanted to marry and he never missed a chance to convince her. He made little attempt to conceal the tender feelings that he had for her and even went so far as to kiss her in the kitchen in front of her master, the Baron de Romilly, who reprimanded him. He also played her the mandolin and he would go down on his knees to her in tears, calling her his dear wife and telling her that he would never leave her and that she was as pretty and fresh as a rose.[8]

These bold ploys were often accompanied by other activities such as renting a room or apartment in which to install the chosen one and even obtaining furniture and belongings as proof of one's commitment. This poor creature who was intended for marriage was tended with such great care only to find that instead of a husband, she had obtained a creditor. There were occasions when the behaviour was downright devious, like that of the tapestry worker from the Gobelins who offered to teach tapestry-making to the brother of his heart's desire so that the former could become a worker in the craft whilst he made advances to the latter.

Twenty or so statements mentioned the existence of letters, some of which are contained in the records. They come from servants and journeymen and, in one case only, from a worker in the printing trade. Not only was the letter a proof, but in a milieu where literacy was far from common, it was a particularly precious gesture by virtue of its rarity. To write that one wished to be married or to be in possession of a letter where words of engagement were signed and sealed gave the promise an official stamp. Not only did the letter surpass any words and gestures, it sealed them, a point made in the statement by Madeleine David, daughter of a lodging-house keeper and which left no room for doubt:

> He was quick to let the plaintiff know the feelings she inspired in him and anywhere he managed to come across her in the house he always talked about them and would add that his own happiness depended on her being his and that he would have no other wife but her. Confident in

his male superiority, he offered to read books to her and each time he returned them he was careful to insert love-letters that were full of tenderness and passion.

How could one resist this combination of male authority with the power of the pen and the word?

Besides the signals exchanged between the couple themselves it also proved indispensable for friends and family to be equally well aware of them: 'They made no secret of their inclinations, especially as the young man's father and stepmother didn't seem to object; in fact they even flattered the plaintiff with the hope that she would become united with their son through the bonds of marriage.'

The parents sometimes knew about the whole affair and, in cases where the banns had even been published, news often reached them by letter or rumour. In some cases they acted as witnesses for the young woman and spoke of the young man's devoted courtship of their daughter in the hope that their approval might be seen as lending the affair an air of public respectability. When Thérèse Bisson, a servant and elder daughter, met Etienne Juffet, she brought him home to meet her parents. Her story was that

> he sought her in marriage from the very beginning and he behaved with all the appropriate courtesy and decency. Her parents took him at his word and received him accordingly. She then set about making all the arrangements for the marriage and had even been to Pithiviers to seek her father's consent. All that there remained to do was to obtain the consent of Juffet's father in Lyons.[9]

Another servant, Marie-Cécile Prévost, said that

> Copreau had given her his word about the execution of the marriage on numerous occasions and that he had paid her all the more attention and was more devoted than ever. So that the marriage could take place, she, the plaintiff, had written to his parents telling them to get a bann published in their church the following day and another the same day in the parish of Saint-Sulpice.[10]

The use of the word 'execution' in connection with 'marriage' certainly indicates the existence of a set of priorities and a code of practice and a ritual which, if followed, should eventually lead to the marriage ceremony. Anything else was betrayal. Admittedly not every couple got as far as the publication of the banns or an official announcement but in the mind of the young woman, it was as good as, and the seduction itself was taken as an indication that it was all obviously leading up to marriage. Therefore she could relax in complete confidence.

Because of their intimate relationship, the young couple were obliged to adopt an often contradictory approach, for they had to keep their secret as well as showing their feelings in public. Friends, neighbours and parents all saw the signs of affection between the two partners and when giving evidence of their obvious closeness they said that the usual signs of tenderness which would certainly have led to marriage had been clearly recognizable. The sincerity of one's feelings had to be seen and not hidden, for the promise of marriage needed the support of the neighbourhood whose recognition would thus render it authentic.

In this matter, the district was all-powerful. It passed judgement on the normality of the relations between the young people and decided whether everything was proper or whether there was a scandal. Its judgement was fearsome and its definition of right and wrong absolute. For some, it was able to confirm that they had appeared very close and that they had never been seen with anyone else. Or it might affirm that they were like 'a lover and his mistress, that they were very much in love, kissed frequently and addressed each other as "tu".' In short, they showed all the signs of closeness which indicated their intentions.[11] But for others, the district decided that there was a scandal, corroborating the view that the behaviour of the young people had been shocking and that 'they had been fondling each other all over the place and had even been heard taking their pleasures in the bedchamber to the point where they had heard the bed knocking against the partition wall and the girl shouting out, "Have your way, my sweet one, I would die for your beautiful eyes".'[12]

The union between a man and a woman needed the respect of others who, being in possession of their secret, interpreted it and restored it to the community in accordance with what they had seen and made of it. It was inscribed within the confines of both private and public spheres and obeyed the rules of obvious material circumstance as well as the intimate collective imagination which together created harmony and deployed hope.

Reason, tenderness and decency are all evoked in the account of the possible union but at that point where the woman allowed herself to be caught in the trap of carnal love prior to the promised marriage, she became entirely constrained by the need to convince the court that the sexual act was a perfectly normal occurrence, that it was impossible to avoid and that it was something which had to be done at the time. She was preparing the ground for the commissioner to hear the most difficult thing for her to speak of, namely the point at which she had succumbed – and that it was not her fault. And thus the consummation of their love was pronounced and the impossible statement made.

## The Sleeping Beauty

'He closed the door of his apartment and told her that she would not return the same way she had come.'[13] Just one example of an event which, itself, scarcely varied. And in the space between the 'before' and the 'after' when there was no hope of going back, everything was turned upside down. The words used to describe this state were those of captivity and imprisonment – having 'captivated heart and soul', the body also yielded for it could hardly do otherwise under the pressure.

The man fastened the bolt. The house was empty as the masters were away and all the windows were shut. There were no servants around. He stuffed a handkerchief into the woman's mouth, held his palm over her face and 'threw her onto the bed'; he grabbed her by the waist, jabbed her with his knees and brought her roughly to the ground, caressing and threatening her all the while; first he made her talk, then told her to shut up again, and 'he was all the more attentive, promising again and again that he would never leave her and swearing his undying love'. When describing those minutes preceding lovemaking, the woman nearly always stressed that mixture of vows, embraces, violence, and rapacity which alone, in her opinion, were capable of explaining what was to follow.

'She remained unconscious, overcome by the shock of his brutality and he took her without her knowing it.' In the majority of cases, the woman claimed to know nothing of the sexual act which had made her a mother and brought about her subsequent ruin. Nothing. Why? Because she was in such a state of shock that she had lost consciousness whilst the man enjoyed himself with her. Nothing; because she was too distressed, dazed, faint or blind, and because she had no idea what was happening. And then at last 'he had done with her' and his 'success was established', unless of course her own efforts to forge her innocence could undo it.

There. The impossible thing had been said; the commissioner had been told. But in order to make this difficult statement which would affect the successful outcome of the complaint, the woman had assumed the vacant expression of someone who was not quite there, describing herself like a lifeless doll plunged by fear and brutality into an everlasting faint and profound state of torpor. Absent, languid, blind, unconscious and out of touch with reality, she only awoke once it was all over; but from that point on, none of her protestations or indignation could efface any of it.

Who is this if none other than the Sleeping Beauty with whom the Prince made love without waking her?[14] Impregnated, but unconscious of it, Sleeping Beauty had no part in her deflowering; she remained unsullied by the unfortunate events taking place in her body; and her passivity being absolute, her loss of consciousness even precluded any enjoyment on her part. The form these statements take reminds one of a very old version of the story in which Sleeping Beauty is a virgin impregnated unawares and hence without suggestion of sin. Untainted by pleasure or sin, the Sleeping Beauty is thus 'in the same position as the Blessed Virgin, who is both Virgin and Mother at the same time'.[15]

Here one sees the real borrowing on the imaginary to create a convincing yet commonplace drama. The woman's presentation of the union and the breakdown of that union is such that the sexual act, which cannot be erased, might at least obliterate culpability. Here the imagination borrows on descriptions stored in the memory of woman over a long period and then transformed, so that although the theme of the Virgin-Mother can hardly be used because of its sacred nature which sets it apart from the common experience of most mortals, the story of the Sleeping Beauty, heard over and over, provides a much more subtle adaptation. It has almost pagan overtones; for one knows for instance that fecundity and unconsciousness occur in a great many pagan legends, like the tale of Danaë's golden rain, for example. The traditional tale and its sacred or mythical counterpart say what the woman does not want to say; namely, that furtive pleasures taken by two people can be construed without too much shame and that they constitute an acceptable, albeit regrettable, adventure.

At this point in the story, highly involved as it is, events have been presented in such a way as to make the commissioner understand that everything had happened quite normally as it should have, except.... And even the 'except' becomes a symbol of innocence because it is part and parcel of a whole scenario of loss: the woman was not there – only her body. Yes, it was true, the man took the woman and that was itself a serious matter; but it was unavoidable. A passion long repressed has to be sated one day or other. It was more of a misfortune than an abuse, because up till then everything had happened with a reassuring order and sincerity. Yes, the woman did give her consent, but she was not to blame because, as pale as absence – she was not in possession of herself.

## Happiness undone

Time and the obvious appearance of the pregnancy eventually wore away the enthusiasm of the first seduction and earlier promises and there came a time when previous trust collapsed. There were some who saw this coming and tried to avoid it by taking precautions. Take the case of Antoine Sabatteau, for instance, who made Anne Aubry drink something to induce an abortion directly after making love with her. She said that

> when she came to her senses two hours later, she scolded Sabatteau over and over again for his unseemly behaviour and told him that no decent

man would dishonour a young person. He simply replied that he loved her with all his heart at the same time as handing her the drink, and telling her that if she were pregnant then it would get rid of everything. This the petitioner refused to do and repeated her previous reproaches which she had every right to do. He told her that she was trying to trick him but, in any case, if she were pregnant he would marry her and if his father wouldn't give his consent, he would do all he could to get it and until he did, he would pay all the necessary expenses for the birth; and if it was a boy, he would take responsibility for the child and prove to her that he was an honest man.[16]

His evidence provides us with a very good summary and illustration of the difficulty of accepting the arrival of a child if only on economic grounds. In this case, the man had already worked out his strategy; firstly, there was his decision to offer the woman an abortifacient immediately after the sexual act and then, secondly, if this failed, to make provision for the future. If she were indeed pregnant, then he would marry her, or should his father refuse consent, which was always a possibility, then he would guarantee the costs of the birth. He added that these were the words of an honest man, but failed to mention what would happen in the equally likely event of the birth of a girl.

Other men were probably not quite so well organized, at least not in their own minds, but the appearance of the pregnancy beneath frocks and skirts often marked the beginning of negative attitudes ranging from desertion pure and simple to more subtle negotiations which prolonged the time, allowing for the beginnings of a tentative retreat.

The women's statements relate in minute detail those first few anxious moments when they say they initially sensed the beginnings of this disloyalty and betrayal, to be followed later by lying and ultimate desertion. Sometimes the time would be dragged out by publishing the banns for instance, but still there was no wedding ceremony. The reasons given were largely economic, for example the need to pay off debts before getting established, or waiting for creditors to pay back sums promised to the man; or else it might be the parents who refused their consent, on the pretext of moral grounds which often concealed their more immediate concern for material benefit.

It was a long time before the woman understood what was going on. She waited patiently, reassured by the publication of the banns, for instance, or a present, or by the departure of her intended to obtain his parents' consent. In fact her dream could go on indefinitely even when, in some cases, the child had already been born and the woman had taken on the costs of the birth by herself, like Thérèse Bisson, for example. At the request of Juffet, the father-to-be, she had sold 'her room to pay for the birth'.[17] Juffet, however, had still not returned from his trip to Lyons to consult his father. A few letters turned up explaining that he was prevented from returning to be with her because his mother and father were both ill. Thérèse went on waiting and carried on breast-feeding the baby until the last letter finally opened her eyes. In it, Juffet expressed his anger that she was nursing the baby herself and gave her orders to put the child into an orphanage: 'What do you think people will say,' he wrote,

> when they see a young woman on her own? I have been advised by a close friend, who found himself in exactly the same predicament, to do what he did and put the child in an orphanage, making sure that he could be recognized so that he could have him back when he wanted, and in fact he took him out a year after he was married. And so, dear friend, this is what I advise you to do. We can have the child whenever we want and it won't set people talking so much. Anyway, we won't be the first ones. It goes on all the time nowadays.[18]

That was that. Thérèse decided to lodge a complaint.

Anne Adot, a chambermaid 'woke up' even later. She placed her first child in the orphanage on the advice of her friend, Jean Grosse, who kept on putting off the marriage. When she became pregnant for the second time, she decided to lodge a complaint in which she expressed her grief at not being able to have her first child back with her. When summoned to appear, her partner revealed to her that he would never marry her as she had no fortune and he had no intention of ending up in poverty.

For others, desertion came more quickly, almost immediately upon announcing the pregnancy. 'When she realized that she was pregnant, she told him about her fears, whereupon he made some indecent remarks and said in public that he had had a good time with her on several occasions but that he had no intention of marrying her and would get away with paying 20 écus';[19] 'now that he had seduced her, he refused to marry her';[20] 'as soon as she realized that she was pregnant he went away and refused to see her';[21] 'when she was pregnant he told her that he would live with her but he would never marry her'.[22]

Betrayed, deceived and abused, the woman had lost her honour. The dream that had been made possible by someone else's words had turned into a tragedy, both materially and morally, and it had to be lived out in full view of the neighbourhood. 'Her misfortune is twofold in that she finds herself deprived of her honour as a result of being five months pregnant and while he now refuses to marry her she cannot conceal her pregnancy from the public.'[23] The only hope of restoring the lost honour was to lodge a complaint with the commissioner. The actual amount of damages and interest obtained was derisory ('getting off with 20 écus', as one man put it), but honour was re-established. In order to do that it was necessary to admit one's error at the same time as showing that it was not one's fault, by denouncing the underhandedness of an untrustworthy partner. The complaint before the law had the effect of restoring honour and providing a few *écus*; but it was also much more than that. It was the only means available to the woman of stating her innocence in public. This explains the length of the statements and the structure of the accounts which constitute a slow and laborious presentation of a union that was anticipated and hoped for, only to end in deception.

## The self-assurance of the male

If the commissioner were convinced or if the facts seemed to be over-whelmingly against the partner, then he would be summoned to appear and undergo an interrogation. The examination of the man reveals an altogether different facet of the truth and draws on a vocabulary and code of behaviour not found in the woman's account. There is a strategy here and a male–female game which have little in common with the evidence established by the woman. All in all, the affirmation of the male role is quite cut and dried.

Some denied ever having frequented the woman, but they were not the majority; others recognized the facts but attempted to discredit the woman with age-old arguments suggesting that she was no more than a libertine or that he could not be identified as the father because she went with anyone and everyone and besides, he'd paid her each time, hadn't he? And she was well known in the district for running around, wasn't she? There were female 'libertines', granted, but they would hardly have had any interest in being domesticated and if this were the case, there would have been no question of their seeking marriage or proof of paternity. The masculine defence slid with easy self-assurance into the traditional argument which said it was the woman's fault because she was always the one who was 'surrounded by lovers' and always took the initiative. In other words, what we have here is simply another well-known slant on the male–female perspective but instead of the woman as captive, passive and overcome, we have the voracious female Siren whose favours it was no sin to enjoy.

Perhaps what was more surprising were the numbers of male statements confirming such opinions,[24] although the commissioner appeared not to be taken in. But the gross nature of the suggestions could only have had the effect of devaluing the personality of the woman, as in the following case of the gentleman's valet whose partner had already had two children by him and who, in his defence, accused her of being a prostitute. His evidence was 'that on one occasion he had had her whilst standing beside the fire in a *cabaret* when she got her skirt burned all the way up to the belt'. Another man was very pleased with himself for 'being her "first" and seeing her underclothes covered in blood'. Someone else asserted quite arrogantly that he had taken some of her pubic hair and could show it to anyone who wanted to look. A fourth male declared that she was so stupid that anyone could do what they liked with her and that it was very bad of her to let herself go like that. This pathetic catalogue of petty triumphs and the typically salacious details of jokes amongst the boys set the man at a considerable distance from the space that the woman had so delicately created for him back in her own evidence. It was a far cry from the tender love-letters, the chit-chat, the teasing and the laughter on the stairs. When called to appear in public, the man resorted, in his defence, to the most stereotypical male role of them all, namely, that of the man who gets what he wants and then goes on his way, pays up and has done, taking his pleasure and leaving with contempt. Why believe him any more than the woman talking about being swept off her feet and losing consciousness? These two inverse images are typical of the preconceptions and pre-existing order of things which the documents have preserved intact. Before the law, no one wished to be marginalized.

But the commissioner was no fool. In certain cases, in spite of the male denials, the man was obliged to pay the costs of the birth and, if necessary, additional damages and supplementary interest; in this way the separation was made public, and honour restored; and thanks to this passage through Justice and the courts, an official reconciliation between the public and State was made possible. At the heart of it all were the police, acting as the cement necessary for this process of harmonization. The union, for which public recognition has been demonstrated to be so important, could only be severed in public, if it were not to become a mark of shame. And thus the personal grammar of the self encountered an almost universal repertoire which required one to expose oneself in order to be acknowledged and rehabilitated within the traditional codes of honour and reputation which the neighbourhood imposed. In order to do this, each party – both male and female – slipped into traditional roles and presented themselves in images that were almost petrified. However, the story told by the woman was her own, as was that of the other. They had both seen each other in private and they were now expecting to be regarded according to the ways in which they had described themselves. They had both, in quite different and opposing ways, appropriated their own novel. Our job is to decode the novel, but not their secret.

# 4

# Concerning Parents and Children

---

'Marriage is also a place', we wrote in *Le Désordre des familles*.[1] Before looking at the marriages that broke down, we should first recall some of the essential characteristics of the happy couple. Their story hardly features in the judicial archives, of course, although there is ample evidence to suggest that they do have a history – and a remarkable one.

Setting up together was a risky business, not to be undertaken lightly. One had to be able to guarantee a decent level of economic survival, for 'it was criminally thoughtless to marry without having the capital needed to maintain the future children'.[2] Being socially and economically established lay at the heart of the relationship that was harmonious both sexually and emotionally, with honesty and understanding playing a large part in maintaining this relative economic stability.

Respect for other people's property or for public property was an abstraction. What really brought a brutal end to a union based on trust was the man who squandered his wife's dowry; the woman who got into debt, or the man or woman who sold off the furniture or the sheets while the other was away. Financially, men and women seemed on equal terms, the woman being no more prepared to tolerate anyone having a prior claim on her earnings than the man; nor was the man entitled to spend the fruits of his labour entirely on himself.[3] The couple was an association in which each partner had rights and responsibilities, particularly where children resulted from the union.

Domestic harmony was also the result of mutual concern and respect for one another. It was quite common to find the wife accusing the husband of abandoning his usual involvement with the children. Such a brutal and abrupt change of attitude was regarded as a sign of misconduct elsewhere, usually outside the home. Whether it was problems at work, an affair with another woman or spending too much time in the *cabaret* etc, it was still an accepted fact that the common man played a natural and equal part with his wife in the nurturing and education of his children.[4]

In this respect, the amount of space played an important role, which might seem surprising seeing that the lodgings, as we know, opened straight out onto each other, allowing for very little intimacy in the modern sense of the word. In spite of this, conjugal space did exist and the man wanted to see it respected just as much as the woman. Staying away from home, sleeping elsewhere or repeatedly coming home late were just so many signs of disaffection. For no matter how transparent, indiscreet or vulgar the room or lodgings, it was still 'Home' – the place to come back to and a source of contact. It was frequent, unwarranted absence in the course of the day (not including regular long-distance journeys, travelling and long-term absence) that was the most common complaint made by husband and wife.

Wife-beating, although widely recognized in ancient custom,[5] did not appear to be approved of. There was immediate outrage on the part of the wife and neighbours and public opinion was firmly behind the victim. It was not unusual for the commissioner to be alerted quickly to such behaviour and for him to intervene in a decisive manner, usually admonishing the husband and even, on occasion, throwing him into jail if the beatings had been repeated and dangerous.[6] Often promiscuity acted as a guarantor of a certain degree of normality in marital relations and yet, no matter how frequent, this type of violence scarcely went unpunished; but paradoxically, this almost daily violence, although common, was not even admitted, let alone rejected.[7]

Hard work and temperance together with honesty were the measure of good intent in one's relationships just as in one's work. Instability, idleness, thieving or regular drinking were hardly likely to guarantee the fragile economic balance on which a part of the conjugal arrangement rested. All this was well known to the district commissioners, who each day received numerous complaints from husbands or wives no longer prepared to tolerate the excesses of their partners. When this happened to a couple, that was the end of their credibility in the neighbourhood and of their good name amongst working people and artisans, without which it was difficult to sustain employment or retain the goodwill of customers.

The union could not have a life of its own without the approval of others. The couple found themselves mutually entwined in a narrow triangle comprising the man, the woman and the neighbourhood. In their capacity as witnesses for one another, they understood the nature of the arrangement and the ease with which it could crumble, not to say, shatter. But for all that the doors opened permanently onto the landing and the dividing walls were thin and, in spite of the ever-present neighbours and regardless of the inevitable fusion of fact and fiction, truth and rumour, interrogations and witnesses' accounts seldom reveal indiscretions about each other's sexual behaviour.[8] Terms like 'debauchery' and 'lechery' were used in condemnation, and 'honesty' in approval. Details that might allow a glimpse of the real life of the couple were rare. Even though every other aspect of life was common knowledge, it is perhaps anachronistic on our part to view such discretion with surprise. It could be anachronism or possibly a form of intellectual blindness which prevents us from imagining an unabashed sexual freedom and an absence of privacy where there was, nevertheless, still a place for secrets.

As far as the couple were concerned, both the man and the woman had their own individual honour to defend. If the husband or partner was debauched, he brought shame on himself in the eyes of the neighbourhood, where he was hardly likely to be excused on the grounds of his sex. If the wife or mistress drank or fell into bad company, she in her turn provoked a hostile reaction. It was up to both of them to maintain their own pride and reputation, in short, to hold their head high. The man was no more the keeper of the woman's reputation than she his. Significantly, witnesses' comments are no more harsh on her than him. Moreover, the disgrace of the one did not automatically rebound on the other; the neighbours certainly knew where to lay the blame without necessarily holding the couple responsible for the bad behaviour of one of its partners.

This was due to the structure of the couple and the perception of the prospects of each party. To assume mutual and yet individual responsibility for one's own honour so that repercussions were not necessarily felt by one's immediate family was to affirm a certain way of life which meant making one's own choices and accepting responsibility for oneself. Marriage, as an arrangement for mutual understanding and economic survival, created a set of relations where it was out of the question that the bad conduct of the one should adversely affect the chances of the other. If the drunkenness or self-indulgence of one of the partners inevitably disrupted the economic stability of the family group, there was no need to stigmatize the entire family as well. Where the offences committed were serious enough to undermine the reputation of all, there was, in the last resort, a call for the imprisonment of the whole family as a means of correction. But usually, each party accepted responsibility for his or her own honour, thereby reflecting the manner in which the association came about – a courageous journey for the majority.

Having left one's relatives behind in the provinces to go to the capital, one set up house in order to become established. Between the man and the woman there existed a kind of equality in their relationship to the outside world; each one worked, went about town, joined in with celebrations and was fully involved in the social round. One did not have a situation where, on the one hand, there was the man as the dim figure flitting between the inside and outside world in his capacity as defender of the family faith and, on the other hand, the woman, turned inward on her world. Rather, there were two people engaged in living and working to the best of their ability in the face of a neighbourhood which they watched and by whom they themselves were watched. To this extent one might say that the progress of the couple did not inhibit the personal development of the individual. Certainly, where an individual was capable of fending for himself or herself, independently of the other, then the honour of that person was capital to be invested only with extreme care.

In a society like that of the *Ancien Régime*, where the Third Estate had no rights and where tradespeople and small businessmen had no political representation or public voice such as the more hierarchical trades' associations might have, there was less rivalry between men and women, and for the couple, more equality in terms of personal worth. But as soon as one moved up the social ladder, the story was different. Conflicts between husband and wife were far from rare. An analysis of their disputes reveals their manner of addressing each other, the nature of their quarrels and their mistrust of one another. It further underlines the extent to which the neighbourhood was involved. When it came to going to law or assessing the rights and wrongs of a matter, the neighbours established responsibility and apportioned blame with scrupulous accuracy. They testified to what they had always seen, heard and understood. They defended the one and accused the other, revealing the strength of their hold on social practice and the consensus around which the collective life of the community revolved.

In these disputes the spoken word was undeniably binding. This produced a strange situation and we have already mentioned, for instance, how talk circulated in this urban microcosm. We have seen how it transformed and was transformed and the extent to which it could make or break reputations. However, when one gave one's word it was taken as concrete evidence and tangible proof. The written word was so rare that what was said between people took on a sacred character, proof of which, paradoxically, remained impossible to establish, the more especially as it was perceived and experienced as being the only proof worth establishing. Mobile, swift, disfigured and disfiguring, it was talk that was the maker and breaker of friendships, creator of upheaval as well as solidarity; and talk, in spite of everything, was taken at its word.

## The historian and the child

The lithe and mischievous silhouette of the child merging effortlessly with the activities of the city is a familiar one for us; Louis-Sébastien Mercier also has a description of the child's slender profile and his easy at-oneness with the life of the town, whilst the iconography of the day delights in sketching his agile presence in the urban landscape. But if we had only one picture of him in our memories, it would surely be that of the *petit Savoyard* encumbered by his sweep's tools and brushes.[9]

The judicial archives contain other images. They are much more shocking and there is absolutely no feeling of folklore or quaintness about them. They contain the annual registers of 'Abandoned Children' kept by the district commissioners; they include records of cases against parents who had failed to pay their fees for wet-nursing and requests for imprisonment by *lettres de cachet*[10] (in this respect, one could remain a child up until the age of 32). Abandonment, wet-nursing and imprisonment were all realities for which we have some evidence even though it is rather patchy.[11]

The main body of complaints and actions brought before the courts of the Petit and Grand Criminel[12] contain references to the child in the context of the evidence and examinations. This might amount to no more than preliminary questions put to the accused in which they were asked to state the number of their children, living or dead. The child was also a cause of disputes between parents, for his games and pranks quite often upset the neighbourhood; and his placement as an apprentice could also give rise to conflicts between the master of the workshop and the mothers and fathers. As a result the child was often to be found at the forefront of a host of quarrels with which the urban scene was studded.

It is difficult to form a clear and precise picture of him, however, or to make out his exact place and role, even though one does have a number of detailed texts on the subject, such as one particular dossier on the affair of the abduction of children in Paris in May 1750.[13] It presents, in all its brutality, a population and its police face to face with its youngsters.

Recent historiography has cast the whole subject of the child in a new light, so that it is now possible to think one knows not only how he came into the world, but how he was fed, clothed, nursed, loved and educated. Segments from his history have been reconstituted and a very different interpretation of his place in the family and in society has come to light. Today, as is often the case, however, the images occasionally become blurred and the actual reality becomes as elusive as ever. In the end one discovers that the source work is confined almost exclusively to what is said **about** him and, very rarely, from what he himself **is**, or from what his parents can say about him or what he himself can say about his activities and his own network of friends and acquaintances. We discover him through moral and educational concerns written on the subject by enlightened elites, or else from graphs showing birth rates, statistics of infant mortality and the numbers of abandoned children. Rationalizations are made based on 'official' attention given him by society without ever really considering his links with the family and other social structures, thereby denying him the possibility of becoming the subject of his own history.[14]

This has made it possible to outline a number of themes which, although divergent, depend in the main on the same basic questions; for instance, does the love for a child remain one of the unchanging constants of human history, whether or not its exteriorization is affected by the attitudes and behaviour appropriate to the time? Or is its appearance a historical occurrence which we can date? This automatic insistence on associating 'childhood' with 'love' has contributed to the absence of new modes of enquiry which might allow different aspects of the history of children to be discovered. Perhaps one part of the field of investigation has unwittingly been rendered sterile by limiting this new object of history – childhood – to one or two questions which are far too closely linked to our own concepts of childhood, such as the following: In view of the frequency with which children were abandoned in the past, or inadvertently suffocated, could one say that they were loved? Or, could one be affected by the death of a baby when death itself was such a frequent and familiar occurrence?

By focusing the research primarily on the extent and amount of love, which is in itself difficult enough to define, let alone evaluate, one limits the possibility of uncovering other modes of relating and socializing between parents, children and adults. This constant association of childhood with sentiment and sensibilities ultimately produces a thick screen from behind which the imagination finds it cannot quite escape.

It is particularly in the studies of poor families where this association gives rise to most difficulty. As far as the nobility or the bourgeoisie is concerned, historians of the eighteenth century have an abundance of literature on the child at their disposal. They can take account of its impact on the reading matter of the period, and assess its evolution and influence on the parents. The mastery of reading and writing, the taste for knowledge and new ideas, the practice of writing journals or memoirs and the habit of letter-writing have all left numerous traces which allow us to see the changes in thinking with regard to behaviour and custom, and provide us with reflections on emotions and the expression of feelings within the family.

Of course there is nothing of the kind for the popular classes. In spite of the compilation of statistics for literacy and well-researched studies of popular literature and the cultural differences between various social groups, it still remains very difficult to describe ways of behaving within families and their evolution. The task of interpretation is much more sensitive here than elsewhere. From factors such as economic fluctuations, price indices and rates of mortality and abandonment, the historian has to deduce a certain number of resulting practices. Apart from judicial archives and the all too rare autobiography, one can call on very few texts which allow a more faithful reconstruction of the exact place of the child amongst the people.

In this context poor families, who were usually more affected by death and disease than others, have often been interpreted in economic terms and nothing else, thus precluding any kind of affection as we understand it today. Some years ago, for instance, one of our most serious and imaginative historians working in this field said that 'the family was a moral and social reality, rather than emotional. In the very poorest families, it corresponded to nothing more than the material installation of the couple within a wider milieu. . . . For the poor, the family as the centre of emotional life scarcely existed.'[15]

It is perhaps surprising to find that not even recent work on the subject has succeeded in providing a different view, and while not necessarily linking economic difficulty to an absence of feeling or relating childhood simply to bonds of affection, it does still create stereotyped images of the child of the people fleeing the house 'to bronze himself in the sun's rays', for instance, or learning about life in the workshop to the crack of the cane or from jokes and obscenities. 'It is said there were no children among the popular classes. Children were abandoned or put out to nurse, they ran away from home, were collected into schools or spent their free hours in the streets, only coming home to sleep.'[16] However, Jacques-Louis Ménétra, journeyman glazier, when writing the *Journal* of his life, begins by recording the death of his mother when he was 2 years old and his very great affection for his grandmother from whom he could hardly bear to be separated. 'I became sick with boredom from not seeing my grandmother.'[17]

When it comes to characterizing the people, one is constantly coming across contradictions and shifts in vocabulary and occasionally tone, which suggest a remote, almost other-worldly quality and one finds that their behaviour and actions are interpreted as being the very essence of popular culture and thought. Popular activities are certainly described better than previously, but at the risk of their being encased in a vocabulary which exudes the odour of sweat and the gutter.

The same ambiguities affect the history of feelings amongst the people as that of popular culture. For if it is generally agreed among historians and sociologists that 'the criteria of beauty are determined by knowledge and discernment and what is generally considered agreeable to the finer feelings, both of which lie well outside the field of competence of the common people',[18] then it is hardly surprising that they have no reservations in contrasting the refinement of bourgeois emotions with the brutishness of the people. I am convinced that like Jacques Rancière in his commentary on Kant, one has to 'give up once and for all this notion that the world must forever be divided up between "cultured" man and "natural" man'.[19]

There is no reason to suppose that aesthetic forms are necessarily linked to knowledge any more than that feelings should be associated with the degree of civilization and refinement. We must stop attributing to the oppressed our own laborious interpretations of their daily activities as though these were their culture on the pretext that the people neither possess nor have mastered the elements of traditional culture. It is time to put an end to this way of looking at things, which is largely due to the intellectual or specialist who applies his own rules and mechanisms to what he has discovered, and puts together what he calls popular 'habits' under the heading of 'thought' or 'view of the world' so as to avoid looking elsewhere. Just because the people have to associate, eat or house themselves in such and such a fashion due to economic constraints, it would seem that there is no other way of categorizing them apart from these practices derived solely from necessity; and, for the common man, it is as if, between necessity and himself, there were no space of his own in which he might think, express preference, criticize, concede, refuse and appreciate. 'For the paid parquet-layer, liberty begins with and depends on reversing roles, by being the one who looks, and not the one who is looked at.' So writes J. Rancière of the carpenter Gauny, whose philosophical propositions he had discovered.[20]

This almost impossible quest to understand that intimate space that the human being puts between himself and his sense of self is the real work of the historian and, occasionally, when faced with this blank space which has to be unearthed and rediscovered, there is a strong temptation to let the documents from the police archives speak for themselves. Quite often they are so superb that one would like to give them to the reader as they are, without changing a single word; this is as much for their aesthetic value as for the depth of their significance. The temptation is there because it immediately acts as protection against those possible shifts in meaning about which we have just spoken. Rather than betray, distort or even conceal, why not lay the texts bare, just as they are? But it would obviously be a mistake to be lured into thinking that the nakedness of the document was a test of the truth or failure of the assessment of its meaning; for history cannot be reduced to a simple display of texts and ancient documents. Like it or not, history is a considered account which each generation dedicates to its past, thinks through anew and reformulates as new events and problematical questions arise.

The work of interpreting texts and situating them in relation to others and to social and political phenomena has to be done. It is essentially that which engenders the search for models, rules and mechanisms which allow one to find order and rationality in the totality of popular behaviours so often described as being the fruits of compulsions, irrationality or primeval tendencies from which all reflection has been totally excluded. Hence we have the people as instinctive animal, or the crowd as impulsive woman, weak and violent; these images are so close to us that they form an unconscious and undeniable part of our mental horizons even if one is sufficiently alert or cautious enough to be on one's guard against them. In searching for this order, which might include the study of irrational phenomena (the world of feelings, beliefs or superstitions etc.), one gradually has to start filling in the generally perceived gaps between bourgeois reason and popular primitivism.

The concern to keep popular childhood quite separate from questions of love or the lack of it (which up until now have been an almost statutory requirement and additional appendix), springs entirely from this pre-occupation. One is thus free to study, one by one, the child's activities in the city such as his comings and goings, his favourite haunts, his relationship with the neighbourhood, his work or trade, forms of collective life and his links with institutional structures (be they parish, family, school, police or prison). Once one has demarcated the processes and procedures of his daily practice, one is free to introduce the question of the nature of the links existing between himself, the family and the social group; the interest shown in him by the adult world and the ways in which it perceived or availed itself of him. From that, what one eventually finds out about feelings will be as a result of thorough research into his place in the fabric of urban life and not by asking a priori questions born of our own concept of childhood or of the people which tend to suppose that the structural reality of childhood can be reclaimed from rather poor updating of this kind. The careful establishment of modes of rationality avoids the arbitrary nature of hasty judgements or of changing ideologies and also avoids falling into the trap of constantly describing the people in the images of Epinal,[21] left forever on the margins of self-awareness. And although highly regulated and rigorous research of this kind cannot give the life of the people its full dimension, I am deeply convinced that it is one of the few methods likely to reveal any popular forms of coherence. But in spite of that, my reading of the archives has left me with a kind of conviction that no amount of analysis, no matter how detailed, can ever take account of those extra qualities of life and thought that come through in each document. One can never have the measure of everything – there is always something left which is important but unpronounceable. Nor does it do any good to appropriate it on the pretext that one is aware of it, even by communicating it lyrically in a form which addresses itself to the senses; this would sound too much like Michelet,[22] or someone of the same school. There is a risk that a rigorous and methodical intellect might lose, on the lower slopes of knowledge, those high points of life and the senses. We never fully discern them by means of the 'sense' we manage to make of them through our own understanding, but we nevertheless still need to grasp the ruggedness or gentleness of the terrain. We should not lose them from sight nor leave them fallow; nor should one immobilize them beneath a pen welling with easy emotion and all too ready to cover over our enormous vats of ignorance with a passing fad. Thus what is said here about childhood and the people is a deliberate attempt to avoid these traps; but I cannot help thinking that scattered somewhere in these documents are small strands of meaning which I have been unable to thread together again, yet which upset the order of things even as I have begun to set it in place.

## Contrasting silhouettes

We are familiar with the great ferment of ideas and philosophical reflection that took place during the eighteenth century and which put the child very much at the centre of its preoccupations. There is no point in our mentioning here the discourses by moralists and philosophers or treatises by those involved with public health who were concerned to introduce new regulations to help stem the tide of infant mortality and the death of women in childbirth. Many historians have already worked on these themes, highlighting, for instance, the conflict between doctors and midwives or the need for the child to be breast-fed by its own mother, to take but two examples.[23]

The moral teaching of the Church at the time on family matters and relationships is also interesting, and J.-L. Flandrin has produced a detailed study of an important text written in 1713 by Antoine Blanchard, Prior of Saint-Mars-lès-Vendôme. In it he expounds on matters of sin and transgression and offers some commandments whose wordiness provides us with a good deal of information.[24] Respect and kindness, for instance, were to be a natural part of the relationship between parents and children. There had been efforts in the sixteenth and seventeenth centuries to stifle this natural affection, which was regarded as ungodly; in the eighteenth century, to be overly demonstrative (particularly between man and wife) was still viewed with suspicion but there was greater freedom in the expression of feelings between parents and children. Confession manuals lay particular emphasis on respect and fairness; parents should not stir up envy or jealousy amongst their children, nor should there be any trace of harshness or indifference in their behaviour. These negative recommendations left the field wide open for all kinds of positive attitudes if so desired, as there were no impositions of a specific nature contained within these moral teachings of the Church. There was some room for manoeuvre, with parents and children having mutual functions to fulfil which were likely to determine attitudes and other matters of significance.

As for the police archives, they offer such a variety and multitude of conflicting, contrasting and contradictory images of the child that on first reading one is overwhelmed by a feeling of incoherence and disorder; being a child would appear to be a space which knew neither laws nor limitations but was rather a zone of confusion in which it was difficult for ways of being to assume any kind of order.

On closer examination, it becomes apparent that the reaction of the parents vis-à-vis their children and their coming into the world lay within the only two spaces available to them, namely the hope for life and the immediate contradiction of their hope due to the deathly landscape by which it was surrounded.

Economic difficulties, constant migrations, the search for work or lack of regular employment forced the parents into putting their children out to nurse;[25] on some occasions they abandoned them,[26] a practice which could sometimes reach plague proportions and fill entire mortuaries with abandoned children. Lack of hygiene, appropriate care and epidemics did the rest. Up until 4 years old, the chances of survival were very slim. At the birth of one of their children, the parents spontaneously welcomed the idea of its life at the same time as accepting the possibility of its loss. The texts reflect a state of tension between several possibilities: abandonment or sending away to nurse; sickness, or indeed death, due to ignorance of basic hygiene.

Louise Brulé was the wife of a servant. Being ill, she wanted above all else to have her son brought back from Montargis where he had been sent away to nurse. On 8 June 1766, when he was only one year old, a driver had brought him in a water cart as far as Port Saint-Paul in Paris, accompanied by his nurse; but on arrival, all that remained was a little corpse. The Watch went to let the mother know and the booking clerk for the Briare coach waited for her to come. He put the child's body on a barrel.

> The woman, who was unknown to us, came to the guardroom. She was all in tears and told us that she had come to see her child and when we told her that he was dead we asked her to give her name. Louise Brulé, wife of Damideaux, a servant to Jannier, rate-payer in the Rue du Sentier and herself resident of Rue de Cléry, recognized the nurse of her male child to whom she had entrusted his care on 25 February 1765 together with the appropriate layette. She confirmed that she had been notified of her son's illness in a letter received ten months ago and that a short while before that, this same nurse had let her know that her son was in very good health and now needed putting into frocks, so she had sent

him one. She said she wanted to see him but the foster-father had said that the child was in no fit state to travel and so she assumed that they would do all that was required and she had offered to pay for his treatment. Since then she had received two letters from the foster-father giving her news of her child. He said that her child had been ill on and off and that he had had a slight fever which was due to teething as he had had four teeth for two or three months now. As they had not had any further news and wanting to see him on account of her feelings as a mother, they had decided to send their cousin with two letters, one for the priest and the other for the foster-father. She could not recall the content of the letters as it had been her husband who had written them, and she herself had not read them. Her cousin had set out and she was very surprised to see him again today telling her that her child had died on the way. She could not recognize him in his present state as the only time she had seen him was the day she had brought him into the world, but she said that she recognized the linen of his layette. Her husband was not there; she thought he was in the country with his masters.[27]

The nurse explained that she had not wanted to undertake the journey, given the state of the child's health but as the parents had insisted, she had resigned herself to it, and that 'in order to meet this request, she, the wife of Beauvais, had left Ferrière with the child yesterday, the seventh day of the month at 6 o'clock in the morning and boarded the Briare coach. This same Jean-Baptiste had died in her arms at 2 o'clock.'

The identification of the body makes a moving account. Louise Brulé had been forced to separate from her new-born child after only 24 hours because of her way of life and its economic constraints (she and her husband could not have been living under the same roof). A year later she had been obliged to state to the commissioner that apart from the layette she had sent him a short while ago, she did not recognize him. The clothes were her only proof of kinship. From this text, one gains a better understanding of the basis of the relationship between parent and child which consisted of enforced separation from birth, concern for him in spite of the distance, ignorance of the risks involved in the journey and the absence of any real married life for a couple where one of the parents was a servant. There is also the lack of confidence in the nurse and her relative incompetence. Louise Brulé was a mother in mourning for a son she did not know.

This scene, which was almost commonplace, illustrates the disruption of the family. In such unfavourable conditions it is hardly surprising to find texts referring to the mother's lack of care for her children, or in which one finds a father complaining before the law of neglect that was potentially harmful to the welfare of his family. Familiarity with risk led to fatalism and then to neglect but this negligence should not be confused with indifference, as indicated by the following example of Marie-Jeanne-Françoise Dupont, who although condemned by her husband, was supported by the neighbourhood:

> On 27 March 1778 at midday, Mathieu Legendre, chief clerk at the office of the King's Privy Council and resident of the Rue du Paon Saint-Victor, came to lodge a complaint of neglect against Marie-Jeanne-Françoise Dupont, his wife. He had agreed that his child of 4 should be weaned provided that he was properly fed and brought up by his mother; but owing to her lack of care and failure to take him out walking in the fresh air or keep him properly clean, he was unable to walk or make use of his limbs. Although his wife had initially agreed to put him out to board at the Barrière Saint-Jacques she had this day prevented him from doing anything, for when they reached the end of the Rue Paon she had started yelling, which brought everyone out onto the street, and they had tackled him and snatched the child from his hands, pulling off his wig and scratching his hands.[28]

At first sight the father appears to be a concerned figure but this rather contrasts with the image of indifference of a man who had no qualms about placing his children in an orphanage because at the time they were preventing him from getting established.

There are also sketches of the woman with hordes of lovers who had brought a large number of children into the world only to dispatch them to the wet-nurse with never a second thought and without notifying their respective fathers.

After several liaisons, Marie-Geneviève Demaisne, a mother already, had set up house with Bordier, secretary to a member of the *parlement* during the year 1768.

> During the time of his liaison with her [affirms Bordier] she became pregnant several times, but she took sole charge of the confinement and the baptism of the children and sent them off to nurse so that all he had had to do was to provide the money needed to cover her expenses. He never knew where she sent the children and in fact she told him almost every time that she had given birth that the children had died shortly afterwards.

Bordier seemed to recall that Marie-Geneviève was probably pregnant 'in the course of the years 1769, 1770, 1771, 1772 and 1773 and that when they were not dead as she had often told him she had put some of them into the orphanage'.[29]

Migration, the high incidence of illegitimacy, the problems of contraception, poverty, infantile mortality, together with the practice of abandoning children, created a landscape in which people managed their insecurity in their own particular way, torn between the desire for life and all the other circumstances which made success a gamble. Closely parallel with these examples in which the mother and father failed to look after their children are contrasting texts illustrating the parents' obvious concern for the child. The new-born child, abandoned at the church door, might have a note pinned to his jacket or else one might find parents concerned about the good behaviour of their children, or even scenes of despair in the event of a fatal accident to a child. (The accident of May 1770, the day of the Dauphin's marriage when 132 people suffocated to death, is a good example of this.) Attitudes were shaped by the hope for life, about which they obviously had good cause to be concerned.

### 'They're taking a child!'

From December 1749 to May 1750, Paris lurched from one crisis to the next; in fact the seasons and months were punctuated by 17 revolts in all. Meanwhile the police took on the strange task of picking up children and beggars right in the middle of the street. They were carrying out the orders of Berryer, the Lieutenant-General of Police who had issued them on the pretext that the children were up to no good and that the others were asking for alms.

In the spring, popular anger intensified and the month of May turned bloody; outbursts of anger which turned violent flared up more and more frequently and brought the populace together, leading to conspiracies and threats against the Lieutenancy of Police and its henchmen. Several commissioners' *hôtels* were besieged, police officers were pursued and shops looted. On 23 May, a police spy was beaten to death by the crowd who had turfed him out of his rather precarious hiding-place in a building on the Rue Saint-Honoré. They took him to a commissioner who was so terrified that he released him pretty quickly, thereby delivering him into the hands of a crowd who were obviously determined to beat him to death. That day, Lieutenant-General Berryer, surprised at discovering events so widespread and finding his own life in danger, was obliged to flee his *hôtel* by a back door.

The day after the disturbance, the *parlement* ordered an investigation, and for the next three months about 30 suspects were interrogated, including rioters and police agents accused of the abduction of children. Two hundred and twenty-five witnesses were heard including those who had seen the riots either close at hand or from afar, those who had been there when a child was abducted and also those who had happened to hear any 'dangerous talk'. The parents of the children who had been taken prisoner as well as the children themselves were also summoned to appear. There were times when procedures went to as many as three interrogations in a row as well as the inclusion of 'additional information', all of it recorded in minute detail.

The *parlement* returned its judgement on 1 August 1750: three rioters, one of whom was just 16, were sentenced to be hanged, and six policemen were either reprimanded or received a warning. On 3 August the three young men were executed at the Place de Grève before a crowd who had begun by demanding a pardon but who fell silent in the face of an impressive police presence. At the end of the day a few police subordinates had had their feathers ruffled and three troublemakers were put to death. Nothing had changed.

How could a society which was otherwise so preoccupied with education, population and the excessive rate of infant mortality have possibly embarked on an enterprise such as the removal of children by its police? In fact, ever since the end of the seventeenth century the population had been shaken periodically by the sound of the arrest and abduction of children which gave rise to numerous royal decrees requiring the commissioners to investigate the matter.

It was the new policy of imprisoning beggars and vagrants which had provoked the events; and as earlier in 1663 and 1675, the *archers* of the *hôpital*[30] were the targets of serious rioting because they were suspected of operating large-scale raids which included children. There had been a similar situation in 1701, and in 1720 the situation was even more serious,[31] with the result that on 4 May, following serious confrontations in the street, the King had issued a decree prohibiting anyone, on pain of death, from interfering with the *archers* responsible for the arrest of vagabonds and beggars, disabled and able-bodied alike.

The youngest were to be sent to the French colonies of America and Mississippi but the arrest of any bourgeois, artisan or workman was to be avoided. In fact, on 29 April a number of *archers* had been massacred by the people of Paris at the pont Notre-Dame and the rue Saint-Antoine and for several days there had been wholesale arrests of men, women, children and young girls with the intention of deporting them.[32] In their haste, they had taken away the sons and daughters of wealthy traders, causing an immediate popular reaction, for *their* children were certainly not going to have any part in the opening up of Louisiana or Mississippi.

The authorities had been looking for a way of populating the colonies for some considerable time already and the idea of sending out abandoned children was not new.

It is a matter of considerable importance to find the means whereby abandoned children might be sent to the West Indies and maintained there until they are of an age to earn their own living. The climate and temperature would help them to gain in physical strength and they would no longer wish to return from a country they considered their own. Harsh as it might seem to engage against their will children who were born free, it could hardly be considered unjust if, for three or five years, say, between the age of 14 and 19, they were to be in the service of those people who had put them in a position to earn their own living.[33]

Of the abandoned children, those who were the first to come under attack were the beggars and tricksters, the dissolute and the idle. After the riot of 1720 the Lieutenant of Police asked the *syndics*[34] of the trades-guilds to give him a list of their journeymen and apprentices. At the same time each master was required to issue a certificate to each of his employees in the absence of which, if taken by the *archers*, they would be 'sent to Mississippi'.

All of this certainly makes it easier to understand the violence of the days of May 1750. Paris had known for a long time that the disappearance of her children might be due to police involvement – the knowledge was still fresh in her memory. It was in their name that her citizens had risen up and directed their anger at the door of the Lieutenant-General. The response, though violent, was a rational attitude to this very real threat which went on largely unseen. In fact, many of those police officers who had been arrested appeared to feel guilty about obeying the abduction orders. For them, this work was not at all in their normal line of duty and in fact some of them even disguised or camouflaged themselves in order to do it. They knew that their actions were provocative and would inevitably exasperate the crowd.

The dossiers of both parents and children produced during the investigations of the riot contain details of the reactions of each party to the events as well as of daily activities which allow us an inside view of the complexity of the relationships existing between children and adults. The parents' evidence given in the course of the enquiry provides us with an account of their reactions from the point at which they first learned about their child's sudden disappearance. These texts, plus those provided by the children who were also called to give evidence, outline the habits and patterns of family life, making them rare and exceptional accounts amongst the police archives. One can see that running throughout the majority of the parents' accounts, there is all the evidence of a consistent and sustained concern, even if one does find contrasting evidence here and there of the kind we have discussed elsewhere. And, in turn, when the children give their evidence they almost always make mention of the interest shown towards them by their parents. There are no elaborate comments, just simple acknowledgements which show in their own way that the parent–child relationship was often symmetrical.

The news of the child's arrest was always deeply felt by the parents. The comments they make about the moment when they first found out what had happened are vivid and they describe how they immediately interrupted their normal activities to set off in search of the child. They stress how in a matter of moments, they felt that they had been sent reeling into another dimension of time which required precipitate action and urgent steps to recover him. One parent started running after the *archers'* prison coach which was still visible on the corner of the square; another man was so overcome with fright that he came out of the bar where he had been having a drink and started shouting for help; a third interrupted a meal with friends; one mother immediately made her way to the prison of Le Grand Châtelet, whilst another woman hastily found out about the habits of Lieutenant-General Berryer in order to lie in wait for him and ask for her child back. The first thought was often to warn the district commissioner. Jérôme Taconnet was a master butcher. He related how his '15-year-old son was at catechism and at about 5 o'clock a girl who was a stranger to him had come and told him that his son had been taken away by the *archers* who picked up young lads to send them off to the Indies. Not realizing what the time was, he thought, good, the boy's at catechism,' and he went off quickly to look for him. The doors were closed, however. This frightened him so he returned home and then went with one of his friends to see Commissioner Le Comte.[35]

Balthazar Lucas, a soldier in the Watch, found out about everything that had happened from his wife as 'he was at vespers with the Jesuits of the Rue Saint-Antoine'. He came rushing out of the service and ran across to Commissioner Rochebrune, only to see his child in handcuffs.

One Sunday at the end of September, Anne-Françoise Cornet was returning from a visit to one of her children who was apprenticed to a clockmaker when she saw 'a band of children from the area coming up towards her. They told her that her child had been arrested and that he was at Le Grand Châtelet [the prison] so she went over there straight away'.[36]

Both father and mother reacted with the same speed and they usually took steps together. Sometimes one of them would be reluctant to warn the other for fear of contributing to the other's grief, like the wife of Millard who, upon seeing her son arrested, 'returned home promptly in order to prevent her husband from finding out, but he already knew'. Once the family was reunited with uncles, aunts, cousins and brothers, it acted swiftly and in unison. This is not surprising – the importance of family networks is well established.

In the end, feelings of shock, fear and hate gave way to grief and its associated behaviour, such as the child crying in the prison yard, or the mother breaking down in tears on hearing of the arrest. Marguerite Ollier spoke about the evening when her only son was taken away from their home: 'The officer said to the son, "Get up and get dressed, you young layabout." Her child got dressed and she was crying a great deal, but he said, "Don't cry, mother", and she followed him outside holding him by the hand.'[37] It was not just women and children who responded in this way. Elsewhere in the records, a witness referred to the pain and grief 'of his neighbour whose son had disappeared', and Balthazar Lucas, a 58-year-old soldier, 'fell to his knees before Inspector Brucelles and kissed his feet'.[38]

The imprisonment of the child, following his arrest, saw an increase in the parents' initiatives, and the days that followed were a race against time in an attempt to avoid the worst, namely official entry and due registration at the prison of Bicêtre following several days in custody at the prison of Le Grand Châtelet. The typical expressions used by the parents to describe those moments spent attempting to extricate their child from the hands of the police are like these by the following two mothers which illustrate the depth of their anxiety: 'The very next day she took it upon herself to make every effort to get her son back', and 'as soon as she received the news she went into action to find him'. The action was swift and imaginative and neighbours and family were all brought in, in a variety of ways. Some asked their neighbours to sign petitions of good character in an attempt to bear witness to the honesty of their little prisoner; then, armed with this precious bit of paper, they would go as often as twice a day to show it at the Lieutenancy of Police where as often as not they would be met by a minor employee or secretary.

Others used their distant relations to make approaches directly or from afar to a police inspector or, better still, to Berryer himself.

Cousins, friends or servants working in large or small households were sometimes able to provide the odd bit of information. Perhaps they had heard that the inspector lived here or there or that he took this or that route or came out at such and such a time. Occasionally they remembered themselves to a former employer who was well established and perhaps able to make an approach to the Lieutenant-General or some of his entourage. This immediate resort to a conscious use of the social channels and protective mechanisms (feeble though they were) does give an idea of some of the links and points of connection between the nobility and the ordinary people. Some of them told the commissioner, for instance, how they themselves had kept watch on the movements of the police inspector after a friend or neighbour had told them that he sometimes went to dine at such and such a house. Thus, what we have here is the minute detail of popular knowledge which was clearly capable of recognizing everyone's comings and goings – evidence, in short, of the 'body social' made visible.

Take the case of Anne Cornet, for example. 'She was tipped off somewhere between 8 and 9 o'clock at night that Brucelles [an inspector] was passing by on his way home to the Hôtel Nicolaï. She ran over there so quickly that she found him at the entrance porch.'

Along with all these comings and goings, the parents also took care of their son in prison. They visited him several times a day, brought him food so that he would not go without, gave money to the prison guards and even to the other prisoners to make sure that he was well treated and, above all, to ensure that he was not beaten.

Gabriel Laurent, apprentice joiner, aged 16, told how he was taken handcuffed to Le Châtelet, where he stayed eight days and 'came out as a result of the interventions of his mother's friends. During this time he had been put on straw,[39] and his mother had brought him his food every day.' Georges-Jean Bacheviller was 15 years old. He was arrested upon becoming involved in a quarrel between some women in the street. He was 'on straw for 15 days at Le Châtelet where his mother and father came to see him two or three times a day'.

The amount of concern shown by the parents was not just related to the age of the children. Marguerite Simon, mother of an older boy of 19 who had just finished his apprenticeship as a cobbler, 'took her son soup twice a day and was distraught at seeing him covered in vermin'. Marie Magnieu, a market trader, stated clearly that she had been 'constantly at the prison with food for her son' and he too was almost a grown man. Fear that prison might be the ruin of both body and soul was very evident in each testimony. One father was saddened to say that whilst his child had been there, 'he had contracted scabies from which he was still not quite recovered and that while he was there he had also learned a lot of filth.'

Now and again one comes across a concern for education. Laundress and widow of a journeyman joiner, Marguerite Ollier had only one son and he had been taken away. She was very grieved by his loss and she got her neighbours to sign a number of petitions proving that she was an honest woman; but in spite of her efforts, her son was taken to prison at Bicêtre. At the time of making her statement her son was still there and had been there for just over six months. She gave the following details: 'She had given 30 *sols* [Old French for 'sous'] a month so that he could learn to read and write and the Governor and the prison masters had said that they were very pleased with him.'[40]

This was not an isolated remark. The interrogations and the statements both show an almost constant preoccupation with education. Whether it was a matter of learning to read or write, or of forming letters (one prisoner revealed that he could only read capitals and another explained that he could write an A, a B and a C), or whether it concerned attendance at school or at catechism, the dossiers give a good account of the obvious importance attached to reading and writing amongst the least privileged social groups and of the concern of most parents to provide their children with some education. Of course, in these archives one does occasionally turn up some statements by parents who showed little concern for their children, thus providing a contrasting picture, as was pointed out previously. It is worth noting however, that they were in the minority compared with the others and perhaps this is because it was a question here of a collective threat coming from a police force supposedly there to protect its population.

Marguerite Lebel, for example, heard a noise in the street the day before the Feast of Pentecost. A neighbour shouted up to her that it was children being arrested and so she went down to get two of hers in, never thinking at the time about her other boy of 11, who had already been arrested.[41]

We find care and neglect living together side by side. Another woman, for example, who found out that her child had been picked up at a fair, decided not to bother doing anything 'as their eldest son had said that there wasn't any point, as the boy was already in prison'.[42] There was no rush in this case, just the inevitable submission to fate. Elsewhere one finds a defenceless woman just waiting and making no attempt to get her son released; she did not want to pay anything as she was convinced that the courts would return him to her because he was an honest lad. The following is the account of her 13-year-old son, François Lefevre, imprisoned for 17 days:

> His mother was asked for 6 francs at the prison to get him out earlier, but his mother hadn't got it, so she told the gaolers that her son hadn't done anything wrong or done any harm to anyone and when they got tired of guarding him they would send him back to her. He came out eight days later without costing his mother a thing.[43]

Whether one is dealing with the disturbance of 1750 or the occasional rare text in amongst police proceedings, one comes to realize that rather than a duality in the attitudes towards children there is a coexistence of different views which sometimes contradict and appear entirely foreign to each other as though there were no logical connection between them. The same person, the mother or the father, seems to hold different attitudes, sometimes at one and the same time, sometimes one after the other. This raises a number of questions. When we read, for instance, that there were some who did not know the number of their brothers and sisters or whereabouts they were serving their apprenticeship, is it really a case of disorder or incoherence when, on the other hand, there were some who had a surprisingly precise knowledge of their lineage, including distant cousins? In actual fact, the whole of these reactions needs to be related to the child and the family and to the circumstances engendering them as well as to the position and functions held in the city by the members of the family.

The child was as much a sign of life as of impending death, a fact which was constantly brought to the minds of his parents by the environment in which they lived. The existence of physical, material and moral danger (accidents, illness and loss of employment) created an insecurity which fashioned the shape of the collective mental horizons where the web of both individual and social existence was woven from an awareness of the potential threats to it. As a result, it was risk, whether real or imagined, which produced that coexistence of attitudes which was in itself a means of responding to the situation. One could deal with the risk or defy it, tackle it head on, or resign oneself to it; it could drive one into submission through anxiety, or else one could confront it with an indifference which was intended to make the days and hours more liveable. It was in fact risk which constituted the general matrix around which a large part of the relationship between parent and child was constructed. Subsequently, it is no longer a question of assessing or measuring positive or negative attitudes in the hope of ultimately drawing a conclusion about the presence or absence of affection in childhood. It is something entirely different. The simultaneous existence of conflicting and contrasting behaviour was the means by which the Parisian population attempted to cope with childhood and to live with risk. 'In a number of everyday situations, risk is found at the heart of a mesh of constraints and contradictory motivations where contending "realities" collide.'[44] This is really what it was about.

As well as the risk and insecurity that each one had to deal with, one should also include the way in which the family lived amid the structures of urban life and the relationships which developed between parents and children at the heart of this mishmash, such that the diversity of attitudes matched their corresponding functions, which we must now describe.

### The messenger

One's eye is caught first of all by a somewhat nervous and slender form whose familiar presence in Paris was punctuated by an incessant activity. Aged between 10 and 16 years, he lived mainly out of doors on the streets, squares or thoroughfares or on the restless banks of the Seine. He had things to do . . .

Depending on his family of origin, he might do this or that job or he might intend to be a tradesman after a period of apprenticeship. In this case, on completion of the contract between his parents and the master, he would live with his master and be dependent on him for several years. His removal from his parents' influence could often cause problems and conflict.[45] If he were really poor, he might be an odd-job boy, a shop hand, woodcutter or floor-polisher, unless he happened to come from further afield like the mountains of Savoy, for example, or Limousin or the Auvergne and then he might find himself swelling the ranks of young chimney-sweeps, sleeping with his companions in dormitories overseen by ancient old men and usually to be seen wearing the reminders of his work about his person. He merged with the world of adults, and was only distinguishable by the smallness of his stature and his cunning agility.

The child also took the time to go to school, however, and to receive instruction; in fact the position of Paris in this respect was somewhat exceptional as 'the Paris school system offered those who had access to it (almost all males of established families and a good proportion of females) a wide range of choices: the system comprised nearly five hundred schools of all kinds'.[46] In fact, in the spring of 1750 at the time of the abductions, a good many parents expressed their fear of sending their children to school and the small schools became empty. Jean-Baptiste Feuchère, assistant to the Parisian diocese and employed in the instruction of poor children of the parish of Saint-Gervais, was called to give evidence on 27 May. He told how

> the fear of abduction of children was so great that a good many mothers and fathers of the children who had continued coming had sought to share their anxieties with him. He had told them that they could come with them or keep them at home if they were afraid and, in fact, after the feast of Pentecost, only about 12 of the 85 children who had continued coming to the school still remained and they were all in fear and trembling, and it had been the same in all the schools of the parish.[47]

This evidence was corroborated by J.-L. Ménétra in his *Journal*.

> In those days it was rumoured that they were taking young boys and bleeding them and that they were lost forever and that their blood was used to bathe a young princess suffering from a disease that could only be cured with human blood. There was plenty of talk about that in Paris. My father came to get me from school as many other fathers did, along with seven big coopers armed with crowbars.[48]

There was school but there was also catechism and religious ceremonies. Some would go to vespers, others might go to hear prayers or prepare for their first communion. The police archives make frequent mention of such religious activities involving children. We also know that at this time a good many priests were involved in the somewhat difficult task of catechizing this world of working children and in particular, those children who had come from outlying provinces to perform the humble task of chimney-sweep or cleaner under the control of their elders. An enquiry into this matter made by the Abbé du Breil de Pontbriand reveals how these little Savoyards lived: You will find them living

> in the *faubourgs* (outskirts), eight or ten to a room which is supervised by a leader. They do not return until late at night, bringing back their paltry takings until they have enough to be able to make some use of it according to the advice from the rest of their room ... their steward and their tutor.[49]

Those children living with their families lived according to its rhythm; and a few apprentices in nearby workshops might still remain at home whilst others spent Sundays with their parents. Embedded as they were in both family and neighbourhood networks, these children performed all kinds of functions, ranging from running errands, carrying parcels and making deliveries to looking after their parents, passing messages and accompanying younger brothers and sisters. If we take the timetables of the children abducted in May 1750 as an example, we see that François Gautier, aged 12 years, was taken right in the middle of the street. He was on his way to fetch some black soap costing 3 *sols* and some brandy to clean up a leg wound his father had received while working on some driftwood. After running his errand, he should have gone to school. Then there was young Joly, aged 9, an apprentice workman in gauze. He was arrested on 1 May 1750 by the *archers* while on his way to bring his little niece back from his sister's as his mother had told him.[50]

Another child was waiting for his mother at the Place Royale. She had asked him to wait outside until she had finished her prayers at the side of a neighbour of theirs who was dying and she hadn't wanted to leave him on his own. In the meantime, a carriage had stopped and a hand had reached out and taken the child.

François Lefevre was 13. He was a ropemaker's boy and his master had just finished giving him some work to do at home by his mother's side. She had told him to 'finish this task' and added, 'then I'll give you a *sou* and you can take this bundle of clean washing to the tailor's'. He hadn't been gone long, apart from a short stop to look at the cattle on the market for the fair of Saint-Germain, when a hand had grabbed him by the shoulder and arrested him.

Then there was the little Taconnet boy who was running errands for his father. He had just finished sprinkling some holy water over an exposed corpse in front of a carriage entrance when he was picked up.

Others tell how they sat down and played games with friends between errands or after catechism and went off for a walk around the town gates, stopping now and again to play a game of hopscotch or have a bit of fun and mischief which was not always appreciated by the adults.[51] Ménétra called them his 'escapades'.[52]

Thus we see the many different facets of the child: apprenticeship, parents' daily help, mass, vespers, catechism, encounters with friends, games in the street, etc., etc. – and the constant coming and going between childhood and adult life, dependence and autonomy, economic responsibility and unbridled mischief; it is impossible to fix these children in a definite role because they contained within themselves that diversity of role and function which allowed them to exist simultaneously as both child and adult. They are best characterized by the notion of movement – the movement of their comings and goings and of their errands and wanderings but also their to-ing and fro-ing between the world of the child and that of the adult. At the in-between stage of 10 to 16 years, whether they helped their parents or went strolling in the meadows, they nevertheless played a full part in the economic transactions of their society in which they were already perfectly adept actors. This detail from the account of Little Copin (11 years old), who was taken off in a coach, provides good evidence of this awareness. He eventually managed to escape from the coach bringing along with him two little girls. He knew as well as they did the financial implications of his action, and when the two little girls, whom he had insisted on accompanying as far as their father's door, began 'to remove the gold cross and earrings they had been wearing in order to give them to him, he said that he did not want them and told them to take them back home with them and to tell their father to send him something instead. So the eldest came back with a 12 *sol* coin.'[53]

They all knew the price of life, the difficulty and uncertainty of their parents' work and the rules of ethical exchange and reward; and they played their part in that life both as child and as adult. This way of being both one and the other, and of being regarded (or used) as such by those around them was thus their status. As a result, they were both rascals and earners, pranksters and responsible persons, in short loyal adherents to the social and economic space allotted to them in which childhood and responsibility held them by the same hand.

A good many parents stressed the primary importance of the child's economic future, and numerous reports made at the time of their disappearance during the 1750 affair alluded to this. The child's absence was certainly costly and buying him out of prison was an intolerable expense. The two examples that follow are good illustrations of this:

Jean-François Joly, a worker in wire-mesh, himself pointed out the problems which his abduction had raised. He said that:

he stayed in prison for 11 days and that he was the last to come out. His father was a porter and his mother shelled peas and earned her living as best she could. They had had to replace him with a small boy at the place where he worked drawing wire gauze; he knew very well that they would have had to have given some money when he came out of prison.[54]

There was Millaud's wife who was not the only one to relate how costly her efforts to free her young son had been: 36 *sols* for the clerk, 50 *sols* for the prison and 36 *sols* for his safe passage and she was unable to give anything to the police officer'.[55] In addition she said that she had found it very difficult to cope with the loss of money caused by the absence of her son who used to run errands in the streets of Paris.

Thanks to the great variety of his tasks and the diversity of his attitudes, the child was the one who kept people linked together, acting as a social cement in his capacity as errand-boy, helper and assistant. In workshop and family he was the most mobile and therefore the messenger known to all. He glided between the family and the social networks, thereby fulfilling a particularly important function at a time when inner and outer worlds were so compounded. As a child, he belonged to his parents, was a part of their intimate experience and thus confirmed their image of him; and as an adult, he was entirely integrated into public life. In this way he brought together within himself both public and private spheres which even today are still not separate and whose fusion is one of the characteristics of popular living.

Indeed, as messenger, he was the one who established the links between family and neighbourhood, family and work, family and district. His exceptional mobility plus the many and varied roles and forms his timetable had him assume turned him into a privileged agent of communication, living particularly off rumour and announcement and all such oral forms of news. A reflection of his family, he either reinforced or ruined their reputation according to his own modes of existence and thus he too acted as a location of the family honour. This aspect is clearly evident in the requests for imprisonment made by the parents and also in the statements of May 1750 which show how intolerable it was for parents to find out that a child of theirs was in prison when he had never been caught stealing before or had never committed any other kind of offence. This accounts for the rapid collection of testimonials from the neighbours to prove that the child had never stained the honour of his family. Françoise Linotte, a widow and vendor of seafood, explained that 'what caused her most distress was that one of the *archers* who had been disguised as a cook had said that her son deserved to be hanged for what he was doing, which might have made the public think that her son was a thief.' Charles

Laporte obviously had the same feelings. He flung himself at the prison grille and shouted through the door, 'Have you arrested him for picking pockets or for thieving, because if you have and he's a thief or a swindler, I won't answer for him, but you will have to prove it to me first.'

As well as the site of family honour, the child was also the locus for the respectability of the district, for he belonged to it; thus at the time of the abductions, we find the district standing up for him and defending his cause. There is some evidence in the archives of people who, having recognized their neighbour's child, had run after the *archers'* coach or who had 'with their own hands' pulled out one of the little ones whom the sergeants had grabbed by the scruff of the neck. Several cases underline the speed with which the women reacted: 'Thirty women got together to prevent them from taking a child away.' 'The market women ran after the Watch', etc. A police officer, charged with the abduction of children, stated at the time of his examination that one of his neighbours had shouted at him, 'Don't do that child-snatching job or the women will beat you.'[56] The police were well aware of this female solidarity, which is hardly surprising here, given the circumstances. The men did not stay on the sidelines either; and the strength of their reaction was also felt very quickly. As the signing of petitions indicates, the link between the child and the district was a real one. Marie-Madeleine Bizet told the court that 'she had a little boy who did errands for the whole district. He was very sensible and did needlework when he had nothing else to do. When her little boy was taken away, the whole district was concerned and had got up a petition to send to the Lieutenant-General of Police aimed at securing his release.'[57]

This alliance between neighbours and acts of mutual assistance turned the arrest into a public event in which all appeared to be involved; and the manner in which the search was undertaken and the protection given were reminders of the way in which the child or the apprentice formed part of the daily landscape. This was the case of the young baker's apprentice of 11 who was able to slip from shop to shop in search of a refuge whilst being pursued by the Watch. As a bread delivery boy, he was indispensable to his district and everyone took care of him in their turn and protected him. The baker's wife hid him behind her counter, someone else opened a shop door thus allowing him to escape by the stairway where he stood with his nose against the window waiting for the sergeants to leave.

It was equally effective in the case of young Regnault. A neighbour, a vendor of herbs and fish, claimed to have

> seen two children being abducted in the cemetery of Saint-Jean on the day of Palm Sunday. Young Regnault was being held by a burly chef and an *archer* was holding the other child. All the women who were at the

market got themselves ready to go and get the child. She said that it was Officer Danguisy who was in charge of the operation and that a million souls on the market that day had demanded the release of the child.[58]

A million . . . so the story went, but not without reason, for the abducted child belonged to the district and as such had stirred its soul. The outcry was unanimous.

There we have it – the plural status of popular childhood in the eighteenth century – a pluralism which allows one to distance oneself from the temptation to define the child by viewing him through the prism of affection given or received. His multiple roles and facets made him a financial support, both autonomous and dependent, part of the family yet apart from it, social link, site of family honour and of the respectability of the district. Because of the great diversity of the often contradictory positions he occupied, he occasionally aroused opposing attitudes with respect to himself, but these nevertheless had their own coherence to be found in the way in which each one dealt with the risks by which he or she was encompassed.

## When the law got involved

When confronted by the parents, it was often quite hard for the police and the law to understand their often contradictory attitudes, which frequently resulted in considerable misunderstanding.

We are now familiar with the mechanisms the parents used to demand imprisonment and the workings of the *lettres de cachet* which offered a family a means of escaping the disgrace of normal judicial procedures if it were attempting to have one of its own members punished. In Paris, in the event of the family honour being besmirched by one of its members, the family could appeal directly to the King through the intermediary of the Lieutenant-General of Police and by means of a petition written with the help of a public scribe. In this way, and depending on certain conditions, a request was made for the imprisonment of one's son or daughter in one of the King's prisons. It was a means used by the poor for at least two reasons: firstly, the *lettre de cachet* avoided the disgrace which accompanied the 'public hue and cry' of judicial retribution (it would have been intolerable, for instance, to have seen one's son or daughter in the stocks at the nearest thoroughfare or taken off to the prison hulks in front of the whole neighbourhood); secondly, recourse to the King preserved a family secret even though the route taken might be somewhat strange:

What an unusual journey for this secret which had to be divulged and then confided to the King in order to regain its original obscurity. It was the royal personage itself that guaranteed this unlikely metamorphosis, thanks to which the secret completed its prodigious itinerary and having travelled as far as the King himself – the supreme authority – it remained within the family. The King was acting here as exorcist, cancelling out what was 'writ'; and the convents and royal prisons acted as a sombre belly engulfing its abject secret, never more to reveal it.[59]

In this way contact was established between the lives of families and the royal authority. The parties concerned appropriated for themselves the instruments of royal sovereignty in order to re-establish their own system of allegiances which had come under attack, and thus became in some respects spontaneous agents of the public order, 'the natural objects' of the police. These were the people who from time to time might turn round to the royal authority and ask it to come down on one of their own so that they could repair some of the shameful ruptures taking place in the family group, although their attitude was no doubt equivocal. In this detention requested by the parents and conceded by the royal authority by means of a simple letter, private and public spheres came together. In 1750 the Lieutenant-General of Police, Berryer, took considerable satisfaction in being able to state that 'by this means, I have succeeded in rendering a service to honest folk by ensuring that the disorderliness of their kinsfolk did not rebound on them.' Later, Lenoir wrote in his unpublished 'Mémoires': 'During the period of M. de Sartine's administration, there grew up between himself and many of the families a kind of relationship of pure trust.'

In fact, during Berryer's Lieutenancy regular use was made of requests for imprisonment and they were still not subject to the criticism they were to receive towards the end of the century. (It was Mirabeau, Malesherbes and then Breteuil who established themselves as the mouthpieces for their abolition or at least their drastic modification and Breteuil's memorandum, drawn up in 1784, when he was made Minister of the King's Household, laid down a number of amendments and several limits to their arbitrary power.) But in the middle of the century, they were used as a matter of course and police personnel who were familiar with this procedure had numerous demands brought before them by mothers and fathers who hoped to use it as a means of correction for their child. Sometimes they complained about the child's dissolute behaviour or the bad company he kept or it might be that he ran away too often or got up to 'tricks and pranks' which were putting the harmony of the family at risk. It was within this traditional context that we find police instructions being given to clear Paris of beggars, rogues and young scoundrels. It was the same in 1750 as it had been in 1720, but in 1750 Berryer must have known that thirty years previously, a riot had broken out. Notwithstanding, he ordered his officers, agents and employees to remove from the squares and thoroughfares those young persons found playing around and disturbing the public peace. When the facts emerged, the people duly rose up.

The investigation which was set up following the death of one of his officers even placed the police officers who had carried out Berryer's orders amongst the ranks of the accused. And what was more, they had actually been paid for the job, with remuneration being offered for each child taken. When obliged to explain themselves before the Law, the police inspectors and officers were indignant, and they were quick to point out many times, in their statements, that these same parents who were so shocked by the removal of children were also the ones who had petitioned for the arrest of their own children. One inspector told the court how, three days before the disturbance, he had found a runaway child some considerable distance from Paris. The child claimed to have been mistreated by his parents; but when the mother was summoned to appear, she had said openly that her son was a good-for-nothing and that she had requested a *lettre de cachet* against him on many occasions. Other officers related how, when the raids first began in December 1749, a number of parents had been very pleased and had approved of their action. They were plainly burdened by their young children who were 'in bad company, thoroughly dissolute and always on the look-out for trouble'.

The police rested their case on the same procedure that the parents were familiar with, in order to assure them that they were acting in good faith, as they were only responding to the wishes of the parents themselves. They were unwilling to see any difference between a deliberate decision taken on high to rid the town of young troublemakers and the private initiative of parents availing themselves of a means of repression emanating directly from the royal authority. As far as the police were concerned, the two initiatives sprang from an identical perception of public order, namely that this order was controlled by the authorities and that the only thing the people were required to do was to comply with it. As the parents had complained about the excesses of their children, that step in itself took them into a logical framework, the terms of which it was not up to them to decide. If Berryer chose to arrest children and thereby clean up the streets, the only thing the parents could do was to recognize the validity of these measures.

However, it was quite the opposite. The parents' logic was quite different and they remained unconvinced by the police. For them, there was no connection between their private initiatives and the reactions of the authorities. Under no circumstances could the use of a royal *lettre de cachet* authorize the police to decide the fate of their children. The gap between the two procedures was quite significant; private and public order were not to be confused. Berryer's authoritarian measures were a totally unjustifiable abuse of power, particularly in this century which was so preoccupied with the common lot of its children. Earlier, in 1734, there had been a commotion amongst the population when the bodies of 16 new-born babies and infants were discovered dumped at the mortuary of Le Châtelet. 'This spectacle attracted a great public gathering and frightened the people', wrote Barbier in his *Journal*.[60] It was in fact a doctor who had gathered all these little bodies together with the intention of setting to work on them for anatomical experiments.

There were other stories and examples one could quote which testify to the contradiction that, on the one hand, one could abandon a child and yet, on the other, find it particularly offensive that the authorities of the kingdom should decide quite arbitrarily to ship off young people to Louisiana. It was only a contradiction in the eyes of the police. The people did not see it that way. Whilst refusing to accept that the fate of its children should be decided by the authorities, it could nevertheless be driven into the position of having to abandon a child. There was thus an absolute gap between popular thought and the system of interpretation of those in power, and a complete gap between the two visions of public order, even if both, parents and police complained about the problems caused by children.

This discord and failure to reconcile the two forms of power, the one private and the other public, were to give rise to the bloody days of May 1750. Discord there certainly was, but there was also failure on the part of the police to understand the popular mechanisms and processes involved.

## Bread and mothers

As already stated, the intention of this study is to find a means of looking at the child other than by the automatic linkage of childhood to feelings of affection. To this end his functions within the city as well as the social and economic situation of his parents, have been examined, with a view to a different kind of analysis of attitudes towards him. Reaching a conclusion on this difficult subject is impossible; perhaps it might be better to let this child speak for himself. He was summoned in 1769 to a hearing of the *Parc civil*,[61] where two women were claiming rights of maternity. The judges held two interviews with him which were transcribed in their entirety. According to the preamble,

> the child stood alone, confused and awkward, but less so than ourselves who cast our eyes over this precious investment on whose behalf Nature and the Law would presently require us to give account. We felt a secret shudder penetrate the very depth of our soul. Here before us was a child whose very condition and mere youth left us with a lasting impression of

respect and pity. After contemplating him for a moment we took up our pens to write questions prior to asking them, and recording his replies word for word as he gave them, we began.

In the course of the interview the child made it clear that he knew very well who his mother was but that he did not want to live with her, and that he was very attached to the other woman who took good care of him.

'What is your reason for not wanting to go with the Widow Brie?'
    'I don't want to, Sir, because when I asked her for bread, she hit me.'
    'But you did eat when you were with her?'
    'No, she was letting me starve to death.'
    'And if we should return you to the Widow Brie?'
    'I don't want to.'
    'You don't think of her as your mother?'
    'No, Sir, I like my mother Noiseux best (the one looking after him). I'm not saying the name of the other one.'
    'But what if we asked you to give the name of the other one?'
    'No. I like my mother Noiseux best.'
    'But if she had always given you bread, would you recognize her as your mother?'
    'Yes, I would recognize her as my mother.'
    'But even if she did not give you bread, she could still be your mother?'
    'No, Sir.'
Thus ended the second interview.[62]

# 5

# Undesirable Alliances and Times of Disruption

---

### Foolish love

Some relationships were banned on both moral and religious grounds, as well as being unacceptable to civil society and condemned by their families. These were those couples who had decided to leave the paternal home and live together as man and wife or those who had left their spouse to live with someone else in 'shameful concubinage' (as we wrote in *Le Désordre des familles*), there being no divorce at the time. Their traces are to be found in the files of the Arsenal archives, where family requests for imprisonment are kept. Reference has not been made to this 'illicit trade' in lovers as such, and preference has been given to looking at the ways in which parents and children, husbands and wives, were torn apart; but often the cause of such family disruption lay in the illicit existence of an unofficial couple formed outside the normal, legitimate channels. For, although forbidden, concubinage was a reality.

Some periods have valued their bastards more than others; medieval history, for instance, is full of their lofty deeds;[1] but irrespective of all that, not all social classes viewed concubinage in the same way. What was a kind of polygamy for the very rich was usually a case of love and poverty for the rest, made even more miserable by the fact that one did not have enough money to marry. In the sixteenth century, however, the Church crushed this practice and extolled the virtues of the social institution of marriage. Concubines were denounced from the pulpit and priests for their part could no longer be seen living blatantly in this way.

We have already shown how, for the least well-off, concubinage was often a means of awaiting marriage, that is the day when, finally better-off, one could actually afford the expenses of a wedding. Lieutenant-General of Police Lenoir alludes to it in his 'Mémoires': 'Amongst the local people there were households of young unmarried men and women who passed in public for man and wife.'[2] Lenoir tells the story on this subject of a water carrier and his 'alleged wife' who lived together in the parish of Saint-Eustache. One evening, the man came home drunk and attempted to kill his wife, who mortally wounded him.

> The Law found that the killing had been unpremeditated and was therefore pardonable and that the woman had not been married. She declared that the deceased, whom she continued to call her man and her husband, had only shirked the sacred rites of marriage on account of the church expenses and the cost of a wedding. This particular incident occasioned a display of zeal on the part of the police among the parish priests. The priests conceded that marriage should be celebrated free of charge and as a result, there were some, although not many, poor people who presented themselves and their children to the Church and asked for the sacraments of marriage.[3]

In eighteenth-century Paris, one also saw a number of couples actually making an official declaration of their status of concubine before the district commissioner of police.[4] Thus the situation of concubinage amongst the poor found itself somewhere between express interdiction and a good-natured tolerance, even if families would have nothing to do with it.

Lenoir also makes mention of another kind of concubinage which had been fully considered and deliberately chosen. He was quite shocked and surprised by it, and he describes what happened as well as all the forms of repression used to defeat a choice of lifestyle which was considered altogether too libertarian. Some 'visionaries and devotees of no particular religion living in the Rue Quincampoix' got together to live in concubinage around the year 1778 in the area of the parish of Saint-Leu. They were 'a number of male and female workers in the fan trade who lived together as man and wife. They neither attended church nor partook of the sacraments.' In actual fact, these artisans and workers had very strict habits, took great care of their children and frequently held readings together. Given their refusal of marriage and their lively contempt for cults, religion and priests, their otherwise impeccable behaviour was to no avail. The district commissioners set up enquiries and reported on their habits and in spite of their seriousness, the young men and women were to be 'enclosed in institutions designed for the correction of immorality'; those men and women who seemed less 'set in the error of their ways were left at liberty and entrusted to the clergy for instruction in religion'. Some of the others put up a fierce resistance; 'three of these girls stayed at the house of correction for quite some time, and after their detention, they were exiled a long way from Paris. . . . They continued to maintain that there was no need for baptism or marriage and that they were united to their men and fathers of their children by their own free inspiration.'[5] This 'free inspiration' had nothing in common with loose living or immorality but they nevertheless warranted imprisonment in the eyes of civilized society.

The 32 dossiers containing family requests for imprisonment from the years 1728 and 1758 reveal the two types of concubinage which were not tolerated: but as they only deal with those couples who were driven out and banished by their families and who felt the full weight of the *lettres de cachet*, it is not possible to draw any conclusions about the general threshold of tolerance of society in their respect. All we can do is to look at the lives of those couples whose destruction was desired by another party and consider how those illicit passions which broke up homes and families in the name of 'foolish love' (as someone wrote in a letter to the King), were perceived.

As one might imagine, there was a world of difference between a woman who decided to go and live with her lover well away from her parents, and the husband or wife who left the domestic hearth in order to live with someone else. In the first case one is dealing with a family who saw itself as dishonoured by the 'scandalous' life of the son or daughter. The family tried to regain control and to assert its authority over this child, who was probably quite old already and who had chosen to live as he or she saw fit but whose inclinations were not recognized by society (18 of the dossiers refer to cases of this kind). The other type of case (found in 14 of the dossiers) concerned a home that had been ruined by the adultery of one of the partners. Adultery was often the means chosen for divorce and an attempt at a new life. In both cases the proscribed couple were the subject of serious criticism, especially if the partners concerned were already married. Such a union broke the recognized forms of the established social order and broke the legitimate family chain of reproduction. Although the couple might appear acceptable and be regarded favourably by others, there was still likely to be a scandal because traditional images were being shattered. Thus the family, the neighbours and the police came together to bring about its demise. The union had to be broken up and the only way they knew of going about it was imprisonment, decided from on high.

## The lovers' fears

Overall in the records, there is a marked disproportion in the requests for imprisonment which is of some significance. Although large numbers of parents demanded imprisonment for the offending daughter, when it came to their sons, they seemed in no great hurry, unless the moral problem happened to be bound up in some more pressing question of self-interest. This lack of symmetry was even more apparent where adultery was concerned; the wives demanded the imprisonment of the concubine and not of their husbands, whilst the husbands sought imprisonment of their wives and not of their lovers. So, out of a total of 32 dossiers for concubinage, only three were aimed at the male partner. (Cathérine Morin was the only wife to request that her husband be detained in Bicêtre);[6] she appears to have suffered so much physically, morally and materially, that in her appeal to the King she expressed the desire that not only the concubine but also the husband of the latter be put away. In this drama with a cast of four, Cathérine Morin had been robbed of her rightful inheritance, beaten black and blue, and was further humiliated to discover that 'the concubine and the latter's husband had allowed all kinds of vice and corruption in their home'. She was insistent in pleading for the indefinite removal of the three persons who had wrecked her life over the last thirteen years.

There are two reasons which no doubt account for the general lack of symmetry and explain why it was so much easier to demand the imprisonment of a woman. The first, as we will see later, is connected with the notion of the woman's role in distracting the man from his duty and her passionate image in what was an affair of instinctual attraction. The other is quite understandable: the deserted woman could barely survive and so attempted to re-establish the economic and social stability of the couple. She only wanted one thing, and that was the return of her husband and the removal of the one he had chosen as his companion.

Often in these weighty dossiers in which letters followed petitions, and enquiries resulted from the views expressed, one can feel the unrelenting hatred of the families towards the son or daughter who had dishonoured them. The vocabulary one finds is not that of grief or sorrow but of an anger and revenge which is exemplary in its severity. One finds requests for life imprisonment and, where money or inheritance were concerned, the expressions used were even more vicious and implacable. There are references to that 'squalid and scandalous business' and to the son who was 'no more than a bad medicine for honest folk'; there was the girl who deserved to be sent off to the Indies or who was 'so ungodly that she deserved to be sent to La Salpêtrière [madhouse] for the rest of her days'. There is a denunciation of a 'wicked concubine and a spendthrift with a heart of stone', and of the woman who was 'beyond the bounds of respect', a tart, a thief or 'a prostitute for the asking'.

These descriptions which came from the families or the spouses contain a violence which is especially disconcerting when one considers that some of these couples who were denounced in this way had been living their lives together for quite some time and often had several children already. Words like 'debauchery' or 'squalid behaviour' were hardly fitting terms to describe a couple who had been living together illegally for 10 to 15 years, sometimes with five or six children.

What about the strange and unique case of Anne Gille, for example?

The lover she had been living with for 40 years suddenly demanded her imprisonment, supported by the rest of his family. Claude Serré, a gardener in Paris, said in his statement that

> Anne Gille had crept her way into living with him more than forty years ago and had continued to live with him as husband and wife wherever he was. She had come to his place one day, asked him for something to eat and come nightfall she had got into his bed, which she had continued to do ever since and had become his mistress.[7]

It would appear that the gardener could not bear the fact that his companion had managed to keep such a grip on his affairs over the last 40 years. However, the inspector responsible for the enquiry and investigations made a note on 22 May 1728 of the following, rather strange phrase, 'having never wearied in 43 years of leading a bad life'. Finding herself threatened in this way, Anne Gille had tried to throw herself down a well, apparently still not tired of what they called 'debauchery' and of living in flagrant companionship.

In similar vein, a brother denounced his sister, Jeanne Le Maréchal, because she had been living with a married man for eight years 'in a squalid affair in which she was pregnant again with her third child'.[8] Elsewhere a young widow was threatened with prison by her in-laws who could not tolerate her long-standing liaison with an officer and deputy engineer in fortresses and fortifications, although she had had several children by him.

In the majority of cases, the demands were made for reasons of succession or vested interest and only arose when the parents felt they were getting older. Invocations of immorality or scandal which were intended to break up a long-standing companionship which had posed no problems up until that point were used to conceal otherwise inadmissible reasons. Lovers pursued in this way took fright and lived clandestinely or even turned to violence. They lived from day to day, seeking refuge with obliging landlords who 'conspired to conceal their debauchery' or paying a high price for a discreet midwife who would keep quiet about their periodic confinements. When harassed by her brother over a liaison which had lasted for more than ten years, one woman decided 'to get out of the district and, in fear, camped from room to room' like a fugitive. Others became hysterical at the slightest hint of an enquiry and attempted to frighten those who were threatening them. Marie Feuillade was a widow. She had been living with a soldier for almost two years but her mother and family simply could not tolerate this arrangement and talked of sending a petition to the King. The hot-tempered soldier 'with whom she had set up home threatened them every day and told them that if they came to lock

her up he would blast them to the back of beyond'.[9] Understandably keen
to remain where they were, the parents hastily drew up a petition and
Marie Feuillade was imprisoned in La Salpêtrière.

Those who lived in concubinage were perfectly well aware that a *lettre
de cachet* followed by imprisonment was no mere myth and so they
lived, caught between clandestinity and violence, an understandable
response, knowing as one does that there were no fixed rules to arbitrate
in this utterly expedient system which some individuals had learned to
appropriate.

In this context, widowhood, so frequent at the time, was a freedom that
was closely watched, leaving as it did so many available partners in the
field of sexual exchange. One-third of the dossiers concerning parents
who were objecting to the concubinage of a son or daughter concern a
widow or widower. Their reasons were plentiful; some parents and in-laws
were worried about questions of descent and future succession; they also
expressed concern for the education of the offspring of the first marriage.
A couple of silk-workers from the Faubourg Saint-Antoine were very
angry with their son-in-law for setting up home with a married woman as
soon as their daughter was out of sight. The son-in-law had made the
mistake of leaving his 4-year-old daughter in the care of his parents-in-law
and bringing up his son of 7 whilst his new companion abandoned the
fruits of their union to the orphanage. The parents-in-law were scandalized
and wanted the woman to be locked up. In fact, they had no rights over
her but in their argument they said, 'What was most shocking was the
sight of a child of 7 sleeping with them and they were bringing him up
very badly.' The son-in-law got into such a temper one day that he broke
all his father-in-law's tools, obviously a very serious thing to do. However,
following police investigations, it was his companion who was summoned
to appear and who subsequently admitted to being 'out of order'. She was
the one who was put away. The dossier ends with one short sentence: 'I
think she should remain there for some time.'[10] This one particular case
allows us to assess the impact of the *lettres de cachet*. In this instance, a
woman was to find herself detained on the request of persons who had
only very distant connections with her partner.

Apart from this one example, the theme of the 'forsaken widow' was a
recurrent one. For those parents who had already seen a son or daughter
satisfactorily settled, having managed, for instance, to achieve a balance
between the occupations of the father and son-in-law, breakdown of the
union as a result of death was a permanent danger. The concubinage
which followed and the children which ensued were seen as an intolerable disorder and disgrace which deserved to be punished regardless of
the strength of the feelings or the duration of the liaison. Widows and
widowers were easy prey in the cut and thrust of emotional life.

Concubinage of one's nearest and dearest was a disgrace which families took action to expunge, in the name 'of an honour more dear to them than life itself'. But for the inspectors of police and district commissioners, who were often involved in the affair, the first concern was the attitude of the district, that living entity and civil personage whose actions and reactions were as important to grasp as the inclinations of the parents. From these dossiers, it is quite easy to see the police response and the reticence of the administration which would think twice about interrupting the course of a liaison if it caused no disturbance in the district or if the family seemed to be exaggerating the scandal owing to its own feelings of resentment. This hesitation was all the more apparent because the final decision rested with the police and because the commissioner, who was one of the central figures, was quite often the only one capable of assessing the impact of the situation on the district. His approach to government was based on the idea that one should not 'upset' the neighbourhood. There was one other person who also had considerable influence over the final decision and that was the parish priest who sometimes added a letter or recommendation at the end of the petitions. He also took the reactions of his parish into account and used them in his argument. One such was the priest of Saint-Séverin, whose verger had informed him about two lovers who had been meeting in the church every day while he had been there. Thus all the decisions revolved around the idea of scandal, whether it was in the family, the parish or the area; but we have seen just how tenuous, relative or arbitrary that notion might be and how, on occasion, it might serve as an alibi or somewhat hasty justification. We know even less about how much the police might have managed or even manipulated it in a manner which would often appear to be contradictory.

Catherine Louis was an embroiderer.[11] When she was 22 she left her parents to live with a young man and soon afterwards found that she was pregnant. The commissioner felt that, from the beginning, the young woman had always been very serious, indeed very industrious, but her parents had always been hard on her. 'They wore down her spirit,' he wrote, 'and in some respects they have pushed her into deserting their house.' Nevertheless he showed himself to be in favour of imprisoning Catherine on grounds that were altogether political, namely that 'the district needs an example; it is full of people who can only be restrained by fear. Do we know how many useful subjects the State loses on account of the decadence to which the majority of the girls of the common people surrender themselves?' It seems a rather curious observation when one considers the outrageous behaviour of the high and mighty and the aristocracy as reported in the bulletins of the secret police.[12] In fact, the commissioner's argument had nothing at all to do with the concubinage of Catherine Louis. No doubt he thought he would gain the approval of the

Lieutenant-General of Police by applying the much-used rule: 'The people need an example' – whatever that might be.

The district was quite capable of being stirred up of its own accord and of showing its discontent when faced with a situation it did not like. Some domestic arrangements could upset the equilibrium of a neighbourhood, threaten the harmony amongst the inhabitants and disturb the collective order which was forever being marred by outbreaks of violence and upheaval and constantly needing to be re-established. The woman who went from man to man was a social danger and a threat to existing couples; her drifting disturbed the fragile consensus of the community and whipped up anger or revenge.

The curate of Saint-Médard denounced a situation of this kind to the first secretary of the Lieutenant of Police. It appeared that a woman called Thérèse Boisselet went about quite brazenly with as many young lechers as there were passers-by and, as everyone could see, she was anybody's. So said the curate and he went on to say,

> I am sure you will not take it amiss if I continue to press you to do all you can to procure a place for the Boisselet female in La Salpêtrière. A new scandal has arisen in the district because of her; the said Boisselet was discovered with a man called Cauchois last Sunday night and they were given a good thrashing by the populace. The time would seem right to me to go ahead without further ado and inflict a punishment which would act as an example capable of putting a stop to anyone else in the district who might be disposed to do the same. (signed) Graffazt, curate of Saint-Médard.[13]

There were occasions when an entire town was stirred up, as when the local worthies of Saint-Quentin demanded the detention in Paris of one of their inhabitants, who was the daughter of a respectable draper. She was the concubine of an officer over whom they had no authority. Their argument may be broken down into two distinct parts and goes as follows: order had to be re-established in that town ('all it needed was for this outrageous woman to be punished to cause a panic amongst others who were beginning to lose their way'); and secondly, didn't the town pay taxes each year for the upkeep of institutions in Paris? This fiscal arrangement was surely sufficient in itself to justify the imprisonment therein of one of its citizens: 'In view of the considerable amount of tax that is provided annually by this town for the maintenance of prisoners in the houses of correction in Paris, the family and local dignitaries believe they have found good grounds for anticipating this favour.'[14]

Support for the imprisonment of illicit lovers was often conveniently provided by the town or district either by acting of their own accord and meting out some kind of corporal punishment on the wrongdoers or else by buttressing up the authority of the powers that be, whether politically or financially.

## Outbursts of passion

In more than one-third of the dossiers one comes across indications of the passion that existed between the lovers. Threats of imprisonment and denunciations only served to heighten the violent intensity of their feelings, so that when they were asked to break up, the couple resisted or refused, or else they promised to separate and then sought every possible means of getting together again. When this occurred the hatred felt by the families and the spouses became even stronger and the fervour of the vocabulary used to notify the Lieutenant-General of Police mirrors the passionate outbursts of the lovers themselves. This passion is referred to as a bewitchment, a charm or a spell which needed curing and healing as well as stopping up at its instinctual source. The petitions plead for a return to reason and suggest that the means by which this might be effectively achieved was by putting one of the partners away definitively (into prison or exile, for instance, sending off to the Indies or into corrective retreat with ladies of virtue), in the belief that the cure lay in preventing the lovers from seeing one another. In a century of rationalism which was still a good way off from the dawn of Romanticism, was it really so difficult to foresee how this cruel absence might heighten the senses and imagination and thus whet the appetite for the missing person?

'Foolish love' only exists in dreams and novels or in the nineteenth century; but in these inglorious texts produced by people of humble origin there is a passion both real and imagined. Accounts, often given by a third party to convince the police authorities, are often portrayed in all the colours of hell. Then there are times of particular emotional intensity when the vocabulary and descriptions are especially intense and acute such as those moments of conflict aimed at causing a breakdown in order to re-establish – for better or for worse – the legitimate bond, of either the marriage or the family.

In these descriptions one feels the convulsions of unbearable grief at being torn apart in this way, and the writing confirms the violence of the feelings or expressions of repentance and regret. There are also descriptions of the horrors of separation or prison, as in the case of a semi-literate woman who wrote to her partner telling him to take care of the children as she had nothing else to lose at the present time:

> These lines I am writing are for you. I have fled. There is nothing left in the room that needs attending to, all I ask you to do, for God's sake, is not to abandon the child, for it is not his fault, the poor wretch. I close

now. I am lost forever. I sleep like a pig on a pile of straw. I have endured great misery already. It is my own fault because of my bad behaviour.[15]

Sometimes the writing is better, if somewhat clumsy. On occasion, the words portray the women like so many animals seizing their prey, as in the case of this mother describing the woman who had ravished her son 'for six years by using her womanly charms to flatter and deceive, in spite of all her tenderness as a mother'. One finds the same devastating rivalry between mother and concubine, mistress and wife or the father whose daughter allowed herself to be fascinated by some other man besides himself ('he made himself more of a master than me').

The dossiers draw very firm portraits of the persons concerned; they are presented as hardened, impulsive or temperamental characters and they also attempt a psychological explanation in which death is often proposed as a final resort in the face of misfortune. One might die for love, or even kill, as in the case of Marie-Antoinette Guichard, a woman already in her thirties, whose mother said of her: 'She was always inclined to violence even as a very young child. One day when she was still quite young she very nearly stabbed herself with a knife in a moment of defiance.' When they wanted to separate her from her lover, she tried to set fire to the house, saying that 'she couldn't care less if she died, like Lescombat,[16] and so long as she had her way she would die at the Place de Grève.'[17] They attempted to cure her by bathing her and by trying to bring her back in the way of religion with the help of two priests. But to no avail; she was destined for La Salpêtrière and was not to be released until much later. The lawyer in charge of her case fell mildly in love with her and pleaded for her to be set at liberty, adding the comment that 'at 30 years old she should be free to take care of herself.'

The deserted wives wrote long desperate petitions blaming the woman who had been chosen in preference to themselves for every conceivable ill and recording the changes in their husband's character. Once captivated, he seemed almost bewitched and became 'very fierce' and aggressive and indulged in 'mad bouts of spending'. The husbands felt the same bitterness and thrashed their wives rather than the wives' lovers.

With regard to passion, the woman was always perceived and portrayed as being much more active and tempestuous than the man. Jean-François Oriol, requesting that his wife be imprisoned, stated that

she had slipped off in secret seven or eight years ago so as to be at liberty to follow the stormy tide of her desires and licentious pleasures and live a life of sin. Four children had been born of this adulterous affair. She had taken leave of her senses and was no longer in control of her own heart or of her tears and laughter.[18]

What was one to do in the face of such a flow of passion? Even when Marie Jeanne was imprisoned she wrote to her lover every day, saying, 'I am writing to tell you about the horrors of my detention here.'

In the end, although these dossiers are concerned with the couple, they mostly refer to the women, who are made to bear the full brunt of the blame by implying that they were more responsible than the men for the intensity of the feelings which caused the collapse of family honour and marital harmony. The story of Le Blanc, a sergeant in the Watch who had already drawn attention to himself for his corruption and his part in the affair of the abductions of 1750, says much about such traditionally held views on women. Six years later this thoroughly unsavoury character showed himself for the lecher he was.[19] He attracted and seduced young girls with no hint of remorse and when questioned he admitted that 'marriage had never been his intention and that pleasure was his only aim. He had done just the same with other girls and he happened to be having a similar affair with a girl at the moment and he would do the same with anyone else who came along.' Inspector Meusnier was shocked at this attitude and wrote to the Lieutenant-General of Police that 'this kind of life affected the social order and family harmony. I think it will be necessary to impose some form of correction.' In the margin of the letter, Berryer's secretary jotted this short sentence which needs no comment: 'It's up to the girls to watch out.' Seduced or seductive, the women could scarcely be defended in the eyes of civil society.

The lovers found life very difficult if they were harassed or if they did not become absorbed in the life of the district. Death was occasionally the recourse chosen by the couple as in this case of a young ironmonger of 26, established in the Ile Saint-Louis and married to an agreeable young woman. He became besotted by his kitchen maid, a much older woman, however, and one morning they were both found dead, poisoned by a brew of arsenic made by their own hand. A note left on the hearth explained that they did not want 'to worry anyone' because of their union. It fell to the three priests of Saint-Louis-en-l'Ile to bear the bodies of 'these unfortunates to a corner of the cemetery'.[20]

## The dispute

There was one exceptional document which came to light and relieved the monotony of the usual complaints contained in the archives of the Petit Criminel. In the middle of the records of Commissioner Convers Desormeaux, there was a bundle of papers classified under the brief heading 'Documents of diverse nature' and with an index which gave some indication of the contents, 'problems of inheritance (17th to 18th century);

documents relating to the administration and distribution of produce in Seurre (17th century); complaints of a husband deceived by Demard, journal kept since 1774.'[21] The designation was incongruous; however, there in the middle of this bundle was a slim handwritten notebook consisting of about 70 sheets which should not have been there. It was completely isolated, without explanation or comment from the commissioner, and with no outline proceedings or trace of a signature. The notebook (of the type used by a schoolchild), was written in a close hand and had only one title which was as follows: 'Details of all that has happened since 30 March 1774.' And immediately below it, one reads, 'She left for Gisors on 30 March with her eldest daughter, Mme Cochereaux and M. Demard and she stayed there for three months and three days before coming back. She created a terrible scene in front of her father.' Having begun, one keeps on reading all the rest of these lines written between March 1774 and January 1775 and which tell the tale of unrequited love between a certain M. Demontjean (or Montjean) and his wife, residents of the Rue Croix-des-Petits-Champs in the centre of Paris and working in the fashion trade.

It is a document of no little feeling. In it, a humiliated husband relates in great detail his wife's every deed and action and it is, in short, a kind of journal. It was obviously recorded whilst he was still suffering the effects of pain and grief, a time when the memory attributes an exaggerated importance to even the smallest incidents which punctuated the story and were proof upon proof of the wicked intentions of his wife. The overall effect is hardly literary. It is simply a succession of events strung end to end with the resonance of a score of litanies. On the last page, there is an abrupt change of form and 'I' is no longer used although the handwriting is exactly the same. References are made to 'the plaintiff' and 'the wife of the plaintiff' instead of the previous 'I' and 'she'. The document comes to an abrupt end, without any conclusion, as though it were never finished and were possibly to be recommenced at some later date. Inside there was an addendum comprising two loose sheets consisting of a few supplementary details which had been omitted.

As one reads, one begins to reflect on the nature of the text. Supposing it were not a daily journal kept by M. Montjean but rather a kind of enormous oral deposition, or an infinitely long complaint in the form of a journal or an account dictated to an official writer and intended for presentation as legal evidence. The oral style of the writing would certainly make one think that might be the case but it is not sufficient proof in itself. On the other hand, the style of the last page, which is completely different, would seem to indicate that Montjean was in fact a plaintiff and that, having made up his mind one day to speak out and tell all, he had related this long oral journal in order to convince the police of the validity of his grievances against his wife. Unfortunately we are never likely to know anything more about this document, as further searches among the archives were to no avail. Only the notebook is there. Alone and enigmatic, yet rich in meaning. It reveals for us, as documents rarely can, the history of a confrontation between husband and wife over the respective roles desired by each of them in society and over which they were in total disagreement.

This text has to be seen as an unexpected opportunity. It cuts a swathe through so much of the usual collection of domestic disputes, the causes of which were customarily regarded as violence, drunkenness or adultery, because here the argument is quite different. The quarrel is about roles. There is a tension between two diverging concepts of the functions of male and female in the society of the small trader and artisan at the end of the eighteenth century, resulting in an immense breakdown in understanding over the allocation of tasks to be performed by the man and the woman. It becomes abundantly clear that this total disagreement could only result in one thing – breakdown. But, paradoxically, the 'friendship' or love that Montjean has for his wife underlies the whole of the account, thus maintaining a certain degree of unity.

## Montjean's complaint

Montjean and his wife lived in the Rue Croix-des-Petits-Champs. They had two children, the eldest a girl of 4 and a boy who was younger and about whom not much is known. The couple manufactured fashion garments assisted by one employee, and a servant or cook kept house for them. It was the typical small unit of production of the artisan in which the work was done at home, with the man taking care of orders and deliveries (some from as far afield as Holland), whilst the woman worked at the job in hand (often working on Saturdays and Sundays in order to complete on time). There was nothing unusual about this domestic economic arrangement. It was the traditional lifestyle of the artisan in which the man dealt with business matters and went off into the outside world to obtain orders and materials whilst the wife and employee busied themselves at the needlepoint behind the window overlooking the street.

The drama unfurls with a journey. Montjean's wife went away to stay with her father in Gisors and whilst there she came into contact with a rather nice kind of society which smiled appealingly at her. Her time spent there was so agreeable that on her return to Paris she wanted to live as she had done over there, refusing to work at the trade but preferring rather to surround herself with friends who would take her arm and go walking, eating oysters or drinking wine. A quarrel between husband and wife ensued, the account of which follows the rhythm of the wife's distractions with the husband's swinging between patience, sulks and anger, and finally ending with a complaint brought before the commissioner, followed by a visit to the Lieutenant-General of Police.

Whether dictated by Montjean or written with his own pen, the title of this little book is quite significant, for it shows the intention of the author (or whoever added it), to define the subject-matter. Although the text deals with biographical facts it is not really an autobiography but a phased account of a period of a few months (March to January), and a series of episodes which effectively transformed a life and, as a result, necessitated their being put down on paper. There is certainly no evidence of a desire for publication in this notebook, which assumes no literary or ideological form; there is simply the need to make a denunciation and a determination to expose some of the daily events with the intent of showing how one life had been rendered unbearable. The title, 'Details of all that has happened since 30 March 1774', says nothing about the content, but everything about its purpose. It is the nitty-gritty of everyday history and it was intended to provoke a reaction in the reader (presumably a magistrate or judicial figure), in respect of the merits of both writing the text and the steps taken; and it is the minute detail of the days and hours of those few months which was aimed at demonstrating the misery experienced by the author and his own innocence in the matter.

The title announces from the very beginning the purpose and function of the text and in itself evokes a kind of *déjà vu*. Tales of the dark deeds of bandits and brigands often began in this way – 'Details of what really happened'; 'The true story of what happened' etc., etc.[22] These accounts could be bought in the street from hoarse-throated hawkers and vendors. No doubt Montjean was familiar with these broadsheets and would have bought them and read them himself. In choosing to use this title, Montjean puts himself in line with this kind of 'rag' which moulded the mentality of the street by turning crime into something familiar yet unheard of and by elevating the monotony of human events to the level of history itself. And the title assures us right from the start that in this matter of self-explanation or reflection, there is nothing which might be considered too petty or unimportant. Indeed, the title announces (perhaps even demands) that detail is in fact history.

Presented with this text of ambiguous status (is it a journal or is it a dictated account?), one experiences the usual excitement and eagerness of all historians and researchers. After all, the discovery of an eighteenth-century artisan's account is so rare that there is the temptation to make it say everything. Temptation there certainly is, but there is also risk – risk of verification but, more importantly, the risk of looking for some largely mythical truth in precisely those places where the document will always remain indecipherable. It is a particular risk for the person who naturally revels in the civilization of the written word and who reads what someone else has written according to his own thought structures.

One must respect the text as the inalienable property of the one who produced it and thus allow it to retain its uniqueness. One can then work on its background and context whilst keeping sight of what there is that is both specific and general. From the personal thoughts of an individual as he recorded them in writing, one's task is to gather up and pick out what he saw when he took a look at himself and his matrimonial dream. It is not our task to fix him definitively in one of those so-called satisfactory interpretations which can be placed side by side with all the rest for the pleasure of having one's knowledge neatly arranged. Perhaps this amounts to saying that one has to stay as close as possible to the text whilst taking every care to remain at the furthest possible distance from it. To do otherwise would be equally difficult to envisage.

Montjean chose a chronological setting as a means of making himself understood but when he makes jottings or adds the exact date between the lines, it is purely for the convenience of the reader. His chronology is first and foremost his own rather than that of the calendar. Dates and times which were clearly added later are quite specific and if there seems to be no ending, the beginning is equally abrupt, commencing as it does with the specific occasion of his wife's visit to her father, which is forever being brought to mind and constantly referred to as being the root of all ills and source of all his problems. This journey is recalled time and time again in the text and the date of it is even incorporated into the title, 'Details of all that has happened since 30 March 1774'.

On that day she left for her father's and stayed there for a month and three days. She came back on 4 May and that was when everything began. From 4 May 1774 to 20 February 1775, the account proceeds date by date describing daily events and recalling conversations between different persons. In the course of the writing, dialogues and arguments between the married couple and angry altercations with parents and friends are all noted down without too much comment. Montjean neither embellishes, rationalizes nor attempts to argue: he simply relates, exposes, amasses the detail and gives a blow by blow account of the quarrels. The result of all this is a dense and tightly packed narrative offering no relief from the facts. All this cramming together and piling up of precise details one on top of the other creates a particular state of mind for the reader. Awash with this endless enumeration of incidents, one begins to identify with Montjean and with his frustration in the face of a wife who is not just fanciful and capricious but who also shows contempt and spitefulness. Without even so much as an internal monologue to analyse the circum-stances, the subject, by his manic recital of daily trivialities, places himself in the position of innocent victim and, with ne'er a sigh, he querulously stacks up the minutest disorders of his household.

The text gushes and spills out like an overflow and then reaches a kind of crescendo. The situation worsens between the couple and the account becomes heated; the tone becomes increasingly heightened and angry whereas the vocabulary used remains the same from beginning to end; that is, modest, familiar, unpretentious and with expressions that are overall more or less trivial. A false friend is referred to as 'that beast of a...'; the comment after an outburst of female anger is, 'I thought the glasses were going to crack'; some friends who had gone off to the pleasure gardens spent their time 'throwing up on the floor'. There are few original turns of phrase, the style is stilted and is more akin to the type of speech that rolls off the tongue with the conviction that the weight of the content is likely to take precedence over the vigour of the expression. It does take precedence since it is only towards the very end of one's reading that one begins to question Montjean's sincerity, particularly as it is not entirely clear what the problem really was that was keeping himself and his wife apart. It was also well known that a complaint brought before the law was not necessarily synonymous with the truth.

But even if Montjean's wife was not so difficult to live with as Montjean hoped to make out, and although he was no doubt more difficult than he would like to have been thought, it does not really matter. The truth does not lie there any more than in the search for a truth which is supposed to become clear at the end of it all. The essence lies in what Montjean has to say and what he describes of the conflict between two distinct modes of life, masculine and feminine, as they come up against each other because they are separate and remote visions of the world. The rest is merely 'detail'.

It is this opposition between two contradictory images of social life which in the end provides one of the principal motives for the form of the account. In the end, the chronological approach adopted by the author is subsumed by a different scansion consisting of a succession of events in which each episode, practically the same as its predecessor, runs into the next, ultimately to be bound together by a single dialogue which remains identical and recurs constantly. This dialogue is repeated, retold and reformulated a dozen times over with scarcely a word of it being changed. It is a dialogue consisting of five or six lines in which, following on from the day's events which are almost the same as those of the previous day, Montjean's wife repeats over and over again, with no alteration, how she wants to live and behave, which is completely different from what her husband wants. The text drags its way along through a never-changing, almost ritualistic procedure, in which events and their respective interpretation alternate continually as time passes. One is reminded of a long, slow and involved lament in which the refrain serves to separate the stanzas from their immutable rhythm. Though the verses move the story along, thanks to new circumstances ever more intense and serious, they unfailingly come up against the refrain which marks the boundary of the dispute, definitive and impassable, with all the poignancy of a musical theme. There is something almost fascinating about reading this obsessively repetitive text which seems to have no end. Is it really a coincidence if it resembles a long winter's tale intended to amuse, frighten or disturb? Montjean would surely have read more than one of them. At the same time one cannot help thinking that it was a form that was imposed on the author in the same way as the events which beset him relentlessly for 11 months were also imposed upon him.

## A woman at her window

She told me that she would not work, that she had not been made for work, and that it was up to a man to look after a woman. She said that when she was at her father's she had seen any number of women who didn't work and their husbands had employees. If I stopped her from receiving Demard, she said she would definitely not do any work. She said I was a jealous old devil and provided Demard could come, she would work....

She wanted to be by the window reading a book....

She tapped her foot and told me that she was not made for work and that she had seen lots of women in her father's village who didn't work; they stayed in their apartments reading a book and that she was made to be like that and that it was a man's job to provide for his wife. She said her sister was very happy and kept a good table and that she had servants to wait on her and that there was always good company in her house and that she put rouge on her cheeks....

She had plenty of work to do but she took a book which she didn't put down until 9 o'clock at night and did nothing all day....

I reproached her for going out walking with that young man and for putting on rouge the way she had because if someone she knew had seen her they would surely have taken her for a strumpet which would have been a great dishonour....[23]

What is important here is contained in these endlessly repeated phrases in which Montjean's wife opposes the traditional norm of the wife of the artisan-cum-merchant as fellow worker in the trade with another way of life she has seen elsewhere. This 'good life' consisted in having leisure and domestic service, keeping good company and going out whilst the husband was off on business.

Montjean confronts this feminine model constantly hankered after by his wife, and which he himself cannot recognize or accept, with two realities of his own, the one economic and the other social. In the first place he pursues the loss of earnings due to his wife's indolence and the heavy expenditure caused by drinks, strolls and outings; in the second place, he reads dishonour and bad reputation into the flirtatious involvements of this woman who was on the arm of one man or another nearly every day.

Strangely enough, although she never wearies of insisting with dogged conviction after each quarrel that it was the woman's place to be at the window and the man's to be at work, he himself never argues or reasons with her and he makes no attempt to persuade her, so convinced is he of the serious distortion she is making of their social situation as Parisian artisans. He has a few orders for Holland, some customers in the city, and a few small business dealings with some banker friends. They have only one employee and a domestic servant, and although he might have said somewhere that he had a little bit of money, in all truth he just did not have the means to take on the social dream of his spouse, which was grossly out of line. No amount of obdurate tenacity on the part of Montjean's wife could alter their basic position as artisans, a relationship in which marital harmony was essential to their economic partnership. Montjean was also very fond of his wife and could never make the decision to part; he soothes, calms and concedes and often pays obedience to her emotional blackmail as in the following: 'If I can have company, I will do my work.' Once he even had to pay three employees for several days in order to complete a job on time for a customer who would have been extremely angry if there had been any delay. All this simply to compensate for the unyielding idleness of his wife. Nor did he want to listen when he was advised to have his wife put away in a convent; he just seemed surprised that so much could have happened since those happy times when he enjoyed sitting by her side on a Saturday or a Sunday while she finished off a piece of work. He was also afraid of losing his reputation and, although he remained fairly discreet on this point, he went to some trouble to explain to his wife that she should not allow her behaviour to alarm their employee who was quite new.

All this kindness and forbearance (Montjean's own description, please note) in spite of the pain, the arguments and the bad moods, rolled off Montjean's wife like water off a duck's back. Her mind was elsewhere, off into the country where she had seen those women at their windows. There were two images that haunted her: the one of good society and the other, like a scene from a minor work of art, the book held in the hand in front of the window. Read and see. Read and be seen. The window was the rim of the world in which she wanted to live and to be recognized, and the book was the symbol of this recognition rather than a cultural object. The book held in the hand was a way of being, a gesture signifying a pleasant ease and time at one's disposal.

It is difficult to know where she may have come across this model; her father confirmed that her mother and her sisters (except one) all worked and although we do not know the trade in question it is still adequate proof that she was not from a milieu of the upper bourgeoisie. Could it be that the Montjeans were somewhere in the middle, on the fringe of a society where it was possible for the woman to dream that things might be different and thus attempt to realize the dream at the expense of disrupting the marriage? We are at the end of the century here and the wife of a merchant in modes and fashions with customers on the Rue de Buci was sufficiently familiar with current tastes and practices to want to appropriate them for herself. In addition to her model of female leisure she also sought an atmosphere of pleasure and conviviality. One had to keep a good table and cellar and if there were going to be strolls and outings it was also necessary to have the pleasure of masculine company (well away from her husband). Of the exact content of these pleasures, we know little except for the following refrain intoned periodically by each of the spouses. Her: 'It's a terrible thing to be jealous.' Him: 'What is everyone going to think if they keep seeing you out walking on the arm of a friend?' He says several times that he is not jealous of her body as he has plenty of confidence in her and says the following, which is rather quaint: 'I told her that I was not jealous of her body because I was sure that she was not made to be unfaithful in that direction.'

And Montjean was probably quite right there. What his wife wanted above all was to participate in the great social spectacle like the libertines at the end of the eighteenth century who knew so well how to go about it.[24] She was so utterly stage-struck by this model of parading and display, of *mostra*,[25] which forbade her from working, that she was entirely 'at her window'.

And thus, two different wills make themselves apparent; the one, the woman's, was to make an appearance in society, and escape from her situation of too great a dependence on her husband; and the other, the man's, was to guarantee the economic life of the marital/artisan unit without being made to feel humiliated. And so the theme of pleasure and play on the urban stage without regard for cost or expense comes up against that of economic obduracy.

### Friends and pleasures

As always when faced with a text so rich and original as this one, it is tempting to tell all; but one has to be selective and simply show the different stages of the dispute as they are determined by the bid for emancipation by Montjean's wife.

Each quarrel ('the man was made to look after the woman etc.') is preceded by a recital of the wife's pleasures and distractions. One of the most amazing aspects of the journal is without doubt the way she manages to surround herself with the company of a new friend from one week to the next. It is possible to count up to nine of them in the account; nine men to accompany her on her walks or to shows and then to come back with her and eat and drink her wine and apricots in brandy whilst Montjean went around with a long face, or even went so far as to state that he objected to their coming and the daily invasion of his four walls by the kind of company he had no time for. When pushed to the limit, Montjean's tone occasionally became resentful and then it would be arguments and angry scenes all over again. His wife would tap her feet, yell at her jealous husband and exercise a remorseless blackmail from one scene to the next. She would decide not to do any more work so long as her husband refused to let her receive her friends; and he would soothe and calm, plead with her to resume her work, only to find 'her friends' at his own table that very same evening. 'Let me receive my friends, and I'll get on with my work,' she would say, and each time Montjean believed her and each time his trust was abused. He was still fascinated by this vivacious woman whose wit and repartee meant that 'she always gave him as good as she got, tit for tat'.

If this scenario was acted out once, it was acted a dozen times but at the same time events grew progressively worse. In the month of June, Montjean received word that a tobacco warehouse was 'up for offer' in Gisors. This enterprise had no particular appeal for him but his wife saw it as a way out of her own situation. In a fit of temper, she made a scene in which she said to him that 'she did not want to work and that I could see what I had to do'.

She harassed him until he finally decided to go. His thrift bordering on the miserly, he refused to take a coach and set off on foot, with a heavy heart. 'If this place doesn't work out, it will be money spent to no avail,' he said. He managed six leagues in a day and felt very pleased to be able to say that he had only spent 26 *sols* throughout the whole day, but he was unable to get his father-in-law to lend him any money.

Things came to a head after this failure. In her disappointment, Montjean's wife went on one outing after another, running through money as she went. The less than gracious kind of guests she invited home never tired of guzzling his wine, their drinking and carousing going on *ad nauseam*. 'There was no point in my telling her that the money was going fast and that we couldn't go on like this much longer, for she just gave me a short sharp answer, and I gave her a cold look.'

The limits were overstepped and one evening, when coming home with friends he found no one at home and nothing to eat. Later he happened to run into his wife at the Palais-Royal. 'She was on the arm of some handsome cavalier and she was dressed in a gown of bronze taffeta trimmed with gauze with a hat *à l'anglaise*; and she had so much rouge on that I couldn't tell whether she blushed or not.' The scene which took place later between husband and wife quickly turned very violent. Montjean's wife called him a tiger and a monster and yelled at him that 'she would leave him for a chimney-sweep and make a cuckold out of him'. From that point onwards the life of the couple was turned totally upside down. He said that she had continued to go out at all times of the day and night without any sense of proportion. He became angry with her friends, then pulled himself together again. He scolded and chided her and then pleaded with her. She shouted, tapped her heels, got drunk and said that since she earned the money, she was the mistress. This all went on until one day when he had finally had enough, he had an argument with her guests who subsequently set about him with a club and challenged him to a duel. He was the one who went to the rendezvous in spite of his wife's sarcasm about his cowardice, but the others failed to turn up. He could see no way out of it all and so he went to Commissioner Laumonier to tell him of his woes whilst she went on a precautionary visit to the Lieutenant-General of Police in an effort to avoid a demand for imprisonment. Their matrimonial convulsions were still not over when the journal came to an end on 28 February 1775; the final image is of Mme Montjean at the ball, having deserted her children.

Running through this account are one or two key figures. What they say and do provides us with a precise description of the social context without which this dispute would be mere anecdote. And neither did the couple live in isolation, a part of them is bound up in the family, the neighbourhood and the district.

Take the father first of all. He is a central character who acts as a reference point for his son-in-law, Montjean, and who is seen in two different lights by his daughter: on some occasions as an obstacle and at other times as a refuge, depending on the circumstances. He is present throughout this long story and he is also the unwitting starting-point for the subsequent misfortunes (the drama took shape following his daughter's departure to stay with him), but he is also the firm voice of authority and advice.

The possible threat of detention in a convent for Montjean's wife which is outlined throughout the journal, and which Montjean himself cannot decide on, is largely due to him.

He told me that he did not want to see my wife as she had shamed him in his village by letting herself be influenced by all sorts of little madams and coquettes. Because of her behaviour she had dishonoured herself in the minds of many of the people where he lived; and he wanted her locked up but I did not want that.

Montjean's father-in-law, Rohault, advised detention in a convent for his daughter on several occasions and his interventions are a good indication of just how well known and commonplace these procedures for imprisonment were; in fact, they were very simple. He said to his son-in-law, 'If you want to, you can give me your signature and I'll go and find your father, and 24 hours from now, she will be in the convent. I will pay her board and I won't ask you for a thing.' So all it took to have her imprisoned was some money and the signatures of three men. 'I was still fond of my wife and I could not agree to it.' Without this continued attachment, Montjean's wife would have been quickly removed from society.

As well as an authority figure, the father was also important financially. Montjean had to go through him when he was attempting to procure the tobacco warehouse, and in spite of his failure he still remained on good terms with him, which could not be said of his daughter. She was so terrified as the prospect of the threat that he kept hanging over her that she launched into a flood of invective against him and even wrote to the commissioner speaking ill of him.

One can see here the detailed workings of the strategies adopted by families vis-à-vis authority and how the commissioners found themselves implicated in the private lives of those under their jurisdiction, whilst the latter found it quite easy to appropriate the instruments of justice which had been left at their disposal. Even family friends, in their roles as dispensers of advice or as conciliators, used the argument of the *lettre de cachet* as a means of bringing the wife back to her duties. Some even went so far as to say that she deserved to be put in Sainte-Pélagie, the notorious prison for women of ill-repute. This line of argument provoked her to dreadful outbursts of anger but also reduced her to nervous girlish panic and trembling which softened her husband's heart. One day, overcome with panic, she paid a visit to the Lieutenant-General of Police to make sure that he would not sign any order against her should her husband ever request it. Then she came back 'in floods of tears and all of a tremble. I sat her down and told her that I was ready to forget everything... that I loved her and that I would do all I could to make sure that she had her pleasures.' The next day it started all over again – the wife's little pleasures, an angry husband, threats from the father.

Of Montjean, the author of the account, we really know very little. He is so taken up with the tantrums and unreasonable activities of his wife that he scarcely speaks about himself or dwells on private thoughts. He no doubt presents himself as he is, namely a man broken on account of his choice of wife, yet still full of affection for her and continually torn between tenderness, reasonableness and reproach. Concerned as he is with his reputation and the smooth running of his business, he has an obsession with money verging on the fanatical; his arguments are almost always economic and very rarely emotional. He keeps accounts of his expenses, is economical with what he has, despairs in the face of unfinished orders, takes stock of the number of bottles of wine and jars of apricots in brandy that he has left, quotes the cost of meals eaten at the restaurant with his friends and makes constant reference to the incessant expense imposed on him by his wife for the hire of cabs. The meticulous detail with which he lists one by one all his expenses, such as the loss of earnings and the breaches made in his economies, are an excellent indication of the importance which he attributed to a form of married life which was first and foremost economic. The expressions he uses are revealing:

'It's true that since that wretched visit to her father I no longer know her. She doesn't know the value of 6 *livres*, in all this time she hasn't done any work . . . cabs don't seem to cost anything to her, she sometimes takes as many as three or four in a day.' And then if she returned from a trip out, it was, 'You've made a fine old dint in my apricots, there are only three left.'

However, this finicky, niggling fellow was also a sensitive creature, always holding back from provoking a final rupture with his wife, always talking to her kindly and always hoping for a lasting improvement from her. But in spite of that, if one had to add up the number of reproaches he made to her and the reasons for his daily surprise at seeing her thus elude him, the economic details would largely prevail over the marks of jealousy or arguments of an emotional nature, although these were there too. Economic accord was one of the fundamental components of the marriage of artisans as was the managerial and financial role of the husband, and this particular example is an outstanding confirmation of that.

Also taking their place in this family whirlpool were the children. Montjean talks about them, or rather about his little girl of 4, on several occasions, although they never occupy the centre stage. Right at the beginning of the account, on the return of his wife, he makes it clear that it was he who put his little girl to bed, even though he was tired and weary from the journey. Later on he becomes angry at his wife for dragging her off so much with her on her totally unreasonable outings and making her ill as a result. 'She came back at half-past midnight with my little girl of 4 and I had hardly finished putting her to bed when she vomited all over the place. She was so ill, I thought she was going to die. Goodness knows what on earth she had allowed the child to eat and drink.' What his wife thought, we do not really know except on those occasions when she burst into anger and shouted at Montjean that it was up to him to look after his children, or when she yelled at him that he was a monster and that she hated her children because they came from him. Paternal attention in the eighteenth century was not an illusion and this is certainly not the first time it has been brought to our notice.

Montjean's wife, around whom everything revolves, is a fascinating figure – at least if one believes her husband. Entirely absorbed as she is by an all-consuming passion bordering on the obsessive, the sole purpose of her life was to nurture it at every possible opportunity and to impose it on her husband. What passion? A passion for society, passion for position and social standing other than her own, passion to be elsewhere, free from marital dependence, passion to be the woman who was sought after and courted and to be on view at the very heart of the show itself, namely the society life of Paris. Headstrong, obstinate and obsessed by the style of life she wanted to lead, she considered that everything else stood in her way. This provoked extreme outbursts of anger in which the one cry (repeated 19 times) to be heard could be reduced to two sentences, namely that she did not want to work and that it was up to the man to look after his wife and children. She maintains this categorical refusal to work throughout the account and it is firmly supported by a somewhat peremptory vision of the social order, or rather the male–female order. Man has to work while woman makes appearances, pleases and entertains. The cry she utters at the height of her anger is particularly violent because it is the expression of a need which is urgent both personally and socially. So completely enthralled is she by the spectacle of the world above her and which, on account of her trade, she is condemned to serve, that Montjean's wife wears herself out in the costly work of appearances.

Her daily timetable provides an illustration of some of the pleasures of the period enjoyed by that middle rank of society who were just comfortable enough to be able to afford the expense of regular outings in Paris, for which the essentials consisted of strolls, meals, clothes, cosmetics and outings by cab, especially if these also included the arm of a man friend. This latter she chose with an acute sense of the social hierarchy and was always ready to drop any one of them in favour of another who might be better dressed, all in the space of the same evening.

> She dined with the boy who worked for M. Simon, the printer, and after the meal they went to take a boat to go to Saint-Cloud, but they didn't find one and so they took a cab in which there were two people. One of these was Dubois, a dancer at the opera whom I had known when he was a boy and as he was better dressed than the printer's boy, she took his arm and walked down the grand avenue with him.

The favoured places for walking out were apparently the Tuileries and the Palais-Royal, with the occasional venture further afield to more exotic places such as the Gros Caillou (where one could eat gudgeon), Saint-Cloud or Pré-Saint-Gervais. There, one might go for a stroll, dressed in one's best and then stop off to drink a beer, a carafe of redcurrant or a glass of white wine – an ample watering for a somewhat fanatical taste for fish, oysters in particular. Montjean never stopped deploring the indulgence in oysters which were so expensive and with which his wife regaled her companions. 'They have eaten 12 *livres* worth of oysters, drunk the white wine and eaten the peaches in brandy.' Grand reunions were occasionally held at his house and while he did his best to put the guests off, telling them, for instance, that 'all we've got in the house is some bread soup and stew', his wife would have ordered '50 *sols* worth of fresh pork, and sent to the oyster lady for 4 *livres* worth of oysters to eat and five bottles of wine to drink'. Recurring constantly throughout the text is this consumption of seafood and fish, much to Montjean's regret, but very much vaunted by his wife as a mark of good taste and *savoir-faire*, which it most certainly was.

Who were these friends then with whom she ate and drank and generally amused herself, and who constituted this society so dear to her heart, this social mirage she preferred so much to her work? We know very little about their trade. One of them was a printer, another a dancer and a third one she met at the home of a young woman who 'drew portraits' and for whom Mme Montjean posed. There were probably a lot of them in any case, and most of them were men who, it would appear, had little concern for the husband. They were forever at the Montjean abode taking advantage of the wife's thirst for society in order to wine and dine and go off on outings at the expense of the couple, without the least sense of shame. They pretended not to notice the husband's anger and were even prepared to assault him when he disturbed their cavorting. Montjean was often the plaything of these 'young masters' about whom we know very little except for their frivolous behaviour. Some of them led him a merry dance and on the pretence of getting *la belle* back to work, they called more frequently each day to take her out.

One can see in the description of their fun and games a kind of infantile *marivaudage*[26] and small-scale libertinism. It had been the same when his wife came back from Gisors (her father's village where she had found this model of womanly life which had thereafter continued to haunt her), and she had told her husband all about the games and tricks she had got up to. There had been a lot of 'squeezing and pinching, silly pranks and friendly smacks' and with her sister 'the two of them had unbuttoned M. Demard's hose and given him a whipping'. One of their friends had said apparently that if they had done it to him, 'he would have spanked them on the behind'. At the thought of this, Montjean laughed out loud. Later, when Demard was ill, she had sent him a nightcap and two very attractive kerchiefs. Once, while walking in the Tuileries in very good company, 'they had all amused themselves by jumping down off the top of the terrace several times, which had made my wife laugh'. When they had had enough, they took a cab to the Boulevard to drink white wine. Card games, gambling, tarot, etc., etc. – it was one long round of pleasure, appearances, games and spectacle. Such was the way of the world in 1774 and Montjean's wife wanted her share of its follies.

Making an appearance was a necessity and a way of life and Montjean himself was not unsusceptible. Once when accompanying his wife and friends to the Palais-Royal, he noticed that he had a hole in his stocking. 'I said to my wife, my goodness, I've got a hole in my stocking; I'm going home quickly to mend it. Go round again with them once more and then come back home to eat.' Going out walking was the focus for the spectacle they all offered each other. If it was unacceptable for a man to have a tiny hole in his stocking, then the woman must have been on show in her entirety – Montjean's wife was happy to be totally engulfed.

From what Montjean says of her, two essential images emerge: one of uncontained impetuousness which required the availability of everything which helped one forget about the workaday colours of daily toil; and the other of the butterfly, the prisoner of her own dreams as well as her status, forever tapping against the window-pane of evasion. In short, a woman eternally at her window.

What of the other important characters in this fresco, the servants? There were not many of them (the Montjeans only had one maid in addition to their workshop hand) but they made their presence felt, as one might expect, and could always be relied on to play the role of go-between, acting as intermediary between husband and wife or of confidante first of one, then of the other. Acting both as discreet counsellors and docile servitors, they carried *billets-doux*, posted letters, tried to obtain information and intercepted messages. Beneath them, and under their orders, there lived the little *Savoyard* who was regularly called on to keep a lookout for the comings and goings of the friends or instructed by the wife to inform her when an escort was waiting for her down below, which was not in the best of taste and put Montjean out quite considerably. 'What?' he said, 'He sent a chimney-sweep to fetch her? An honest woman sent for by a chimney-sweep at 4 o'clock, what kind of example is this in this area?'

The domestics were party to all the adventures. The cook, for instance, helped Montjean's wife to doctor the wine when the latter had drunk too much of it with her friends while her husband had been away on a trip to Thiais. Later she reproached her for exposing her husband to a wicked duel he did not deserve. The masters always had need of their respect, evidence borne out by this strange little scene where Montjean returned home unscathed from his duel for the very good reason that his partners had not turned up. He collapsed in a heap on the dining room floor, sobbing and yelling in order to make his servants believe he had been wounded. Abandoned by his wife and despised and mocked by her for his inability to fight, at that particular moment he had needed a theatre in which to demonstrate his prowess, and the domestic servants, of course, were the only public remaining to him. And thus he acted out the scene he most needed to play, that of courageous virility, wounded but strong, and the one he would have liked his wife to have watched. It did not matter that the servants were the only ones who had to look and not see; at least they were there – and gullible.

> I had the girl and the young lady believe that I had fought and that I had been wounded and so I stretched myself out on the sofa. One of them got out the brandy and all the dressings to put on my wounds and all of a tremble, they asked me if I was badly wounded. I started to laugh and they saw straight away that I was doing it on purpose and that there was nothing the matter. I told them because they were trembling more than my wife.

Because of what they saw and heard and got to know, the servants had difficulty in keeping the secret and, as in many novels, it was through them that Montjean learned about a good part of his misfortunes. This would end in tears and threats of dismissal and then everything would return to normal again, all that is except for the Montjean couple. The account ends with a picture of the wife dragging the cook off to the pleasure gardens in the Bois de Boulogne and of the *Savoyard* left to keep watch over their possessions in an empty apartment.

One could have commented on each phrase, explained each detail and interpreted each event which is so rich in precise detail about daily life. Instead, a number of images have been selected, to bring out this unusual combat between two marriage partners whose quarrel revolved around a fundamental disagreement over the distribution of male and female tasks. The end of the eighteenth century dragged along in its train the mirages and illusions of high society to which the world of the artisan and small trader dreamed of acceding. The woman here is the decisive actor in a desire to rise socially, passing in turn by way of the 'spectacle' put on in good taste for oneself and for others, to reading and the descent into horseplay and revelling with company. Into this dream, aspired to daily, should one not also read the utter weariness of the wives of artisans employed by their husbands at the same time as a distaste for marriage very typical of certain aspects of the eighteenth century?

'Marriage is a tyranny exercised over Beauty; it is a monster which devours the marks of favour given you by Nature. What should make ladies tremble is the loss of liberty in marriage. Belle Angélique, there is no marriage amongst the angels.'[27]

# Part II

# Work and its Margins

---

We know the broad shape and outline of the world of work as we do the organization of the city; there are great numbers of studies which have shown us the strength and vigour of the craft-guilds with their festivals and ceremonies, as well as their constraints and restrictive practices. We also have other studies which provide us with sketches of the tissue and fabric of urban life, with its streets and trade, its passers-by and the population on its margins. However, the desire to uncover events other than those usually described has led to a journey across the spaces of town and work via their internal conflicts, with the effect that the resulting images are either sharper or in need of modification, thus making it no longer possible to remain at the surface of things.

League and counter-league; the need to get together to celebrate, cheat or rebel; the desire to rally others around oneself in order to avenge or defend oneself against injustice – these all produced a particular climate in which one might express or justify oneself, or reflect on one's conditions of existence and vulnerability. Then there were crucial moments such as the formation of an alliance or its breakdown (whether in the workshop, in the town or well away from work altogether); there were times when truth and falsehood crossed paths, when proposition met with opposition within which desire and intent were often sealed in the impossibility of their realization. Whether such activities brought people together or stirred up a hue and cry, they were all a part of the convulsions through which society inevitably passes in the course of its transformation and construction.

These are the concerns of this book for it is in the rediscovery of this kind of behaviour and activity that it might be possible to discern the thinking and understanding that ordinarily are so well masked by the documents.

# 6

# In the Workshop

The picture of the Parisian workshop of the eighteenth century is a familiar one which the historiography and iconography of the period has made more immediate (the image of the sansculotte workers of the *faubourgs* has been fixed for ever for instance by the Revolution of July 1789).[1] Nostalgia has also helped sustain the memory of the craft workshop as that familiar place of old-world courtesy where the master shared his expertise and pride in his work with his journeymen. Nevertheless, we also know that the tissue of daily life was interwoven with intrigue and grievances; but memory has somehow managed to accommodate these clashes without too much difficulty, so ingrained is it by the school texts.

We know that the corporatist policies of Colbert played an important role during the seventeenth century. Not only did the number of corporations increase (in Paris the numbers rose from 60 in 1669 to 129 in 1691), but the machinery was put in place for the regulation of the trades to be made subject to the State Inspector-Generals, who were responsible for bringing everything under central control. The Lord Chief Justices were no longer allowed the right of regulating the trades and crafts which had hitherto been under their jurisdiction. This attempt at centralization which was so obviously intended to serve the interests of the absolutist monarchy naturally provoked a good deal of resistance, and in Paris several enclaves claimed the right to maintain their privileges like the square and cloister of Notre-Dame, the Temple, Saint-Jean-de-Latran, Saint-Germain-des-Prés, etc.

Ideally, the whole body of corporations was to be directly dependent on the King, but this desire for unity was never in fact realized as the corporations were so ill-adapted economically. The philosophers of the Enlightenment were themselves advocates of freedom in this area which had become so stifled by an abundance of rules and regulations and nervousness about the possibility of conflict.

The workshop was both repressive and cautious; and the fear of conflict weighed so heavily that the authorities often trod on each other's toes and lost their footing in the face of the extent of the problems. The law affecting the trades and professions was normally administered jointly by the craft-guilds themselves and by the King's own officials; but it was this apportioning which proved stormy and uneasy. Strikes, on the other hand, were repressed by a wide range of authorities depending on the particular region and occasion, with everyone getting involved from the King's Procurator and the Chamber of Commerce to the Lieutenant-General of Police, who could be found wielding his *lettres de cachet* with great aplomb.

Little by little, throughout the eighteenth century, disorder crept in amongst the ranks of the guild-masterships and so long as artisans were excluded from paying municipal taxes, a close *esprit de corps* prevailed, paralysing everything. Even the guild officials (*jurés*) abused their rights and found themselves in serious contention with the masters, whilst journeymen and apprentices continued to shake the yoke of the masters' authority.

Throughout the period, philosophers and economists were rethinking the industrial question and it was no mere chance that in 1757 the subject of a competition held at the Academy of Amiens was concerned with 'The obstacles to work and industry created by the craft-guilds and corporations'; and it was no coincidence either that the prize was carried off by Clicquot de Blervache (under the pseudonym Delisle), whose paper was a lengthy discourse on the sclerotic condition of the corporations and the masters' obsessive concern with training an excessive number of apprentices through fear of competition.[2]

The police, for their part, had to sail daily in stormy waters. On the one hand, acting on behalf of the Lieutenant-General, they had no hesitation in issuing police orders, itself an indication of the extent to which the life of the trades had been disturbed by conflicts, regulations, orders, interdicts and instructions which were always transgressed and perpetually repeated.[3] On the other hand, the police were prevented from intervening directly, since traditionally the guild's own police was directly responsible to the juries of their own magistrates; but in actual fact, things were not so simple, as the police were also responsible for all matters affecting public order and what is more, some of the more serious and prolonged disputes occasionally called into question the authority and honesty of the officials themselves. But the dream itself remained pure and clear, thus ensuring the firm hold of the existing system which integrated the police within the corporation, which in turn subjected the members of the crafts and trades to the body as a whole in accordance with a model upon which the whole of society could be based. In his 'Mémoires' Lieutenant-General Lenoir makes constant reference to this perfect ideal of the 'domestic chain' by which masters were subject to their juries, journeymen to their masters, apprentices to the journeymen: the desired (and disputed) model was that of the relationship of servant to master.

As the atmosphere progressively deteriorated, it became increasingly difficult to control antagonisms and conflicts. Those *syndics* who were afraid that they might not be able to assert their own discipline chose to be accompanied by the police commissioners and on top of all this, the adjutants of the Lieutenant-General came along on the King's orders and put the more recalcitrant characters into prison. Under such conditions, recourse to the police archives should allow one to examine in detail the fever which was shaking this milieu.

It is still difficult to approach things in this way, however, as the archives of the corporations disappeared in the fire of 1871 and it was here that the greater part of those conflicts settled internally were to be found. Direct recourse to the police commissioner was altogether more rare and this explains why systematic searches have failed to turn up many hundreds of conflicts. It is thanks to the commissioners' archives, however, that it is possible to describe this world of the workshop which has been too much the prisoner of a historiographical image which has fixed it either in the nostalgia of 'the job well done' or in the ideology of the Revolution to come and the class struggle of the future.[4]

As with the case of the child, we need to question our own syntax and collective imagery. Our memories have been left with a glossy picture of the cheerful journeyman, proud to be so, who is safely ensconced within a culture of work and *cabaret* where friendships and hostilities collided over a glass of wine. Any resentful or unpleasant traits in his character could be explained by his common origins, where brawls and beatings were known to be almost a ritual. With its banquets, secret traditions and 'well-chosen' vocabulary, it is tempting to think of it as another world which 'we have since lost' or as a popular way of life with which one has lost touch and whose spontaneous as well as more exotic aspects it is now fashionable to resurrect.[5]

By looking at the workshop 'cell', which was quite restricted, it is possible to gain a clear insight into the nature of the social stakes at play; for this reason, the repression of infringements of working practice is of less interest to us than the emergence of conflict and encounter. But before penetrating into the workplace itself, let us recall some of the difficult conditions which inevitably made life so precarious for workers in the eighteenth century. The two following examples will suffice:

Suzanne Lavallée, an invalid-attendant, was the wife of a journeyman cooper. Their home was at the Cul de sac de la Forge-Royale, parish of Sainte-Marguerite. On 11 November 1761, they made a complaint before

Commissioner Crespy that they had been robbed of all their linen. She said that

> fifteen days ago she had left the house where she lived alone (as her husband slept at his master's), and she had gone to look after her invalids. She had left behind her a woman by the name of Manon, who had come to stay with her whilst she recovered from an over-production of milk. This same Manon had remained at the house while she was away as she was fostering a child. Eight days after, on getting back from work, she had gone into her room to look for her but could not find her as she had gone and had left the key with a neighbour as well as the child, and everything had been stolen.[6]

The situation for this couple, who were unable to live together, was indeed precarious; the husband stayed at his master's and the wife had to be away several days at a time to take care of the sick, leaving behind a woman who was convalescing and nursing a child. The convalescent went off with the linen, leaving the key and the child with a neighbour who seemed to accept everything. When the invalid-attendant returned, she no longer had any clothes, all she had, in fact, was a child who meant nothing to her.

The other example comes from the milieu of the lodging-house, where conditions were by and large promiscuous. Françoise Torpied, a shop girl, recently arrived in Paris, was lodging with a man by the name of Pelletier in the Rue Saint-Martin-au-Grand-Cerf. He put her in a room with two beds. One of the beds was occupied by a nurse and a guide for the blind and the other by herself and a nurse who was a complete stranger to her.[7] The following morning she could find neither her box nor her money and strongly suspected her bedfellow.

Four women to two beds, and two straw pallets beneath which one might place the odd item – risky cohabitation indeed; but for some, it was a way of life.

And as for the way of life in the workshop, the traditional and hierarchical structure of work (the number of masters in Paris at the end of the eighteenth century was put at 30,000 over all trades[8]), which grouped together the master and his employees, this was also markedly precarious and more or less affected by the general ups and downs of everyday life.

## An open space

The order of things was not as one might have expected. The workshop could hardly have been that place of domestic intimacy and expertise where the apprentice took his time becoming a journeyman, and where the journeymen took pleasure in getting together for celebrations whilst awaiting their mastership. Nor was it always a warm, enclosed space where the stability of the employees aided production and promoted the interests of those working there. In fact, the statements made by workers and journeymen reveal a space that was constantly disturbed by comings and goings and the disruptions caused by various hirings and firings. Such conditions were hardly conducive to calm and steadiness.

The timetables we have been able to piece together from the interrogations would seem to bear out this fragmentation of time as one moved from job to job and from one master to the next, like the journeyman joiner who had served more than ten masters in three years.[9] He had been in a workshop in the Rue Maubuée before installing himself in another in the Rue Aubry-le-Boucher and then he worked in another one at Saint-Germain for a year. He then left for Vernon and proceeded to Rouen before coming back to Paris, where he again worked for several masters, finally ending up at Villeneuve. His case was by no means exceptional; in fact it was one of the most common causes of conflict between masters and employees and one of the major preoccupations of the police. Notice of leave and the statutory authorization required before leaving a master as laid down in the edict of 1749 did not seem to have made much impact on these customary practices of arrival and departure.

Not only was such mobility a fact of life, it was occasionally asserted as a right, as in the case of the cabby who was arrested in the popular uprising of 1750. When questioned about his reasons for leaving his master, he replied that, 'he hadn't liked it there, and besides one didn't always stay with the same master',[10] a phrase which would seem to signify an almost permanent desire to be off, to be elsewhere, to seek something better and to make that mobility a personal choice (certainly, it was often experienced as such). It was, in effect, a kind of refusal to adhere to the ideal model of the workshop as a structure of authority in which employment was motivated by dependence and domesticity as propounded by the police and the monarchy.

The workshop was not then, as one may have been quick to assume, a system based on the bond between the master's family and his journeymen where all lived together in blessed intimacy and familiarity. A bond was made on the basis of a specific contract which only ran for a certain length of time and which might be rather quickly undone. There was life outside the workshop. Information circulated, and the desire to find better pay elsewhere gave life a gypsy-like rhythm and almost nomadic quality. As for the boys and girls who worked in the shops and the simple domestic servants, their situation was even more unstable; they lacked qualifications and regarded their job as no more than a way of earning a living for the time being, with no future.

One might think that this situation was essentially Parisian, but this is certainly not the case, and a study based on employment registers at Rouen gives similar results.[11] Not only did workers do the rounds in one town before moving on to the next, but a half of the jobs only lasted for a couple of weeks, while 20 per cent stayed where they were for a month. Very few stayed in the same place for more than three months. Obviously in the course of all this moving around, it was not uncommon for an employee to find himself back again at some time with one of his earlier masters.

That one went from master to master was a fact; but the uncertainties of economic life also gave rise to other types of mobility, such as changing one's particular profession. It was not unusual to find a journeyman with a different trade from the one he had learned from his father because he had been unable to carry it out as there was no work or because he lacked the means. For the majority, work was a necessary activity and not a personal investment in a chosen field, with the exception of the sons of masters who did not need to bother themselves too much with this kind of problem. Theirs was a sheltered life within a trade which guaranteed them a secure future. For the rest, work was not necessarily an expression of oneself.

Even if one had been doing a definite kind of work for some time, one would find one's time divided up in a particular way. The seasons, for instance, were marked out by a whole variety of different tasks and by lengthy dispersals from Paris. During the eighteenth century there were many building-workers in the city and in winter some of them returned to the country, while others stayed where they were, getting by on whatever meagre means there were available (for example polishing the silver in the grand houses of Le Marais or doing the occasional odd job). In the spring, they returned on site to be set on by whichever master paid best or had a shortage of manpower.

Having drawn attention to this itinerant way of life and its displacements, and having recalled the fact that the workshop was far from being that settled and enclosed space where a journeyman always remained with the same master, we need to take this description even further. Within the workshop, a place of forced cohabitation between family, employees and servants, specific tasks were not allocated to each person once and for all. Although it is difficult to find detailed sources providing information on the exact type of work performed by each person, or the manner in which masters and employees perceived their relationship to their work, it becomes apparent, as one works one's way through testimonies and interrogations that the tasks varied greatly. It is also apparent that much of the time was taken up here and there with a number of small ancillary jobs, some of which are quite surprising, such as taking letters, going to fetch a jug of wine for the master, running errands, fetching the master from the *cabaret* (if he were still on his feet...). All of these activities, which are referred to quite often, were all part and parcel of the work one was expected to do. One of the strangest of these tasks was imposed on a young apprentice who was made to hide behind the window and watch what the neighbour was doing: 'Yes, that's you, the neighbourhood spy! It's a well-known fact. You're the lowest of the low,' exclaimed the master wigmaker as he looked at Guesbois, the master hatter.[12] He told them how Guesbois spent his time making fun of him and looking out of the window to see what was going on at his place:

> He went up into his room at the time when he knew Guesbois would be there watching him, but it was so bad that he had to look away and draw the curtains. At 10 o'clock in the evening he had had some trouble with one of his boys. This had created a noise which had caused Guesbois to send his apprentice over to look through the window to see what was going on. This seemed to be a source of great amusement for Guesbois, who was laughing.

In this case, the apprentice was up late keeping watch, and in another case there was the journeyman sculptor who was sent to play messenger and go-between for his master and a neighbouring manufacturer of fireworks.[13] Elsewhere a journeyman joiner seriously mistreated one of the house-boys whom he had ordered to go and fetch the boss, yelling after him as he went that 'that was what he was there for'.[14]

Each workshop obeyed the law of its master and of his wife, which created diversity in working-practice and a looseness in the definition of tasks which was often a cause of argument or fights. Such conflict was felt particularly acutely because it brought the journeymen into outright confrontation with some of the most dearly held convictions of the police and the authorities, who tended to see employees as domestic servants subject to the authority of the powers that be, whereas many journeymen could not tolerate having to carry out tasks which they considered to be the responsibility of the boys or apprentices.

The apprentice, of course, was himself directly threatened by this servile perception of his work. He often complained of doing servants' jobs all day and of being expected to do anything and everything, although he was not a liveried servant. Far too often his time was confined to cleaning and running errands when, as he complained, he should have been learning the trade. The apprentice was often treated like a servant and the following case in point concerning a young girl of 15, the daughter of a bourgeois, is particularly telling. She had been apprenticed in 'hairdressing and fashion' but asserted that 'she had done nothing at all to do with hair or fashions, and had merely acted as a servant',[15] and she had been courted by the master into the bargain. With the exception of women who were incorporated within those trades that were specifically female and controlled by female magistrates and officials, the main body of women workers in Paris was spread thinly throughout a variety of largely undifferentiated small trades which did not require any qualifications and which were ill-thought of by a bourgeoisie who did not wish to see its daughters working:

'Imagine, if you will, a creature so peaceable, so tender and so delicate. Do you think it possible for her to survive more than two hours without a migraine? Could a girl escape unscathed?'[16] In the poorer milieux, they obviously did remain unscathed, and in the workshop the lack of work definition led more often to the status of servant than to a professional qualification. Certainly this was one of the ways in which their work was regarded.[17]

The workshop was nevertheless a place which was easier to leave than one might think; it lived in keeping with a complex and fragmented rhythm; nor did it operate in isolation like a recluse – quite the opposite! It was a space that opened up onto the outside and was constantly cut across by outside influences. The journeyman, the shop boy or girl brought into it with them many different worlds; they did not live day-in and day-out from dawn till dusk within the strict hierarchy of work or the household. They all had their time taken up by a wide range of family commitments and other matters which obliged the workshop to be a porous place where all kinds of social relationships overlapped and thus prevented it from being that tight structure which one finds described so often.

Because the employee was working virtually unprotected, he very rarely took on a face-to-face confrontation alone with his master; that would be too risky. As the archives plainly attest, however, the journeyman would be supported by a decidedly strong family presence. There was often a brother or a sister, an uncle or parents around to give support or show solidarity in the event of a disagreement. The respective wrongs were weighed up and assessed, with the characteristics of each party well known to all concerned.

Even the architecture of the workshop opened it up to outside view. Overlooking the street as it did, with its windows open, its journeymen carried out their work in front of the rest of the district, who passed comment and criticism, gossiped or remained indifferent. The narrowness of the streets also made for close encounters of a mischievous or cheerful nature but in either case, as neighbour or competitor, one saw and was seen. Rumour, the current gossip, rude comments made on the market, chit-chat – these were all a part of workshop life. One might try to lure the neighbour's customers away or put them off; or perhaps nip into the *cabaret* for a brandy with a fellow journeyman who had been hailed over.

Then came the rallying cry that travelled faster than the wind or the abrupt lay-off without notice on the same day as one found out that offers of work were at a premium at the Place de Grève. This ebb and flow of news and comment and movements affecting the individual heart or the street were regularly experienced in a life where things seen and heard were responsible for making or breaking solidarity, for prompting revenge or the like, or else were just so many of the various ways of breathing in the air and the difficulties of the time. The workshop found itself engulfed with no possibility of holding itself aloof. Honour and reputation, tossed by talk and chatter like trees in a storm, lent it a fragility which could on occasion undermine the master's discipline. In this open and exposed climate so subject to knocks and buffeting, friendships and social groups were fleeting and mobile, and while the networks and channels formed outside decreased the forms of social dependence, such alliances and understandings always needed to be recreated and reconstructed as arrivals and departures were so frequent; in fact it was movement which was the permanent feature and characteristic of social groupings of this kind, which makes it necessary to reconsider the type of friendships and intimacies which might arise as a result.

The workman, always torn between the desire for wealth and his own free space, inhabited the workshop out of necessity and in keeping with his own plans, the conduct of which remained therefore both solitary and collective. Any intimacy he might know on the shop-floor was most likely to be at some particular moment and liable to interruption for any number of reasons. Whether it was fleeting or lasting, the experience of such moments was constrained and confined by life inside and out, since the workshop was neither a well-defined shelter nor refuge, but a place dominated by tensions and power relationships and by simultaneous systems of alliance and dissension. In this place, private and public spheres were conjoined without distinction and the structure of the space itself reflected this intermediate state in which choices between the inside and outside were not even open to consideration but simply became immersed in the flux and flow of city life. It is difficult to catalogue habits and rituals; it is rather a matter of showing how exposed this place was and how it served as a focus of resistance for those who wished to establish a mode of being and an order of things quite different from the dreams of the masters and police. Defence mechanisms and utopian projects shook the guilds and the authorities without cease.

## Feverish interludes

One should not imagine the workshop as being solely disrupted by conflicts between masters and employees; that would be oversimple. The

trades were in fact disturbed and shaken by scores of feverish movements and activities which spread and reverberated, provoking an almost
permanent state of *malaise*. Several dramas were acted out on this stage of
work and on each occasion loyalties shifted and the confrontations which
arose created new connections which thus modified the map of alliances.
Serious problems arose at every level and confrontations between master
and journeyman were no more frequent than those which brought the
masters into violent conflict with their guild officials and no more common
than the differences which divided the world of the journeymen themselves. Cracks were visible at every point and no one was spared. Each
type of conflict established its own forms of agreement or rupture causing
earlier alliances to break up and new ones to form.

The complexity of the forms of social opposition which occasionally
brought together those who moments ago had been in conflict with each
other allows one to grasp something of a workshop thus caught in the
peculiar stranglehold of opposing forces which did not necessarily respect
the forms of solidarity or antinomy one might have expected; and if one
moves beyond the complexity of the situations, one might possibly find out
something of the modes of thought.

Given the state of conservation of the archives of the craft-guilds and
corporations and the diversity of the authorities responsible for maintaining order in the world of work, it would be unrealistic to think that the
police archives contain the only records of these conflicts. Thus the 170
workshop disputes that were singled out from the middle of the eighteenth
century (see n. 4), can only serve as a framework on which to reflect. It is
difficult to know at what point matters were considered serious enough
to go before the commissioner of police and how representative these
disputes were. What is evident is that a detailed analysis will benefit us
more than a quantitative outline of the conflicts of working life.

The evidence we have shows that all the disputes collated here involved
a great deal of violence. Conflicts did not take place with buttoned foils.
Violence and brutality erupted very suddenly into a climate of aggression
with no attempt at containment. It was as though there were no other
means of expressing what one found unacceptable other than by blows
and punches and that there was an underlying hatred which only needed a
pretext for it to spill over. The workshop, however, was no more violent
than the tenement block, the *cabaret* or the market-place, especially if one
considers how its authoritarian and hierarchical configuration might easily
give rise to opportunities for discord.

When a disagreement did arise, anger, blows and insults were all dragged
in and things would finally reach the pitch where the whole neighbourhood became involved. The fight was rarely with bare fists, as there were
far too many wooden or metal tools about the place for them not to be

used. If one did not want one's adversary to die, things had to be brought to an end quickly or the participants restrained by the others. Paring-knives, hammers, nails, lumps of lead and glass were all lethal and costly. The insults, however, knew no bounds and so there was no shortage of them. Loud shouts of 'Filth!' 'Beggar!' 'Rogue!' or 'Wretch!' hardly made much of an impression, for they were part and parcel of the whole business, just like the expressions aimed at the women, such as 'Bitch!' 'Whore!' and 'Madam!' From time to time one finds an effort to make them more specific and then they resound all the more intensely: 'Money-grubber!' Villainous cheat!' 'Dealer in human flesh!' – terms which evoke exploitation and economic difficulty. Or one might declare oneself ready to do anything: 'I'll gouge your heart out and eat it, you rotten slut; go hang, you're not fit for Bicêtre!' In this case the insult was combined with the hope for justice which would see the other dead or imprisoned.

As usual the more foul and salacious insults were reserved especially for the women and these included images of the punishments traditionally meted out to persons of ill-repute. It was not uncommon to hear such remarks as the following: 'I'll rip the frock off your backside, see if I don't', or else, 'You soldiers' moll', and 'Your bitch of a cousin will be put on a donkey one of these days', a reference to the punishment of miscreants by a humiliating public donkey-ride.[18]

Blows, wounds, insults and a neighbourhood in uproar were the main characteristics of these disputes. There were also tears and sobs but they came mainly from the young apprentices who, because they lacked the physical strength of the adults and were still quite close to childhood or were indeed quite simply children, could not offer the same opposition, force of arms or argument. As far as they were concerned, we are talking of pain, sorrow and tears.

### The master's wife

In the midst of all this disorder, there was one figure who stood out like a target – the master's wife.[19] Although her professional situation was utterly ambiguous, this had the effect of making her an even more important personage, carrying out as she did a wide range of managerial tasks in the workshop and helping create a pleasant ambiance for entertaining customers and clients. In close parallel with her husband she exerted a powerful influence over day-to-day matters and as wife of the master, merchant or landlord she was the inevitable bustling, busy servant of her husband (not of course to the liking of all, as we might recall from the case of Montjean's wife). She was also the mistress who exercised her authority over journeymen, servants, apprentices and shop hands. Her tasks were vast and imprecise, creating a distortion of power which gave her even more influence and meant that she was present at the workshop much more than her husband, who was often out on business (or as we shall see later, involved in disputes between guild officials, *syndics* and masters). Accountant, manageress, giver of orders, she demonstrated her authority whilst lacking any qualification and only held this power on account of her marriage. Because of her many titles, which in fact were nothing of the kind, she was both a central character and a vulnerable figure. She was vulnerable even at the very heart of the alliance formed with her husband, for everything depended on the coordination of their lives and their mutual understanding. In fact she was infinitely vulnerable, for although she was one of the essential figures in the success of the business she represented the weak link.

Given the importance of the fact that gossip and rumour were the common property of the district, it was easy for anyone in disagreement with the master to avoid taking on the master directly in person simply by resorting to the alternative of lashing out indiscriminately at the honour and reputation of his wife. There were all kinds of ways of undermining the image of the couple, such as a careless word spoken in the *cabaret* or at the market or the spreading of suspicion by dropping the odd suggestive comment. It was a serious business, for the artisan could lose his customers. The life of the workshop being a constant combination of 'inner' and 'outer', the wife of the master represented one of its most private aspects at the same time as being obliged to present an image of herself to the public which was trustworthy and reliable. When conflict arose, however, it was she who became the obvious target. Furthermore, everyone knew that once she became a widow she would be the real mistress of the place unless one of the journeymen managed to marry her. As a woman and wife of the master, she had a dual image in which weakness and power were intermingled. Her private life was more exposed than that of others since her marriage gave her an effective power which would be hers officially in the event of her becoming a widow or else it could make her the object of a new matrimonial strategy for a man who may have spent a long while awaiting the position of master and the death of the husband.

Given all this, it is not surprising that she found herself implicated in nearly all the disputes no matter what they were about. Insulted, mocked, or even manhandled, wounded and beaten, it was always her sexuality or dubious associations that were called into question. What else could one say about her? On 1 November 1760, Marie-Angélique Pillet went to register a complaint before Commissioner Hugues as a result of being profoundly humiliated, which had also caused her to be subjected to the full weight of her husband's anger. He was a master wigmaker in the Rue

Saint-Sauveur and a short time ago he had dismissed his boy, Baptiste, whose only aim was to get his revenge in the only way he knew how, this being to attack the virtue of Marie-Angélique in the absence of the husband. He 'kept on making the most disgraceful comments about her, saying that Linelle, another boy who lived with her, had obtained her favours and that she had given him presents every day. He had even written a letter to her husband telling him that he too had had everything he wanted from her and her husband had been furious.'[20] The authors of some of these stories did occasionally end up being right about what was happening between the couple; but resistance to the over-inflation of this gossip and rumour was difficult, as was standing up to the insinuations which caused stirrings in the district and upset the neighbours. On 17 July 1765, Jean-François Vandelle, master and merchant hatter living at Rue Pavée, and Marie-Elisabeth Fleury, wife of a butcher in the Rue Montmartre, but who herself lived in the Rue Pavée, brought a complaint against Antoine Hardy, apprentice to her husband;

> further to the complaints that they made to us about him, it was plain that he was the author of the current misunderstanding between Bougueul and his wife, the plaintiff, who has been obliged to leave her husband as a result of the wicked comments made by Antoine Hardy, on whose authority the husband had seen fit to strike the plaintiff while she was pregnant. Since she had left her husband, which was two months ago, he had kept repeating shocking comments to persons of her acquaintance and she wished to have him punished so as not to lose her reputation.[21]

When there was a fight or scuffle it was rare for the master's wife to remain untouched and more often than not it was those parts of her body denoting her femininity (breasts and belly, for example), that were quite deliberately abused. It was not just a push and shove or a slap round the head, there were also the words and gestures intended to recall her sex. Wherever the master's wife was to be found, one also found the union of weakness and strength – an inevitable line of weakness and an obvious target.

To be fair, there were some master's wives who abused their position and took advantage of their situation in order to impose excessive discipline even going so far as handing out blows and slaps to dreamy or careless apprentices. On occasion there were husbands who complained about their wives but it was rare. The following text allows us a better understanding of the status of the wife of the artisan:

> Summoned to appear before the court was one Sieur Delamothe, wood-merchant and supplier for Paris, living at the Quai Saint-Bernard in the parish of Saint-Nicolas-du-Chardonnet. He brought before us a

complaint against his wife, saying that he thought he might have done better than to put all his trust in this mistress Hardy and to leave all the care of his household to her. When he had to go away on journeys required by his trade, he had even handed over to her the keys of his study and his strong-box. However, he soon noticed how he was suffering as a result of this blind faith and, seeing how his wife was indulging in every variety of outrageous dissipation whose consequences he wished to forestall, he had seen fit no longer to leave the management of his money to his wife and to take care of expenditure himself. This wise precaution which alone was capable of preventing the ruin of himself and his children would appear to have launched the wife of the plaintiff into such a strange fury that it was no longer possible to have any peace in his own home and his wife had turned all the other merchants away from him and had spewed out enough insults against him to ruin him.[22]

Here was a powerful woman – no doubt too powerful; and when anger exploded, it was the ambivalence of her person that it went for.

## The apprentice

The 170 disputes studied can be divided almost equally into four types of conflict, namely: master–apprentice, employee–master, master–official and disputes between journeymen. Not only were there disputes between those involved in the intolerable relationships of dependence but quarrels also occurred between those of equal status, thus introducing rivalry where previously there had been solidarity.

Entry into an apprenticeship was a solemn occasion whereby the contract made between the master and the parents of the child was signed in the presence of a lawyer:

> This day, before the King's counsellors, notaries of Le Châtelet de Paris, here present be Jean-Baptiste Desseigne, burgher of Paris, and his wife, Marie-Françoise Régout who, desirous of advantage for their son, Claude Desseigne aged 17 years, do recognize and accept the obligation made on the part of their son to be engaged in the service of Sieur J. N. Richomme, master printer in fine print, for the space and time of four complete years in succession...[23]

The contract stipulated the duties of each of the parties: the master had to teach his craft 'without concealing anything' at the same time as keeping the child fed, warmed, washed, lodged and lit. The parents, for their part, undertook responsibility for providing him with a bed and clothing as well as a certain amount of money. The child, in his turn, promised to obey, and not to absent himself nor work elsewhere. Parents and masters agreed upon the necessity of good manners and healthy conduct.

The contract, which was generally quite precise, is a good indication of the apprentice's situation. Here was a young lad suddenly subjected to two authorities: his parents, on the one hand, and the master on the other. This one short agreement, covering his work, his obedience and the money he brought with him, offered ample scope for day-to-day difficulties. Relationships between the three parties were often stormy and the apprentice himself, still a youngster, found the framework allotted to him difficult to endure. Moreover the great majority of complaints brought before the commissioner relate to the physical maltreatment of the apprentice. It was an intolerable situation highlighting certain aspects of the daily life of the workshop and revealing how its apparent closeness was often troubled and oppressive. But it was also a situation which revealed the anxious concern of the parents for their children. They took on their defence, harboured the child who might have fled from the blows that were being dealt out to him and even protected those who might have been old enough to stand up for themselves. Though the parents themselves might use their children to do their work, badgering them or taking them to task until the work was done, they were swift to demand that the training of their children as set out in the contract should be respected without incurring either violence or abuse, especially where the apprenticeship provoked a situation in which there was an intolerable clash between parental authority and that of the master. Even their excessive tiredness was closely watched and condemned over and over again but the guild officials were apparently powerless to put a stop to such excesses and found themselves on occasion advising the parents to complain directly to the police.

The position of the parents was difficult, for the apprenticeship contract cost money and the eventual dismissal of the child was a serious matter for the family. Witness for instance the case of Jeanne Bro, a cooper's widow. Her son Nicolas had been in apprenticeship with a master confectioner for three years, and for the last few months the master had been giving him an excessive amount of work which was absolutely beyond the limits of his strength. One evening when he was 'thoroughly worn out', he had refused to do some extra work which consisted of washing-up and scouring some kitchen utensils. The mistress, who was very angry, gave him orders to get out and he returned to his mother at Poissy. Jeanne Bro was extremely worried as the period of apprenticeship of five years was far from being complete. An attempt at reconciliation needed to be made but the master refused to come to any arrangement so long as the guild officials declined to intervene. It was Commissioner Crespy who was finally informed of the affair and who had to settle it on the advice of the officials, who refused to exert their influence over the offending master.[24]

One further example, taken from among many, effectively sums up the whole nature of the problem which apprenticeship was up against. It illustrates the exhaustion, the unwarranted claims on the apprentices' time, the bad treatment, and the cruel role of the master's wife: the son of François Hocquin (widow of a journeyman carpenter), had been serving an apprenticeship for two years with a master enameller. He was aged 11 at the time and was subjected to so much violence and harassment that he was totally exhausted. His arms were 'black and blue with blows and cuffs' he had received from the master's wife. He had learned nothing and he felt ill. His mother, heart-broken, explained to Commissioner Hugues in July 1761 'that it pained her to have to see her child obliged to do work that was so much beyond his years that even the most sturdy journeyman would have had difficulty in doing it'. In fact the master's wife had been expecting him to produce 4,000 pearl beads a day; if he didn't, she hit him with a bull whip so that some evenings he preferred to sleep on the stairs. His mother was indignant and demanded the annulment of the apprenticeship agreement.[25]

Condensed in this one example are the principal problems posed by apprenticeship, namely: forced production; the impossibility of escape from a domestic authority which had been accepted by contract; the absence of tuition in the trade; total dependence on an utterly unscrupulous master or, in this case, on a woman 'whose conduct was not reprimanded by her husband', as the mother pointed out. Not all the apprentices were treated in this way, but all the conflicts relating to apprenticeship are illustrative of this daily enslavement to the wishes of the master and of the claims on the time of his employees which was abusive. For some, the main tasks were to sweep and clean, run errands and act as servant. For others, their time and hours were so constantly occupied that they were virtually robbed of their lives; they were made use of without respite, not even for a little religious education. If first communion had not been made, as was the case of a little niece of Gulnet's, a lemonade seller, the master should normally have left some time for the child to receive instruction in the mass. Tourié, an orange merchant, had not understood it this way and, although he had given his word, 'he had not even given her the time to go to mass on feast days'.[26]

Another cause of serious differences between masters and parents lay in the behaviour of the child, but here the complaints were mutual. The master might express his concern about the doubtful habits of an apprentice who had been tempted to spend the night away or who whiled away his time. The parents also kept a watch on their children to see that they did not come under the bad influence of the master. Thus the apprentice found himself watched on all sides.

The apprenticeship contract could be renounced at any time, like the following between the daughter of a journeyman fancy goods-maker and a master button-maker. The latter was accused by the parents of allowing her to make too many rendezvous with another master who worked with the plaintiff.[27] There were so many eyes watching and following the apprentice that they were too many to count. Servants and journeymen also had their bit to say. Some of them warned the parents about what their son was up to even at the risk of their initiative not going down particularly well.

The apprentice found himself at the centre of attention as his young age and his period of training made him the property of everyone around; conflicts were thus complicated and compounded by the degree of this collective appropriation of his body and his time which characterized his social and professional status. Moreover if it were a young girl apprentice she was at risk of being led astray by the master, pestered by the pressure of his demands or his banter which was not always 'very Catholic'. Thus it was that Chantelle, master wigmaker, had to appear in court one day to give account of his strange dealings with Charlotte, aged 15. According to the girl's parents, 'he had sought to corrupt her morals and her heart by asking her if she were a virgin. As she replied that she didn't know, he told her that he could see from her eyes that she had left her virginity behind in the country and that she did it herself every day in her bed and that in any case he would take a look at her nipples and see if that were indeed so.' The following day his behaviour was too blatant for her not to inform her parents.[28]

To this feeling of total belonging to the master, so often resented, the apprentice responded in several ways. Some sabotaged the work, wasted time or offered passive resistance. Others resorted to insolence or guile, treating the master and his wife with contempt, insulting or even striking them. Many preferred to flee and go on the run or to look elsewhere and thus break by stealth a contract which others had drawn up for them and which was costing them far too dearly. And it nearly always caused a drama because not only did parents and masters lose money as a result, they also lost their good name – both of which were needed, the one as much as the other.

There was the case of Antoine Flamant, apprenticed as book-keeper to Lecointre for four years. He owed him the sum of 200 *livres* but after two years he left without paying, 'taking his clothes with him without the plaintiff knowing or being aware of where he was living'. The master therefore asked for the apprenticeship agreement to be annulled.

If the masters were very possessive of their apprentices and some-what less than delicate in the way they appropriated them, which led to complaints and legal proceedings, it was because they derived enormous profits as a result. This regular use of young people in their workshops allowed them to bypass the journeymen and obtain servants and assistants on the cheap. The journeymen were very well aware of their little game and tried to protect themselves against this utterly unfair competition by condemning the corrupt practices of their masters. Once again we find the commissioner brought in as witness to resolve those questions which the craft-guilds themselves, too paralysed by their own internal differences were not able to resolve.

In 1750, for example, a complaint was brought before Commissioner Mutel by five journeymen tilers.[29] They drew attention to one of their guild's statutes which prevented any master hiring out his apprentices unless they had served at least three years' apprenticeship and had been deemed 'capable of journey work by the guild's officials and custodians'. They asserted that several masters were contravening the regulations, like Vamousse and Magdeleine who hired out youngsters with barely a year's apprenticeship behind them and were employing them 'in preference to journeymen'. Quite unusually in the course of this affair, one of the apprentices was called to give evidence after a visit by the commissioner. In contrast, in March 1766, the Lieutenant-General of Police gave his assent to the guild of master tilers who were seeking authorization for a master to have three apprentices instead of two on account of the upsurge in the building trade which had created a veritable 'dearth of journeymen', and thus an increase in their daily rate. As Sartine wrote in his police deposition:

> There are two grounds for this demand, these being:
> 1  The current shortage of journeymen in the trade together with the vast number of buildings under construction at the present time.
> 2  Journeymen taking advantage of these circumstances to demand 3 *livres* to 3 *livres* 10 *sols* per day although by decree of 4 October 1756, based on past performance, the daily rate has been fixed at 45 *sols* for the period between All Saints and Easter and from Easter to All Saints at 50 *sols*.
> This demand deserves favourable consideration.

In the end, the nature of apprenticeship came back to the status of the young. It allows one to see the difficulty of making agreements without the principal party being one of the signatories of the contract. The apprentice's only hope was that he should not be submitted to undue dependence and that he might navigate the best course between whatever authorities had control over him, even though they had made an agreement between themselves over his head.

## Confrontation

They worked together, took their meals together, and often slept under the same roof; and one of them employed all the rest. Their daily familiarity, however, if indeed it did exist, did not imply the use of 'tu', which in fact was likely to lead to an argument. In the eighteenth century, the existence of face-to-face confrontation between the master and his journeymen was always a reality and police officers were very well aware of it, as were social reformers and inspectors of industry and manufacturing. Anger was provoked on all sides by insolence and insubordination on the part of those whom one would have preferred to see obeying like servants in this chain of authority which went right down from the King to the very least. But this indignation was tinged with real fear, and *syndics* and guild officials were afraid to intervene without the commissioner, who was himself hesitant or discreet about his involvement or else made improbable attempts at reconciliation. There was one way out, however, which was used quite often and this was the *lettre de cachet*, that instrument of royal command, swift, impartial and able to effect the overnight disappearance of the troublesome worker. This practice, more common than one might have believed, was used even more frequently when there were protest movements or serious strikes.

The complaints brought before the commissioner show us a workshop at grips with two kinds of conflict headed as much by the master as by the journeymen. In the one case, this arose from the journeyman's need to take his leave, to be off elsewhere, free and better paid and to be able to depart as and when he wanted. This led to fighting and quarrelling, with insults and threats of revenge provoked by the master, frustrated at seeing his world of work destroyed without warning. In the second instance, we are presented with an authoritarian master insulting or maltreating his employees or dismissing them on occasion without paying what he owed. In this case the journeyman immediately lodged a complaint.

Each example is the inverse of the other but in either case it was always a matter of departure which might be voluntary or inflicted, according to the particular case, but it always had serious consequences. It was no coincidence that it was the idea of departure which was central to shielding a turbulent workshop given that a workman's time was punctuated by dismissals, lay-offs, voluntary departures and disruption and the only need for an agreement with the boss was in order to make another one which was less restrictive. This refusal to be bound down indefinitely, which was perceived as a form of imprisonment, was the hallmark of the world of work and because of this continual need to be off, the journeyman marked out a solitary route in which his desire to climb the social ladder and to be integrated within his society was combined with his concern that he should never be bound in servility.

To leave, yes, but also to return when one chose; if one had forgotten something, say, or if the master owed one money or perhaps (and why not), if working practices and conditions of dependence had changed. The masters were not at all happy with such a tradition of liberty or with the displacements and comings and goings.

Cadet had been a journeyman butcher for five months with the widow Thénard in the Rue de l'Oursine. Four years previously she had dismissed him for his disloyalty and yet there he was back again, but she did not remember him and it was only later that she recognized him. By then he was trying to 'introduce new practices between himself and the other lads', wanting them all to have a share in the little bit of profit they made on the side from their dealings. When she wanted to dismiss him once again, he made a terrible scene and threatened to 'finish her off'.

To stay? Yes, provided the type of work were different and there were alterations in the relationships. This was the case for Adam's three journeymen, monumental masons in the Rue de Fourcy. They had been there for eight years and in fact one of them had been there twenty years, but from one day to the next they had managed to 'cause trouble', 'play around', slip off from the workshop, distract the others and generally upset their work habits. The master thought that all this would improve by setting on a kind of supervisor, but his wife, who was getting on in years, paid the price and she was insulted, humiliated, and beaten. If the neighbours had not come to her rescue, she would certainly have been beaten to death.

When the work was not to one's liking, or if the master were too strict, it was quite easy to have one's revenge on the material one was making or on the goods one was producing or selling. There was a journeyman butcher who had to untie the calves' hooves each day. One day, in a rage, he slashed them through to the bone 'which affected the quality of the merchandise'. On being dismissed he shouted 'that if he was thrown out he would see to it that he [the master] got a knife in the gut at the first opportunity'. Another employee who usually 'kicked his heels and annoyed everyone' threw everything on the ground one day and went off to think over something his master had just said to him.

To be dismissed was one thing but what if one could get one's revenge by ruining the master's reputation or driving away his customers or even threatening him with death, and not just in any old way. Take the case of François Berton, for instance, whose rather remarkable scheme deserves a mention. When he was dismissed by Letesne, master button-maker, François went from street to street denigrating him and saying how he was going to get his revenge in the future. 'In order to do this he signed himself up for the Gardes françaises, which gave him the right to carry a sword which he intended to put right through his body.' What was the point in obtaining one right in order to transgress another? Well, killing the master was one thing, but killing him and having the right to wear a sword was much better because it annulled the position of subordinate, established a truly different situation and allowed one to reclaim one's own self.

The right to carry a sword was one of the popular demands of the time. In 1764, Police Inspector Damotte found himself embroiled with some milliners' boys who had gathered in a crowd at the Porte de Chaillot and were making it loud and clear that they did not agree with the ruling of their guild which forbade the carrying of swords or of hunting knives on pain of a fine of 20 *livres*. On this occasion, one of the boys was arrested, but his master took up his cause and went off to see his district commissioner. He protested strongly for the release of his assistant and, overcome with anger, he shouted out that his boys were 'worth a lot more by birth than Monsieur de Sartine'. The commissioner said nothing but wrote off immediately to the Lieutenant-General. The boy was released a short while later but in the meantime his master had written to Sartine: 'We know that no one has the right to do it, but the practice is tolerated and if we might be so bold as to say it, even necessary so as there can be no confusion between servants and domestics' (AB 12261). Wearing a sword was a sign of distinction, and its absence was an affront to dignity and a testament to servility. Moreover, in order to obtain this right, the milliners had dressed themselves in 'braided garments worth from 300 to 400 *livres* and with lace cuffs costing between 3 and 4 *louis*': an observation on the part of Inspector Damotte which says a good deal. For by means of their external appearance, the journeymen were seeking to demonstrate that in no way could they be included with that coarse body of tied servants and domestics.

Debt was sometimes the basis for some departures and dismissals and the complaints made in this respect cast some light on the way in which the accounts were organized in the workshop and how the journeymen were paid. It was quite common for the master to make irregular payments and it became very difficult to keep a track of the money. Others made an advance for the week if that is what was required. In any case, it appears that the accounts were often quite complicated, especially if the journeyman was paid on the basis of the number of his clients and the master and his wife were not in agreement with his calculations. This whole system of advances, debts, loans and sums conditional on a sale wove a web of obligations between master and employees such that a simple quarrel might arise quickly and make the whole financial situation inextricable, even if the journeymen kept a detailed journal of their accounts and showed them to the master at the slightest hint of a doubt.

Of equal importance with money, debts or salary were the tools. They belonged to the journeyman and never left his side. If he decided to leave –

they went with him. His tools were a part of his patrimony and his traveller's back-pack when he felt the urge to take a look further afield. Some tools belonged to the master and they remained in the workshop. In the event of a dispute, some gestures assumed a symbolic significance such as refusal to work which was accompanied by throwing the tools on the ground and trampling them underfoot. Leaving with one's head held high having thrown down tools (the master's as well as one's own), often indicated that one would be back in the morning to pick up one's things. It was not always to the master's liking of course, especially if the journeyman had left with his work unfinished.

In any case, what the tools signified was the possession of a personal qualification. One not only possessed the tools of the trade, but the trade itself, which indicated a relative degree of liberty and freedom to choose one master over another. On the other hand, work-clothes and overalls usually belonged to the master and in most cases handing in one's apron had the opposite symbolic effect, for it marked the end of that particular dependence.

These two types of item, tools and clothes, illustrate the two opposing poles which constantly put a strain on the life of the workman. The implement was the privileged means by which he created his own free space between himself and his master, whereas the clothes were a constant reminder of his dependence and of the fact that he was owned by another. He was forever playing on this contradiction, hoping to achieve something better out of a reality which was ultimately very limiting.

At other crucial moments, when workers were being taken on, for instance, things seemed rather precariously balanced and rivalries and disputes were easily engendered. The demand for employment was increased by the fact that the masters played on the apprenticeship system to avoid taking on too many journeymen. The Place de Grève, the place where people were traditionally hired, rather resembled a *cabaret* in that everything there was always ripe for the eruption of a fight or for tempers to get overheated. Masters and officials were often thought of as 'assassins' who were ready to take advantage of the workforce without paying a fair price and accused of spreading poor reputations about journeymen who wanted to leave and look for better conditions. In either camp, the weaponry was the same, namely to cause discredit, that deadly poison which could shackle people for life and cost them very dear economically. Journeymen were officially procured by the guilds' own employment bureaux but in order to speed things up, the masters often did business directly at the inn or the *cabaret*, and certain hostelries were renowned for this type of activity. There, one might find employers and those seeking work engaged in animated discussion over a glass of wine. The contracts that were signed, were necessary but never final and they were always drawn up with the prospect of leaving which the master had some difficulty in stifling.

The authorities were growing worried;[30] there was a swell of paid workers who were becoming increasingly isolated from the bosses and who were quite blatantly seeking their autonomy. Keeping the worker tied to his work was a recurrent theme but there tended to be more boldness when it came to issuing writs and regulations than when it was a matter of action in the street. It was in this spirit of constraint and of illusory struggle against a rebellious and self-confident body of journeymen that the *lettres patentes* of 2 January 1749 were issued, the purpose of which is made quite clear in the preamble:

> We are informed that a number of workers in the trades and in manufacturing are leaving the manufacturers and entrepreneurs employing them without first having obtained in writing notice to quit, or without completing the work in hand and, in many cases, without reimbursing advances made to them on the basis of earnings from their output. We are also informed that some of these persons having formed a kind of body are holding meetings and laying down the law to their masters, doing as they choose, depriving them of workers and preventing them from taking on those whom they want.

There then follows a number of specific prohibitions, for example, that in order to leave a master one had to obtain written notice from him on pain of a fine of 100 *livres*. If the journeyman had been maltreated, however, it was possible for him to lodge an appeal with the police judge in order to obtain a leaving certificate but he first had to complete his work. Furthermore, groups and assemblies were forbidden and the masters were to have the right to choose their own workers themselves.

In September 1781 during the reign of Louis XVI, it was felt necessary to consolidate these letters and the notice of leave was replaced by a booklet of successive leaving certificates issued by the masters – the passbook...promise of a fine future.

The whole of the second half of the eighteenth century resounded to the noise of three opposing concepts. Firstly, there was the desire of the authorities to see that the power of the masters was not undone as this was the indispensable link in the chain guaranteeing the policing of the realm; then there were the economists who were on the lookout for every possible opportunity of suppressing the corporations which held back industrialization, and also the wage-earners who, on the one hand, wanted to make use of a system of alliances with their masters which allowed them to envisage the possibility of setting up on their own one day, and who on the other hand were intent on undermining this same system by constantly breaking one contract in order to choose another which was more advantageous to them.

The workshop was the place where all these disagreements were formulated and made concrete and where confrontation, which had previously been face to face, often became limb to limb. At the same time it was swept by intrigues and collective actions which punctuated city life in vast convulsions,[31] dragging along in their wake not only isolated individuals but also groups of men and women.

## The anger of the officials

The further the century progressed, the more the guild masters found themselves grappling with difficulties on two fronts: inside the workshop management was no longer a simple matter so greatly did the spirit of individualism reign and the need for liberty express itself; outside, the officials and *syndics* elected by them and responsible for their governance, committed many abuses and took advantage of their authority which they (the masters) could no longer tolerate. Thus the masters in their turn proffered their own type of insubordination and resistance by shaking the power of the officials, such as refusing them admission when they turned up inopportunely on one of their authoritarian visits. They had had enough of what were usually quite brutal descents on their workshops to collect, amongst other things, the dues of royal visit and they were tired of their ineffectual controls. These were usually carried out with such brutality, and more often than not in their absence that it was their wives whom they bothered and mistreated. Normally things should have taken place without any trouble. In fact one of the responsibilities of the *syndics* was to monitor the workshops to see that masters, journeymen and apprentices did not break the rules of the guild. To this end, it was often necessary to take legal proceedings, with the result that they were occasionally accompanied by the district commissioner. The following is an example of their normal activities:

> Tuesday 25 January 1785, we, Commissioner Hugues, Médard Arnould, resident of the Quai Pelletier, Augustin Passinge, resident of the Pont Notre Dame, and François Debians, resident of the Rue de la Lune, each being master sculptors, gilders, monumental masons and *syndics* and wardens in charge of these guilds, on the request of said guilds, and for the purpose of the execution of the police ordinance of 2 October 1784 published on the 27th of that same month concerning apprentices and journeymen gilders, did proceed to various masters of the guild, accompanied by other officials and Sieur Marcel Patté, Inspector of Police, with the intention of verifying whether these same masters were observing the prescriptions of the ordinance and in order to assess

whether there were any contraventions on the part of the masters and to make a report in the hearing of the police and in respect of the journey-men and apprentices to instruct them in the course of our visits of their obligations and matters affecting them. To this end we entered the workshop of Sieur Presle, painter to the King in the Rue Poissonnière, where we found eight journeymen who gave their names as Gori, Meunier du Pré, Danton, Augibout, Bouclé, Husneron, etc. All of these masters and journeymen thus far named, having hitherto failed to comply with the aforementioned ordinance of police, were duly warned to conform at risk of the penalties which we explained to them. We continued our visit up until 8 o'clock in the evening without further interruption save for refreshment.[32]

Here everything was calm but quite often the artisans did not take kindly to these official visits and suspected the officers of underhand dealings amongst themselves or of setting rates which favoured some masters depending on who they were. The visits were often occasions for disputes and violence with neither side inclined towards conciliation such that the situation could turn nasty very quickly. The guild officials complained of lack of respect and hid behind their titles, which obviously did nothing. Disputes broke out on all sides attesting to the growing rift between the artisan and his representatives.

The whole thing might begin with quibbling over prices. In 1765, for instance, the amount levied in dues from the cobblers was 20 *sols*. When the guild officials arrived, the master's wife came forward and presented them with half of that amount, an obvious strategy on the part of the master, as the officials were more likely to settle things amicably with his wife than himself. This was not the case, however, and when the officials refused to accept it, she flew into a rage and complained that they had always favoured some in preference to others and that they did just as they pleased. After discussing the matter, they admitted that there was a problem and then proceeded to reason along the lines that it was true that this had sometimes happened but that this was in the case of poor masters who had no work, which was obviously not the case of this particular workshop which housed four journeymen without counting the father-in-law who was still at his job. At this moment, the master, who had deliberately remained in the background, allowing himself to be taken for one of the journeymen, stood up, and making threats, he grabbed hold of a paring-knife and rushed at the officials shouting 'insolent rogues of *syndics* and book-keepers, inmates of Bicêtre, if you get my 20 *sols* all you'll do is to go and swill down a bottle costing 12 *sols* at the expense of all of us!' In the face of this unbridled anger, the officials backed off, intimidated or, as the legal proceedings state, they withdrew 'with the utmost moderation'.[33]

Many of the other dossiers record these same outbursts of anger and the fear of the guild officials. Their anxiety had grown to such a point that more often than not they preferred to exit backwards from the workshop and on the tips of their toes. Subjected to sarcasm and abusive comments and threatened with rough treatment, they did not even feel supported by the police commissioners, who also preferred to make themselves scarce. Accused as they were of 'lining their coffers and money-grubbing' their image had completely deteriorated and nothing seemed to come to their aid, not even public opinion which in fact had very little time for them. They made their excursions to the accompaniment of rough and ribald comments and at the first suggestion of a dispute, the neighbours weighed in against them with a vengeance. In 1775, one official related the details of a somewhat perilous escapade:

> They had hardly got out when the public, who were only aware of the more unpleasant side of their responsibilities, trooped over towards us and, yelling and shouting, marched us back to our premises. [The gang of traders who had gathered shouted that] they would wipe their arse with any legal proceedings and that as for these clever dicks, they would beat them all the way to Peru and back and that meanwhile they ought to have their arms and legs broken.

The arrogance of the masters was equal only to that of the officials, and when it came to the iron fist, their contribution was impressive. When there were heated and violent exchanges, these artisans won the day over their representatives and the police authorities and it was this fundamental rupture which brought one of the greatest cracks in eighteenth-century society into full view. The police acted on their own hopes and aspirations whilst the population resisted and prevented itself from being taken over. The masters entrenched themselves in a negative position, refusing to obey the *syndics* and claiming that they no longer recognized them.

From there on, anything went. Witness the shameless attitude of Chevreuil, master outfitter of the Rue Saint-Honoré, who 'replied quite arrogantly that he did not recognize the officials and had no respect for them. As far as he was concerned, he could just as easily shit in their face.'[34]

Of course things did not always turn out to be so straightforward. In order to put up this kind of resistance and to make such serious comment, one had to be sure of the backing of others. On one's own, things could take on a completely different appearance for, in spite of everything, the police succeeded in imposing a frightening presence which allowed them to maintain order in the face of insubordination. There were some who were so terrified that they preferred suicide to suspicion and constant surveillance. On 8 April 1775 an employee at the gold-mark office slit his throat with a razor, and a note on his person gave details of all his linen and the following moving note consisting of a few scrawled words: 'If I'm desperate, it's because I can see that the *mouchards*[35] are still after me and I have done this. It's because I am terrified of being kept in jail. I am innocent. I have never done any harm at all in any way.'[36]

With the exception of particular cases, the balance of power between masters and officials was decidedly not in favour of those who represented the authorities. What lay behind this hostility were the strange goings-on when guild officials were elected and started wheeling and dealing amongst themselves. Some received back-handers; others disregarded the rules relating to elections; and others, swollen-headed, insulted their colleagues and formed cliques without consulting their fellowship, following their often quite brutal visits to the workshops. Quarrels broke out almost everywhere between old and young officials. The young ones refused to take an oath and insulted their elders, treating them as though they knew nothing, and spread themselves around Paris making use of their new powers and enthusiasm.

In the face of so many irregularities, it was hardly surprising that the visits made by the officials often turned out so badly, especially as their tasks did not stop at workshop visits and the collection of dues. They also had to pursue those who were on the margins of legality and membership of a craft-guild and who were in fact attempting to exercise their trade in their own home. It was a daily, unrelenting struggle which contaminated the atmosphere of the city and was the cause of a good many periodic explosions.

The workshop, that ideal place where work combined with authority, and training with subordination, found its structures shaken and turned upside down by this constant cry for individualization compounded by a desire for social and economic stability without constraints. In this dual movement, which was as paradoxical as it was strong, one refused to acknowledge the master at the same time as one aspired oneself to be one.

This attitude of refusal coincided with the atmosphere and spirit of the times and with the reforms of the intellectuals and philosophers. In the desire to be a master oneself, however, there was the unchanged reproduction of those same well-worn structures from which one had originated. It was at the heart of this contradiction, which paralysed and stifled the workshop, that the strategies of the one group and the insubordination of the other found themselves bound together. Faced with the depth and extent of this movement, the authorities grew frightened and ineffectual; they knew that the exercise of conventional justice had little effect on it but there remained, nevertheless, the rather more discreet machinery of the orders of the King.

# 7

# At the Workshop Door

---

Gravitating around the workshop were those individuals who either looked on enviously, or who, having perhaps decided to live on its margins, had not been invited to its banquet. On the whole they did not burden themselves with masters, but practised their trade only amongst themselves or with their customers in a rather desultory way, stealing in and out of the mesh of city life and as often as not finding themselves up against the authorities rather than in accord with them. Their main preoccupation was to live. It would have been impossible to contain them indefinitely in any one place, thus shattering any definitions one might have liked to have made of them. They came together, formed associations, separated, and never saw each other again; and yet there were so many of them that they occupied a significant position on the social scene. They ripped apart the unrealistic dreams of the police whose obvious intention was the classification of each and every man in society by assigning him a place in it, thereby guaranteeing the smooth running of the whole for ever and ever. At the same time, however, they afforded the police great incentives for their activity, provided ample work for its employees and spies and felt the full weight of its repression in their respect. They 'visited' the prisons as often as they filled the police registers with their names and nicknames; and it was to them that justification of the King's orders might be owed.[1]

## Dealers and chambrelans

There are so many people living on the fringes – outsiders, beyond the bounds of that chain of individuals who were considered easy to deal with by those like Lieutenant-General Lenoir, who in his 'Mémoires' constantly harks back to this same theme. He states that 'it was possible for the police to exert their influence over a crowd of 200,000 people where some were under the direction of others and where everyone, from first to last, was well classified, registered and bound by rules of discipline and subordination.'² It was precisely because they were not integrated into the craft-guilds and their associations that they were the stumbling-block for this social utopia. The police already had their work cut out controlling manual workers, day labourers, small traders, odd-jobbers and errand-boys; how was one to control them, given that they were not bound by any overall body? Simply seeing that they did not create any disorder or provoke a potentially harmful gathering or assembly was in itself a constant worry: 'They somehow managed to keep them in separate groups and thus avoided the possibility of large gatherings of these men who, due to their sheer brute strength, were considered highly dangerous.' As far as Lenoir was concerned, these lawless men were capable of anything, even if some of them were 'classified', such as the cabbies and market hands from Les Halles, for example, who having an order, a number and reserved place were thus under the surveillance of the inspectors. As for the rest, they were inevitably under suspicion, particularly if they were prone to getting together and becoming a crowd, that malevolent spectre of the century.

But what could be done with these people who had neither status nor domicile, who were workers without work, or possibly *chambrelans*, that is, those who had set themselves up on their own account in private rooms outside the traditional circuit of the craft-guild? How was one to watch out that they did not turn into 'hordes of miscreants'? And what was one supposed to do with all those wheeler-dealers who were more or less scattered throughout the whole of Paris, on its bridges and in its *faubourgs*? How, in fact, was one to avoid trafficking, receiving, fraud and all manner of swindling and conniving?

The authorities were indeed worried when faced with this mass of men and women on the borders of the world of work, who were constantly on the move and defied all classification and permanent control. Economic instability was such that no single building project and no amount of workhouses could ever manage to contain all these folk who were pushed and pulled between the urgent need to stay alive and settle down and a total disregard for conventional rules. The police themselves had to admit that they spent so much of their time pursuing this 'floating population' that on occasion they failed to arrest the real delinquents, deceived as they were by their official status as workers. When Inspector Poussot wrote to the Lieutenant-General to let him know of the arrest of a number of thieves in February 1750, he apologized for not having jailed them earlier and gave the following explanation for his failure:

I should point out to you, Sir, that two of the persons in question are journeymen joiners and the other a marble-cutter. They all live and work in the Villeneuve district, which is why there was no reason to suspect that it was they who were the thieves, thus making it all the more difficult to find them. Parisien [a *mouchard*], had told us several times that he thought that they were thieves, but as we had nothing against them and because we knew they were working, we did not arrest them.[3]

From indications like these,[4] we are given to understand that the police registers were more likely to be darkened by the names of unemployed workers such as odd-job men and those with no particular status and hence the obvious importance of placing them on police records.

Not everyone was a Ménétra, that journeyman glazier and son of a master who, after many adventures but without too much difficulty, finally acceded to the position of master in accordance with a route which was, in spite of everything, quite traditional.[5] For others nothing was quite so simple. One might be a journeyman yet never achieve a mastership. Accession was very costly and positions as master were exceptionally limited; it was by thus refusing to open up the profession and to take on much greater numbers, at the obvious expense of progress, that the corporations protected themselves. Let us take the example of the wigmakers in 1765, whose written memorandum appears in the manuscripts of the Archives de la Bastille.[6] It was felt by the *modernes* of that guild that the number of situations (of master) was quite enough and that on no account should others be created. It was also their desire to convince the King's Procurator-General on this matter as well as the Lieutenant and the *syndics*, with the effect that a dispute set in between ancients and moderns. The latter described themselves as 'convinced from their all too painful experience that there were too many of them already since the greater part of them did not have the wherewithal to make ends meet.' 'And this,' they affirmed, 'would lead to the total ruin of the whole guild community', much to the annoyance of the *anciens*, who vehemently upheld the opposing view. Moreover, the *modernes* expressed their deep regret that the new statutes imposed too short a period of service on the masters-to-be which thus devalued the profession. It was a shocking fact, they said, that 'positions were being bought by valets and manservants.'

The situation was growing worse from one day to the next. After passing through the hands of a few masters, some apprentices took away their customers and set up on their own account without attaining the position of master. Having become *chambrelans*, they were then liable to distraint, but their defence was that they were awaiting a position and that it was absolutely essential to create new ones. The *syndics* were weighed down with more complaints than they knew what to do with.

This statement, which was printed and posted everywhere, was not to the liking of the Lieutenant-General of Police, Bertin, who put his inspector, Bourgoin, in charge of the case with instructions to find its authors. Suspicion fell on Grignon, an assistant wigmaker to his father, a master wigmaker in the Rue Saint-Honoré. The inspector was faced with a difficult task. If he arrested Grignon it might upset the whole of the wigmakers; therefore some shrewd tactics were required. First of all, they had to disguise the spies in order to discover the hiding-place of this man who had temporarily disappeared; it was also important not to alarm folk by a rather inopportune enquiry which was liable to be disapproved of by public opinion. Matching disguise for disguise, we learn from a subsequent police report that Grignon had taken refuge, also in disguise, with an ambassador who was also one of his customers. The Lieutenant-General of Police was angry. 'He'll have his head swabbed, for his insolence,' he wrote to Bourgoin. But in spite of being permanently posted in front of the Grignon domicile the latter's efforts were in vain. However, on 9 January 1765 he made so bold as to call into question the Lieutenant's somewhat injudicious conversation, which had destroyed all hope of finding Grignon. 'What has made Grignon suspicious', he said, 'is the fact that on the Eve of Epiphany, you told your wigmaker that Grignon was to be arrested on your orders, and your wigmaker warned Grignon.' 'This has been a costly business for me,' he added. Hairdressers' tittle-tattle has presumably been the same throughout the ages and Lieutenants of Police were no less susceptible than anyone else when it came to being washed and powdered.

One is tempted to ask whether that rather strange affair might not explain with hindsight the behaviour of one Abbé Belichon, who in 1732 sent out countless numbers of letters to wigmakers asking them for the names and addresses of all the others. The letters were interspersed with comments on the Bull *Unigenitus* and invective against women who bedecked and bewigged themselves. They were intended

> to root out the crime in our midst by preventing women from doing themselves up with hair-curls and every other sort of ornament. He protested that such affectation caused more fuss and palaver and the wearing of three times as many garments as was necessary to the modesty of the sex. In fact the whole business was more immodest than if the women had been wearing nothing at all.[7]

If the wigmakers had listened to him, the problem of admissions to the mastership would perhaps have sorted themselves out.

In any case, Grignon remained invisible, whereas two of his accomplices were finally arrested, but they only remained in jail for a few days. It would seem that Lieutenant Bertin himself must have bent under the pressure of events.

Leaving aside the rather amusing nature of this unusual affair, it does demonstrate the difficulty the authorities had in getting people to respect the regulations. Although the pursuit of all those who had set themselves up privately without holding the mastership was the responsibility of the *syndics* and guild officials, backed up by the police, it was one of the most unpopular measures there was and thus one of the most risky for those who had to see to its enforcement. The commissioners' archives, like those of the chamber of police, are awash with legal proceedings drawn up by the *syndics* duly rebuffed by those whose tools and merchandise they had been sent to distrain. This forcible and authoritarian expropriation of the means by which a man or a woman managed to survive was resented by the population as an intolerable violation. It did not really matter that the *chambrelan* lived outside the rules; but removing the means by which he earned his living could definitely not be tolerated. Such incidents added to the existing number of small street protests in which the neighbourhood wasted no time in showing its solidarity; its riposte was rapid.

Distraint was considered one of the most unfair and abusive practices of them all and everyone sought protection against it. It was a persistent threat which pursued the out-of-work journeyman or the vendor with no seal of quality as well as those who did not have the means to make the entry into the mastership.

The wife of Leroy was a vendor of glazed ware but she did not have a seal; nor did she or her husband have the means of keeping a shop, so she had been setting up stall illegally in the street for some time. On 16 May 1766 her basket of pottery was abruptly seized and the 'money-grubbing officials' called for her arrest. 'She started to cry and said that she had been selling glazed ware for almost ten years now and in that time had had the misfortune to have been 'seized' more than 30 times.'[8] If we work this out, we can see from this example just how common it must have been to witness such seizures. At the same time it must have been extremely provocative and would have disturbed the order in the street by creating an atmosphere of almost permanent confusion, but more especially, a climate of defiance in the face of authority.

Those who had been distrained felt no sense of guilt or shame, for they knew that they would start up again as soon as possible and that it was their only means of avoiding being reduced to begging; they even said as much. Martin Pillon was setting out his poultry stall at Versailles when he was asked whether he held a mastership or whether he had permission. 'He admitted that he had neither the right nor the seal of quality for the sale of poultry but as he had no other profession by which to live he confessed to contravening the law and selling goods dishonestly. He said that he had been doing this for 11 years now and, if it please God, he would do the same again unless he were able to do otherwise.'[9]

Seizures and contraventions occurred on a daily basis, but so did revolts; popular resistance was tenacious and no incident was allowed to pass unheeded. On the markets, stall-holders defended themselves and abused the guild officials as soon as they turned up, for they were recognized a long way off by their aprons, a pathetic disguise which utterly failed to deceive the street-people, who rioted immediately and surrounded them with jibes and jeers, making faces at them and throwing stones. The various trades had an understanding amongst themselves and chased off the officials, creating an atmosphere which was often very tense, for the guilds' men were not gentle and hardly acquitted themselves with finesse. Nevertheless, when they saw a threatening crowd advancing towards them, they were often the first to back off and quite often the police themselves were called in. In 1772, jurors from the guild of instrument-makers got inside the cloisters of Saint-Martin-des-Champs to seize some violins from a tailor. No sooner had they reached the interior of the cloister than the occupants closed the gates and threatened the officials. The revolt turned nasty and three sections of the Paris guard were required to restore calm.[10] One could recount no end of such happenings – the archives overflow with them – but they have been completely forgotten by the historiographical memory. In fact, it was these daily incidents which led to the creation of lasting allegiances and the advance planning of strategies by which one might better defend oneself, as with the cunning of the flower-girls, for instance. They had no authorization to sell but joined together to write a letter to the Lieutenant of Police.[11] They based the merits of their case on the fact that they were married to soldiers who gave both their time and their bodies in the service of their country. When they found themselves confronted by officials from the florists' guild they stood their ground, shouting out that 'they would gladly spill the guts of any mistress'.

In the face of so many difficulties the guild officials felt afraid. Their rallying cry of 'Houette! Houette!' when escaping or trying to identify themselves with their fellows hardly allowed them to pass unnoticed. Consultations with the police often resulted in instructions to withdraw, which gave cause for much misgiving. When the guards of the mercers' guild, accompanied by Commissioner Dudoigt, wanted to seize the merchandise of Lefèvre, there gathered 'such a great crowd of people that the commissioner thought it better to give orders to retreat without doing anything'.[12] In the margins of this file which led to the imprisonment of Lefèvre by order of the King, the commissioner noted, 'I tend to be of the opinion that in order to bring authority to bear on those who set up stall illegally it is necessary to send them to Bicêtre.' Seizure was proving impracticable, and so the solution was an imprisonment order issued by the King. The Archives of the Bastille thus contain many personal files on *chambrelans* and workers without qualification who were put in the Bastille by means of *lettres de cachet*. It was an impeccable strategy, and in order to carry it out, inspectors and commissioners made use of the unstable nature of the milieu. The large number of street-traders who were always on the fringes of legality were readily open to pressure, and it was easy to find narks and informers who thus made it possible to make a few 'proper' arrests by order of the King, without going through the burdensome procedure of distraint, which was much too dangerous and provocative. And even if none of them could be found to make any denunciations, there were always the *mouches*, who were there to keep a close eye on the milieu of the street-traders, where there were any number of unemployed youths and workers involved in the illegal sale of the odd worthless item pinched from some place or other.

The year 1763, selected at random, is interesting in this respect. Arrests following the issue of *lettres de cachet* are recorded in 458 files preserved in the Archives of the Bastille.[13] The greater part of the imprisonments concern those people, both young and old, who did not have any particular status and who were taken whilst they were trying to sell some small object, no doubt stolen, on the market or below the Pont-Neuf. This might be a handkerchief, a key, an implement or some item of clothing or whatever, but as often as not a wretched theft by some poor wretch. Defending oneself was an impossibility, even though the odd sentence in the dossiers does show that the arrested persons protested they had done what they did in order to survive and that it was a legitimate way to earn a living, justified by their loss of employment. The commentaries by the inspectors, on the other hand, indicate an utterly arbitrary desire on their part to rid the streets of all this *hoi polloi*. 'Because they are poor, these sort of people are inevitably suspect.' 'I consider imprisonment necessary even though the item concerned is trifling [in this case, a pillowslip], but this sort of thing is going on every day.' It was all a far cry from the great legendary prisoners of the Bastille – the *lettre de cachet* was decidedly an easy and well-tested measure.

No one escaped its net, especially not the Jewish population, whose every activity came directly under surveillance. Lieutenant-General Lenoir, in recalling the broad outline of this surveillance, states that

> During the period of my administration, they were no longer subjected to treatment as foreigners, but every Jew in Paris had to present himself for registration and he had to be certified as being well-known to a Jewish syndicate. This syndicate had to see that the religious practices in their synagogues took place calmly and quietly and had to act as a special police force responsible for the Jewish community. By the edict of August 1776, they were excluded from the corporations.[14]

An inspector of police was given special responsibility for Jews and kept registers in which he made a daily record of the names and addresses of those who had settled in Paris together with the reason for their being in the city, the date of their passports, reasons for their absence as well as regular observations on their behaviour.[15] When the police received a request for a visitor's permit or rights of residence, the inspector would make enquiries and then send his recommendations to the Lieutenant-General of Police.

But in spite of all these regulations and efforts at surveillance, they were still surrounded by a great deal of suspicion and, following the orders of 1763, two Jews were arrested, even though they had never given any occasion for complaint. The reason offered was simply that 'they were poor and found wandering around with no passport and that people of this ilk could only be very suspect.'[16] The craft-guilds kept a keen eye on this milieu and distraint of goods caused as much uproar as usual. However, the verbal reactions tell us a great deal about the way in which the Jews were commonly perceived. In 1778, a fight broke out over a seizure and the Jews who had been accused fought hammer and tongs. It is stated in the report that 'They struck out in such merciless frenzy as to make the blood of humanity run cold, whilst two other angry Jews set about the goodly cook.'[17]

If hawkers and *chambrelans* worried the authorities so much, it was because they were to be found on the margins of work in those shady areas which obsessed the police. Even so, they were still more or less observable, whereas a population which drifted in and out of begging, prostitution and crime was more threatening and more difficult to control on account of its mobility and its ability to associate freely and easily. It was a population which had lost its moorings but which the inspectors hoped to channel. Whether on their own or in alliance with each other, they represented a permanent danger. It is interesting to study their way of life as well as the methods used by the police to arrest them. We do have a register in our possession which makes it possible to narrow down the enquiry on this particular milieu which is so difficult to pin down. It belonged to Inspector Poussot and was kept between the years 1738 to 1754 in the district of Les Halles.[18]

### Thieves and crooks

For 16 years in succession, Inspector Poussot kept a great register, in which he noted down, in alphabetical order, all those men and women who had been arrested by him in his district of Les Halles. It was a painstaking and detailed work of great precision. Each page was divided into five columns. In the first column on the left were written the name, forename and nickname, age, occupation, abode and place of birth of the arrested person. (One should point out that occasionally certain information is missing such as the age or type of activity, for example.) After this, one finds the name of the prison to which the offender was taken and then the exact date of the arrest and the name of the authority whose decision it was. And then at the end, in the final column, which is the most important and often full of long, detailed notes, one can read the reasons for the arrest, the conditions surrounding it, the offender's past and many other pieces of information. At the same time as allowing one to see the methods used by the police to infiltrate this milieu, these commentaries recreate for us a particular social atmosphere and climate.

Since 1740 there had been 20 inspectors in charge of the districts, and Poussot found himself in charge of Les Halles.[19] It is difficult to assess the work of these inspectors as the sources are patchy – some of them have been burned, others, no doubt found to be compromising, have disappeared. Moreover, the activity of the inspectors was so wide-ranging and intense that it hardly lends itself to being quantified. According to the surviving registers or the reports to the Lieutenant of Police extant in the Archives of the Bastille one could put the number of matters dealt with annually by each inspector at 1,500. But even that is an approximation, as certain inspectors were responsible for a particular department in addition to their normal work in a district. Furthermore, one has to take into account the zeal of the three, then four inspectors appointed after 1776 to the Bureau de la Sûreté,[20] which specialized in the pursuit of large-scale crime, organized aggression and theft.

The arrests made were obviously fewer than the staggering totals of cases, enquiries, reports, surveillances and appeals which passed through their hands and which, particularly towards the end of the century, were intended primarily for the prevention and deterrence of crime.

Inspector Poussot's register contains information on 2,692 persons arrested between 1738 and 1754; that is approximately 168 persons per year. We cannot even attempt to interpret this figure. Was it a lot? A little? Or was it representative? Enough said. It would seem more important to use such impressive material (which is actually very informative in spite of being presented in a series of large tables), partly to find out about a type of police work which was different from that of the commissioner and partly to shed sufficient light on a population and social scene which in some respects were the same as those dealt with by the police commissioners (many of the arrests were made in common), but in other instances opened up on to horizons which were slightly different.

The register sheds light on the inspectors' methods, indicating the importance of the social groups about whom they provide information. The need to proceed in alphabetical order suggests that particular attention was being given to the compilation of a record-system, a systematic approach to the work and the need to clarify procedures.

This enormous filing-system of Poussot's opens up with the letter 'A' and here we find solemnly recorded the movements and tracks of thieves and robbers whose names were written down in the book day by day. Thus the names of those who had defied the law could be retrieved quickly along with previous offences, current habits and activities. All it needed was a glance through this great book which was so impeccably maintained to make everything clear and legible.

There is a definite desire here for classification, for the keeping of records and the production of 'memoirs' which was common to the period. In this case the concern was with deviants but, as we know from other sources, the idea of the modern index-system was making great strides. It was an idea that was in keeping with one of the utopian dreams of Guillauté, who in 1749 wrote his 'Mémoire de réformation de la police envoyé au roi'. (Memorandum to the King concerning reform of the police)[21] He dreamt of the setting up of a central register, not only of all offenders but of all inhabitants, in other words, a complete picture of the whole of society, no longer just that of its lawbreakers. In his own way, Inspector Poussot was faithful to the spirit of the age.

Half of the arrests (1,648) were made by order of the King; others were imprisoned following a police decision which was something quite different. Poussot was working as a direct agent of the King, which completely set him apart from the commissioner. For the most part, the complaints did not arise from the populace; it was more a matter of royal directives granting permission for the search and arrest of suspected persons. Thus Poussot's lists enable one to see those areas which were causes of concern for the monarchy.

In this particular field of work, observers and *mouches* were absolutely indispensable. The arrest of a propagandist, for example, implied long hours of observation and following, a knowledge of Paris and its secrets, and the ability to operate clandestinely. In this register one tends to be aware of their presence rather than to see them directly, and that is usually as a result of the arrest of certain people who got too closely involved in the pursuit of *mouchards*.

On 3 April 1744, François, a porter at the Hôtel Parc-Royal found himself imprisoned in Bicêtre by order of the King 'for insulting a number of *mouches* who were on observation in those parts and for drawing attention to them'. Unforgivable behaviour! It was also an indication that Paris was pretty well packed with these individuals.

Ten years later, in October 1782, Jean-Baptiste Préault, nicknamed Luxembourg, a ticket-tout at the Opéra, met with the same fate and was taken to Bicêtre. The note in the margin reads: 'Insolent rogue. Drew attention to the *archers* and other police agents in the process of making an arrest. Thieves and other suspects able to get away.' Things could go even further than that. In 1746, for instance, a woman called Marguerite, who went by the name of Lenfant, assassinated a *mouche* who was arresting deserters in the *cabarets*. The police escorted her to Le Grand Châtelet, where she was duly brought to trial.

The *mouchards* themselves were far from reliable or trustworthy. Some of them had to be brought to book and were even imprisoned on occasion for submitting false reports or for conduct that was patently abusive or licentious. Michault was a *mouche* for Inspector Poussot. He was arrested on 8 April 1744 on police orders because of his disloyal conduct. Observations made on his account read: '*mouche* for Sieur Poussot. Made false reports, led astray other *mouches* causing operations to fail and warned particular individuals involved in these affairs. In addition potentially dangerous dissolute.' Because they were always mixed up with a crowd for whom discipline was not the primary objective, these *mouches* had the greatest difficulty in maintaining their integrity. It became necessary to keep a close watch over the company they kept and the women they met. On 26 January 1747 Catherine Martin who was referred to as Gage, was imprisoned in the jail of Saint-Martin. She was a 'whore who had corrupted a man working for the police'. Of the police employee, on the other hand, we know nothing.

Paris was a city in which spies and spied-upon occasionally mixed and where at other times the two had the greatest difficulty tolerating each other, with the result that there were occasions when attempts were made to reverse roles and to disturb or disperse those whose job it was to establish themselves discreetly in those milieux which were regarded as dangerous by the authorities. As one leafs through this register, reading the names of all those men and women whose nicknames crop up so frequently on its pages, which either say a great deal or very little, one finds a landscape emerging.

There were about 3,000 who ended up in this book, mostly young people and usually living some distance from the capital. They were engaged in every kind of trade and activity apart from the most respectable, and there they stayed, having known at some stage the vagaries of life on the road, the precariousness of seasonal work, or the oppressive atmosphere of the *cabaret* with its trafficking and hasty alliances with those for whom life had scarcely been more indulgent, and who were equally predisposed to mischief. There were the petty thefts and fraudulent deals accepted in haste or destitution; there were also the leagues and gangs one came across in the countryside, and the women of the world as much a part of one's wretchedness as they were the inglorious companions of the 'bad boy's' aspirations. In short, it was a lifestyle without fame or fortune.

Pickpockets, the common soldiery, beggars, ladies of fortune, accomplished thieves, ringleaders and poor devils, they were all there, filling these columns in the course of their brief passage so peremptorily interrupted by an arrest or prison term. That was not the end of the peregrination, however; one might abscond, be set free or transferred, recaptured or eternally at large, 'roaming the countryside', according to the expression of the period.

The register is paradoxical in this respect: it fixes peoples' lives permanently and suddenly, at the same time as it gives an impression of incessant movement and constant coming and going. Although this relates more particularly to migrant workers, the information occasionally available from previous records reveals a world on the move, in flight, everywhere and nowhere. In particular the bands of thieves stand out clearly from the main body and add to this impression of major and minor upheaval, of transience and elusiveness.

Beneath Poussot's neat charts and carefully drawn tables one uncovers a rising tide of malefactors and unfortunates whose swollen and powerful waves broke and branched, swelling and receding or disappearing endlessly into the distance only to regroup in order to reappear once again, all the stronger. And then once again we have the image of a Paris caught in the night – the searches and forays into its furnished lodgings and inn rooms, and behind the closed doors of its houses of ill-repute – revealing its nocturnal life. The inspector could go anywhere he liked; he could disturb folks' slumbers, take lovers and their liaisons by surprise and insist on knowing the whys and wherefores of everyone's activity. He deliberately awaited the hours of darkness in order to hound his prey with the assurance of one who knows that time and darkness will prove him right. Poussot meticulously assembles for us, right before our eyes, all those creatures thus caught in the trap and who, no doubt, had naively believed themselves protected by the night. Here there are none of those thieves arrested in full public hue and cry while pinching poultry off the market, or bits and pieces off a rag-stall or items of linen off a washerwoman's line (although the list did occasionally contain the odd handkerchief stealer caught in the act in church or reported by passers-by). Here we are dealing mainly with that crowd of people who were well known to the police, who were actively looking for them. They would probably have been pointed out by some needy *mouche* or by a superior authority. All that remained to do was to pick them up, usually after nightfall at some illicit spot such as a gaming-room or in those *cabarets* which had not closed their doors for the night, or perhaps in those places which afforded a bed for the night, such as the furnished lodgings, inns and hostelries. This was all made possible thanks to the registers kept by innkeepers and hoteliers, which were strictly monitored by the inspectors, who moreover hardly ever bothered to obtain the proper rights for this purpose.[22]

There we have it, a picture of Paris by night, cramming into its countless shadowy outposts this *canaille*, subject of so much fear and consternation but also an object of fascination. It was this same *canaille* who, it would appear, compounded its actions with the direst debauchery, thus truly warranting the title of 'criminal'; and it was this same *canaille* who knew the thousand and one hide-outs of the capital where evidence of one's complicity, booty or future projects might be concealed and who, as the bourgeoisie was convinced, were one and the same as 'the people', that seamy backstage world which was the justification for all this police activity, including the most sordid.

Gathered here, we have a population whose criminal activity was, for the most part, a way of life. It bore no resemblance at all to the Paris of the mornings and afternoons whose sounds and echoes were received almost good-naturedly by the police commissioner even though there might be the shouts arising from theft of victuals,[23] workshop quarrels, arguments in the street or *cabaret*, infringements of public order, coach accidents, drownings or noisy exchanges in the market-place; all these sounds peopled the day and occupied a population who from time to time was involved in criminal activity, often violent and quick to assemble,[24] up to tricks and whose emotions were easily aroused. By night, however, the image the police registers fix in the mind is that of people who were permanently rooted, rather than occasionally involved, in the margins of criminal behaviour. Were these then the 'murky depths' of the capital which writers like de la Brétonne and L.-S. Mercier were so fond of describing?

It is not our intention to establish a neat set of important and elaborate statistics; there are too many imprecisions and gaps within the document to allow it to be treated with any certainty. Although it is true that we could provide a certain number of figures and make a number of calculations, we have deliberately given preference to an approach which is more qualitative. It consists of a reconstruction of the forms of police control and the workings of the social channels and networks and it is based essentially on a close reading of the reasons for the arrest and the small number of jottings and notes made by the inspector to this end. Our aim is the reconstruction of a social landscape rather than the presentation of precise rates of criminality by the use of figures. It is the register's margins, with their imprecisions as well as their specific but secretive jottings, that have guided our reading and have allowed us to reflect on and raise

Table 1   *Comparison of police records in Paris (1738–1754) and Languedoc (1750–1790)*

|  | Ages where known | | | |
| --- | --- | --- | --- | --- |
|  | 0–20 yrs (%) | 21–30 yrs (%) | 31–40 yrs (%) | over 40 yrs (%) |
| Paris: arrested | 26.3 | 40.7 | 19.0 | 13.9 |
|  | 26.3 | 59.7 | | 13.9 |
| Languedoc: imprisoned | 8.3 | 65.9 | | 25.7 |

questions about this obscure and precarious world. Some of the figures provide the broad outlines of a preliminary sketch:

Of the 2,692 persons recorded on the register, we can count 795 women and 1,897 men. Compared with the usual rates of female criminality, this obvious feminization of crime (more than a third instead of the traditional fifth) needs to be pointed out first of all.[25] It was certainly making more of a mark on the scene and the police made note of the fact that there was a distinct female presence around many of the men who had been arrested and that their role was an important one.

We also know the geographical origins of 915 of the persons arrested; that is, of approximately one-third of all men and women arrested. Of this total 631, that is 69 per cent, were born outside Paris and 284 (31 per cent) in Paris itself. Putting aside the odd discrepancy, this proportion is not surprising; and given that more than two-thirds had not been brought up in the capital, the well-known phenomenon and image of migration in France in the eighteenth century is once again borne out by these figures.

We know the ages of only 999 of the individuals, a little more than a third of the total, and they are distributed in the following manner:

- 263 were aged between 0 and 20 years (26.3 per cent), with a significant number of very young people, born mostly in the capital.
- 407 were aged between 21 and 30 years, which represents 40.7 per cent of the total.
- Above the age of 30 years there were 190 persons ranging from 31 to 40 years (19 per cent); of those aged over 40, there were only 139 over 40, i.e. 13.9 per cent of the total.
- In sum, two-thirds of those whose ages are known were 30 or under; one-third were over 30.

Table 1 makes an interesting comparison of the Paris data with the figures for the prison population during the *parlements* of Toulouse, 1772–90, presented by Nicole Castan in her study on the criminals of Languedoc.[26] On either side of the 20–40 age group, there are two things that stand out: the under-20s are prominent – more than a quarter – and they constitute an impressive band, whereas the over-40 age-group is really quite small. Inspector Poussot's work was in fact taken up with young people; they were the ones who became debauched, indulged in trafficking and theft, lived in criminal bands and were most likely to be found looking for pleasure and excitement. His job was to capture them and stifle their hostility, which was all the more intense for being juvenile. The places he inspected were the favourite haunts of that high-spirited section of the population; and it is for that same reason that the number of older and more mature persons is under-represented.

There is no point either in expecting a traditional socio-professional classification, as professions are not always given, and when they are, they are hardly precise, as a variety of designations is often used and these do not provide an exact location of the individual within the social hierarchy. In any case, we only have information on a half of the persons recorded on the register, which rules out any comprehensive analysis.

It seemed preferable to take as a reference-point those who could be defined more by their status, temporary though this might be, rather than by any professional activity, notwithstanding the possibility that the person might possess a trade elsewhere – information which is not always noted by the inspector.

What stands out in the first place is the number of soldiers: 300 of them were arrested by Inspector Poussot in the district of Les Halles. These figures are evidence of the importance of their presence in the centre of the city as well as of their almost daily activities outside the law. Then, almost level with them, was the group of 200 dissolute men and women, the *débauchés*, which included prostitutes, and the pimps and madams who lived off this activity; there was also the group of beggars, again 200, whose lot it was to see the inside of a prison for reasons of idleness or illegally requesting alms.

Of the 1371 whose type of occupation we know 700 (that is half of them) were not categorized by any stable profession with a recognizable definition but by the practice of some form of social life of a temporary nature (being a soldier, for instance, was only an episode in a man's life). Alternatively it might derive from neediness which imposed its own laws (the beggar often had a profession which illness, the death of one of his relatives or debility had obliged him to give up), or it might be due to transgression of social norms, as for instance in the case of the *débauché* who, having wandered away from the usual channels of employment, lived a life well off the beaten tracks normally trodden by other people.

The fact that there were as many as 700 who had never had any regular professional activity of any kind should come as no surprise. These were the folk whose haunts were those shady spots which were so difficult to control and to keep trouble-free. Seething with problems though M. Poussot's workplace might be, unmasking those individuals who lived on the margins was all a necessary part of the job of inspector. For all that beggars, soldiers, ladies of the night and degenerates of every sort were the direct objects of police attention, they still did not live outside the normal processes of urban life and communication. They too were the city, even if the authorities did attempt to exclude them and repress them by singling them out as being the principal adversaries of public peace and order.[27] They were referred to as being 'outside' or 'elsewhere' in royal decrees and police orders,[28] but the rest of the population did not regard them as such; although not constrained or categorized by the bounds of the professions, they *were* nevertheless the city and like everyone else found themselves organized according to the laws of tension and equilibrium of the urban game.

Unstable and insecure, they kept faith by virtue of their nomadic status with that other group, the migrants, who represented more than two-thirds of those least privileged classes of society and who, having arrived in Paris, still continued to go off for long periods at a time either outside the city or within its walls. It was by way of a response to the instabilities of economic life, as well as to the frequent urge to return to the countryside and thereby increase the chances of survival. For all of them, their experience of the city was one of hope (although those who had actually chosen their own social lot were few and far between); for here risk and anonymity were simultaneous possibilities. In this way, they merged into the crowd, made attempts to find their way into the social networks which were made just as easily as they were broken, and were ready to take on all kinds of risk and adventure which might one day perhaps land them in jail. By seeking pleasure and income from the city, they became immersed in the urban system, living as much off its conflicts as its solidarities, taking refuge where they could from denunciation, searches or enquiries until the day arrived when...

The other half of those arrested had some kind of profession but the vagueness of the information makes classification as difficult as it is unsatisfactory. Thus once more one has to say goodbye to the finer points of interpretation and proceed much more broadly by bringing together certain kinds of information and stressing where it is deficient.

The notes made of the trade give no indication of the level attained by the individual who professed to belong to it. There is just the name followed by a brief note, such as: locksmith, tailor, lacquerware, and so it is impossible to tell whether one is dealing with a master or an apprentice. In this group 180 individuals are included, and one thing worth pointing out is the abundance of those represented by the building trades, accounting for well over half of the total (carpenter, roofer, mason, joiner, locksmith).

In all 140 persons were unqualified and were involved in the small trades, which takes us into that whole wide range which includes water-carriers, washers-up, laundry-workers, cleaners, odd-jobbers, hawkers of sheet-music, vendors of herbs and meat etc.; in other words, the precarious small trades of the street, almost always seasonal and unstable, here today and gone tomorrow; a world where the future was hardly secure and where resourcefulness was essential if one wanted to maintain one's place.

Domestic service stands out as another significant grouping consisting of 130 men and women, 53 of whom referred to themselves as having no particular condition, with another 27 who classed themselves as man- and maidservants in the great houses. Their numbers correspond not only to their representation in the town but also to their role and obvious participation in activities outside the law.[29]

The rest of the population can be divided as follows (note that the same proportion of building-workers can be found here as above): 53 journeymen; 51 apprentices and boys; 51 from the professions, which inevitably entailed a certain number of persons of note, including 20 priests and those in holy orders; 43 masters or merchants; and finally 23 cabbies or carters, who had been deliberately singled out and were particularly notorious in Paris for the disturbances they caused, the accidents they provoked and the numerous quarrels and fights for which they were responsible.

> When a cabbie mows you down in cold blood, the purpose of the commissioner's enquiry is to find out whether he did it with the small wheel or the large and the cabbie will say that it was only the small wheel. If you do expire underneath the large wheel there is no financial compensation for your next of kin. There is a going rate for an arm, a leg or a thigh and that price is always fixed in advance.[30]

As the names of the trades, 180 thereabouts, are mentioned without any further clarification, it is perhaps better to present them in the following way: there were 140 persons exercising some form of small street-trade as against 147 persons who had entered upon a definite professional future, of whom 51 were still apprentices; the others were journeymen (53) and finally those who had reached the summit of their professional aspirations (43 masters or merchants). Culturally and professionally, the 130 domestics can be situated in another area, for their ability to operate within two distinct cultural environments is now well known, as was their manner of appropriating many of the instincts of the elite along with the vivaciousness and impetuosity appropriate to their own estate. These three groups were equally represented and in certain cases were just as liable to break the law.

However, these reflections should not allow one to forget the clear distinctions at work within the two halves of this population, where the one half defied all attempts at strict classification according to profession and only allowed its identity to be grasped through its precarious aspects where drifting, distress, economic and sexual adversity and resourcefulness were sovereign. It constituted a fundamental part of the Paris of Inspector Poussot and the one which he had made it a priority to track down.

Quite typical of a society which was just making its first halting attempts at classification, identification and statistics, M. Poussot's register is a supple blend of classification and narrative. Even though this enormous book is presented in tabular form and consists of columns which are very clearly set out and which demonstrate the organizational scope of the enterprise and the attempt to achieve an overall picture of the problem, it still leaves a good deal of room for improvization and comment. The space reserved for the reasons for arrest lends itself to an enormous number of variations bordering on the fantastic. Sometimes there are no indications and the space remains blank and sometimes there is one hasty word which attempts to sum up the situation such as 'theft', 'receiving' or 'whore'. Quite often one finds a whole paragraph of comments written in a neat and careful hand on the person's situation, the circumstances of his or her arrest and subsequent conduct. It is impossible to summarize this wealth of material in hard figures as though it were a faithful and rigid mirror of reality. Even amidst this abundance of comment and commentary it is still difficult, in some cases, to understand the exact reasons for the arrest. On the other hand, the mass of detail, the originality of the notes and a continuous reading of the material without hope or intention of ascertaining accountability allows one to gain a profound understanding of this population, and of its vast numbers of networks and interdependencies as seen through the eyes of the police. One has to use this register as a discourse offering information on the population in an uncustomary manner, perceiving it through its own eyes and allocating important roles to some of its actors or events by borrowing on the weaknesses of each individual and relying on them like some kind of connecting cable, thus allowing one a better grasp of the workings of a certain type of deviance. We shall see, for instance, how the woman, even if she herself were not directly accused, held a role of the utmost importance.

For the time being a few of the notes and comments concerning the reasons for imprisonment are simply reproduced here:

*Aubert Mte Jne*: concubine of Picard, known as Boulanger, and of others in Rafiat's band; an accomplice.

*Auret Joseph*: beggar, able-bodied, currently in the King's service.

*Auguste Charles*: living in sin with the Croiset woman whose husband is a guard with the Prince de Conti. Very suspicious. When arrested, covered his head with a cloth. Transferred to Bicêtre 23 October 1767 and sent abroad with the Soissonais regiment 20 November.

*Beligant Jeanne*: accomplice's mistress. Kept guard while he was thieving.

*Bontemps Philippe*: bad lot.

*Corblet Fcs*: propagandist.

*Chery*: beggar, smearing his face to make believe he was a leper. Condemned to the galleys.

*Cousim Mie Cath*: prostitute. Left house of correction three months ago. Arrested while on night visit, hiding in cellar.

*Claudor Jean*: five years a deserter. Found in bed with Agathe Thiébaut during a night raid at the home of Chartran, Rue Montorgueil. She is pregnant as a result and suspected of theft. Could be an accomplice.

*Cuvilliers Charles*: for last 12 years, only trade has been as pimp for both sexes. Committed several thefts over the past three months.

*Dutoit Marie Aimé*: arrested on night raid as suspect. Found in bed in her room in the Rue Grenier St Lazare with Belle Amour a soldier in the Gardes françaises. When entry requested, sought to throw herself out of the window and then found hiding in the chimney.

*Gandoche Nicole*: found in bed with militiamen.

*Gilles Pierre*: trouble-maker and rabble-rouser.

*Grenier l'abbé*: has written three tracts against religion.

*Giard*: suspected of highway robbery.

*Paul Jacques*: arrested three years ago and taken to Grand Châtelet for stealing fish from shops and other effects from housebreaking. Stayed 2 years in prison at end of which he received an extension of 6 months, then a term in Bicêtre where he became ill; transferred to the strong room at the Hôtel Dieu from where he absconded 3 or 4 months ago.

*Rémy Nicolas*: thief and pickpocket.

*Renault Marie*: whore, arrested on night raid hiding underneath a bed.

As these brief examples taken at random from the pages of the register show, the work that needs to be carried out on the reasons for arrest requires a much broader and more complex system of interpretation.

A third of the offenders were arrested for theft (the total figure for both men and women was in fact 963), and under this heading we find a whole jumble of rogues and rascals, petty crooks, receivers and dealers in stolen goods – in fact every type of thief imaginable: they were all there. They picked pockets, robbed churches, or committed highway robbery in groups and gangs, committed assault, with or without battery, took vast amounts or not so much, shared out their catch amongst the gang or singlehandedly committed acts of petty theft and larceny. The booty varied; it might be money, handkerchieves, medals or snuff-boxes – anything went. Often, no one bothered to write in what had been stolen and the clerk simply wrote in the comment column: 'well-known thief' or 'one of the country gang'.

Rather than picking off the isolated thief however, the inspector took it upon himself as a point of honour to dismantle the bands of thieves and their accomplices by finding the ringleaders or their successors on the arrest of one of their number. Always on the move and acting with *carte blanche* from the King, he would already have had wind of such and such a crime and the necessary connections between a recent infringement of the law and the passing of a gang of thieves. It was decidedly not the same work as that of the commissioner of police, who himself was more accustomed to receiving complaints in his *hôtel*, and attending to everyone's grievances. Although he too had contact with a considerable number of thieves, they were definitely not from the same population of offenders. When folk came to his *hôtel*, it was to make a complaint about a basket of cherries that had been stolen, the theft of a silver earring or a sheet that had been taken by one of the servants; it was the occasional crime, rather than a case of organized gangs operating their rackets and putting the people of Paris in jeopardy.[31] It was these latter who were the principal targets for the police inspectors' activity and in particular for the agents of the Bureau de la Sûreté.[32]

In his district of Les Halles, Poussot did not have much to do with violence. There are only 54 acts of violence (representing scarcely 1.5 per cent of the total) recorded on the register, and these include acts of rebellion, murder and assassination attempts, some of which had been previously committed by the robbers. Libertinism, on the other hand, occupied a substantial place, on a par with begging and loitering by soldiers absent without leave or deserters. In the course of his pursuit of thieves and libertines Poussot inevitably crossed paths with confidence tricksters and gamblers. On these grounds 71 people were arrested, grouped under a number of different categories such as 'rogue and a cheat'; 'crook profiting from misfortune'; 'billiard-room crook' etc. It was also part of his brief to arrest those responsible for the sale of prohibited goods or for circulating handwritten pamphlets against the King and religion. The number of these 'propagandists', the majority of them male, amounts to 71, all of whom were arrested by order of the King. In contrast, Poussot had very little to do with requests by families for imprisonment, as there only seem to be 47 of these, which is quite a paltry figure considering their popularity at the time.[33]

How does the rest of this nefarious activity break down? We have no idea at all about 300 of the incidents, as there is nothing in the observations and motives columns. As far as the rest are concerned, we find quite a few practitioners of the magic arts and fortune-tellers, whose exact crime is not mentioned apart from that of nocturnal gatherings. These promisers of fortunes and riches reveal a semi-clandestine world where one left one's daytime work in order to organize or participate in nocturnal gatherings in which dream and reality became confused and where one was able to invent and fantasize for a brief while about one's good fortune to come and happiness at last received. Noël, known as La Suze and blind in one eye, was born in Paris. He was exiled by order of the King on 1 August 1741 because he was mixed up with 'spells and magic', a somewhat vague accusation if ever there was one. The same thing happened to Marie Petra, a linen worker, aged 26. She was imprisoned in Fort L'Evêque for superstitious practices and for 'treasure-seeking which she had been born to do'.

Next to be pinpointed were the concubines of thieves or of former thieves and even some who were just suspects and whose only reason for being considered guilty was their occasional association with theft. The same went for the soldiers who were found drinking with prostitutes or bedded down in the grass 'in bad company'. In other words these were no more than the ordinary people of the night. There then follows a long procession of people arrested by the patrols and as a result of night raids and rough searches in the lodging-houses and furnished lettings. Here we have the inspector purging the night of its prowlers and shadows, a political clean-up which affected the streets of the centre of the capital as much as the gaming academies and 'vice-dens' or the *cabarets* and seamier parts. Amongst those arrested there were as many persons innocently in search of a few furtive pleasures and encounters under the cloak of night as there were rogues and brigands.

Amongst all these people thus caught in the net of repression, there is a noticeable absence of the deranged and mentally insane; there are two or three rapes and one or two instances of homosexuality, as in the case of the Chevalier de Castille, who was arrested by decree of 9 July 1751 and jailed in the prison of Le Châtelet 'for committing the crime of pederasty'; there is one condemnation for incest, in the case of Marthe Dardenne, aged 24, who was living with her mother and her stepfather. She was found in bed with him having lived in sin with him for some considerable time; there was another arrest for the crime of bestiality concerning one Joseph Picard from Lorraine, aged 34 years. He was arrested by order of police on 6 February 1748. The notes in the margin read: 'Beggar, able-bodied. Dressed in militia uniform. This man said that he had committed serious crimes. He had lived with the mares and deserved to be punished.' The rest can be divided up between endless numbers of diverse, highly questionable, and reprehensible acts, which include insulting behaviour, blasphemy, sexual misdemeanours or nothing more than suspicious behaviour in places where the patrols were passing. The register contains a wealth of unsavoury details about some of the arrests and the actual process of reading it firms up one's impressions of a Paris that was multiform, sensorial and impetuous.

On 7 September 1750, the writer Lebel was imprisoned in Bicêtre for striking an image of the Virgin Mary with his sword in the Rue de la Jussienne – a blasphemy and an act of sacrilege which was immediately punishable. Pierre Montenet, a wine-merchant's boy, was also to find himself punished on police orders in September 1744 because 'he had associated with a certain two persons for the purpose of collecting money from wealthy wine-merchants wishing to have a *Te Deum* sung for the King's convalescence and who had subsequently appropriated their money.' It was the kind of squalid behaviour which did not go down very well and which often ended up badly. Sexual deviation also led to imprisonment, as in the case of Michel Maisonneuve a master writer, who was sent to Bicêtre in December 1751 for failing to abide by his exile from the city. 'He was banished a year ago for self-defilement outside the doors of the classrooms where the schoolmistresses were giving the cane to their pupils.'

Not even the priests were beyond participating in sexual perversions which could lead to arrest, as in the case of the widow Vatan: 'She has hired out two girls of 14 for prostitution and has been arrested this day, September 1748, at the Porcherons, where she lives and where she kept a young girl whom a priest came to see and who whipped her while completely naked on about 12 occasions.' And then there was the long list of individuals who were considered 'very dangerous' or the 'libertines who were very crafty and degenerate', like Nicolas Godeau, aged 28, born in Paris and a deserter to boot. He was taken to the prison of Fort l'Evêque on 29 December 1750.

Absconding; indecency; threatening behaviour; nimble antics in the hay; defiance; branded shoulders; breaking a banning order; making rude faces; 'found on the slope of the Pont Marie at 11 o'clock at night with his sword by his side and taking his pleasure with a woman on a heap of straw'; woman disguised as a man; young man impersonating a count; drunkenness, false signatures; 'only went out at night', tout – there they all are, the potential prisoners which any night raid might throw up. They serve as witness to the flimsiness of the motives for their arrest as well as to a particular way of populating the capital.

## Family or Gang?

If one leaves aside those who acted independently (who were the majority), the two obvious systems of organization that stand out are the gangs of criminals on the one hand (some of which were notorious and others relatively unknown) with a total of 71 persons belonging to these. On the other hand, there were 71 families who were implicated in illegal activities and proceedings, not to mention the associations formed amongst concubines which were fairly common; the total number of identifiable members of these families came to 170.

It was the association between husband and wife which came up most frequently as well as that between two brothers, who were usually quite young, not much more than 14 or 16 and sometimes as young as 13 and 9. They were usually arrested on charges of 'begging and roaming the countryside'. These young vagabonds who either had no parents or who were living away from them, took to the roads in the hope of finding some means of keeping themselves alive; or alternatively, like Pierre Legeaye, aged 14, and his brother, Martin, aged 13, who were both boot-blacks, they might go off thieving in Paris. This particular pair had stolen some items from a surgeon and were jailed at Fort-l'Evêque in February 1754.

Some families got together to arrange the sale and distribution of prohibited books, like Mazuel, his wife and her nephew, who were arrested and taken to three different prisons – Fort l'Evêque, Le Grand and Le Petit Châtelet. They were accused of 'the sale of books that had been banned on account of their contravention of moral and religious standards'. In 1744, Jean, Jeanne, Marie and Marguerite Paumier were arrested on charges of 'distributing propaganda for Rambault; relaying news and gossip; acting as mistress to the copyist, and newsmongering'. Rambault was certainly a well-known dealer in banned books and he had effectively recruited the assistance of the Paumier family by using their potential for carrying information not to mention some sexual involvement to boot. In this case Poussot had managed to dismantle quite a complex web of relationships: the man was sent to Fort l'Evêque and the three women to Le Grand Châtelet.

Some sisters also formed gangs, but they tended to be older than in the case of brothers. Catherine Morset, aged 27 and the wife of Léger, 'had completed a month's detention for passing on charms and cures' and on 9 April 1750 she had joined up with her sister Marguerite, the wife of Cobet, aged 52 years. They were arrested for theft and note was made that they had already been whipped and branded for the same offence.

There was one group which was not in any way typical of the rest; these were spies from the English court who were imprisoned in the Bastille in October 1746. There were quite a few of them – Lady Morton and her son, Mistress Morton and her sister and the governess of the young Morton, and their servant, Moisson, and four servants belonging to Lady Morton and her husband. The family group was not held separately from the main body of the servants even in prison, thus perpetuating the idea that the household was comprised of servants and masters all of whom were considered equally responsible. Even when imprisoned in the Bastille, the servants did not change their roles, but continued to serve their masters, and the governess carried on bringing up the young child.

The type of collaboration previously referred to underlines in particular the vitality of the family group amongst the least privileged classes. It was a vitality which neither migrations, wanderings, the nomadic life nor extreme poverty or utter precariousness had called into question. Living together as a family, which might include brothers, cousins and nephews, meant an undertaking to stick together for survival through thick and thin. Criminality was typically a characteristic of such families.

Tracking down a family group was one thing, but the business of the composition of gangs was another.[34] The inspector threaded his way in and out of the entanglements of 71 networks, sending out his spies and observers to vantage-points from which they might discover the hide-outs of the ringleaders, or the mistresses of some and the concubines of others. Certain names keep cropping up like the Langevin gang or the gangs controlled by Poulot, Jolivet, Rafiat, Lalande and Sandrin. Their tentacles seemed to extend in every direction, making it impossible to control them, for they always rose up again from their ashes thanks to new arrivals and fresh links in the chain. Although now and again word might get round that one of the leaders had been hanged or that he had had all the bones in his body broken, this did nothing to snuff out their activity and they still continued to attract other contenders. A special mention must be made of Clavier, who eventually became one of Cartouche's accomplices and who caused so much fear that a special stronghold had to be constructed for him and his comrades: 'Pierre Clavier, thief and formerly of Cartouche's gang. Imprisoned indefinitely, God willing. First taken to Bicêtre, 22 May 1749 by order of the King and from there to the dungeons of Le Châtelet built expressly for them, and chained by the neck.'

The odds on gaining a clear picture from amongst this jungle of thieves and crooks are not very high, but one can see three different types of group emerging, even if there are no watertight compartments between the various organizations.

Immediately recognizable were those specializing in church robbery. In their activity they were not unlike a colony of ants: swift, furtive and conscientious, they were fiercely pursued by priests and sacristans and were particularly active in the churches of the centre of the city such as Saint-Eustache or Notre-Dame. The church at this time was a place for socializing; it was busy and noisy, with scant regard for calm or meditation. Into this *brouhaha* slipped the filchers and pilferers, for in the midst of all this bustle what could have been easier than picking a few pockets or emptying a coffer or two. Its architecture and dark corners provided good cover for the accomplice who, with his back propped against a pillar, had the job of giving advance warning to the thief. Between 1750 and 1775, 21.05 per cent of the thieves arrested and appearing before the chamber of the Grand Criminel had committed their crime in a church. The rest of them could be divided roughly between the river banks, the fairgrounds and the boulevards. In Inspector Poussot's register, opposite the name of the thief, one often finds the mention that he was 'part of a gang of church thieves'. Upon their arrest they were nearly always imprisoned in Bicêtre where they stayed for some time, detained by order of the King, which was proof of the importance attributed to the punishment of this type of activity.

Another type of gang consisted of young homeless thieves, who were quite often arrested in the limekilns from which they wreaked havoc in the countryside. Such roving bands, living by what they could beg or pillage, usually consisted of quite young children, sometimes brothers, sisters or cousins who had been left to wander the roads as a result of financial hardship. Surfacing as they did quite spontaneously and intermittently, they had no rigid structure or leader and were formed by chance encounter, as a result of abscondence from orphanages or during the search for work. They were seemingly without future and were only formed out of necessity and in response to economic pressure. When Jean-Baptiste Blanchard, aged 18 and born in Burgundy, was arrested on 9 July 1749 with Bonaventure Ballet, a decommissioned soldier and a beggar born in Paris, he said that they had 'come from Lyons with neither money nor possessions' and that they lived off thieving and begging. The same was true of three youngsters aged 13, 15 and 16, of whom one had escaped from La Pitié, the second was an apprentice button-maker, and the third was unemployed and unqualified. They were arrested as 'thieves without morality, of no fixed abode and sleeping in the limekilns of Belleville and Ménilmontant, where they had been committing all kinds of damage in the countryside and the peasants had complained about it.' The peasants were quick to spot these chance bands of unfortunates, which were not very organized, stemming as they did from poverty and not with the deliberate intent of planning theft and robbery.

What Inspector Poussot applied himself to most diligently, however, was the dismantling of the great gangs of 'infamous robbers' who were capable of reforming their networks and adding other leaders to their numbers even though their previous leader might only just recently have been imprisoned. Like octopuses with innumerable tentacles, these gangs who were constantly chased and pursued stand out from the first page of the register to the last, as though it were impossible to put them to rout definitively. Moreover the notes written in the margin explain the reasons for such pursuits, which though fruitful at times were as often as not inadequate. On 10 January 1750, Jacques Dumont, known as Saint-Paul, a soldier in the guard and born in Paris, was arrested by order of the King. He was accused of robbery and of being 'linked to a considerable proportion of thieves and robbers who were in Le Châtelet and Bicêtre and in correspondence with them', and he was immediately sent to the prison of Le Grand Châtelet. Thus even in prison, the thieves maintained contact with the outside world, made attempts to escape, and wrote to each other regularly about such and such a deal. The police tried to seize the ringleaders and persons of influence and their guards even to the extent of imprisoning them or having them broken; but their very memory provoked new crimes. The arrest of Guillaume Reyne, known as the 'Little Blond', brought the police considerable satisfaction, as the note in the margin indicates: 'The most dangerous thief in Paris. Taken prisoner in 1739 and implicated in the Rafiat affair.' The inspector must have spent a great deal of time trying to track him down with his spies and observers.

The police campaign was a long-term operation. All we have to go by from the register are a small number of fragments and details giving the story of some of these gangs. Take, for example, the case of Jean Poulot, a soldier and 'deserter from several regiments'. First he was a thief with Jolivet's gang and then gradually, after being compromised in a number of affairs, he seems to have become leader of a gang of his own, with accomplices and mistresses of his own. Following his arrest, he escaped from prison several times, which led to the arrest of people who knew him and who had compromised themselves on his behalf. On 4 September 1744 he was arrested on the King's orders and his bones broken; but the talk about him persisted for a long time afterwards. Sandrin, referred to as Pognon, confirmed that Poulot 'had accused him of several robberies' in declarations made before he died but he was not arrested until 27 June 1746. Some considerable time later, it was the turn of Françoise Rousselle, aged 23, the wife of Pierre Dion, an odd-job-man, to be taken to La Salpêtrière, because she was 'implicated during the trial relating to Poulot's escape'. It was recorded that at the time she came out of detention her mother was still there.

Friends of thieves, former thieves suspected of being a member of X's gang, mother or mistress of the thief, concubine, go-between... The register is full of persons and situations capable of reinforcing the determination of the police on the one hand but of prolonging the life and ramifications of these gangs on the other.

Women played a significant role in these gangs, either because they passed from one man to the next or because they were linked to several of the thieves on account of the services they provided or the deals they were involved in. The arrest of Louise Levasseur, a street seller, aged 24, and her widowed mother, aged 45, provides information about some of these female links: 'The two women were drunks; the mother was a procuress and the daughter a whore. They made purchases indiscriminately from every crook and thief in Paris and had relations with them. They were arrested at 11 o'clock at night in a *cabaret* on the Rue du Grand Hurleur where they were making a din.'

Fellow-travellers were often denounced by their own kind like the accomplice of the well-known brigand Langevin, who was shopped by Fanchon, Langevin's mistress. Offering each other little protection because they were primarily concerned with getting their own prisoners off the hook, these fellow-travellers of the thieves dotted Poussot's register with their misadventures. However, what we are dealing with here is not the odd criminal incident but with large-scale crime which spread from one gang to another across the whole of France, taking advantage of a highly organized system of networks.

## Disguise and getting a name for oneself

The inspector's lists do not have a lot to say about the social habits and characteristics of this miscreant population although there are two particular features which stand out: a tendency towards impersonation and disguise on the one hand, and the use of nicknames on the other. It was a practice that was very much alive, as indicated by the 10 per cent of people on the register who gave their nickname as well as their actual name.

As to the disguisers, one finds a number of them among the beggars and vagabonds, who were always ready to use any sort of deception or subterfuge in order to arouse compassion, sometimes with a great deal of imagination. Chéry was sent to Le Grand Châtelet in 1746 for impersonating a leper. He had daubed his face with the white of an egg to give the impression that he was affected by the disease; and Antoine de Claire was also a beggar who in spite of his youth (he was only 20), had fearlessly burned his abdomen in order to inspire pity. Others impersonated the halt and the maimed, even adding a few wounds, as in the case of Jacques Gaillard, aged 40, who 'inflicted a wound on his leg which he had daubed with animal's blood from off the market'. He had been begging in the parish of Saint-Eustache and found himself imprisoned in Fort-l'Evêque in August 1746.

Those who had been branded for a previous offence mutilated their scars by deepening and lengthening them, claiming to have been bitten by dogs or horses. Some even wore masks in order to avoid being recognized by a policeman, as in the case of Nicolas Moussant, aged 32, who had recently come up from Berry. He was sent to the prison of Le Grand Châtelet in June 1746 for 'begging and impersonation of the one-armed man who had led a rebellion. He was found to have a mask in his pocket.'

There were a few women who had disguised themselves as men; this was not altogether surprising at the time, for during this period of the eighteenth century one finds quite a taste for disguise. This was the case of Suzanne Goujon, chambermaid to the wife of the King's architect, Tirot, who was arrested on 22 January 1749 by order of the King 'for writing two anonymous letters and for having dressed up as a man and found lodging in furnished lettings in the Rue Saint-Sauveur with no female clothing in her possession and saying that Tirot had abused her and had made her wear men's clothes so as not to be recognized'. She was to be sent to La Salpêtrière like Marguerite Goffier, who was arrested the same year in a *cabaret* in the Rue Salle-au-Comte dressed as a man.

Some women did it in order to live the life of a man, as in the case of Françoise Fidèle, the daughter of a captain in the Irish regiment. She dressed as a man and enlisted in the Paris militia. She wanted to go to Flanders in this attire in order to find one of her parents. She told the police who arrested her in November 1748 that 'she was a good girl and had done nothing to offend her honour and that she was not the first in her family to disguise herself in order to enter the service', thus presenting the act of disguise as something of a family tradition. What is more, Françoise would not have been the first to have asserted this as a possibility and to have assumed that this subterfuge in no way reflected on her honour.

Bellerose, Vive Lamour, Ménage, Lespérance, Jupiter, Le Bourguignon, Petitpas, Loiseau Bleu, La Gaillardise, Fanchon la Boiteuse – these colourful nicknames are the bitter-sweet windfalls that break up the monotonous terrain of the lists of arrests with their trenchant irony or their scathing assessments. Because Fanchon shuffles along with a limp, she is 'Shuffler'; because Nicolas Merlet is dark and swarthy, he is 'Le Moricault' (from 'Moor'); and because J. Drumont comes from Poitou, he is 'Le Poitevin' – obviously! Consequently, there are a lot of folk by the name of *Picard*, *Le Bourguignon*, *Lauvergnat*, *Flamand*, *La Lionnaise* or *Le Breton*, closely followed by others who are quite simply called after the names of towns like, Namur, Bellegarde, Saint-Louis, Cartagena, or Chambéry. Or they are described by their place of birth – origins which were not forgotten in spite of all the migrations, expeditions and periods of roaming the countryside or returning to it.

The nicknames derived not only from one's village or town of origin; all types of physical appearance, for instance, and all manner of human behaviour and characteristics went into forming some of the names, which were as lively as they were descriptive and as surprising as they were farcical, their very sound opening up onto wide horizons of adventure and fantasy. Reading these nicknames helps us penetrate even further into this unstable and precarious world where one's role, faults or temperament were the means by which one might be recognized by one's fellows. To be nicknamed 'Sans Souci' (Carefree), 'Commissionaire' (The Commissioner), 'Belle Amour' (True Love), 'Tapineuse' (Hell-raiser) or 'La Libre' (Free-for-all), 'Le Sage' (The Sage), 'Cochon' (Swine), or 'Capon' (Chicken) meant the achievement of recognition at a certain point in the human adventure even though distance and derision might have been its precedents. François Estève, known as 'Le Sage' had probably been wise only once in his life; and more than likely 'Harmony' and 'Fantasy' were not expected to abide by the implications of their name. It is possible that Michel Faure, known as 'Sans Peur' (Fearless), was such a coward that he had got his nickname from constant gibes. A nickname offered more scope than a banal surname and allowed some degree of differentiation from one's fellows. It often came up quite by chance as a joke or a statement of fact and could be quite determining. Some people possibly helped create their own nickname in order to equip themselves with a history, to leave anonymity behind, endow themselves with a role, give themselves some colour, or laugh at themselves; or indeed – and why not – to pursue an immense dream.

A good many of the nicknames probably came along in this way, and if some of them raise a smile, almost all of them cause some surprise for they go back to systems of perception existing amongst the individuals themselves and are so rich and varied that they fire the imagination and defy reality. Just listen to the evocative sounds of the nicknames as they roll by one after the other: La Petite Beaulieu, Gueule Noire, La Belle Blonde, Le Vineux, La Lime, La Fleur, Répit, La Grande Gogo, La Goulue, Le Petit Pot, La Caresse, Ciel, Le Chaton, Blambec et Baublanc, La Demoiselle, Le Teigneux, La Raie and La Quarante Coups...

## Companions in crime

*Marie Dyard*, sent to Fort-l'Evêque by police decision 23 July 1747: 'concubine of *Lyot* and *Sans Regret* and other thieves'.

*Marie-Anne Forget*, known as 'La Quarante Coups', imprisoned in Le Grand Châtelet by order of the King on 14 May 1746: 'mistress of Merlet and a fair portion of the thieves of Paris, already in detention two or three times'.

*Elizabeth Guyeux*, sent to Le Grand Châtelet by the police on 3 October 1744: 'concubine of thieves and deserters'.

*Marie-Anne Giroroux*, prisoner at Le Grand Châtelet by royal decree in this same month of October 1744: 'concubine of *Beaufort*, thief'.

*Florence Guérin*, sent to prison of Le Grand Châtelet by royal decree, December 1744: 'concubine of Jean Lainé, member of gang'.

The concubines of small thieves as well as those of the gang leaders themselves were also useful prey for the police, who made assiduous efforts to find them, convinced that they would obtain a great deal of information through them which would enable them to track down not only their present but their past companions as well.

Concubines and mistresses are the leading lights in this register and on the whole there is no record of whether they themselves had committed any crime, for it was in their role as the consorts of brigands, well-known or not, that the police had decided to arrest them and that the orders of the King fell about their heads. In spite of the lack of detail, the portraits of the women sketched in the register are the kind one imagines coming straight from the great popular romances of the day – heroines in spite of themselves, whose counsel was always valued and well respected and who traced their descent from that small class of petty thieves renowned for their spirit and valour. There seems to be little departure from the most traditional typology in keeping, almost without exception, with the most well-worn and familiar of images and stereotypes. They were the passionate lovers so often obliged by misfortune to change the arm on which they leant on account of the frequency with which 'their' thieving-man went off to jail. These women – always so ready to bear the blows and always well informed about the latest plans of their proud companions, paid the price of their love for this *canaille* with frequent spells in prison.

Marie Laplace, aged 25 and born in Paris, cuts a fine figure of a woman. She was detained in La Salpêtrière by order of the King in December 1751: 'Mistress of Poulot, who was broken, and at present the mistress of Renard, a thief in the country. Has already spent four years in prison.' They gave themselves to the most vile it is true, but they remained faithful to their chosen one and these *grandes amantes* seemed to change lovers only to perpetuate the memory or deeds of their previous love. The men fell, were broken or hanged, or at best imprisoned or sent to the galleys. The women were left behind, acting as unfailing links in this network of rogues.

This could certainly be said in the case of Marie-Marlaine, who claimed that she was married to a butcher's boy. She sold greengrocery as well as being 'the mistress of a good few men in the galleys', but in 1752, the prison of La Salpêtrière momentarily put an end to her passions. The almost mythical figures of these great lovers, these women with neither hope nor future, populated the inspector's calligraphed columns. It was well known, and even recorded in writing, that for some of them there was no real evidence of their falling foul of the law; but the simple certainty that they were the concubines of such and such was proof enough. It was this relationship which determined their identity and their criminal status, much more than their name, marital status, trade or even their criminal activity. In the eyes of the police it was this link which was of prime importance and it was a sufficient definition for them to warrant prison on its account.

It was on this charge that the two Renaud sisters, Marie and Catherine, aged 16 and 18, were to go to prison by order of the King – one to Le Grand and one to Le Petit Châtelet – for being the 'concubines of the aforementioned Léauté and Capon and the brothers Babelle, who were thieves and crooks. Arrested at an ale-house in the Rue Saint-Placide and found with handkerchieves on them but, there being no proof, taken into detention.' Here we have the particular logic of the police system working at its best: pulling in the two sisters was especially important because it inevitably led to a pair of crooked brothers and two other thieves. The police were sneaky and well informed; it was no mere coincidence that they fell upon this or that woman and the concubines of these robbers were almost certainly as sought after as the thieves themselves, given the ease with which they passed from thief to thief, which made them the repositories of precious knowledge. They were the living links in a chain of thieves which could never be broken, for if the men died or went off to the galleys, the women bound them back together again by offering themselves to those who remained as their new companions. Is it not the case that this function, which might initially produce a smile (a response which is just as stereotyped as the feminine model which provoked it), has an internal coherence of its own which allows a better understanding of the masculine and feminine roles within this criminal society? And is it not also the case that the internal circulation of the women within this milieu of criminals, which at first sight might appear anarchic, was in fact the guarantee of the stability of the milieu and its desire to endure? In the face of the risks taken by the men, was it not the role of the women to do whatever was possible to make sure that the gangs and their networks did not fall apart? Once some amorous adventure had brought them into the thick of things and integrated them, the women found themselves drawn into a destiny which seemed logical and from which there was no going back. They could not leave without risk to themselves and, as a result, it became their responsibility to see that things ran well and to ensure that they were able to keep well clear of the police net.

This probably explains the activities and *grands amours* of Marie-Anne Petit, known as La Dumont, and the widow of Le Cœur. She was arrested in 1746 as the 'former mistress of *Marrondinde* who was in the galleys. Linked with all the rogues of Paris and also former mistress of Poulot, who was broken live.' The same thing happened to Thérèse Saint-Père, who was taken to Fort-l'Evêque in 1747 as the 'concubine of Lyoteaux, Morneaux, Sans Regret, and other thieves'.

As a concubine of thieves, it was accepted that one would strengthen the complicated ties between members of the same gang or between different gangs; these ties were one form of the organization of the system. Seen in this way, the concubines of the thieves fulfilled a quite considerable role which cannot be overlooked, although their central tasks were the more traditional functions of persuading, influencing and supporting in contrast with the more valiant and dominant duties of the men.

Some of the women's duties can be seen from the lists drawn up by the inspector. Where we have one jotting following from another, it becomes possible little by little to add some finer touches to some of the female portraits. If their lovers were in jail, for instance, the women tried to assist in their escape, a hope they clung to. In fact in the eighteenth century prison escapes were something of a daily occurrence. Thus in October 1746 we see Marie-Anne Dubuisson and Madeleine David meeting up at the prison of Le Grand Châtelet 'to prepare the escape of thieves who had been detained at the Conciergerie'. In December 1750, Jeanne Carrier, 'who claimed she was the wife of Baronneau, a soldier in the guard', was sent to Fort-l'Evêque, and then transferred to detention at La Salpêtrière, finally completing her sentence two years later. She was no stranger to the police, who had her under suspicion: 'she has already been in Le Châtelet twice before for supplying Carter with women's clothes for his escape and still associated with former thieves.' There was no end to this system of escapes, for in their turn the bandit lovers tried to get out their companions, as in the case of Rose, who was imprisoned at Fort-l'Evêque 'for having violently snatched the woman Denis from the hands of the doorkeepers of Saint-Martin, who were transferring her from the strong-room at the Hôtel-Dieu'. Adelaide Denis had first been taken to Saint-Martin, where she had fallen ill and had been transferred to the strong-room at the Hôtel-Dieu before being brought back again to the prison of Saint-Martin. After this abduction Rose found himself arrested whilst 'in bed with Adelaide'. As the men were imprisoned more frequently than the women (and there were plenty of reasons for that[35]), it is hardly surprising that the women were determined to get them out. These 'mistresses' were considered as schemers or sources of trouble and the accusations reveal the age-old idea of the woman as a temptress, cause of original sin, trouble-maker and inciter. This was said of Jeanne de Lespinière, 'the cunning and scheming mistress of Boyer and mixed up in all of Boyer's operations'. The same was true of Elizabeth Demainville, the mistress of a soldier who was hoping to join the Watch. Arrested in 1752 by order of the King 'for causing an argument between her two lovers who fought each other with swords, one of them being killed by the other'.

Occasionally there is the odd detail which crops up unexpectedly and when it does, often in isolation, it is very precious as it helps enrich the significance of the notes and jottings. It is not possible to tell why one particular piece of information should be pinned to this or that thief and not to another, but the fact that it is not repeated is not important. When Marie la Lame was arrested for concubinage with a thief in the country-side, it comes as some surprise to find the following comment written just beneath the indictment: 'found carrying the thief's pistols'. It certainly surprised the inspector's sergeants enough for them to make mention of it; in fact it was very rare for the weapons to be entrusted to the women, if only for the purpose of carrying them. It would appear that even the concubines of thieves had unexpected roles which this particular piece of information seems to bear out, unique and tenuous though it might be.

Prostitutes and women of ill-repute, pimps and soldiers' girls were also pursued by Inspector Poussot. The district of Les Halles was admirably suited to their activity and the register is proof of the frequency of the raids made into the places of prostitution. Searches, forcible entry into bedrooms, raids by the police on 'bawdy houses' and 'brothels' are all a part of the police lists, which are explicit in revealing police actions which were conducted quite overtly and with absolutely no delicacy.

Here too, the police went straight 'to the girls' to find every kind of undesirable male – soldiers absent without leave, deserters, well-known crooks, or thieves on the run. It was always the same procedure: where the girl was, there the trouble was also. It could have been no clearer, there was no room for any doubt about it: 'Found in bed with a whore'; 'found in bed with a procuress'; 'found in bed with Manette'; 'said they were husband and wife, when in fact she was a woman of ill-repute' – the list of accusations becomes quite tedious. Nor should it come as any surprise that the police intrusion went as far as the very beds of the offenders. As the scene of the transgression, it was the bed that made it possible to pursue two targets at once: both prostitute and suspect. It was pointless and a waste of time to pursue them separately since more often than not it was the harlot's bed which brought them together.

The numbers of 'whores and prostitutes' arrested in the street was also quite high, and since they were largely protected by soldiers in the guard, this made it possible to run a number of surveillance and reconnaissance operations amongst these groups where there was a tendency to agitation and upheaval and all kind of criminal activity.

Even if they were not arrested, the women still appeared on the register, mainly in the margins as additional or supplementary information. Although they only appear alongside, or in the shadow of those who were arrested, one nevertheless senses that they were still regarded as an important cog in the criminal machine. Of one man it would be said that 'he had been roaming round the countryside with a woman'; and with regard to another, it would be underlined that 'he was consorting illegally with another woman'; and of a third, that 'he had said that they were husband and wife but this was not in fact true'; or else that someone had been found in bed with a woman. Jean-François Edé, aged 26, a native of Paris and a French grenadier, 'was suspected of several thefts, did nothing and lived with Catherine le Pain, who was supporting him'. If the inspector saw fit to write these things down, that was because they were important. It was possible to identify criminals by means of their associates and other such tokens as might turn out to be useful for making a denunciation. When François Simousse, an accomplice of Langevin, was exiled from the kingdom on 6 January 1746 it was because Fanchon had betrayed him. And because the woman is always expected to be the betrayer in the end, is it not politic to *chercher la femme?*

Because she was the heart and soul of the organization; because she moved and circulated in this marginal world, often acting as the implicit reference-point for those who possessed her; because she was the companion, support and close shadow of the man, yet neither his mother nor legitimate spouse, she was also the temptress, the corrupting influence, the unfaithful one, the traitress and the source of all dishonour and trouble. She was both link-point and the point at which the links were broken. It was in her dual capacity as fermenting agent and hotbed of hunted villains, as well as traitor and informer, that she was of interest to the police. Caught in her ambivalence, she was regarded as an essential link and cog but also as the one who might destroy everything at any moment and denounce the one whom she had adored; and thus she remains true to the descriptions of her as devoted and erratic, perjurer and renegade. In any case, and no matter what she did, she was sure to give the man away – the police banked on it.

This explains the importance of her presence on all the pages of Inspector Poussot's register, a presence which is somewhat surprising as it exceeded the usual rate for women implicated in criminal incidents. In fact this 'excess' was due to the efforts of the police and the inspector, who by focusing their attention on the women were sure that they would improve their chances of tracking down the gangs and their ringleaders. In keeping with the traditional idea that the woman was the surest pointer to the man, they gave her a major place without ever – or almost ever – having definitely established her guilt. Because immorality and concubinage were criminal offences at the time, that was enough to allow the penetration of this criminal milieu in order to pursue this or that person. One finds the same line of thinking when it came to cleaning up the centres of prostitution. It was not so much because the inspectors wanted to strike a blow at prostitution that they were interested in the brothel-keepers and the pimps, but because such establishments were very fruitful breeding grounds alongside which a whole range of marginalized and suspect people took shelter. Inspector Poussot's register singles out in particular very many women whose only criminal activity consisted of the illegal sharing of their lives with crooks, so that, in spite of themselves, they were sure pointers to their delinquent companions. By tracking down their love affairs the police turned up the criminals – they knew what they were doing.

### Attention to detail

What we have here in this register is not a vast amount of bloody crime; for out of the 2,692 persons actually arrested by Inspector Poussot there were no more than 36 cases of murder or attempted murder, and 26 condemnations to the wheel or hanging. It seems clear that the gang-leaders (Langevin, Poulot etc.) had finally been brought to book by the police and that it was rather a matter of dismantling the ramifications of organized theft bit by bit.

These groups were not so much bands of assassins as 'thieves and country rovers' and every possible means was used to get to know who belonged to them and what kinds of alliances there were, which all helped whet the curiosity of the police and which would go some way towards explaining its methods and approach. As for the manner in which the police worked, the register is obviously no more explicit than in other respects, but it does bring to light a contradiction between the luxurious wealth of infinite detail and precision on the one hand and the vague notes on the other which reveal real uncertainties and unforgivable inaccuracies.

The police paid particular attention to the relationships among the thieves whether these were family, emotional or sexual attachments. There are references to so and so's past, or to the fact that one of his parents was put in prison; his connections were noted, as was the role of his wife or concubine. In fact they dwell at length on the person's past and although the notes in the margin may not have been systematic, they clearly show a determined effort at recording events as well as taking account of the historical impact of crime at both family and emotional level. Thus the ancestry and very memory of the thief recalled in this way already intimated his guilt, even on occasion serving as proof.

Aubry, a militiaman and poacher suspected of highway robbery, was arrested by order of the King on 28 October 1748: 'His father was broken for highway robbery and murder; and since he came out of the militia he has been constantly engaged in roaming the highways by night.' It was his ancestor rather than his activities that had brought him to the prisons of Senlis. The same thing happened to Charles Baccard, a young thief of 20. He was born in Paris and sent to Le Petit Châtelet in 1747 with the endorsement that he had 'watched his father and mother being hanged' and that he had been 'taken to Bicêtre without ever having joined his regiment'. The police remembered and made use of their memories in order to incarcerate certain persons. At times one can see their quite frenetic pursuit of the activities of certain persons, their ability to gather information and the obvious degree of their organization. When Julienne Barge, aged 50, was imprisoned at La Salpêtrière in November 1750, the observations noted in the margin show that she had been known to the agencies of the inspector for some time. 'Previously hanged, she was arrested in 1733 for illicit activities and banished.' One has to suppose that she had managed to escape from her hanging. Forget, a native of Lyons, had also been known for ten years: 'He has been roaming around the countryside with his wife these last ten years and two years ago he was arrested by the beadles of the poor. He is the son of a large manufacturer in Lyons and has been wanted for some time.' In July 1746 he found himself in Fort-l'Evêque.

They were also kept under surveillance and were followed, like Jean Poitevin (a carter and militiaman, aged 22), from the village of Lument near Orléans. 'He spent the whole of the winter in Paris doing nothing but play bowls and roulette', and ended up in the spring of 1752 in the prison of Bicêtre by order of the King.

In addition to these clarifications on the offenders' past there is a whole wealth of detail included in the register the purpose of which is not quite clear; however, on essential matters the register often remains silent. Perhaps they were situations or events which had simply struck the inspector's men as important. The apparent lack of order or consistency in these details indicates that as an instrument the register still fell short of any real organization, and was rather a halfway house between disorder and a methodical filing system.

Jeanneton Prudhomme, also known as La Verdure, must have caused quite a stir by her behaviour, for the day of her arrest in March 1746 it was noted that she was the 'mistress of Camaille, who had eaten a loin of veal and peas with her the day Bonnefond was assassinated'. This appetite thus shared with her lover was a scandal worthy of being noted down. It was details such as these which compounded her guilt, for not only was she the concubine of a murderer, she also testified to a healthy appetite the day of the murder – putting her not far short of an ogress.

Details revealing that Marguerite Burette was 'well-versed in thieves' slang' and had been 'found sleeping with Pierre Echy and passing herself off as his wife when she was in fact a beggar roaming the countryside', suggest surprise heightened by the conviction that one had here abundant proof of foul play; for knowing slang obviously put her in the same category as men from the Cour des Miracles.[36]

There is a delicate balance between a sense of precision and detail and a feeling for precedents and connections and the actual apparatus of proof which together contribute to relative vagueness in the drawing up of charges. The important thing was to infiltrate these marginal places, get to know them as best one might and proceed from time to time towards making arrests, at which point the suspect was likely to find himself in prison on the same grounds as the real offender. Drouy, a soldier in the Parisian militia, was arrested at Brie fair in November 1747 'having left his military battalion after the review without leave, confirming my view that he was a good-for-nothing'. An assurance of this kind was sufficient to establish proof. If Jean Groute, known as Bourguignon, was put in the prison of Pontoise on instructions from the provost of the Ile-de-France on 13 November 1747, it was because his particulars suggested 'strong connections with those involved with theft from churches'. When Edme Gaudier and his wife and son were arrested in 1748 as 'beggars roaming the countryside together for 14 years, vagrants and vagabonds the pair of them, and both consenting to live together without being married, already in and out of prison 7 or 8 times', what the police actually wanted was to be rid of Edme once and for all. The notes read, 'there would seem to be enough proof to send Gaudier to the galleys', indicating both their certainty and yet their uncertainty.

The same attitude can be found towards the Renaud sisters; one reads: 'found in possession of handkerchieves on arrest and, there being no proof, taken to jail'. They were in fact taken to the prison of Le Petit Châtelet in 1751, as were Marie Barbe Batiste and her friend Pierre Beaulieu, both arrested at Pontoise fair 'both half-caste, speaking German, Hebrew and quite good French, of no fixed abode and refusing to answer the questions put to them'.

There is a vagueness about the evidence and a significant disproportion between the type of offence and the form of repression. There hardly seems to be any distinction between the deserter, the snatcher of a couple of shirts, the prostitute, the soldier absent without leave, or the beggar or gang-leader. The inspector concerned himself with all of them and the prisons filled up pell-mell even to the inclusion of children like little Martial Desbois, aged 12, who was admonished for being a 'vagabond associated with others, having nothing else to do but play at the end of the Pont-Neuf, or slipping into the laundry presses to pinch handkerchieves'.

We do not know very much about the depth or the extent of the repression. For certain of the accused, mention is made of their being hanged; for the rest there is silence. It is impossible to know whether they remained in jail for a day or a month. Some of the death sentences seem excessive in relation to the charge. Side by side with murder or attempted murder, one reads of the hangings of church thieves accused of taking gold braid and gold pieces or of stealing garments. It is impossible to draw any real conclusions other than for the purpose of underlining this disproportion between the very different charges which led quite arbitrarily to the same punishment.

Does the analysis of such a register really require that we reach any conclusions? The decision to interpret everything without any systematic use of statistical methods and to give preference to qualitative information be it ever so incomplete or patchy is quite deliberate. Attempting to read the register in something of a 'workman-like' fashion is both a challenge and an opportunity, for it offers the possibility of understanding certain aspects of the politics of the inspectorate as well as some of the more delinquent ways of life. In fact the 3,000 persons arrested by Inspector Poussot's men remove the veil from the Paris the prevailing order did not wish to see – the Paris which it sought out at all costs, in order to isolate it the more effectively from the rest of the population. Behind these arrests, one perceives a desire on the part of the police to infiltrate all the secret places of the capital, a desire to intervene at every level, in homes and houses as well as in the street. At the same time one can sense the utter futility of such an undertaking, especially when one comes to understand, from snatches pieced together from other sources, how this world of petty crime actually functioned. Shifting and furtive and already well organized, whether by a type of family association or according to some kind of ritualization of male–female relationships, crime and delinquency always seemed to rise again from the ashes. Poussot's register allows one to accomplish an amazing trip across the histories of certain groups of malefactors that not even death itself could interrupt.

As well as providing evidence of police organization the register reveals its impotence in strangling the existence and activity of the criminals, who were impossible to get hold of because they were so thoroughly a part of a way of life which was uncertain and nomadic, which abounded in broken relationships and which offered ample opportunities for producing rogues and thieves, but also the means of keeping them invisible.

# Part III
# Crowds

---

Crowds and gatherings were a regular part of the everyday scene, and around the urban throng and the powers that be there grew up such a complex web of stories of affection and disaffection that their origins are difficult to trace. The authorities and the mob provided each other with numerous opportunities for regular meeting. These rendezvous might be an occasion for seeking mutual agreement or else they might be a chance for some rather flamboyant behaviour deliberately intended to press home a point. It was then up to each side to make what it would of these signals by means of its own system of thought and its own reading of events. Parallel, and indeed contradictory readings of all these encounters between the crowd and the monarchical authority ran right through the social process, feeding it and nourishing it; it was a process whose dynamics were bluff and counter-bluff, and whose sequences formed the texture of the social and political climate of the city. The crowd had its thinking done for it by the authorities, whilst believing what it was given to believe, and between these two perspectives gaps grew up, were filled in, and opened up again in ways that contemporaries often found difficult to fathom. And if, like dancers in a perpetual set, they did come to some mutual arrangement and recall each other to the paths of law and order, they each did so in terms whose vocabulary differed widely.

The monarchical authority as well as that of the elites who dominated the thought of the time, and who commented on the events of which they were a part, defined the crowd in terms that were eminently contradictory at the same time as linking it irreversibly to the smooth running of the public order for which it was considered indispensable. And thus we have the crowd as animal – impulsive, squalid and dangerous; the crowd as passionate – good and grateful, offering its approval and acclaim; the crowd as friend who might be called on to express its joy and good offices; the crowd as enemy, subject to indefensible furies and gross pleasures. The crowd as indispensable.

Seen like this, the crowd appears to be one solid block; the authorities had great difficulty in seeing any of its differentiations or internal divisions. They found it harder still to make any sense of its many tensions or the various and indeed contradictory attitudes which prevailed within. Its response to being thus treated by the monarchy was subtle and enigmatic. For although its various levels and subdivisions were in fact very different, and even though it got on with the job of sorting out its own internal conflicts, it did of necessity come together as one body at those great public festivals of life and death which took place at regular intervals and where, for a few, brief moments, life was lived in symbiotic privilege with the King and his pomp. Symbiosis it admittedly was, but it was also a means of obtaining a specific reading of matters to which it had no access. Politics, the unthinkable and the supernatural, also received a visit from the crowd and the interpretations which ensued might pave the way for a number of strategies for its defence and integration, some of which might go so far as disruption.

Invited to attend the crowd most certainly was – on an almost semi-permanent basis: religious festivals; entrances of the King into the city; marriage celebrations; occasions of royal mourning; *Te Deums* for victories; the saying of masses following childbirth or on account of illness; public executions at crossroads or right in the middle of public squares. All of these made up a compelling calendar.

Called on to gather together in this way for such spectacular occasions, and obliged to follow the ups and downs of the body monarchical in all its joys, griefs or sorrows, crowds had a duty to mark, by their presence, the irreversible alliance binding them to the royal power. And even when they were not specifically invited to a royal spectacle, the crowds showed a fondness for anything unusual that might be going on in the street, whether it was some kind of game or anything else out of the ordinary. The street was a familiar setting where it was possible to stand around and gawp or chew over all the latest questions and marvels of the time. There was certainly no shortage of these, during an epoch when doctors and thinkers offered new intepretations of society and the social order almost daily according to the progress of their research, and which no longer corresponded to the traditional forms of religion which, though weakening, were still practised.

Whether they were summoned by the government, attracted by what was happening in their own space or stirred up with fear, hatred or revolt, the masses were constantly altering the relationship they had with authority and thereby constantly modifying it. Each event that brought them together transformed them and transformed the object of the spectacle that was exposed to their view.

Always described in the same way by those who looked on from a distance, the crowds were in fact always different, although they did share the same convictions, namely to be legitimate, to associate freely and to make sense. The study of crowds means trying to understand how a population in the process of change is able to produce something intelligible and believable on the basis of its own anxiety to decipher and appropriate for itself events which it had been offered as display and performance.

# 8

# Invitations to the Crowds

In response to the frequent invitations issued by the royal authority to view it in all its aspects, from the sacred and religious to the powerful and political, immense crowds came along 'columns deep' in the course of a day and in accordance with set routes and precise ritual. They came to contemplate the scene of this monarchy which could not exist unless it were seen; and the means used to achieve this, such as spectacles and festivals, marvellous firework displays and illuminations, were just part of the apparatus by which this indispensable alliance between the King and his people was implanted.

And in this respect, the eighteenth century was the inheritor of a long tradition. One only need think, for instance, of that *Tour de France royal* (the subject of a recent study),[1] in which Catherine de Medici, accompanied by her young son Charles I and their royal cohorts, decided to leave Paris for two years to travel to the furthermost reaches of her kingdom. An assembled body of loyal subjects was summoned to greet the passage of the royal nomads who, on entry to each town, put on a full display of their splendour and political will for its citizens. Festivals, tournaments and the processions by the town's institutions provided all the signs and symbols necessary for a monarchy intent on having itself recognized by the established urban elites at the same time as enlisting popular consent. At the town gates, the royal cortège was swelled to almost double by the ranks of the urban militia, guild-masters, town worthies and aldermen. The procession became one great public exhibition of the social hierarchies which made up the town, whilst the people who were not a part of the march-past were called together as one to witness it go by. Likewise the King passed, followed by the urban oligarchies, and the people looked on, contemplating the presentation of this spectacle put on for them by the monarchy and the town hierarchies by whom they were governed.

These emblems and insignia were references to a shared culture whose imagery and symbolism served as reminders of the necessary subjection of the power of the urban authorities to the royal power. The people themselves were solicited to attend by the sumptuousness of the festivities, giving their consent by token of their massive presence, yet not participating. They saw the king, drew close to him physically, but at the same time realized just how far away from him they were. The gap was obvious and it was a gap which could not have failed to make an impression and which such festivities could only have served to increase and heighten by provoking an ambivalent reaction. But in spite of being kept passive, allowed only to look, the presence of the people was nevertheless required. It was still the same in the eighteenth century: every festival decreed, each entry by the monarchy, each mass and *Te Deum* at the church of Notre-Dame, as well as being a gift offered to the people was also a call upon them.

In Paris, in addition to the celebrations on the 52 Sundays and the 32 religious festivals,[2] there were a great number of royal displays and processions. Henry IV himself was concerned about the number of working days lost, which seriously affected farming and other necessary work. In several dioceses there was a constant 'cutting back' of festivals but the custom (obviously considered essential) of turning each and every good or bad fortune of the monarchy into grounds for a celebration was retained. In Paris during the eighteenth century all this was on top of the ceremonies and processions due to the occurrence of serious events. One need only think of the number of times that the Parisians, preceded by their bishops and priests, went to fetch the reliquary of St Genevieve to process with it along precisely ordained routes in order to encourage her to interrupt prolonged periods of drought or heavy rains. Nicolas Delamare says quite clearly that 'Recourse to St Genevieve at every public disaster was a custom nearly as old as the monarchy.'[3] He notes that the first procession took place in 887 in order to bring about the lifting of the siege by which the Normans had beset Paris. 'It was a common experience in times of war, famine, infertility, flood, contagion and threats to public health. . . . It was left to the *parlement* to judge when it was necessary to resort to her. The Archbishop of Paris gave his orders and instructions regarding matters spiritual and the police magistrate then added his.' Thus the way that the government handled public disasters was by publicly requesting the intervention of the Church and her saints in organized processions for which the populace were duty bound to be grateful. And once the danger was over St Genevieve also needed thanking.

There were also many other occasions for processions when the religious and political authorities came together to make an event the theme for popular gratitude and thanksgiving, as the following example shows: on 22 October 1725 a slow procession consisting of slaves bought in the kingdoms of Morocco and Algeria by Trinitarian monks or friars set off on its way.[4] The order, signed by Hérault, the Lieutenant-General of Police, laid down both the precise route (from the church of the Friars to the Abbey of Saint-Antoine) and the conduct of the procession. It was to be led by the 63 slaves, the captain of the town and his sergeants, trumpets, kettledrums, the banner of the brotherhood of Notre-Dame-de-la-Délivrance, the clerics of the brotherhood, brothers carrying relics, the banner of the captives, standards, oboes, choir-boys, religious corporals, two sergeants and six guards. The procession, starting at 10 o'clock in the morning, was to go down the Rue Saint-Jacques, turn onto the Quai de la Tournelle, cross the bridges and follow the Rue de Fourny and the Rue Saint-Antoine before returning to the abbey.

Life in the street was lived in that particular climate where public displays and demonstrations were an extra part of everyday life. The population, always available because they were there, gave each of these events its own specific history. How it took part, the ways in which it hissed and booed or roared its approval, were all taken as significant markers, the computation of which quite often gave the public authorities cause for concern. Should the King come to doubt the fervour of popular approval then he would surely doubt, in the privacy of his own closet, the effectiveness of his counsellors and his own political path.

An echo of such princely apprehensions can be found in Louis-Sebastien Mercier:

> The court is most mindful of what is being said by the citizens of Paris; they call them 'les grenouilles' [frogs]. 'What are the froggies saying then?' was often the cry. And what a happy band they were when the froggies applauded their appearances or clapped their hands at the spectacle in the wake of St Genevieve. But occasionally their silence was punishing. In fact they were able to tell what the people were thinking about them from their bearing; the happiness or indifference of the public had a distinct character. It was claimed that they were sensitive to the reception they got in the capital because there was a vague feeling that somewhere in the crowd, wit and common sense prevailed and that there were men there capable of appreciating them and their actions and that these men, somehow or another, determined the opinion of the populace.
>
> In some circumstances, the police took the precaution of paying the loud-mouths to spread themselves around the various districts on festive occasions in order to liven things up whilst bribing the spoilsports. The real displays of public happiness and contentment, however, had a quality that nothing could upset or interfere with.[5]

This fine text needs little interpretation. If the *grenouilles* (just one of the many animals used to typify the crowd) didn't croak too well or didn't croak at all, then the princes felt punished and humiliated. The people were most certainly vile and coarse but, seeing that the success of so many of their political victories depended on them, it was worthwhile attributing to them some good sense, even though the attribution was likely to be withdrawn as quickly as it had been bestowed. But after all, wouldn't there be some people planted in the crowd in order to promote disaffection? Ringleaders and conspiracies! It was a well-known (and still used) theory; but the spontaneity of the people was a fact which no agitator could really thwart.

When the kings felt that their presence was unwelcome they made themselves scarce if they were worried about their popularity. After the events of 1750 when the people rose up against a police force responsible for snatching its children, one might recall the reluctance of Louis XV to travel through Paris; and after the accident of May 1770 at the festivities given on the occasion of the marriage of Marie-Antoinette, which culminated in the crushing and suffocation of 132 people, it was a long time before Marie-Antoinette came back to Paris. The death of Louis XV in 1774 took place in an atmosphere of indifference and contempt, as noted in scrupulous detail by S. Hardy in his Journal.[6] It was already apparent at the time of his illness that hearts were scarcely moved, and that 'the indifference of people of all estates was very noticeable, which was in complete contrast with the much-remembered demonstrations of affection shown towards him in 1744 in the course of his journey to Nancy where he had fallen seriously ill.'[7] Hardy also notes that in 1757, at the time of Damien's assassination attempt, 600 masses were celebrated in Paris as against a mere three in 1774, and a number of people were arrested each day for expounding rather too freely on the King's illness. The police intervention might have been to encourage caution but it is more likely that the number of discontented had grown. One of the stories going around was that a man in the Rue Saint-Honoré had said to one of his friends, 'Why should I be bothered? We couldn't be any worse off than we are.'[8] On 11 May, the day after the death of the King, the general opinion was that 'far from being affected by the death of this Prince, the people welcomed a change of master with an almost indecent degree of satisfaction; and that although the old King had been naturally good, over the years he had unfortunately become the sad plaything of his inordinate passion for women recommended to him by wicked courtiers interested in distracting him with a view to gaining more power for themselves.'[9]

Contemporaries like Barbier, Mercier, Rétif, Hardy, some thinkers and those close to the King were all familiar with the business of interpreting signs from the people but in fact they very rarely managed to grasp the different levels of awareness amidst the crowd, nor did they understand the desire not to appear as an undifferentiated whole. The crowd was the crowd in the same way that the people were the people. That there were dealings and transactions between an infinite number of hierarchies within that ensemble remained a closed book up until the day when there would be a specific outbreak of unrest which served to clarify some aspects of these differences more precisely.

This was the case, for example, in October 1781 when the festivities for the birth of the Dauphin were in full swing. Lenoir, the Lieutenant-General of Police, freed all the prostitutes imprisoned in Saint-Martin and Hardy relates the incidents which led to this amnesty:

> When the women came to the magistrates in a deputation to offer their thanks and to take part in the public rejoicing, the fishwives and girls who were there when they arrived were unanimous in saying that they did not want anything to do with whores and harlots and demanded a separate district for them to do their dancing in. And the cry that went up on this occasion was that there were still some standards.[10]

Festival time was a compartmentalized space whose individual shapes and separate outlines corresponded to the images and ideas the population had of itself and its own heterogeneity.


## Scenario

In complete contrast with the royal festivities, and yet complementary to them, was the whole scenario of punishment in public decreed by royal authority for those who had transgressed against it. Just like a *Te Deum* which summoned the people to attend its performance, it depended on them to reinforce its significance, and was by its very nature a part of public spectacle.

The execution of public punishment was not, as one might easily believe, exclusively a display of death. In the eighteenth century punishments were many and various, and essentially designed for maintaining a hold over the body and, with one or two exceptions, only making any sense because everyone could see them. Crimes such as begging, prostitution, petty theft and other misdemeanours and offences might warrant the iron collar, the pillory, the placard, the branding-iron, galley-slavery or carting-round. Capital punishment, although less common, was part and parcel of all this.

Pain and punishment were on show almost daily and whether it was on the square or at the crossroads, it was all part of the scenery for Parisians, coming in the same category as street-theatre, setting up stall, job-hunting at the Place de Grève, arguing on the doorstep of the *cabaret* and trooping off to the well to fetch water. It took place wherever there was life and was, in short, both exemplary and legitimate.

The death penalty had a full part in this legitimacy and exemplariness, crimes being defined in relation to it and not the other way about, according to Bernier in his lecture in 1719 on the legislation of Louis XIV where he states that 'the capital offence is, more often than not, considered to be that crime for which the usual punishment is naturally death'.[11] It was legitimate because it embodied the ancient right of the sword, the divine right of authority, the common right of all nations and the respected tradition of all. It existed as the fundamental proof of royal power and evidence of its might. The King, and only the King, had the power to appropriate the rights of life and death over his subjects and to deny them the same rights over their peers. In order that order and tranquillity might remain the guarantors of the royal authority, it was necessary that the monopoly of supreme violence belong to the King along with its obligatory converse, the right of mercy, which was all the more important for its constant reminder that death, like life, was a mere event at the disposal of the royal personage.

The death penalty had three aims: to get rid of 'the wicked', to avenge the victim and, most importantly, to deter others from crime by the horrors of the punishment. Its harshness was intended to make an impression on the minds of the people and in that respect it kept company with the rest of the body of royal ceremonial whose goal was also to stamp the mark of its authority and bounty on a heedful public. Thus, the strands of the social fabric were drawn together around this force which gave and withheld in turn, never delegating, merely endowing the people with the possibility of seeing some of the fragments, so that it might reconstitute them writ large in its imagination.[12] Such daily or weekly shows of royal strength were intended to provoke submission and consent, and not only as a result of the whole spectacular show, whether celebratory or punitive, but also thanks to the work of the imagination developing around it. 'It is the power of the imagination itself that lends power to the discourse of the powerful and nowhere is this more in evidence than in the field of custom and tradition where the whole arbitrary power of the masters is internalized as though it were required thinking.'[13]

For the execution of capital punishment to assume its full dimension, it had to be celebrated by means of an intricate ritual of signs and symbols whose repetition was to leave no room for any other thoughts other than those offered for contemplation. As with festivities, the purpose of the execution was to perpetuate the alliance between the people and the King, with punishment being only one of the more extreme objects of the exercise. The unchanging nature of the ritual was intended above all to fix the significance of this act firmly in the minds of the onlookers and public before whose eyes it was taking place, for here at the very heart of this utopia of power and authority, there was to be nothing which might permit any deviation from its initial intent and primary meaning. And thus it was essential that 'history' should not insert itself between the punishment that had been ordained and the body of the people. By 'history', one should understand all kind of contingent reality, such as the eruption of feelings other than those of commiseration or of a redemptive nature or the welling up of feelings of identification with the victim which might cause any deviation from the obligatory sequence of punishment: royal will–repentance–submission and public order. By 'history' one also has to understand a personalization of the event such as might give rise to a certain number of relationships and connections between the social and political climate, the crime committed and the seriousness of the penalty inflicted. The ritualization of the death penalty also required one to see no difference where differences did in fact exist. Given the arbitrary dispensation of the death penalty, it was essential that a domestic theft should not be deemed less culpable in the eyes of the public than a parricide or a rape, for example. In that spacious wasteland created by the royal authority and the supreme punishment, absolutely nothing had to interfere with the acts committed there, not even a hierarchy.

This sacrificial system, used by the monarchy as one of its instruments of power, can only owe its explanation to the individual and collective religious acts taking place at the same time. The participation of the priest, the ritual admission of guilt and *amende honorable*,[14] the rites of confession, prayers and the *Salve Regina* intoned by the crowd at the point where the executioner made ready to inflict death, were the sorts of gesture designed to hasten the reconciliation of the guilty man with God and through him reconciliation for those participating in the sacrificial death of the victim by virtue of being there.[15] By admitting his guilt, the condemned man (the 'Victime émissaire' [scapegoat] of M. Bee[16]) was taking on the guilt of all, and by being thus immolated as penitent and martyr, achieved a posteriori his only means of social reintegration.

Just as the King had the miraculous power of curing scrofula,[17] he also had the power of offering salvation by expiating guilt.

We are dealing here with a particular kind of alchemy which owed its success partly to the fixed nature of the event and to the absolute refusal to allow the intervention of any possible space between the punitive act and its reception by the people. The whole edifice of execution could only stand up if, based around it, there were a quasi-historic certainty that nothing should be allowed to impede or divert it. It was a certainty which presumed that the monarch, as revealed in this display of punitive activity, could be none other than the very image of perpetual gift, bounty and justice.

It was from this perspective, that is, the refusal of all political thought or interpretation of events, that a lengthy treatise and a massive amount of official action were elaborately formulated the day after the assassination attempt by Damiens in 1757, with the intention of isolating the crime as an act of insanity. Damiens had to be mad...the people could not possibly be harbouring a regicide in its bosom...it was simply impossible for the King to be killed. Derangement was in fact the only possible explanation of such a crime, for the death of the King was unthinkable, in the literal sense of the word.[18] In the masses and ceremonies invoking the King's recovery, there was much rejoicing at the improvement in his health, and constant entreaties were made to God asking Him to pardon the awful defilement this monster had inflicted. The newspapers and official journals only reported popular consternation and dismay and kept quiet about the crime itself. It would have been too risky to do too much probing; the causes of the murder attempt had to remain unknown at all costs and it was therefore essential to avoid any speculation by politicians who might be rather too keen to bring it to the centre of debate in the *partement* with particular reference to the Jansenist dispute.[19] From that point on, censorship was at its height and no interpretation of any such kind was to come out. Blindness was obligatory and blocks and stopgaps were imposed to prevent the news travelling through any obvious breaches, or by more devious routes. History, in short, was denied and forbidden from intruding, for history would only come along and provide meaning, which might overturn the only possible meaning there could be – that an attempt on the King's life was unthinkable. It was constitutionally impossible! The resort to every possible means of denial meant that all the odds were against the intervention of any sort of thought between the monarchy, its representation and its public. One must not forget that even to have considered, let alone to have carried out an attempt on the life of Louis XVI was the occasion of an unprecedented traumatic shock.

> When the revolutionaries killed the King by means of the Law and its formulations they found themselves caught absolutely in the vertiginous grip of evil. They set right against right, order against order and the world seemed turned upside down...as in those Shakespearian plays where the death of the king is presaged by sinister events such as torrents of blood and plagues of toads, or the sight of cemeteries disgorging their contents to reveal the ghastly faces of their corpses.[20]

The only 'ghastly face' one was allowed to see in 1757 was that of Damiens expiring in the course of an unspeakable punishment which had been legitimized by official decree and which inevitably surpassed all previous expression of royal might.

Having said that, however, it would be something of a surprise to find that the model execution or at any rate one faithful to the ideas of the monarchy had ever really existed. Nevertheless it had functioned effectively with the consent of thinkers and jurists up until the end of the seventeenth century, when some doubt came to be cast over its legitimacy as well as concern over its cruelty. The debate widened with Montesquieu,[21] and culminated in 1764 with the appearance of Beccaria's *'Traité des délits et des peines'.*[22] Criticism was both more thoughtful, wider ranging and more dynamic and had within its sights the whole range of criminal legislation with its injustices, arbitrariness and barbarism. Jurists were divided, but the majority of them agreed with Beccaria and the statement with which he prefaced his book: 'What I have chosen to examine in this work is that ill-defined code which is nothing more than the monstrous product of the most barbaric of centuries.' And thus developed the idea according to which the penal law should be the reflection of collective sovereignty constructed on the basis of a contractual relationship with one's peers. At the same time there were reflections on what was wrong with execution in the chronicles of events made by those who were there. It was felt that witnessing the punishment was not noble, and that men were depraved by watching such horror close at hand. Nor was the unhealthy, and at times bestial, curiosity of a people considered a legitimate support for the authority of the monarchy. Accounts of executions dwelled at length on the attitude of the people, whose complaints and rumblings of discontent were frequently heard; occasionally there would be outrage and revolt, with the guard being obliged to maintain order. Any incident could turn into an outburst of popular emotion, for taking place at the foot of the scaffold was a history of violence and passion which could so easily be turned against the current order. The glory of the punishment might be transformed into ugliness by the people who might appropriate that moment and make it their story, make history in fact, and thereby pervert the sacred meaning given to death by the King.

Philosophers and historians have reflected on such changes in emotions and sensibilities and all of them in their turn have offered their own particular mode of interpretation. Norbert Elias (1939) and Michel Foucault (1974) have placed particular emphasis on such phenomena. Elias has explained how a change in the social structures brought about a corresponding change in emotional patterns, so that from the point where there were rival social groups each contending for a small portion of power within the social edifice that had grown up between the King and his people, the whole execution performance was liable to arouse a good many reactions which were threatening for the monarchy. Foucault, researching the shift in emphasis of the punishment from an assault on the victim's person to sequestration of his soul, stressed the importance of punishment as a social and political function such that the method of punishment was not the result of a point of law or an indicator of the social structures but a technique of the power process. When the violence of the King met with that of the people, a transformation of the techniques of power was needed, giving rise to another politics by which to hedge the soul about and to insert the powers of punishment the more profoundly within the social body as a whole.

### The horrors of punishment, or 'barbarism'?

'The populace left shops and workshops and gathered around the scaffold.'[23] In the eighteenth century, chroniclers and contemporaries castigated the crowd for its fondness for public executions and punishments and subsequent historians have to a large extent taken up these allegations, describing the crowd as insensitive, cruel and indeed barbaric. There is no one who has really enquired in any depth into this alleged barbarity and the theme still recurs today. In spite of all possible attempts to explain changes in sensibilities, there is nothing which really explains what this so-called barbaric encounter between a people and a victim actually consisted of. But within this problematic relationship, it is nevertheless possible to sort out and identify some of the elements conducive to a clearer definition of popular behaviour.

There is precious little difference between one account of an execution or another.[24] We find the crowd hurrying along early in the morning, occasionally taking the trouble to hire a window that afforded a better view of the spectacle. Then there would be a long wait for the scaffold to arrive and no one would leave the scene until the whole display of agony was over. Chroniclers took the crowds' readiness to be present at punishments as a sign of their grossness and coarseness. They did, however, note the presence of people of 'quality' mixed in with the others, and this amalgamation consequently embarrassed their attempts to attribute any single definition to so composite a crowd, reproducing as it did all the usual social stratifications.

Louis-Sebastien Mercier's description of the executioner, for instance, reveals some rather muddled thinking, for he says that 'for the lowest class of people, the figure of the executioner was a familiar one', and that 'for the grosser sections of the population who went along in their droves to watch such dreadful spectacles, he was their grand tragic actor'. Not only they, but even 'polite society was drawn in by inexplicable feelings of curiosity whenever the crime or the criminal was out of the ordinary'.[25] Any hasty equations between the death of those condemned for the public good and 'polite society' who came to watch them die, are highly suspect; it would seem that all executions had a very wide public.

It was these same contemporaries who decried such spectacles as these, in which they saw baseness and barbarism reflected, who were the first to find themselves a place and take part. Some of them were particularly fond of describing what they had seen on the day of the execution in minute detail and with a lavish sprinkling of anecdotes. There are torrid accounts of the facial expressions, mannerisms and posture of those condemned or the state of their hair. It is all done with a gloating kind of curiosity which these writers seemed incapable of discerning as a contradiction; for while they castigated the vile behaviour of the mob they were actively indulging in descriptions of an atrocious kind themselves, and yet this dubious coexistence was never called into question.

Louis-Sebastien Mercier seems to have had no problem in handling this type of contradiction; in fact he did not really give it much thought, as the various sequences in his account of the execution of the famous Desrues[26] would seem to testify. He begins by protesting that the Place de Grève was too small to accommodate everyone, and calling for improvements, saying that 'executions should be held elsewhere'.[27] Besides, it did the spectators no good to have their noses right up against all the 'revolting paraphernalia of an execution as that was utterly grotesque and totally unworthy of the majesty of the law'. In short, he feels that a larger space would make the whole business more dignified and seems to be in agreement with the performance itself. He then shifts the argument into another gear and berates both polite society and the vile rabble for having run along together to watch Desrues die. 'And we think we are civilized!' he expostulates.[28] He concludes his sketch with an angry condemnation of the carrying out of executions at night by torchlight on the grounds that executions were only of any value if they were carried out in full light in front of a public which was wide awake and fully aware of what was going on. 'If you can spare him the publicity, then why not also spare him his life?'[29] Here he restates the traditional model of punishment which only attains its fundamental purity by means of exposure to public scrutiny, and thus his request for publicity and spectacle rejoins the first part of his argument concerning the limitations imposed by the location, which thus contradicts his opinions on the baseness and bloodiness of justice.

One finds in these authors what is in fact a very modern trait, namely involvement in one's own times whilst denigrating the greater part of its forms and traditions. They made sure that they were at the executions and provided full and detailed descriptions, but at the same time they were indignant at seeing all the crowds on the move for the very same reason. They seem to have found it impossible to keep any real distance between themselves and this kind of spectacle. It is something which needs further research and an attempt to interpret this attitude as being symptomatic of the population as a whole is required.

In fact, is there not evidence here of the very real difficulty of separating punishment from everything else that was going on in the street? There were so many official and unofficial events requiring one to be an onlooker. That they were taking place beneath everyone's eyes and that they invaded the street with their presence to such an extent meant that it would have required a deliberate expression of political will together with a considered and generally accepted collective refusal in order not to participate and to withdraw physically from what the execution was putting on view. Not only was retreat a physical impossibility, but recourse to such an attitude was also unthinkable. Even to have considered isolating public execution as an attestation of tyranny and to have chosen instead to make it the manifestation of opposition to the established order would have shown that the relationship with the social machine was close to breaking-point. A language by which one might express consent or disapproval did exist however, and it was used, whether this was in the general rumblings or shouts of the crowd or the rude signs and gestures made at the executioner or priest. There were also the tears of anger and pity or of heartbreak and satiation. Such emotions were predictable and the police were well aware of this, with the effect that the ranks of men from the Guard and the Watch were regularly reinforced. But to be absent, to refuse collectively to be there was impossible to envisage for the very reason that everyone, of necessity, lived on the public stage.

One could almost argue that there was in fact no actual displacement for an execution, but that what was taking place was an act of an existentialist nature, something quite normal – and no more than the living out with others of given events there on the very spot where the fabric of social reality was being created. At times of great drought or deluge, off one went in a long procession carrying the reliquary of St Genevieve; at the feast of St John there would be the ritual burning of a few cats and general merrymaking round the fire and at the feast of the Virgin, Count d'Osier's statue would be paraded around the streets of Paris to annoy the Protestants. On the tomb of Deacon Pâris men and women in a state of trance would harangue the crowds who had gathered there to listen, with lengthy testimonies to their faith; straw was spread out on Mondays in the Place de Grève to make it more comfortable to sit down and listen to all the business involved in engaging labour. In the Rue de Buci, a purse-snatcher was put in the pillory, whilst at the Montagne-Sainte-Geneviève, a young washerwoman gave birth to a stillborn child in the middle of the street and, in her distress, put him in her barrow to show him to the district police commissioner and so avoid being accused of infanticide; at the Place de Grève, brigands and highwaymen were executed. Given all of that and the fact that social reality was so ingrained with the constant flow of public displays and popular reaction, how could one possibly imagine deserting the Place de Grève on the day of an execution?

The massive attendance at public executions is borne out by the evidence and to suggest the contrary would be utopian; but this still does not mean that it can be classified as indifference. Historians have from time to time interpreted this massive attendance at punishments as evidence of the familiarity that contemporaries seem to have had with death: familiarity, indifference, insensitivity – literature and historical works abound in these kinds of assumptions and they are never questioned. Admittedly they do keep at bay, and quite rightly, all those anachronistic value judgements about the ultimate 'savagery' of our ancestors but they give way to many ambiguities and stereotypes which adorn even the greatest works. Was it not on the basis of this theme of familiarity with death which verged on the indifferent that we saw the construction of that rather curious intellectual framework concerning the absence of maternal feeling in the eighteenth century and its impact on the culture of the nineteenth? The memories of our ancestors were supposed to have been so stuffed full of accumulated deaths that they finished up with a 'mentality' where human life counted for precious little and this was the reason (according to this kind of thinking) why they had no problem at all in being part of the whole show of public execution, the spectacle of death being one of the best shared things in the world.

If this had truly been the case, why then would the act of capital punishment with its highly complex and elaborate rites of supplication have been at the centre of one of the most fundamental mechanisms of the monarchy? What then was the point of constructing such a costly ritual with such extraordinary pomp, if it was all played out against a background of collective detachment?

Certainly death was omnipresent, in the countryside as well as in the town, and it actively made its presence felt in the rhythm of accidents at work, for example, or epidemics and street violence, carriage accidents and incurable diseases. Graveyards afforded an open exhibition of the centrality of its existence and the number of children abandoned on street corners revealed its threat. Death had a public character. One could hardly ignore the death of one's neighbour, for instance, when it was customary to place the corpse before the entrance of the dwelling with passers-by slackening their pace and making the sign of the cross as they went past. Yes, of course, death was manifest, as was the sight of hardship and physical deformity. Sociability and neighbourliness were founded on this, the utterly discernible nature of the whole social body and its vicissitudes. Such ups and downs were there for everyone to read, in keeping with the whole uninterrupted rhythm of the give and take of urban life.

Death was everywhere and there was certainly a 'familiarity' with it; of that there is no doubt. But how did the idea arise that 'familiarity' could be linked so easily with 'indifference'? There is even a dissonance in the juxtaposition of the terms. To be familiar with someone implies, quite rightly, the existence of privileged ties with that person which is indeed a far cry from indifference and it is a word which suggests a whole range of intense feelings bearing no relation at all to lack of interest.

Thus as the condemned man faced his death it was quite clearly a matter of anything but indifference; in this respect, the eighteenth century contains within itself a formidable number of tensions whose explanation casts quite a different light on the execution accounts. 'The inexplicable curiosity of polite society and the vulgar populace' referred to by Louis-Sebastien Mercier is the result of the paradoxical and contradictory coexistence between the fear and horror of death and a real taste for it. These two emotions which were expressed publicly on the Place de Grève each reaffirmed the other in a way that was so complex that it exhausted all attempts at explanation, with the result that contemporaries preferred to describe the phenomenon as 'inexplicable'. It was in fact 'inexplicable' because any such coexistence was unspeakable; one was only allowed to talk about the horror, which by the end of the century had invaded everything and was clearly visible. The public cried openly, broke down in tears and were moved to revolt. On several occasions Hardy relates moments of great despair when the signs and signals emanating from the crowd left very little room for any doubt about their feelings.

There was an old tradition, for instance, whereby an appeal for clemency might be granted if a woman happened to shout out a proposal of marriage to the prisoner on the way to his death and occasionally women's voices could be heard calling out above the crowd to save the life of the prospective victim. Here and there people closed their eyes or pulled their children out of the way. One priest took ill in the middle of the crowd and another collapsed with a fever simply as a result of hearing the news that a man had been hanged for his part in the corn riots of 1775.

11 May 1775.... No one was allowed into the Place de Grève during the execution and the guard kept bayonets fixed ... A few days after this execution, the mother of one of those who had been thus punished went off to see the priest of the parish of Saint-Eustache where her son had lodged and she said to him, 'Sir, if you had been there my son would not have died'. The priest was so overcome that he was struck down on the spot with a fever and he fell ill. That the news had such an impact was confirmation of the good-heartedness of this pastor who was held in such great esteem by his parishioners.[30]

Some individuals who were rather more bold or perhaps had more conviction attempted to sabotage the structure of the gallows itself.

> Two hours before the departure for the Place de Grève [the hanging in question was for burglary], a chap of about 50 climbed up the ladder onto the gallows and took out the iron pins which held the various parts of it together and shouted out that they were for sale. The apprentice carpenter who had been put in charge of keeping an eye on this instrument of execution fought with him to get back the pins. The man said that 'he wanted to have the pleasure of watching the hangman cut a merry caper'.[31]

In addition to the horror and indignation which came with the dawning of political awareness there was also the horror pure and simple which made the sight of death intolerable from whatever point of view. On 26 May 1773, four thieves were due to be broken live at the Porte Saint-Antoine but 'they were not executed on the main concourse of the Faubourg Saint-Antoine in front of the grocer's house because the lady of the house had been delivered of a child just a short time before'.

Fear and dread of death was a constituent part of the society but one did not become accustomed to it simply because it erupted onto the scene so frequently. Sudden deaths (disappearance in the course of migration, drownings, accidents at work and violent deaths) all had a traumatic effect on friends and neighbours alike. People were horrified and scandalized by this kind of sudden and unexpected death which snatched people away from their loved ones before they could prepare themselves for it with them. Backs would be turned on corpses that had been laid out in this way without first having received reconciliation through the religious symbols of the Church. These were dreadful deaths because 'they upset the usual patterns of consolation as set out by the Church'.[32]

Even if one were prepared for it, death still provoked feelings of grief and revulsion; and the death of a child, a spouse or a loved one are recurrent themes in literature as well as in correspondence and personal journals. The fear of it was so intense that although medical progress offered some hope of rolling back its frontiers, at the same time it also provoked near panic because of fears of being 'buried alive'. If the indications of death could be deceptive, for instance, how was one to distinguish those that were precise from those that were merely approximate?

Two accounts of an execution, one by L.-S. Mercier and the other by S. Hardy, portray this fear that Death, not having quite finished the job, might have the last laugh:

> About 17 years ago there was a very attractive-looking young peasant girl who went into the service of a man corrupted by every vice known

to the big city. [A number of serious circumstances had conspired to bring her to the gallows.]

Things went badly for her as it was the hangman's son's first attempt. A surgeon had bought the body and it was taken over to his house. He wanted to get to work with the scalpel that same night but he became aware that there was still some warmth in the body. The blade fell from his hands and he put the girl he was about to dissect into his bed.[33]

For his part, Hardy tells how one evening following an execution, the barking of a dog at the Cemetery of the Innocents stirred the district to revolt as they were convinced that the dead man was still alive.[34]

Fear and dread of death was a fact; and contrary to received thinking, it would seem that it was all the more terrifying the more obsessive and invasive its presence and the more one was unable to take a step without catching sight of its hideous visage. But because death clung to life in a way that was so unbearable one had to defend oneself against it no matter what, and it was here in this place of anguish that one finds the meeting of the waters where the taste for death sprang up.

'Death, fascinating and seductive':[35] the taste for death is a difficult subject to explore because it flagrantly transgresses so many taboos. Perhaps one should begin by asking whether it was not precisely this paradoxical encounter between the mystery of dying and the permanent spectacle of death that effectively sustained such interest. No amount of bodies laid out in front of buildings nor the vast number of children deceased between nought and four years could stop the questions of what it was to die – that one unique and solitary act which proximity to it could never explain. This is what Mercier is trying to say when he talks about the people gathering together on the Place de Grève to 'see how the patient would accomplish this grand act of dying'. At the heart of that slow ritualization of agony and the prolonged gaze of the crowd upon it there resided without a doubt, the desire to taste and see, to penetrate the mystery of what it was to lose one's life.

When the chroniclers noted this strange impulse which they classed as 'barbaric' and when they discerned some degree of relish in the attitude of their contemporaries, they always held it at a distance so as not to carry even the tiniest fraction of responsibility for it themselves. No one wanted to recognize in himself or herself that 'unmentionable' bit of the truth and so they all kept it at the furthest possible distance in, it would appear, one of two ways: either by transferring it onto 'the other', the stranger in the midst, radically different and usually 'woman'; or else they described the phenomenon as being part of an ancient heritage which a progressive civilization had a duty to see off.

## *The cruel woman and the Iroquois*

The women went along in their droves to see Damiens being punished; and they were the last to avert their eyes from this horrible scene.[36]

The most delicate of women and some of the daintiest ladies from the Court...turned it into a great holiday, like going to watch some grand display or spectacle.[37]

None of the women who were there (and there were a good many of them, some of whom were among the prettiest in Paris), none of them withdrew from their windows, whereas the majority of the men could not bear to watch such a spectacle.[38]

In short, the men did not lose sight of the fear and horror of the scene they were presented with, whereas the women saw it as a great opportunity for a very heady kind of pleasure. The year 1757 was not the only time that women were castigated in this way; the theme of female cruelty stuck fast, as did that of their unbridled violence whenever there was a revolt; but one has to look beyond this traditional formula and examine not only its validity but also the way in which it allowed the taste for death in men to be concealed.

Women, they say, looked on at the spectacle of death more than men. It is certainly true that where riots and revolts were concerned, the women played an active part, especially if these happened to be connected with the price of grain, the high cost of bread or the abduction of children. Woman's flesh knew more intimately than that of man the mystery of what it was 'to live'; her privileged relationship to the child and therefore to survival itself permeated her being through and through. Sometimes the gift of life and the rapid onset of death became confused in her because she so often gave birth to children who were to die only a short while later. It was this, her sullen and violent work, which shaped her body and her spirit, and this strange amalgamation between her reproductive nature and the significant level of infant mortality that gave her a direct hold on the permanent mysteries of life and death.

If a woman were thus capable of feeling within herself both the goodness of nature as well as its maleficence, she then became, in the eyes of men, the one who most easily combined within herself some of the strands of the current thinking of the period whose self-styled harbinger was the Marquis de Sade.[39] For him, the world of Man and the world of Nature were enemies because Nature sought to annihilate everything in order to revel all the more in her ability to give new birth to everything. Crime, punishment, violence and the erotic were some of the ways of participating in this universal destruction and of thus assuring the continuity of Nature.

Death was then imaginary because in the decomposition of the corpses the processes of life were at work. Man had to adapt to Nature and not vice versa, and hence his great delight and pleasure in communing with her in the paroxysms of her unyielding will.

Men have quite rightly distanced themselves from this hopeless outlook to which de Sade's thinking led but at the same time they were incapable of, or horrified at, having to admit that in some sombre recess within themselves, there was a part which was linked to that intellectual and moral reality; and so they preferred instead to see this cruelty and barbarism as something which belonged to the female side and they compounded their observations with the conviction that women entertained particular ties and links with death.[40] Such a conclusion meant that one need not entirely reject the notion of barbarism in human beings but that one could instead situate it in the female, which understandably raised a considerable number of questions for the doctors and thinkers of the century.

Nor were women included in the legitimate or public forms of violence, as they took no part in wars and were not involved in conscription. And so, except in specific cases of criminal responsibility, they were more the spectators of death than its purveyors, in contrast with the warriors brave and true who had no need to legitimate their actions. She, the onlooker, however, had to answer for the directness of her gaze, which neither her public nor her social role could justify. The difference was an important one for it was saying, in other words, that it was one thing to be familiar with death in private – that was a recognized fact – but that this did not entitle one to adopt an attitude in public that was more like a man's. However, having recognized this attitude, the men were then able to lay it squarely at the door of the women and thus disburden themselves of any guilt in this respect.

At the same time, one not only finds the expression of some unease at seeing women give way to cruelty but it was becoming increasingly hard to understand the enthusiasm of polite society for the brutality of execution, which ought not to have appealed to anyone but 'the filthy rabble'.[41]

This visible communion between polite society and the common people gave cause for concern. 'And we think we are civilised!' exclaims L.-S. Mercier in amazement when expostulating on the death penalty. The facts that executions were still being carried out in this way and were watched with enthusiasm by such a mixture of the public, were good enough reasons to doubt the degree of civilization of a nation in which current debate revolved around the idea of progress and which prided itself on its image compared with that of barbaric peoples in far-off lands. Progress, civilization and barbarism were the standards by which contemporaries measured themselves with acute anxiety and from this angle it is interesting to study what is now a well-known text published in 1724 by a Jesuit missionary, J.-F. Lafitau, and entitled *Habits and Customs of the American Savages Compared with the Practices of Former Times*.[42] It was a book which enjoyed considerable success at the time and in it Lafitau drew a parallel between the cultures and traditions of antiquity and those of the Iroquois. He demonstrated to the world that the Greeks had also been savages and yet these very same creatures were revered by philosophers, naturalists and thinkers who made constant reference to them in their books. Furthermore, he draws comparisons between the French people and the Iroquois, most notably in a chapter devoted to the 'Punishment of slaves in the nations of Northern America'. As well as precise detail about their interminable punishments, such as the roasting alive of their slaves, Father Lafitau punctuates his descriptions with comments and opinions and makes several comparisons between the methods of the West and of France.

The Iroquois punishment was horrific. The torture that was inflicted went on endlessly, with each person present seated on a traditional rush mat, calmly smoking a pipe or chatting. He could decide whenever he liked to intervene in the punishment of the condemned person, taking 'pleasure in burning him on any part of his body he might choose; in the end, everyone took part indiscriminately'. There was no hurry: the slowness was an integral part of the ritual and the punishment. It was a bloody tragedy which continued long after the death of the victim. This all provoked considerable emotion in the author, who writes, 'This scene took place in circumstances of such enormous barbarity that the very thought of it makes me shudder', and a little later he goes on to say that these people 'perpetrate horrors [and] have no more humanity than the wild beasts'. Thus, according to traditional modes of thought which governed the thinking of almost all the chroniclers of the day, we have the Iroquois relegated to bestiality. All those who were neither learned nor bourgeois, or who did not belong to the dominant elites, were ranked along with the animals; any thinker observing what he believed to be someone different from himself was quick to call him or her an animal, be they people, crowd, woman, foreigner, savage, negro or Jew. They all provided the lawyers, doctors and thinkers with ample scope for developing a fairly comprehensive bestiary.

But then suddenly one finds the barbarism of the Iroquois confronted with a reality which is quite surprising and which confounds the author and causes him to search deeply within himself for the answers. He notes that the French treated the Iroquois prisoners with equal barbarity and indeed, he has to say, with a refinement of cruelty which even they themselves could not have surpassed. In his attempt to justify their actions, Lafitau resorts to a political bias, arguing that as a result of this 'rigorous' treatment, the Iroquois were obliged to submit. For, he says, 'Even the most mild of peoples are obliged to go beyond the bounds of their natural gentleness if they believe it would only serve as a pretext for their barbaric neighbours to become more proud and intractable.' Hence French barbarism was not natural, merely a political response and thus one could not call the French barbarians. The most one might say of them was that they behaved 'badly' (Lafitau's expression), thus banishing once and for all any other suggestion, although there is some semblance of a doubt when he says that he never knew quite what to say to the savages who criticized the French for their ferocity for, 'it was such an established fact that we did not know how to reply.'

Thus any face-to-face encounter of the French–Iroquois type would be one of barbarism versus bad form; anything else required silence, for there was too much risk in giving a name to it and too much danger in putting down another adjective which might alter the meaning and cause one to shudder.

Lafitau, a careful observer, pushes his comparison between the two civilizations even further in a desire to 'do justice' to the Iroquois and to see his own people through their eyes. The Iroquois had told him in fact of their surprise at seeing the Europeans fight each other in duels or destroy each other over some misunderstanding, or a point of honour, insult or wrong word. How could they be so little concerned about their own countrymen who had been killed by their enemies and find it perfectly acceptable to live with such indifference towards one another? For the Iroquois, the brutality of their punishments was reserved only for their enemies and they did not fight amongst themselves. To do otherwise would have been considered outrageous. Lafitau has no comment to make and once again replies with silence: 'There was nothing one could say to that, and they were shocked.' No other conclusion was suggested nor any means of pursuing an argument that was bound to end up at some point by attributing a measure of equality between the savage and the French-man, which would obviously have been considered inconceivable. Hence the silence, which was not a confession but a response to the unthinkable.

Father Lafitau's writings are only one illustration of a whole host of feelings it was not possible to read about or speak of, including for example barbarism and the fascination with death. Should one become aware of them it was essential to project their existence quickly onto others rather than on oneself and, in this case, female cruelty or Iroquois barbarity could provide a suitable vehicle.

But perhaps the truth lay elsewhere. Understanding this dread of death and yet the taste for it might be overstretching or exhausting the imagin-ation, but the place where they so obviously met up was, in fact, at the execution. It was a tension which might give way to revolt or open up the desire for revenge. The observer of death would himself die, as well he knew, and here in this incontrovertible destiny which so visibly threatened, anguish and rejection were embedded and thus, as Michel Foucault was to point out, violence could rebound, and as Norbert Elias has shown, behaviour could change. In social and political structures that were losing their coherence it was no longer possible to find execution inoffensive and thus the displacement of the taste for death was made possible by its reincarnation in the form of movements of resistance and revolt.

There were two high points in the execution ritual which went right to the very heart of this tension between the horror and the seduction of the whole affair and reactivated feelings of allegiance to the victim. Firstly, there was the *nuit blanche* ['sleepless night'], then the exposure of the corpse, on which subjects much has been said by witnesses; copious notes and comments by S. Hardy and Procurator Gueulette are also outstanding in this area.

## The nuit blanche *at the Place de Grève*

At 11 o'clock on the evening of 16 April 1775, a man guilty of highway robbery was broken at the Place de Grève.

> On arrival there he asked if he could go to the Hôtel de Ville. He was not executed until 11 o'clock at night, by which time he had sent for various people and had eaten an omelette, thereby proving the firmness of his resolve right up until the very last moment, for they say that he had even wanted to get undressed by himself. He was strangled before any blows were delivered.[43]

It was a familiar scene. On arrival at the place of execution, the condemned man could refuse to mount the steps leading him to his punishment and demand instead to go to the Hôtel de Ville to meet with his judges once again and make a fuller confession, giving the names of new accomplices or making interminable statements which held time in suspense. Such time as this snatched back from death was scrupulously respected by crowd and judges alike; secretaries took down the words of the condemned man, whilst sergeants made it their business to go off and look for these newly denounced accomplices on the spot so that they could be brought before him immediately. Confessions and questions came one after the other in this night of last-minute admissions which was also known as the *nuit blanche*.[44] The public would remain there, endlessly waiting for the guilty man to emerge. If it took a long time, the punishment would take place in the light of torches and his cries would be accompanied by the flickering of their flames.

Commentators have always been fascinated by these last tragic moments salvaged from death and they made every effort to find out the details. Gueulette, the King's Procurator, was very well placed to do this, and it is from him that we have the most precise information on those hours snatched back in this way from the jaws of death.

For a few hours the world was turned upside down. The condemned man became the master whilst the judges attached the greatest importance to these desperate measures. Everyone was bent on doing his bidding: they lent him their ear, wrote down his proposals, incoherent though they might be, went to look for whatever food he might occasionally request, tried to calm him down or else he was given orders to take some rest; rapid attempts were made to find the accomplices he had named, or he might be urged to make his confession. This morbid haste to meet his needs was the ultimate gift made to him by society before it stripped him of everything. In these extraordinary *scènes de l'hôtel de ville* ('town hall scenes'), where fears were heightened and raw emotions were on show, anything was possible – long farewells, drugging of the terrified body, or perhaps displays of absolute contempt when the condemned man cursed God and all that lay before him. These macabre scenes, so wretched and inept, were the place where the judges tried to make out who on earth this man was whom they were sending to his death and who made no end to his desire not to go there.

In this situation food and rest assumed a privileged yet paradoxical place which is commented on in turn by each observer. On 30 May 1775, Récollet was hanged for burglary.

> When he arrived at the place of his punishment he asked to be taken to the Hôtel de Ville and was not executed until half-past six in the evening. I found myself on his route as he was descending the steps of the grand staircase of Le Châtelet. He appeared repentant and contrite and I heard him ask God out loud to pardon him. I learned with some surprise that not only had he had the courage to eat some soup and boiled beef for his dinner but that he had even asked for something else which had been refused him. I didn't hear whether or not he had accused his accomplices.[45]

Too many requests for food smacked of indecency and wickedness but for the condemned man it was a kind of revenge. Dying with a full gut, something perhaps never before experienced, was an act of defiance in which poverty and cynical mockery combined. There were some determined to eat a full spread and, to the embarrassment of their judges, invited them to join them.

Jean Marguenne died on 19 March 1765 looking every inch the scoundrel. Before leaving Le Châtelet to go to the Place de Grève, he told the Lieutenant in charge of criminals to make sure that there would be a good meal provided as he had a good twenty-four hours' worth of declarations to make at the Hôtel de Ville.[46]

On the other hand, if one became too weak, by refusing to take food for instance, or by talking non-stop to the point of exhaustion, this might constitute a mortal risk that the doctors and surgeons would then take in hand. Hard as it is to imagine, attention was paid to caring for the body precisely at the point of its entry into death and can only be explained by the intimate conviction that the guilty man should be 'in good health' when he got onto the wheel. Execution was a deliberate punishment and not an unlicensed and unbridled act to be dealt to a body which was already in a state of depredation. Besides, there were things the public would simply not tolerate, such as those occasions when an execution turned into the mere finishing-off of a body which was not even capable of standing up and supporting itself; nor would they put up with incompetent executioners who needed several attempts at the job. There was a definite order to this slow procedure leading to the infliction of death on a guilty man, an order which had to be observed and a respect whose limits were somewhat obscure.

Jean Falconnet was taken to the Hôtel de Ville on the night of 23 February 1732 and during the night of the 24th he begged them 'to let him have a few hours rest as in his present state of mind he would not be able to endure any act of justice, collapsing with fatigue and overcome with sleep as he was'.[47] The doctor who was quickly summoned looked him over and found that his pulse was very weak. He said that 'unless he had a few hours' rest, he did not think that he would be able to keep going for much longer and that there might even be some risk to his life'. The confrontation therefore did not recommence until the morning of the 25th; the punishment was to take place later when all risks to his life had been avoided in order that it might be removed definitively a few hours later.

The same kind of precautions were taken in the case of torture. Desrues, a grocer who had poisoned a woman and her child in order to rob them, was himself of a somewhat 'delicate complexion' and had been subject to only minimal torture, but he was so feeble-bodied that even the reading aloud of his sentence had made him ill, thus justifying the precautions that had been taken. While the details of his sentence were being read out, 'it is said that he had undergone a movement of the bowels which had greatly offended the noses of all present', notes Hardy prior to relating this long-awaited execution which took place in May 1777.[48]

The *nuit blanche* was a time of confusion and intense feelings when everything became blurred and was concentrated in a sense of tragic urgency. There were tears and sobs, involuntary movements of the body, or a need to pray and read psalms of repentance and entrance into the Kingdom of God. Printed copies of 'revelations' of this kind of conversion of body and soul sold in their thousands both before, during and after the execution. Gueulette contented himself with commenting on just a few, in particular the extremely long 'Account of the conversion and edifying death of a young girl, an assassin's accomplice, executed in Paris in the month of January 1737'.[49] All the details were there: the young woman cried and prayed, expressed anxiety in moments of doubt or fatigue, became exultant with joy at feeling in good health at the approach of death:

> At that point she enjoyed perfect health, which caused her to say, with a kind of joy, that God had delivered her from all her weaknesses and had given her to understand that he wanted a victim who was sound and healthy and that there was nothing weak or feeble about her sacrifice.

And according to this text, she died crowned with happiness at the prospect of her future encounter with God.

This period of waiting in the face of death was a place of redemption; it was also the place for love. But among the guilty and condemned there were those who had no inclination to pray, such as Michel Rouleau, a tailor who had been condemned by an order of the court of the *parlement* of 30 June 1760 to be broken live whilst his lover, Marie-Jeanne Oville, was due to be hanged at the Place de Grève. They had both been involved in the premeditated murder of Marie-Jeanne's husband. Gueulette had noted with some surprise 'a rather strange story' on the back of this printed order. The woman had

> asked to be placed on a mattress by Rouleau's side and the request had been granted and everything agreed. The strange thing was that although this woman claimed to be repentant, what she actually said to Rouleau bore no relation at all to her actual situation. She kissed him repeatedly and in her own way said all kinds of sweet and tender things to him, assuring him that she would love him right up until the very last moment of her life.[50]

The prospect of death did not always call forth resignation and repentance. There were those who, somewhat more rebellious than the rest, used the *nuit blanche* as an act of ultimate defiance and as a means of spewing up over a world which had arrogated to itself the right of meting out such dreadful punishment. Others, whose sole aim was to put off the evil hour of punishment, made denunciations of distant accomplices who, when confronted, proved to be innocent.

The scenes between the potential victim, the accomplices who were dragged along in the middle of the night, and the confessor responsible for recalling the future victim to the paths of repentance were indeed violent. Often the condemned man was so distraught that he would go back on his declaration, saying that 'there was nothing true in all of what he had said and that he had only done it to prolong his life as he had been advised at Bicêtre.'[51] Or else, after testifying to the innocence of those he had sent them looking for, he might provoke the Lieutenant in charge of criminals, insult him and roar with laughter at having been able, while all this was going on, 'to get a good meal in at the Hôtel de Ville'.

In amongst all these turbulent scenes of heady words and imprecations which were as desperate as they were violent, the demand was for life. The supposed accomplices who had been freshly denounced and seized in the middle of the night threw themselves at the feet of the condemned man, proclaiming their innocence, as in the following case recorded in the margin of notes made by Gueulette on an order made on 17 October 1764 condemning Pierre Padoix, a cobbler's boy, to be hanged at the Place de Grève for burglary. Apparently a surgeon's wife was dragged out to the Hôtel de Ville to appear before him and 'the surgeon's wife was so stunned by this declaration that she collapsed in a faint and died the same day after being taken to the prison of Le Grand Châtelet with all the others.'[52]

Death for death's sake. Indeed, why not make a denunciation? One can quite easily understand the fear felt by the accomplices and fellow-travellers of those robber-bands on the great highway whose networks of marauding brigands were so efficient and widespread. Their fear could often be the occasion of some rather unusual scenes of trafficking and dealing, as for instance in 1743, when Volteface, a journeyman joiner, was condemned to the wheel for theft and murder. His accomplices went in fear and trembling of being denounced by him and so they made the most of his fear of the world beyond and of Divine Judgement:

The night before his execution a message was passed along to him from cell to cell promising him eight masses to be said the day after his death if he did not make accusations against two of his accomplices who were still alive. He promised not to do this and kept his word by accusing only those of his companions who had died at the Place de Grève. In the time it took to get him down from the cart, it is said that a small boy presented him with a note which was then taken from him. It was a receipt for the eight masses. This information was obtained from Mr Vautroux, Commissioner at Le Châtelet and one of his judges.[53]

Those nights at the Hôtel de Ville took place somewhere between the devil and the deep, in a space between life and death. There were even occasions when the condemned man had been tied to the wheel and yet still demanded to be heard; the clerk would kneel down beside him to take down his final words. Death was not a simple business. The *nuit blanche* was a time and a place which was taken very seriously by the judges and treated by them with great respect. To some extent, a man's word and his repeated confession rendered him innocent of the judgement made by men; but there was also something more to this face-to-face confrontation between a man and his judges, and to this final encounter, be it desperate or provocative, submissive or vengeful, between the wise and wretched. Perhaps it was, in fact, the only moment capable of explaining what remained inexplicable and disconcerting for magistrates and for the public, and by that I mean that enigmatic space between the crime and the man committing it. It was a gap crowned by a *nuit blanche*, where the repeated confessions of the criminal made him more man than monster. There beneath their eyes, the judges could make out their own image, that of a humanity which the death they had decided upon would not be able to efface.

## Stripping the body

Since the punishment was the divestment of the body itself, the *amende honorable* was made 'naked or lightly clad' and, in the case of breaking on the wheel, punishment was inflicted on the body in a state of total undress. The women, however, managed to escape this particular punishment 'on the grounds of the respect due to their sex', and instead they were hanged in a light gown, their hair covered by a bonnet.

Public nudity was at this time becoming less and less common and since the end of the seventeenth century, for instance, there had been regular police orders outlawing the male practice of nude bathing in rivers, which was generally considered shocking.[54] It was no easy battle, however, as bathing trips on the Seine were part and parcel of popular Parisian pleasures.

The struggle was taken up on another front during the eighteenth century by the religious brothers in the Christian schools who attempted to impress a sense of decency and respect for the body on the children of the poor, teaching them, for instance, that they should at all costs avoid looking at another person's body as well as at their own. Boarding-school regulations and the dissemination of treatises concerning aspects of Christian conduct helped convey the new message of bodily discipline and training in an attempt to introduce some order into the kind of promiscuity engendered by popular housing and accommodation in Paris and the urban way of life. By the end of the century, male nudity in public caused something of a scandal and it was a sight that had become increasingly rare.

But for all that, there was still that rather gay abandon of the more rumbustious festivals, or during the dog-days of harvest, for instance, when the harvest workers were allowed to undress and take their refreshment in the nude on account of the excessive heat. On such occasions nudity was tolerated because it was a normal part of festive pleasures or traditional harvest custom in the heat of the sun. It bore no relation whatever to the statutory shameful nudity required in order to pay the price for one's misdeeds. In this latter case, the naked body was offered as a public spectacle bearing all the marks of humiliation and shame.[55] Thus the only occasion when the exposure of someone else's body was permissible was in that final moment when the punishment of the victim came crashing down upon him as a visible demonstration and clear example of its full horror and monstrosity.

Guilty, abominably execrated and humiliated, the body of the victim rapidly attained the status of both the sublime and the obscene, capable of assuming a dimension that was both pitiful and heroic and of arousing as much terror and revulsion as cynical contemplation. As the punishment took place, the world turned upside down and the body, that privileged target of the torture, became the one unique place where all eyes converged in a mixture of dread and fascination.

There are so many relevant manuscripts and printed documents in so much detail on this subject as to reveal quite unwittingly the place of primary importance accorded to it. Because society at that time was so visual and mannered, it was customary to interpret much on the basis of the body's signs and signals; for, before it is anything else, and least of all a public spectacle, the body is a language. Naked and dying, it was both language and spectacle.

Its appearance and constitution afforded the spectators a vast amount of information and nothing was considered unworthy of comment or lengthy interpretation, whether it was a tearful or effeminate face, a wild look, a body that shook and trembled or threatened revenge, or perhaps angry gestures or pleas and imprecations.

There were a variety of ways in which the condemned person might either accept or reject the turning of his body into a public spectacle, as in the case of Billiard, the cashier at the office of postal administration (quoted by Michel Foucault). He refused to lower his hat over his eyes and instead, with clear ostentation, attired himself in the finest apparel previously used to mourn his wife, who had apparently died the year before. He shod himself in fine new shoes and made sure that his hair was 'well curled and powdered'.[56] All this public show was an attempt to transform a pathetic breach of trust into an act of heroism which was to 'impress itself' on the public.

Then there was the young servant of only 20 who was condemned to the wheel for murder. He sobbed and sobbed and was so convulsed with grief that he softened the hearts of all those watching him so that the public were moved to revolt on account of his youth which approaching death had transmuted to innocence (20 April 1773).

In 1775, after the bread riots, the population was sickened at the sight of a thief who was hanged while unconscious and 'frothing considerably at the mouth'.[57] His loss of 'sang-froid' had transformed his death sentence into the vilest butchery. Two years later, in 1775, the same population were concerned at being unable to read anything from the face of Desrues, the famous poisoner: 'His physiognomy was so mute and cold that it was extremely difficult to discern the agitation by which his soul was most surely afflicted.' Giving nothing away about oneself was a fault which the public found hard to forgive, for how could one know what one felt towards this victim, how should one identify with him? Not knowing anything about him took away any sense from his death and removed any meaning from his punishment.

Even in this final chaos, suffering still had its rules and the body was not to be abused needlessly. To be endowed with a robust constitution, for example, was not a reason for the executioner to prolong the punishment; that would have been considered particularly unjust. The judges were well aware of this and attempted to fit the form of the punishment to the resistance of the guilty man. This was certainly the case for a Franciscan friar who was sentenced to the wheel for murder on 7 October 1779. The sentence passed on this man was

> that he should be placed alive on the wheel and remain there so long as it pleased God to spare his life; but, as the life and suffering of this unfortunate man, whose constitution was so robust, would have been drastically prolonged if such a sentence had been carried out, the *parlement* had included in its certificate of confirmation permission for him to be strangled in the event of his remaining alive on the wheel for more than 3 hours.[58]

Moderation for the body in its state of total violation. What respect!

Upon this increasingly precarious balance established between spectacle and punishment, any unforeseen infringement of 'the rules' might lead to rumblings among the crowd or become a source of rebellion. Incompetent executioners who needed several attempts at the job or who set about dismembering the corpse with neither caution nor restraint were hissed and booed by the crowd and castigated by a population who were only prepared to 'accept' a spectacle provided it remained faithful to their own expectations. In 1751, when Jean Masson was hanged at the Place de Grève for domestic theft, Procurator Gueulette protested about the disgraceful conditions of the hanging, for the rope broke and the man was hurt. He was finally strangled to death on the ground only to be 're-hanged' once he was dead. 'The people cried out for mercy and the *archers*, with bayonets fixed, turned on the people and pursued some of them, thereby causing considerable upheaval.'[59]

There was certainly an unwillingness to accept a breakdown of the rules but there was also a collective sense of God's judgement. If death itself did not want any truck with him, could Jean Masson really have been so guilty? One also needs to add that by 1751 the death penalty for domestic theft seemed unjust to more than one or two and for it to be badly administered into the bargain was intolerable.

When it came to handing over the female body in a state of semi-nudity as a public spectacle, this gave the opportunity to some writers to describe details they would not otherwise have thought of mentioning had the criminal been of the male sex. Gueulette, for example, seems to have found it very difficult to put aside the image of the women who were being punished and he usually noted in the margin some observations about their physical appearance such as the harmony of their proportions, an attractive face, the subtle roundness of a breast or even a lock of hair which might suddenly have fallen from the bonnet they were wearing for the hanging: 'La Groison [hanged in 1755] was a strapping young girl, quite pretty and rather well developed.' There were some instances when the women claimed, and were granted, the right to set off for execution wearing a veil; but Gueulette, for instance, was quite scandalized by the according of this 'honour'. In 1743, some women who had been accomplices of the notorious brigand Raffia were taken to the gallows. Marie-Françoise Lefort, a receiver of stolen goods and accomplice of the murderer, was hanged on 4 July 1743 and Gueulette complained that

La Lefort was very reserved but neither I nor anyone else could see her face as she had fastened her mob-cap over it with a pin and all the rest of Raffia's wretched followers had also obtained the right to be taken to the gallows in this way; they still had their faces covered when they were strung up. La Lefort was taken to the Hôtel de Ville and she left there at 1 o'clock in the morning to be hanged with her face still covered.[60]

Here we have a particular relationship to the female body which involves a number of rather grey areas in which anger and indignation intermingle more or less ambiguously with some of the more traditional forms of seduction and pity. One need only read Hardy to see that Gueulette was not alone in feeling this way. The former relates how, following the death of the infamous poisoner Desrues, who has already been mentioned, his widow was herself charged with complicity. Whilst in detention she gave birth to a child and afterwards was sentenced to branding and imprisonment for life at La Salpêtrière.[61] She was due for public branding on the shoulder on 13 May 1779 in the courtyard of the Palais de Justice but just as she stepped down from the prison cart to be branded, she threw herself to the ground between the axles and refused to move. Whilst she was out of sight of the public, the executioner of the High Court of Justice stripped her shoulder bare in order to burn it. A further irony was that all those who had climbed up the bell tower of La Sainte Chapelle to get a better view 'were left looking all the more like fools as the emplacements for reconstruction work at La Palais had prevented them from getting close up'. Only Hardy, it seems, managed to get a good look and he saw that she wore 'her hair like a bather's with only a couple of locks [showing] on either side'.

Female crime and its punishment certainly stirred the imagination most vividly: on the one hand, there was the hatred of this female monster, often expressed in seductive language but which also allowed to creep in the image of the repentant and penitent criminal who possessed redemptive qualities. Popular 'rags', 'true stories' and laments, for example, were particularly fond of celebrating in one and the same account both the heinous crimes of the woman and her virtues. In this way, the punishment was turned into sacrifice, as in the 'Account of the conversion and edifying death of a young girl, an assassin's accomplice, executed in Paris in the month of January 1737',[62] which has already been cited. It tells how the faces of the magistrates were bathed in tears whilst she, the condemned woman, consoled chaplain, judges and fellow detainees in turn. Thanks to her mediation, prison, 'that place normally inhabited by wild beasts', was shown to be a place of affliction, redemption and peace where through the agency of feminine wisdom and gentleness, the crime was transmuted.

This same duality in relation to the punishment of women and its effects on the individual imagination was shared by the popular literature of the period concerning women. In it one finds a perpetual coexistence between these two faces of woman. In answer to the seductive troublemaker and dispatcher of Death, one has the angelic tenderness of the one in whom true virtue abides. These images call out to each other continually, constantly re-echoing and contradicting one another.

Nor did the death of the victim interrupt the work of the imagination or the antinomy it had so ambiguously constructed. This young woman who had thus repented was to receive burial in a Christian grave. 'Some of her own sex came by cab to fetch her for burial. They placed her in a coffin to take her to the cemetery where she remains to this day awaiting the Day of the Lord.'[63]

In contrast, an entirely different lot awaited the widow Lescombat (notorious for having murdered her husband, aided by her lover). While she was still alive and in detention, a cast had been made of her hand and her arm as she was very beautiful. After her death, as was the custom with other criminals, her body was reclaimed by a medical surgeon, in this case, one Sieur Hérissant, whose treatment of her was bizarre. Gueulette, who went to his house to see her, had the following to relate:

I saw Lescombat beneath the glass. She was dressed in the gown she had worn for the execution and placed upright in a cabinet with bare feet and legs which were rather on the large side. Her skirt was a little tucked up on the right because on her hip she was holding a little fox cub which had a goldfinch in its mouth. She had strong arms and beautiful hands and in general her skin was pale and fine. Her belly looked as though she had risen straight from her bed without thinking; her breasts were beautiful and finely veined though her bosom was quite well covered. As to the head, that was somewhat gross – the eyes had been made of enamel and were black, the nose rather snub, the lips bright red and the mouth small and very beautiful. The face was set square and still wearing that affronted look it had had whilst alive.[64]

Undoubtedly beautiful as Lescombat was, she was still 'affronted'; it was in this encounter between Beauty and the crime that the seduction was played out. And so this doctor, over and above the excesses of the punishment and death, had taken the body and painstakingly reconstructed it in a macabre and erotic work of the imagination in which every detail counted, from the fox cub to the finch, not to mention the raised skirt. The tortured body had been forgotten and had been transfigured by means of the affronted seductiveness it suggested. What Dr Hérissant's macabre piece of work illustrates at the crudest level, and in a way one would neither have expected nor sought, is the extent to which the punishment of women was a public spectacle of seduction and death. Lescombat is the other face of the repentant Dupuis and rather than conflicting, the images are actually an expression of the male–female conflict itself.

By now executions had not only become too disturbing for the imagination; they also created a real disturbance in social terms. Anything could happen; the crowds who gathered there were no longer capable of serving as receptacles for the single message emanating from a repressive monarchical authority. They saw the horror of it and felt the impact of feelings which were both clear and confused. The crowds thus summoned by the King could no longer be guaranteed to grant him their popular approval. The allegiancies they had begun to practise were other than those predicted.

## When the Dauphin decided to marry Marie-Antoinette

[*Marking the appearance of a crack at the heart of the performance and when nothing was ever the same again.*]

Cracks begin in the dark. Long before they gape and yawn, they are what one might call mere faults, whose disruptive work is begun along narrow, almost invisible channels. After the split, comes the final breach and collapse. Too late then to warn anyone – only time to fill in at top speed what are by now positively indecent gaps through which come chaotically tumbling out, the many aspects of the truth.

Feasts and festivals were all repeats of the same thing – from the mounted portraits of royalty to the bounteous hand-outs accompanied by the sound of trumpets and the burst of fireworks. They shed their light, wealth and pomp on a people who were requested to assemble together with unshakeable loyalty, rejoicing and content. To have taken time to perceive these men and women as any other than as passive receptacles of the royal spectacle would have been rare indeed; and should one have happened to discern a crack there, then all that was required was the lavishness of the royal bounty and the blaze of the illuminations, to stop it up. The mask was superb, if nonetheless derisory.

In 1770 the crack had already been deepening for about 20 years.[65] There were murmurings among the people and in the street it was hardly quiet. Preparations were underway for nuptials, and the Duc de Choiseul was putting everything into what was an affair of the utmost importance – the opportunity for securing an alliance between France and the House of Austria. The marriage was to be the occasion of great pomp, more superb and dazzling than any other celebrations given even during the time of the Great King. On 30 May 1770 Paris witnessed the marriage of the Dauphin and Marie-Antoinette, 'one of the most important marriages in the reign of Louis XV', according to Moufle d'Angerville.

### Inauspicious omens

Arrival in France; meet the Dauphin at Compiègne; entry into Versailles; marriage in Paris: the celebrations were spread out over more than a month and they were not always so fine as envisaged. In that year, poverty had invaded the towns and the countryside; but that was a mere shadow to be brushed aside with impunity – the show must go on.

To give you some idea, it was estimated that 30,000 horses would be needed for the journey and there was some talk of a detachment of tapestry-workers travelling in relays from town to town in order to appoint and decorate the various places at which the Princess was to stay. That part of the cortège that had gone to fetch her from Strasbourg consisted of 60 brand-new chaises.[66]

While back in Paris the crowd were all off at the Royal embroiderer's having a look at the princely 'outfit', the provinces were being shaken by a number of revolts brought on by famine. Tours and Besançon were particularly affected by the disturbances, whilst in Manche and Limousin around 4,000 persons died of hunger. It was vital that this news should not get about and there was a diversionary article in the *Gazette de France* of 14 May 1770 which stated that there were large grain reserves in Nantes but that distribution had been held up because the rivers were in full spate. It was just possible to prevent the cries of the people reaching the throne for a brief while but it was not possible to stop the spread of news from the provinces to Paris. Pamphlets and broadsheets sold under the counter were easily obtainable; these attempted to show, for example, how all the money that was being spent on the celebrations might actually be spent at a time when famine was making its presence felt throughout the realm. One such was entitled *The Singular Idea of a Good and Honest Citizen Concerning the Public Celebrations to be Held in Paris and at the Court on the Occasion of the Marriage of Monseigneur le Dauphin*. It was a lively attack on royal ostentation and pomp and a plea for a deduction of the cost of the festivities (estimated at 20 millions) from that year's taxes, and the *taille* in particular.[67]

> Thus in place of entertaining the wastrels of the Court and capital with idle distractions of a fleeting nature, joy might swell in the soul of the farmer; and the whole nation might participate in the happy event.... History would dedicate this deed to posterity more gladly than all the frivolous details of a magnificence which is burdensome to the people and far removed from the true grandeur of a Monarch who is indeed the father of his subjects.

Was it a sign? At the rendezvous at Versailles, there seemed to be no great pomp or ceremony and neither the illuminations nor the fountains worked very well on the arrival of the Princess. As for the poor, according to accounts by contemporaries, they were obliged to beg instead of receiving the customary hand-outs of bread, wine and sausage.

In Paris, however, every preparation was being made for the day of the marriage.

The grand finale of the celebrations was set for 30 May 1770. In the evening there was to be a grand firework display by the celebrated Rugiéri on the Place Louis-XV whose crowning glory was to be a gigantic volley of 30,000 rockets and just for that one brief fairytale 'twinkling of an eye' an immense crowd was expected.

## A night of disaster

'Carnage', 'dreadful butchery', 'the aftermath of battle', 'a city under siege' . . . Contemporaries were dumbfounded by the injustice and the extent of the accident that occurred on the night of the firework display.

The fireworks had just finished: everyone was a little disappointed as the best part of the display had gone up in flames before there was even time for the explosions to cascade in patterns of light. The crowd was preparing to leave the square to head for the boulevards and wait for the illuminations; the shortest route was by way of the Rue Royale and they proceeded quietly along it. Equally quietly but in the opposite direction, those crowds of people who had been at the entrance to the boulevards and who had not been able to see the best of the displays were trying to make their way towards the square. In order to do that, they too took, or attempted to take, the Rue Royale. At the same time the carriages which up until then had been parked behind the colonnades quite brutally cleared a passage for themselves.

An altogether ruthless scrummage then ensued; the two columns of people in party-going mood came together in a dreadful crush. A 'river of people' was now split up by vehicles 'driving in different directions along the street in tightly packed clusters. Some of the men and women who had been tossed about in this way were already too weak to stand up to further pushing and shoving and some had the misfortune to catch their feet in drains and gutters and on stones.'[68] There was general disorder, with whole sections of this human tide affected by panic. Some of the frames supporting the illuminations and a couple of carriages were overturned. These were immediately trampled over by some of the crowd who perched on top of the debris which they used as a refuge for catching a breath of air.

The horses went mad in the crowd of men and women who, already half-suffocated, expired beneath their hooves. There were some who were so squashed that they died standing on their feet, one against the other as they had no other recourse. A police report notes that 'there was blood coming from their mouths, noses and ears and they only fell to the ground when the crowd no longer supported them.'[69]

Death such as this, occurring right at the heart of the celebrations, was perceived as a serious tragedy. Such negligence on the part of the police and the organizers at an event like this was taken as an obvious sign of lack of concern for the safety and security of ordinary people who had been invited along to the feast to clap their hands. So bound up were the celebrations in the desire to see the people go through the required motions that the very conditions which might have made their enthusiasm possible were forsaken. Once the accident had occurred, it was time for all the actors on the social stage to undertake their own interpretations of events, which obviously conflicted with one another as various interests were at stake. It was impossible for the King to emerge any the greater for this day, if for no other reason than forgetting that the terms of the alliance could not work unilaterally.

The figures given the following day conflicted, and there was no real agreement on the number of victims.[70] In his *Tableau de Paris*, Louis-Sébastien Mercier mentions the accident on two occasions.[71] As an eyewitness, he first of all refers to 1,500 persons who died of suffocation and then some considerable time afterwards he recalls that there must have been about 1,800: 'I witnessed the catastrophe of the 28 May 1770[72] ... and I almost lost my life myself. Between twelve and fifteen hundred people perished either that same day or as a result of that dreadful crush.'

However, one thing seems almost certain (corroborated moreover in the police archives), and that was that 132 bodies were picked up from the area of the celebrations and they were set out in a line at the Cemetery of La Madeleine for identification by their neighbours and relatives. Each corpse had a card with a number on it and a detailed report on the physical appearance and clothing of each was kept in the dossiers. Furthermore, any articles found on the person of those who had perished were returned to each family by the registry office.

In spite of these precautions, rumours still circulated and contemporaries make reference to them here and there. Someone was sure that he had seen the number 134 on the front of one of the unfortunate victims. And elsewhere Hardy reports in his Journal of 4 June 1770 that the public had received definite information from a police bulletin 'that the estimate of the number of deaths had risen to 367'.[73] In fact the number of injured was so great that it was scarcely possible to know the exact number of those who had died as a result – 500? 1,000? 1,200? It was impossible to be any clearer than that, as d'Angerville explains in his commentary on the incident:

> In addition to the injured, there were those who had been lamed or were suffering from suffocation and were taken into hospitals or neighbouring homes to die shortly afterwards. There were also those who thought they were unscathed but who afterwards found they were spitting up blood and within six weeks or so discovered that they too had become victims

of their curiosity, making in all anywhere upwards of eleven or twelve hundred.[74]

The public were kept regularly informed – indicating the extent of police diligence in the affair – and then after a short while a fresh estimate was circulated in the city through the distribution of police bulletins: 688 persons were pronounced dead excluding those who had subsequently been taken to their homes. The bulletin was at pains to classify them and Hardy gives the details: 'Religious, 5; priests, 2; distinguished persons, 22; bourgeois, 155; common people, 424; unidentified, 80.' As one can see, there were no subdivisions among the ordinary people; artisans and odd-jobbers were all lumped together under the same heading. Police bureaucracy remained true to the prevailing ideology of the day; only the people themselves were aware of the numerous subtle differences by which they were constituted.

In any case, at the time of the first count Hardy assures us that 'they had picked up enough corpses to fill 11 vehicles'; in fact there were 132 dead: 89 females and 43 males including 11 children aged between 6 and 14.

Were there more women than men at this celebration? In the event of buffeting by the crowd, were they more vulnerable? Items in the dossier occasionally mention that a husband was waiting for his wife to return, an indication that people did not necessarily go as couples to such festivities, but then there are other examples that would seem to contradict this and of course there are any number of examples where no evidence of this kind is available, so regrettably one must leave this to one side. One can be more or less certain, however, that these ordinary folk were not well off and yet strangely enough half of the women were designated by their husband's profession, although it is hardly likely that they would have had no employment themselves.

In any case, for the most part they would have belonged to the world of the menial trades or domestic service. Where in fact the personal profession was indicated, these were most often as workers in establishments connected with laundry, lacemaking, dressmaking, spinning or as kitchen maids. The wives of artisans (engravers or locksmiths) were few and it is unknown whether their spouse was a master or journeyman. There was only one woman who was a member of the master class and she was a master dressmaker. It was easier to distinguish between the men: 4 of them belonged to the world of the bourgeoisie (lawyer, shipowner); 4 were traders, 2 were masters, 9 were journeymen, 3 were apprentices or shop hands and 9 worked in menial jobs such as cleaning or as clerks.

For the most part these were ordinary, undistinguished folk, who had slipped in with all the others to go along to the festivities that had been provided for them – people from the world of work and small artisans from the shop and workshop. They took with them those small items in their possession which were both the marks and signs of belonging and the means by which they were socially inscribed.

In the middle of the general panic, petty thieves took advantage of the night and its disturbances to grant themselves a small haul with very little difficulty. Some of the injured who were still sufficiently conscious of what was happening recounted their misadventures to the police a few days after the accident. Marie-Françoise Rivaudon, 36 years old and wife of P. Bardeuil, a casual worker and odd-job man, and herself a vendor of apples and resident of the Rue Planche Mibray in the parish of Saint-Jacques-de-la-Boucherie, gave the following evidence:

> she said that she had lost consciousness but had got up four times, her body broken and shattered. She had felt someone cutting beneath her left ear with scissors in order to rob her of a lace trimming which was tied beneath her chin . . . she had been taken by street cart to the *hôtel-dieu* in the Salle Saint-Nicholas where she was wrapped in a lamb's fleece. This did her a lot of good and she had been more fortunate than those who had died next to her.[75]

The police officers made scrupulous notes about each of the bodies, recording every item of clothing, all pieces of jewellery worn and whatever happened to be stuffed inside pockets. All personal belongings had to be handed over to the family. Of course, one would never really know what had actually disappeared in the frenzy or as a result of foul play; and there are no hats, caps or shoes on the lists – they probably remained on the streets. Many of the women must have had their pockets (worn over their aprons like a handbag) snatched, but in spite of this there was still a large number of items and traces of lives. Four-fifths of those picked up on the spot had something on them and each person also had several items in their possession.[76] It is worth noting that the average was around five items per person.[77] It allows us to gain a better idea of which items were usually carried around and considered necessary to have about one's person. It would in fact appear that the people did not get themselves dressed up to go to the festivities (as evidenced by the lists of clothes as well as the condition of the fabric, which was often referred to as worn or of poor quality). The pockets were those worn every day although here and there there might be a lace bow or tin crucifix on an extra ribbon; but nothing to suggest definitely that one had dressed any differently for the occasion, which is another indication (if one is required) that the population received its celebrations in the same way as it greeted everything else that took place daily in the street. When all was said and done, festivals and celebrations were just like everything else, with everyone enjoying it in his or her usual way. And so on that evening, at 9 o'clock, what one had on one's person was what one had been using all day in the normal concerns of each passing moment. That is the reason why the pockets of men and women alike contained so many small tools and instruments which would have been in constant use each day: 153 knives, dice, scissors (large and small) and corkscrews were recorded. These were indispensable items and everyone would have had at least one of these on his or her person, going everywhere and used for everything. But does this come as any surprise for a population which lived essentially by its hands and know-how and which, on account of the small trades it pursued, was more or less obliged to live in the street?

In addition to the utilitarian, there was a quantity of other items indicating strong links with other spheres of cultural life such as the literary and the spiritual: 90 items had some connection with the worlds of reading, writing or the practice of religion. The 25 reliquaries, pocket crucifixes and rosaries were matched by 24 small books, of which 9 were books of the offices or pious works whilst the others were almanacks, stories or, in one case, a calendar. The rest (41 objects) consisted of all kinds of papers with addresses written on them, receipts, a few letters, notes, cards or just simply one's name written down. Maybe it is unacceptable to combine 'devotional items' with the books, but as the sample is small there is no question here of attempting a cultural approach in respect of these victims; it simply appears appropriate to point out that the objects carried on the person would seem to indicate references to another universe beyond the material world of work. Whether this 'other place' can be divided and categorized according to items and objects relating to reading or to evidence of religious practice is, in fact, another matter.

As far as the items which testify to the existence of the religious life are concerned, and in spite of the fact that there were not very many, it is interesting to draw a distinction between the men and the women. A quarter of the women had on them a book of offices or some other devotional item whereas only an eighth of the men had bothered with such things.

In contrast, a large number of small containers were being carried around: 34 snuff boxes and 83 cases, mugs, cardboard boxes and flagons of every kind. Some of these boxes were quite flimsy, and there was one old case with nothing in it. But there were other items which were better made, sometimes with enamelling or silver-work. The types of snuffbox, for instance, would seem to suggest that these were not so much utilitarian as little luxury items. As for the cases, which contained all manner of things, they were a fair indication that life in the city provided the wherewithal to raise one's flagging spirits and that the street afforded the passerby with the odd temptation, whether found or purchased. Why else should there have been so many empty cases and such great numbers of mugs and jars unless they were used to draw water at the public fountains or wine at the pleasure gardens?

And not forgetting hygiene, the pursuit of which fell largely to the lot of a single object, the handkerchief – 77 of them in fact, whereas only one comb was found (and that was broken); there was also a tongue-scraper and three ear-cleaners. It was the handkerchief which was the central and indispensable item, serving on all occasions and for every purpose. It was a highly prized accessory – one may recall, for instance, the numerous references made in the archives of the police commissioners to handkerchief snatchers who were always vigorously pursued and severely punished when arrested. Thus, there were more handkerchieves than there was money (only 67 persons had some coins on them, roughly half of the individuals involved); even keys (52) were a long way behind. Such low numbers, especially if one thinks that two or three items were contained in one pocket whilst some had none at all, again sketches a picture of an urban landscape which was open and where the distinction between inside and out was blurred. Doors did not lock and neither did drawers; there were no watertight spaces and Harpagon-style strong-boxes were not the lot of the bulk of the population.[78] The key was not a distinctive feature of the Parisian worker.

There were not many spectacles or watches (these may have been stolen early on); there were a few tokens or lottery tickets and an insignificant array of bric-à-brac which defied classification (a dog-collar, a lamp, a pencil, a lorgnette and three pieces of bread).

For the most part, it is possible to see some degree of homogeneity in the categories of item: tools, books, papers, handkerchieves, cases, etc. Persons whose possessions were different or original enough as to fall outside the common lot were few and far between. Even more than the type of trade or employment, it was the street and habitat that determined the interior of the pocket.

## Identifying a friend or relative

The day after the disaster, at the request of the King's procurators, an enquiry was opened headed by Sirebeau, advocate to the *parlement*. The work of the enquiry was divided between Belle, Guyot, Thiéry and Coquelin. Sirebeau himself went in person to hear the accounts of the wounded and the workers who had helped recover the dead and wounded. The other commissioners were instructed to listen to the evidence of those persons who had identified the corpses which had been taken to the little cemeteries of La Madeleine and La Ville-l'Evêque.

All these statements were brief and for the most part repetitive. But if one also reads between the lines, it is possible to make out the ways of life, habits and customs on festive occasions and also the mode and manner of social relationship; there are also discreet, almost imperceptible glimpses of poverty and grief.

On the one hand there was the family, and on the other, the neighbour-hood around one's work or place of abode (the two often merging) which formed two living networks upon which men and women were essentially dependent. In fact, half the bodies in the Rue Royale were recognized by a member of their family and half by a neighbour lodging in the same block or working in the same workshop. All in all, it is a further confirmation of a way of life among the popular classes in which individuals found their place amid a network of family relationships and encounters in the workplace or dwelling.

The knowledge they had about each other was often telling and quite precise, allowing of course for the fact that the majority of the statements were made two weeks after the catastrophe, by which time everyone had had a chance to find out about whomsoever had died; but what matter. The place of birth was recorded as well as the trade or profession, remarriages and the number of children. Each identification process also took into account what was known about the family – its comings and goings, its ups and downs; and, as already mentioned, the contents of the pockets often indicated names and addresses which had been written down.

Within families there were occupational similarities: for an uncle work-ing in casual employment there might be a niece who was a laceworker and an aunt who was a washerwoman; dependent on the father who was a journeyman in inlaid-ware, there was the mother who had been married twice before, twice a widow and a vendor of fruit with three children from two different marriage beds. The four daughters of the mother who worked as a carder were employed as domestic servants in the big houses or inns. There was certainly little social extravagance in this milieu and definitely nothing to spare. The only thing of any importance and in fact itself something of an adventure was to have one's family (brought to Paris from the country) around one and to try to provide them with a life that was more or less decent. For some of them, there was not even time to accomplish this aim: two cousins who were natives of Limousin, one a journeyman mason and the other a quarryman, had migrated to Paris and stayed in La Nouvelle France in the same dwelling. Jean Burau, the quarryman, planned to bring his family up to Paris with him, but on 30 May he was asphyxiated in the crowd and his cousin, who came to identify him, stated that 'he had left a widow, Jeanne Lafoulle, resident of the village of Laveau Bourgoin, and two children, a boy aged 5 and a girl of 8 whose future was totally dependent on Jean Burau'.

There was the same solidarity between partners as in the following moving example of G. Peignen, a blind man and his wife. She died on the pavement, having left her husband at home as he was not in a position to enjoy the spectacle. His brother-in-law, a journeyman mason, came to the cemetery to identify her body and to fetch her belongings back for her husband. He remarked that 'Sieur Peignen was in a worse state than previously because of the accident to this his wife who had acted as his guide.'

The statements often stressed the state of material deprivation in which wives and children were likely to find themselves. In the following case, it was a market assistant who had died and was recognized by his workmate, who added that he knew how much poverty his wife was in at the present time and that she had been obliged to do some cleaning jobs. Then there was another case of a wife who 'did the finishing-off on the small number of jobs that her husband was able to do', and now that he was dead, there was a great risk that the family would slide into complete and utter poverty. Such cases show not only a precarious financial state made absolutely intolerable by the incident but also the almost total dependence of the members of the family on each other, it being the group as a whole which ensured its survival. When one of them faltered or, worse still, disappeared, the future became extremely difficult for the others.

Belonging to the same trade or being under the same roof was also a means of being recognized and identified, and in these networks of urban life where everyone knew everyone else, servants and domestics had a special place. Going as they did from place to place they usually ended up getting to know each other quite well, and so they would all know that young lad who was workshop assistant for 18 months with the master tailor and who had left a few days before the arrival of a new servant who had not stayed long herself. Some of the servants even admitted that they had come to the cemetery of La Ville-l'Evêque 'to look at the bodies out of curiosity', pretty sure that they would recognize someone or other of those who were being brought in.

A master haberdasher who was a shopkeeper in the Rue Saint-Denis stated that he had recognized four of his employees and, without attempting to elaborate, simply gave the numbers written on the cards that the police officers had fastened to their chests. Other masters identified their journeymen or apprentices in a similar manner. Shop and workshop were matrices of social life.

Some of the statements were made away from the scene by people who had come to the help of neighbours or friends in mourning, who were also seriously hurt themselves and unable to leave their homes. The injuries were often quite staggering: vomiting blood, crippled feet, crushed hands, broken legs and shoulders, collapsed rib-cage, etc. Then there was the shock of being trapped for a long time beneath a pile of dead or unconscious people or having been too close to men and women who were desperately trying to breathe: 'their eyes turned up towards the sky, their stomachs protruding and bleeding from the mouth.' Panic, the fear of losing a member of one's family, or the grief at discovering one had lost a child or spouse marked a good many of the statements. Their accounts referred not only to those they had lost, but also to those they had almost lost, only to catch up with them and find them in the last throes before suffocating to death, including the following clothier who

> had the misfortune to lose his son aged 7 in the Rue Royale and who very nearly lost his wife who had been picked up as dead and whom he hadn't managed to get to until 3 o'clock in the morning. He had her taken home where she was still ill and he had then gone and identified Eustache, his son.

Sometimes the bodies were so severely injured that it was difficult to recognize one's own relatives. A brother-in-law recognized his sister-in-law by a beauty spot on her left breast (the visible breasts suggesting a promiscuity even among the dead). Then there was Potel, a contractor, who went looking for his friend and thought he had found him laid out at the cemetery. He picked up his belongings and made a statement, only to bump into him on the way back and find him alive and well and hard at work. His friend came back to give evidence of the fact that he was in good health and to bring back the things as they did not belong to him.

On that day they had gone off to the illuminations in good spirits. Some of them had gone together in a group 'sometimes six at a time, as many boys as there were girls and as many men as women'; usually there were parents or relatives with them or else, according to workshop practice, the master would go to the festivities with 'his young male or female apprentices'.[79] After an hour or two master and apprentices would usually have become separated from one another with each going his or her own way. One of the young girls might be among the corpses; when she did not return, the night would find the master searching the places where she might have been hurt. In this and many similar cases, the parents would not be informed until later; the apprentice was first of all a resident of his master's house.

## When the priests did their reckoning

A royal celebration which ended up by causing the deaths of men and women was a threat to the established order and status quo. The Dauphin intervened immediately in an act of compassion and money was distributed to the poor unfortunates. The Lieutenant of Police was quickly informed of this decision and Hardy makes a note of it in his Journal of 3 June 1770:

> The news is that Monseigneur le Dauphin, being so moved with compassion at the terrible consequences for those poor wretches who perished amid the disorder of the festivities has written to the Lieutenant of Police sending him the 6,000 *livres* that he is usually allotted each month so that he can spend it as he sees fit in the relief of the suffering of the poor.[80]

In her *Mémoires*, Mme Campan, a chambermaid to Marie-Antoinette, was more hagiographical:

> The Dauphin and Dauphine sent their entire year's revenues for the relief of the unfortunate families who had lost their relatives on that day of disaster.
> It was an act of generosity which will be numbered amongst the many outstanding rescue efforts dictated as much by compassion as by the politics of princes; the grief of Marie-Antoinette was profound indeed and lasted several days.[81]

In order to distribute the funds, the Lieutenant of Police first sought the help of the police inspectors and subsequently the parish priests, who were sent a circular to this effect followed by a second issued on 12 June 1770. They were asked to draw up a list of those who had died as a result of their injuries. They were also asked to point out those families in a state of financial hardship.[82]

The priests made enquiries in their parishes and then sent their replies to the Lieutenant of Police, often accompanying their findings with a personal letter and comments on the situation. On 2 July, the Lieutenant drew up a table of the parishes in the city, but it comes as some surprise to find that this document combines detail with the most amazing lack of statistical precision (see Table 2). The age of meticulous statistics had obviously not yet come and one might indeed wonder by what standards one should assess the 'few' or the 'many' when on the same table one finds 66, 2 or 'several'.

The powers that be were disturbed. The Lieutenant-General of Police quickly tried to get together as much information as possible. Loaded with money and beset on all sides with demands and requests, the police inspectors visited the most unfortunate and delivered alms. What was more, it was all done rather too quickly so that the parish priests immediately took umbrage and made complaints in their letters to the Lieutenant of Police. It was all a matter of their own power over their own parish territory of which they were the proud and ferocious defenders. The undue

Table 2  *Survey of the parishes,* faubourgs *and outskirts of the city of Paris in which there were those wounded in the events of the 30 May 1770 in the Rue Royale, some of whom died from their injuries*

|  | Dead | Injured |
| --- | --- | --- |
| **Parishes** | | |
| La Madeleine | | 9 |
| Saint-Germain-le-Vieux | | 8 |
| Saint-Pierre-aux-Bœufs | | 4 |
| Saint-Barthelemy | | a few |
| Saint-Germain-l'Auxerrois | | 8 |
| Saint-Roch | 1 | many |
| Saint-Leu | | 3 |
| Les Innocents Saint-Jean-en-Grève | | several |
| Sainte-Opportune | | a few |
| Saint-Nicolas-des-Champs | 2 | several |
| Saint-Sauveur | | 22 |
| Saint-Gervais | | several |
| Saint-Paul | | many |
| Saint-Benoît | | 10 |
| Saint-André-des-Arts | | 2 |
| Saint-Hyppolyte | | 3 |
| Saint-Sulpice | | 10 |
| Saint-Jean-de-la-Boucherie | | a few |
| Le Temple | | 8 |
| Saint-Jean-de-Latran | | 2 |
| Les Quinze-Vingts | | 3 |
| Saint-Merry | | several |
| Saint-Louis-en-l'Ile | | several |
| Saint-Séverin | | several |
| Saint-Nicolas-du-Chardonnet | | several |
| Saint-Eustache | | |
| Saint-Symphorien | | 2 |
| **Faubourgs** | | |
| Sainte-Marguerite | | 43 |
| Bonne-Nouvelle | 1 | 10 |
| Saint-Etienne | | 6 |
| Saint-Médard | | 10 |
| Saint-Jacques-du-Haut-Pas | | many |
| Saint-Laurent | | 66 |
| La Madeleine | | several |

haste of ill-informed police officers was not to their liking and undermined their considerable influence over their parishioners, to which they attached so much importance.

The letters from the priests were short but precise, attempting to put things back in order and to show how much they were masters in their own house and would brook no rivalry with the police, as this letter from the parish priest of Saint-Louis-en-l'Ile illustrates:

> The person whom you sent to me, Sir, conducted himself in the act of distribution with the utmost prudence but I fear there has been rather undue haste and that it would have been better had he known beforehand the extent of the poverty and deprivation of each person. In this respect, there is no one better informed than myself and consequently the allocations would have been made proportionate to the actual situation of the persons concerned, which would seem to be more in keeping with your own views. I fear that he may have been wrong, for instance, in giving 2 *louis* to a mother and her daughters who admittedly had been injured but who since then have been receiving our support, whereas he gave only 3 to a poor man who has been left with seven children on his hands.

What use therefore was royal charity if it was being administered by incompetent officials who were too hasty and unmindful of the consequences?

> I believe that if you had been kind enough to consult each of us variously you would have been better served. Instead, your officials suddenly turned up full of fervour, hardly giving us time to draw up a hasty list. They really ought to have come back to find out about any new cases that had been discovered and yet I have not seen a soul. (Parish priest of Bonne-Nouvelle)

Each passing day lengthened the list of the deceased or those for whom misfortune had become a definite reality. In spite of the firmness of purpose there was more than an ounce of servility in the affirmations of loyalty and deference expressed. The preamble to the letters is quite stereotyped and gushes with flattering attestations to the good grace and bounty of the Lieutenant-General. Expressions such as: 'We all know the inclinations of your heart' or 'We know the soundness of your sense of honour' are matched by references to 'your zeal for law and order' and 'your great love for the poor and unfortunate'. The priest of the parish of Saint-Nicholas-des-Champs was even more enthusiastic; he latched onto an expression which history retained for someone else much later: 'You are the first father of the people this capital has had, being touched by their misfortunes as a natural consequence of your great kindness and tenderness of heart.'

Although there might be differences and divergences between the Lieutenant-General and the parish priests there was no question of any disagreement over the ideology which they held in common and for which they strove with the same tenacity, namely that order must be upheld and that the public had no grounds for complaint. The clergy clung to this authority and whilst making sure that their own share of this power was preserved, they signalled their indispensable connivance with the man who held the highest police authority after the King.

Submerged beneath this flood of comments and polite formulas, there appeared one or two details on the state of the injured. The notes are strangely loose and fluid like the table already mentioned: 'the washer-woman's husband is quite poorly'; 'seven or eight of them are injured'; 'most of them are all right'; 'three or four are in distress'. There are no names, no exact figures and yet at the same time there are also precise details which suggest a real concern on the part of the priest. For example, the parish priest of Saint-Pierre-aux-Bœufs made a point of stressing the courage of one of his priests and of his servant who were responsible for saving the lives of many people. He also refers to 'a poor family who have lost a great deal, even having to pawn their chairs which they had been renting as the result of a fire'. There were many others for whom that day had dealt the same misfortunes and it was true that it was only the priests who could have really known the exact details.

There was no doubt that on the day following the accident, rumours spread around Paris and the number of dead, which was not something that could be controlled, rose or fell in accordance with the gossip and the feelings aroused. Statements and contradictory statements ebbed and flowed; false lists as well as genuine probably circulated and everywhere there was talk of pillaging, rifling and plotting. In short, there was talk – a lot of it – and that is what had to be stemmed. As soon as the news got out that there were sums of money to be distributed, there was the increased risk of the least seriously injured becoming convinced that they had been afflicted with a malady that was incurable or indeed fatal. The police inspectors were flooded with demands and their hasty attempts to try and please everyone and stop the whisperings were hardly likely to assist the just and fair administration of help and support.

This was an area in which the parish priests had a long history of experience: 'This is how I go about it,' wrote the priest of Saint-Nicholas-des-Champs, as he proceeds to explain the ingenious and authoritarian system that he had set up to stop things getting out of hand. Each family who had requested help and support was required to write a note accompanied by a certificate signed by a doctor known to himself. If the parties were reluctant to take these steps he let it be known that he himself would come and pay them a visit in order to establish the truth of the situation and that in the event that they were lying, he would deprive them of any help whatsoever, now and in the future. Furthermore, he sought the help of the nuns who regularly distributed alms in the district. They provided him with a list of the most needy so that he was able to verify whether the requests were indeed justified. 'I heard not a single murmur,' he said, the phrase itself a clear expression of infallible authority as well as an admission to the most acute fear of all – of murmurings or complaints on the part of the people, for the spread of rumour was considered most dangerous and threatening.

An incident of some significance occurred in the parish of Saint-Paul; the rumour got around that there had been an unfortunate incident involving some young communicants. 'But, thank God,' wrote the priest, 'not one of them has gone from us.' His expression conjures up the typical image of the young female communicant, caught like a bird in a cage. The papers seized on this potential newsworthy item – death of young communicants during the celebrations – and it would have no doubt made a good story. The priest himself was worried and upset and began to suspect the girls themselves of making up the stories and spreading them, being prey as they were at their age to all kinds of impressions and imaginings. He put considerable energy into 'keeping an eye on the whole circus' and finally had the pleasure of announcing that 'the charade was falling apart bit by bit'. After several days, the communicants of Saint-Paul were of no more interest to anyone.

In every parish, priests used the pulpit and the system of public announcements to control what was going on as well as the parishioners themselves. As one of them said: 'I made it quite clear before a public audience that it was my intention to make donations to the poor of my parish twice a week.' But as everyone well knew, it was not possible to quell a rumour and pursuing it required authority and influence: 'Permit me to disabuse folk and put a stop to all the shouting that is going on all over the place' (parish of Vaugiraud). Others gave up the struggle more easily and simply shrugged their shoulders in the face of a continuous succession of vague pieces of information and incessant fancies: 'I became so used to hearing folk tell me what they had heard and seen when they had never done any such thing that I gave not the slightest credence to any of these tales.'

Authoritarian or indifferent, the fact remained that the ideas they held about the poor and the people were more or less the same. 'The genius of the people, and particularly of the poor' consists first of all in taking advantage of everything and then in deception – the conviction was that they were all rogues unless they were kept well bridled. The accident of 1770 moreover had given rise to waywardness and a descent into cruelty and deception. People had taken advantage of the injured, rifling bodies and stealing from corpses; they had removed jewellery and cut off purses. When faced with the task of separating the wheat from the tares, comforting the deserving poor and leaving aside the bad, one needed authority and the ability not to be taken in by attempts at deception. But in the distribution of alms it should have been possible in the end to classify those 'poor families who were essentially honest folk'. So who then were these difficult, if not wicked, people who went about murmuring discontent?

There were several answers to that. The priest anxious about the practices of his parishioners might say that in the face of the considerable spread of irreligion it was hardly surprising that the world was so unjust. Other priests were even more ready to attribute some fundamental characteristics to the people for which, apparently, religion would be of absolutely no help at all. In this respect they wrote some political proposals which the Lieutenant of Police would be quite happy with: 'Long experience has made me recognize that one always has to treat the people well but also remain alert and ready to ward off any surprises without stirring them to revolt' – tightrope equilibrium as befits the notion of the people as impressionable and liable to revolt at any moment. But the final word remains with the priest of the parish of Bonne-Nouvelle whose irrevocable definition of the people is charged with significance, foreboding things to come: 'As you well know, Sir, the people will always remain people, which should not give you any cause for concern.'

On 22 June, armed with the information collected from the priests of Paris, the Lieutenant addressed himself to his commissioners. It was now up to them to give out the exact figures (132 buried at La Ville-l'Evêque, 2 in the parish of Notre-Dame-des-Champs, two in Bonne-Nouvelle and another in Saint-Roch). They were also required to give news of the injured: 'It is hoped that there will be no further deaths,' he stated. It was then necessary to stop the rumours by being firm and convincing: 'Do me the pleasure of destroying the impression that these lists have been making on the public by their exaggeration of a misfortune which is already too great by half and by which I have been greatly afflicted.'[83]

How the commissioners dealt with this remains to be seen; more than likely it was by means of public notices posted in their districts and a quiet but reassuringly firm word in the ears of persons under their jurisdiction. As for the priest, he possessed a distinct advantage in being able to get up in the pulpit.

## Whose fault?

If public opinion was aroused, if genuine and not so genuine lists were doing the rounds in Paris and if there was a growing discontent, it was because the population had realized as soon as the accident had happened that there had been gross negligence on the part of the police; in fact, there had been an indifference that just about everyone had been able to note.

There had been indifference at the time of the accident and worse still, which made it all the more hard to bear, indifference less than a week later. The casual attitude of those responsible proved this quite clearly and the population noticed and, like a whipping which added insult to injury, they bore the full brunt of it.

On the eve of the festivities it was quite apparent that the Place Louis-XV had not been properly cleared to receive the crowd and it had been considerably narrowed by the construction work in hand. The city architect had not taken the trouble to level the terrain nor had he capped off the trenches on some of the passageways.[84] There were also obstructions on the site which restricted movement and the circulation of traffic. As for the swing bridge which usually gave access to the square in the garden of the Tuileries, that had also been closed.[85]

Furthermore, immediately after the fireworks, the carriages parked on the side of the colonnade had decided to force their way through in order to get onto the Rue Royale and it was this movement that had made the crush lethal. Guards had been stationed there to bar their way and to prevent them from using that route but the coachmen, spurred on by the incitements of their masters, had ended up ignoring their prohibitions. It came to light later that not only was the guard insufficient at that precise point but that Jérôme Bignon, the *prévôt des marchands* and the city administration chief, had withdrawn the order preventing the carriages from passing because of pressure from persons of quality who were travelling in them. The fact that the carriages had been allowed to crush the crowd without the authorities even intervening was an unforgivable insult and a decision not likely to be forgotten. The symbolism is so poignant that there is little point in dwelling on it; it is sufficient to read the pamphlets of the day to understand how the whole business was instantly perceived. The following song reproduced by Hardy in his Journal of 9 June is from one of them:[86]

> Sartine's[87] concern will not avail –
> God knows full well how he'll be met.
> Mistake it was to fear the herd,
> Who gathered in great numbers there,
> Where honest man, or so I'm told,
> Did cab and carriages prefer.
> Take care all good Parisian folk,
> Lest ye be murdered, broken, choked.
> Did ever France see such punishment?
> Oh woe for those poor wretches all,
> Their cry for vengeance goes unheard,
> And there's none other 'cept they alone
> To pay the price of broken polls.

Nor did the hurt end there; not only was Jérôme Bignon, administrative head of the city, vigorously attacked, he also 'had the indecency to be seen at the Opera the following Friday, which so aroused indignation amongst the citizens that rumours of his fall from Royal Grace and his possible demise began to circulate'. It would seem that on that particular Friday, the population was only too well aware of the factors responsible for precipitating the catastrophe and was truly in a position to allocate personal responsibility. They were therefore expecting the findings of the enquiry that had been commissioned by the King's procurator to indict and punish those who were to blame, or at least strip from office those in the front line who had lost the confidence of the public. Such expectations did not prevent pamphlets from circulating, however, and one of their favourite targets was Jérôme Bignon. He was the subject of a pastiche based on the lamentations of the prophet Jeremiah and entitled: 'Jeremiad concerning the conflagration of June 1770 in the city of Paris for the marriage of M. le Dauphin as ordered by M. Jérôme Poignon, *prévôt des marchands*; the disorder being so great that seven to eight hundred persons were either crushed or grievously injured in the ensuing débâcle.'[88]

The pastiche itself was decidedly mediocre; it made use of simple literary techniques and was based on an inversion of meaning intended to hedge one's adversary about with derision and ridicule. In the course of reading it, one begins to realize that each time the description of what happened appears absurd ('I arrived in a large square that was small'; 'they had shortened it with planks to contain the multitude', etc.), this is in fact borne out by the concrete facts of what had actually happened. Indeed, the large square was small because it had been narrowed and blocked by building work which was still in evidence; and indeed the crowd was expected on a building site that was not yet ready to receive them, etc.

This play at standing logic on its head is pursued at length, justifying each of the incidents in turn: if the horses happened to terrify the people, that was because they were too content; and when the show of lights that was expected to rise heavenward only produced a cloud of smoke that rebounded on the people, that was because it was the one and only distribution of royal gifts, for as everyone knew, there had been no hand-outs of bread and victuals that day.

Lacking as it does any literary polish – in fact it rather resembles an almanack with the odd pleasantry thrown in here and there – its repetitious use of illogicality and fallacy ultimately proves quite effective in achieving its purpose. The text itself, although weak and struggling to sustain the irony, is rather droll at times and succeeds in the end in conveying a certain sense of tragedy; and though it is imperfect – even crude from the point of view of form – it nevertheless carries along the content, even lending it additional meaning at times: 'They have eyes, but see not'; 'the mothers would crush their daughters and the young men would rip open the bowels of their fathers'. At another level it denounces those responsible for the catastrophe and, more than that, manages to portray them as smug and detached, rendering them not only odious but dangerous to boot. The humour turns to satire; and from treatment as an unfortunate mishap that was obviously of no consequence, the accident becomes charged with criminal intent. It ends with a view of the rows of corpses in the cemetery yawning and falling asleep one by one. And thus any feelings of pity or horror one might have felt are undone by the lightness of the allegory and replaced with a kind of perverse yet innocent game in which J. Bignon might regrettably have participated – 'He put on a show, but it's not the way I'd have done it', is the final flourish which brings the text lightly to its close.

Like a papal 'bull', this jeremiad is unpretentious; and although the words trip lightly and produce a smile, its effect is quite profound, for it succeeds in convincing us that not only was there a casualness on the part of those in power but that nonchalance and indifference were the very hallmarks of power itself. It was a flippancy that was quite ostentatious, sure of itself, and confident that it knew what was right no matter how absurd or deadly it might be; it was equally self-assured in its indifference and libertinism which it knew were guaranteed to provoke. The eyes of the great and mighty were wide open – and blank. Exactly! That was precisely the root of the problem and – make no mistake – everyone knew it.

While the crowd awaited the conclusion of the enquiry, they whispered among themselves the names of the two men they considered responsible, namely Jérôme Bignon and Chevalier Rocquemont, who was in charge of the Guard and the Watch. But while they hoped for their disgrace and disappearance off the public stage for having been so publicly and glaringly at fault, the conflict shifted its ground elsewhere. It was, in effect, to be taken away from the populace who were gripped by a legitimate desire for punishment, in order to be carried on well away from the people where it would be used in support of machinations of a quite different kind between the *parlement* and the Crown, from which the people themselves were obviously excluded.

And so the initial attempt by the crowd to denounce those whom they knew to be responsible and whom they had named found itself juxtaposed with a quarrel in high places. The latter was sufficient to erase all traces of the initial conflict based as it was on ancient rivalries between the Parisian police forces over the division of judicial responsibility.

One should note that Paris was an area of conflict for the police on two fronts.[89] The *prévôt des marchands*, who was the city's chief administrator, had responsibility for the banks of the Seine and its immediate vicinity. This jurisdiction, which was quite specific, brought with it untold quarrels and legal cases. For instance it was not uncommon to see criminals or thieves who had escaped from the street police finding a brief moment of respite on the banks of the Seine as this restless and turbulent place came under this other jurisdiction. The interaction between the Lieutenant-General of Police and the provost was one of constant rivalry and abuse of privilege with endless arguments over powers and priorities.

On the occasion of the marriage of the Dauphin, the policing of the firework display had been entrusted to the *prévôt des marchands* as it was to be situated by the banks of the Seine and thus in his locality. It was anticipated that the rockets would fall back into the Seine where everything was to be arranged so as to avoid the possibility of an accident or drowning. But as it happened, a serious quarrel had arisen between the office of the Lieutenant of Police and that of the provost. Jérôme Bignon had lacked the generosity to award the regiment of guards the payment of 1,000 *écus* required by the Duc de Biron for putting them in place to supplement the bourgeois Guard. What was more, besides leaving responsibility for the Place Louis-XV in too few hands he had also given way to pressure from persons of 'quality' who were travelling by carriage.

The *parlement* rapidly shifted the enquiry's brief and after finding, upon examination, that the activity of the Guard had been deficient, it attempted to find out who was in charge of this body of a thousand or so men (both Guard and Watch combined).

The Guard and Watch were both under the authority of the Lieutenant-General of Police but they were totally different in their composition. The officers of the Watch had responsibility for those in their charge and answered directly to the parliamentary court whereas the Guard, much bigger altogether, consisted of salaried men and were dependent on the Crown. The latter had been trying to diminish the Watch for some time and in 1765 it had nominated Rocquemont, who was already Commander of the Guard. The purpose of this was perfectly clear – namely, the amalgamation of these two bodies to create a single body tied to the Crown.

From that point on, the *parlement* concentrated all its efforts on bringing out the responsibility of the Guard for the accident of 1770 and making it loud and clear that the Watch had behaved not only correctly but efficiently at all times. In discrediting the Guard, the *parlement* sought to gain absolute power over the Watch.

Just when the quarrel was at its height, the Lieutenant of Police took everyone by surprise by publishing a hasty edict maintaining the separation of the two bodies and which was intended to resist at all costs any attempt at recuperation by the *parlement*. The death-knell had been sounded and in 1771 the Watch was to be suppressed by the chancellor, Maupeou, and the *parlement* lost its battle.

During this significant episode between the Crown and the *parlement* which took place at a level at which the population could obviously not participate, the city authority issued a variety of bulletins in answer to the attacks to which it had been subjected. It attempted to explain by every possible means that 'this misfortune was the result of extraordinary circumstances'.[90]

It was not long before an official version of the facts saw the light of day; its main task was to restore and relay calm amongst the population and it dwelled at length on the theme of fate and fatality and the risks arising wherever there were crowds. The following is an example:

finally all precautions had been taken and orders given in a manner so as to ensure that everything ran smoothly and this would have been the case had it not been for the sudden and unexpected influx from the opposite direction with the effect that all the measures which had been taken were momentarily thrown into confusion. All this occurred so suddenly that some distinguished persons who at that same instant had set off from the colonnades without even realizing what had happened and believing that they would be hemmed in, only extricated themselves as a result of the brave efforts of the people who were accompanying them.[91]

Order and control were re-established for the time being – political machinations taking precedence over the events in the street, from which attention had been diverted. In a sense, the accident had been taken off the street which had been thus summoned to celebration and catastrophe, thereby removing the means of keeping up the murmurings against the monarchy.

Contrary to other events where there was collective involvement and where it was often the rule to leave it to the crowd to punish the person responsible, the system on this occasion operated quite differently. There could be no doubt but that those who had been designated as guilty by the crowd were too well placed in the political hierarchy to be abandoned to popular condemnation. Thus it was necessary to rearrange the order of play and so divert attention towards other types of responsibility.

It was no mere coincidence that the *parlement* should appropriate this conflict, thereby depriving the population at a stroke of all possibility of influence or action.

# 9

# The Crowds amongst Themselves

---

In Paris no one needed an invitation to get together or to go off in a group; the natural corollary of living outdoors was the permanent attraction of whatsoever was happening and whatever presented itself before one's eyes or ears or called for one's attention in one way or another.

> Thus the Parisian inhabitant is never indifferent to what is going on around him. The least little novelty is likely to make him pause on his way. Take, for instance, the example of a man who has his head in the air and is looking intently at some object or other. You are bound to see several others stop immediately and turn their eyes in the same direction thinking that they will see whatever he is looking at. Little by little, the crowd will grow, each of them asking the other what they are looking at. All it needs is for one poor canary to escape and perch on a window-sill for the whole street to be blocked by the crowd. The moment he flies from one lamp to the next, shouts and cries will go up on all sides, windows will open and there will be faces at each. The brief and momentary independence of one small bird will become a spectacle of general interest.
>   If a dog were to be thrown in the river, the banks and bridges would be covered almost immediately with people, some of them concerned about what might happen to it and others saying it must be saved, watching it closely in whatever direction the current happened to take it. This spirit of curiosity is not necessarily lacking in sensitivity; it is not unknown for instance for the people to separate two combatants and for the women to harangue them so fiercely on the advantages of peace and harmony that they would settle their grievances on the spot.[1]

It is easy and, in fact, customary to interpret this kind of up and run behaviour as evidence of the immaturity of the crowd with their taste for the fortuitous and the accidental. Chroniclers, contemporaries, the literati of the period and modern historians have all described these irrational impulses of the crowd and its inability to separate the real from the imaginary, allowing itself to be carried along willy-nilly to whatever speechifying or spectacle might be on offer.

Scientific progress had also had a hand in putting all sorts of odd inventions within the bounds of possibility and, whilst religion was becoming less satisfying, there was still the possibility of acts of God with their power to incite or punish. And so from time immemorial one has been led to believe that the crowd or common herd has submerged its fears and ignorance by submitting to immature systems of relationship with reality which were no more than pure fancy, thus providing obvious proof of the need for constant control of these potentially dangerous excesses and enthusiasms.

Strangely enough, it was a work by Nicolas Ledoux on the city and urbanization (something of a utopian dream) which expressed another view of these continual gatherings of Parisians and what it was about the daily goings-on that attracted them all so much.[2]

For Ledoux, festivities were not so important if everyday life were sweet and pleasant. The real value of the festivity was in the fact that 'the community had the opportunity to contemplate itself and rejoice in one another.'[3] It is an approach well worth considering and singling out from some of the other well-worn tracks. What better way of re-appropriating for oneself not only one's essence but also one's meaning than by seeing oneself and each other for oneself, and by being oneself the spectacle of one's perceptions of self and one's own attempt to make sense of events. The King's celebrations or punitive events offered the people an opportunity for consensus. The taste for freaks and curiosities (the expressions of the period), evinced different attitudes, among them a desire to offer one's own pronouncements on the significance to the day's events. Furthermore, there was a feeling that the experience of the many lent sense and meaning to whatever was seen or heard, thus making it possible not only to gain a collective grip on reality but also, and why not, a potential mastery of events such that one need never wait for meaning to be attributed or suggested by those who knew, controlled, commanded or governed.

This unfailing attraction for the strange and the improbable was referred to in the texts of the period as 'credulity'. It was a recurrent theme to be found as much on the pens of justices as in texts by ministers or writers. The people had to be gullible: this was the basis on which the elites needed to act and react and an assessment which they quite often 'worked on'. Because it was so apparent to everyone, popular credulity was itself the subject of vast analysis. The difficulty of questioning it or even approaching it is that there is a permanent risk of being tricked by the initial position of 'looking at' or of the desire to dissect things up into small parcels of meaning. Even if every precaution is taken to distance oneself as much as possible from this position, other risks arise, most notably in the subtle shifts and shades of vocabulary employed and it is this surreptitious betrayal by means of language that is perhaps even worse.

However, one thing is certain – popular credulity is not an entity in itself; nor does it constitute anything objectively capable of defining, once and for all, the essence of a social group. It is an opinion and that is an entirely different story; it suggests a relationship, made by others, between a form of action and a mode of being, but learning unfortunately does not usually preoccupy itself with its own received ideas or its stereotypes and archetypal assumptions. That the people were obviously gullible was useful more often than not as a point of departure for other forms of reasoning shored up by this principle, which is no principle at all. That credulity was a form well suited to the intelligence and social arrangements of the aristocracy, for example, is very rarely taken into account – or at least very rarely analysed in these terms.

Credulity, as one knows, was far from being the prerogative of a single social group and the kind of peculiar events and curiosities which the people enjoyed so much and which are so complacently related by chroniclers and archivists of the time were in fact central to a complex system of beliefs that were more or less shared by those of different social spheres. It was not really until the eighteenth century that the break with a common basis of belief took place, thereby marking the appearance of an elitist culture which strove to distinguish itself from the people and the weight of past archaism. It was a rupture which is relatively recent. It is more apparent in its desire to maintain a distance and instigate a definitive separation between the upper and lower ends of the social hierarchy and is more convincing in its strategy for the installation of cultural supremacy than in the actual content of its knowledge. Although cultural unity may have been breaking down, abundant traces remain, clearly measurable in the beliefs and activities of the elites, as well as in their treatises.

Even the *Encyclopédie* found itself grappling with fascination for the extraordinary; and not even its reasoned attempts managed to refute what was, and still is, a common vision of the world.[4]

Furthermore, life in the city (particularly between society and the authorities), saw the emergence of a number of variations and combinations as to what ought, and ought not, to be believed. The field of play might include, for instance, phenomena that were purely intended to incite; deliberate construction of events in order to make them believable; sudden attempts to repress and control what came to be termed 'sheer fantasy' where previously it had been considered 'news' or novelty; all this helped give 'credulity' a number of facets and thus enabled it to engage in a field of activity which was both productive and destructive and in which the ordinary people and the elites played their part, each echoing the other. For the elites as well as the mob were equally keen partners in their enthusiasms for the extraordinary, the sensational, the 'scientific' (or at any rate, the 'hitherto unheard of') but in the treatises and discourses of the great and mighty responsibility for credulity is assigned to the backward and boorish masses. It was rare for the elite to perceive its own taste for these same items; and when it did, it did so badly. It was even worse at seeing the ambiguous nature of its own conduct in the thick of an event in which its own complicity helped render it an object of credulity.

It is possible to gain some idea of this complexity from some of the famous events of the century and some have already been analysed from this perspective;[5] one need only think, for example, of the phenomenon of mesmerism or of the ecstatics in the cemetery of the church of Saint-Médard. There were also some small events that were so insignificant that contemporaries did not think to write about them but which nevertheless reveal, at the most basic level, an overview of the whole of the social scene. Because they were so small and unimportant one might believe that they were entirely the upshot of popular emotion and only relevant to that particular type of credulity, but not so – even the least of these rather strange and peculiar little affairs can conceal within it a set of mechanisms which provides a rich picture of the social world as a whole with its hierarchies, challenges, disruptions and acts of common faith.

In 1756, the story of a little girl of nine and a half, Madeleine Ernault, was to arouse a great deal of astonishment and one can find traces of it in the judicial archives.[6] The story was such that she managed to mobilize around her the police, the aristocracy, the medical bodies and the people. The bizarre nature of the phenomenon, the tender years of the child, the occurrence of something that had hitherto been unheard of, and the obvious references to sexuality, all helped set up certain ideas and beliefs and led to the printing of accounts and spread of various rumours which were effectively taken in hand by the police. The field of play might well be tiny but in so far as the archives allow us to make sense of it, it was in fact immense. First, there was the event itself – everyone believed it. It was true. Then it turned out to be false. As one follows the route from belief to rumour and then to error, one can see the complex social tangles which shatter the simplistic assertions which so confidently establish clear divisions between people and elite, rational and irrational, truth and error, news and rumour.

## Little Madeleine

On Friday 12 March 1756, at 5 o'clock in the evening, Commissioner Roland received in his office a little girl of 9, accompanied by her parents, salt and tobacco retailers in the Rue Saint-Victor. They had come to register a complaint against Denis, a bar hand for a wine vendor in a *cabaret* not far away known as Le Petit Trou ('The Little Hole'). Madeleine asserted that she had been touched and fondled by this 18-year-old and that he had penetrated her. This had taken place each time she had gone on an errand to the establishment over the summer. Denis of course had intimated to her that she should not tell anyone, with the result that there she was, pregnant and unwell.

Louis Ernault and his wife, La Flèche, had taken every precaution, presenting the Commissioner with a diagnosis and report made by Jeanne Bary, midwife in the Rue du Fauboug-Saint-Martin.

From here everything proceeded very quickly. The Ernault parents who were anxious to have the matter dealt with at the highest level had taken further steps and had also appealed to the Lieutenant-General of Police for the immediate arrest of Denis. The usual procedure was to register a complaint with the district commissioner – an appeal direct to the Lieutenant was quite unusual. Their intention was to obtain from him an order of the King against Denis which, as we know, would have effectively prevented any trial.

From this point, Lieutenant Berryer took the matter in hand with his usual firmness but also with a degree of circumspection. It is important to remember that this affair took place six years after the popular revolt of 1750 caused by the abduction of children on the streets of Paris and which had been carried out by the police on the instructions of Berryer himself. The authorities had been on full alert that year and it was still a source of trauma for the King, the police and the people. Berryer had nearly lost his position and the King was still reluctant to travel through the city. Thus the fact that a little girl had been raped and violated by a youth and was pregnant as a result meant that the matter should be taken in hand quickly and receive immediate attention for, as Berryer knew, one did not touch children with impunity.

There then followed enquiries amongst the neighbours, a statement by the midwife, and visits by the police inspector to the parents and the little girl. The probity of the parents was acknowledged and not a soul would have dared suggest that it was the little girl's fault for 'enticing him'; therefore action was needed. A brief comment in the margin of a letter from Berryer to Commissioner Machurin indicates that legal proceedings should not go ahead and that in this case it was a *lettre de cachet* that was required: 'What needs to be issued here is an order [from the King]; this case is not suitable for consideration at law.' Indeed, how was one to make a legal decision on the basis of this unspeakable incident which not only defied both nature and the law but medicine itself – after all it was a 9-year-old child who was pregnant. On 25 April, Denis (Denis Guillemard in full) was taken to prison at Bicêtre to be detained there. He made no attempt to deny what had happened, at least as far as the fondling was concerned and as for the pregnancy, his opinion was not sought on that matter.

Denis in prison and Madeleine pregnant. The news spread like a cloud of dust. The 'epic' did the rounds right up until the end of the month of October 1756, or perhaps one should say until February 1757, if one takes the final conclusion of the saga to be the release of Madeleine's mother four months after her imprisonment for deception. It was a tangled history: populace, folk in carriages, important men of medicine, all trooped along to the Ernaults' house to watch the child's belly swell and to make on-the-spot comments about this prodigy. Nine, ten, eleven and then fifteen months went by without the child having given birth. The police were mobilized and the crowd too. Printed accounts were sold in the streets; the birth was announced, then denied and finally attempts were made to justify the fact of having been deceived.

This story of a little girl, commented on day after day by the police, was a strange business. False and unfounded, it was a story of credulity and an example of the mechanisms and processes by which a piece of news might become an item of belief, an error, a rumour, and the motive for police activity. Above all it perhaps best illustrates with what natural inclination an insignificant affair among the popular classes of the Maubert district was taken up by those of bourgeois and aristocratic estate and their predilection for the extraordinary. As we shall see, the house of little Madeleine was a veritable social observatory.

## Setting the scene

From 4 May, the crowd began to gather in the Rue Saint-Victor and the mother, without wasting any time, gave her permission to allow in only 'those who had something for little Madeleine – to put in her purse'. The child herself sat with outstretched hand, whilst outside, the Guard were obliged to keep the peace; the shop windows were shattered and the 'mob were prepared to use violence to get in'. There were not enough men from the Guard at Pont Saint-Michel or from the New Market and the sergeants of the Watch indicated their disquiet in their accounts of the day's events. These accounts are quite detailed and from day one they mention the arrival of persons of importance:

5 May 1756. The Guard maintained good order until 9.30 in the evening. At around 6 o'clock there was a visit from Monsieur le Comte de Lancy and Madame la Marquise de Senelet, accompanied by several other lords and ladies. Good order was maintained.

> 7 May 1756. I [Durier, sergeant in the Watch] went over to the
> Ernaults' this morning at 9 to prevent a disturbance among the populace
> who were wanting to see the child; there were also a number of honest
> members of the public and persons of quality who had arrived by coach
> and horses.

And thus the whole world came running – important doctors and
surgeons came out of their way; the Dauphine and her midwife were
interested in the affair, and coaches and carriages passed in procession
beneath the windows of the Ernault family. The clergy also took up their
positions. Shocked by the displaying of the pregnant child, the superior of
the Bons-Enfants seminary and the Grand Master of the Cardinal Lemoine
College together with several clerical professors wrote to the Lieutenant-
General on 6 May when the file-past of visitors first began: 'The young
mother Ernault, who according to medical reports is in fact pregnant, is by
virtue of her singular condition causing a scandal bordering on a state of
public commotion which seems to us as prejudicial to the State as to
matters of religion.' They strongly recommended that matters be taken
firmly in hand, for 'the evil is widespread', they protested.

And thus, all at once and all together, the whole world came rushing to
take a look: ordinary people, doctors, the high and mighty, the bourgeois,
the police and the clergy. There was no shortage of 'visitors' to join in such
a prodigious and disturbing phenomenon as was this, the pregnancy of a
young child. Between them, each social group, either jointly or separately,
lent authenticity to the incident for no other reason than by virtue of their
being there. No one made any attempt to prove anything; each of them by
their very presence confirmed the singular reality of the situation without
the slightest doubt being expressed. It had happened. It was unheard of.
One had to see it. At the same time there was really no need to rush for, as
everyone knew, it took nine months to deliver, although that in itself was
enough to alarm the clergy. As they saw it, most strange events usually
passed like a thief in the night, but in this case, the scandal promised to
go on indefinitely, which was an unbearable prospect.

Then there was Medicine. That was certainly one of the preferred
terrains for various forms of credulity, for in many areas there was still a
great deal of ignorance, whilst at the same time great advances were being
made. A privileged space was readily available for the prodigious, or
such as might defy knowledge or nature, and when it came to the female
body and sexuality or maternity, the space was even more propitious. A
woman's belly was a centre of contradiction in which unprecedented
fragility met up with extremes and excesses that were impossible to chart.
Nine-year-old Madeleine was a captive person, appropriated because her
body had become the meeting-place between utmost vulnerability and

exceptional and hitherto unheard-of forces. Why should one not believe it? How could one not believe it? Then there was the fact that this incident had been preceded by a rape – innocence stained; then there was the fact that the crowd, which included doctors, people and marquesses, had only appeared the day after the boy's arrest. Denis's confession had thus cemented the incident. From probability, it had become certainty.

One might with good reason suppose that this tale was untypical and that the fact that it had brought together a cross-section of the public was exceptional; but if one reads the newspapers and journals of the day as well as the memoirs and chronicles, one would see that this was not in fact the case and that the opposite were true. Nor is there any need to go far afield in looking for examples; they abound in the manuscripts of S. Hardy's Journal and there is also L.-S. Mercier, who has the additional advantage of offering the odd item of useful speculation on the problem. Usually laconic, although occasionally chatty, Hardy's manuscript gives consideration to minor items of news as well as to the more grand and newsworthy pieces, with the result that episodes in the street feature as much as political intrigue and scandal. Precise and to the point, Hardy makes his reports with apparent detachment and little comment, from which neither public executions, nor popular uprisings, nor the death of Louis XV gave him cause to deviate. His ability to maintain this distance is due in part to his style and the manner in which he prefaces his news with phrases such as 'it is said that': 'it was reported yesterday'; or 'much has been said about'. These expressions invariably followed the day's date and preceded all information whether it was political, anecdotal, social or quite simply surprising, because it arose from the realm of the sensational or the irrational (miracles, cures, departure of hot air balloons etc.); so that in between hangings, the announcement of an epidemic, periods of brutal cold, or the birth of a prince, one could read, for example, that on 27 February 1777,

a natural phenomenon has been reported which is most extraordinary. It would seem that the wife of Sieur de Barentin, the first President of the Cour des Aides, has recently given birth to a bush which has been identified as a currant bush, although it was not bearing currants at the time – only cherries – so it is said. This monstrous new species bore absolutely no resemblance to anything human and was quite inanimate. This strange birth has obviously been the cause of great sorrow to all the family.

That is all – just these few lines; the Journal then continues with other news. There is little point in looking for a refutation or confirmation of the facts in the following months for that was not Hardy's intention or purpose. For him, the news occurred, it set itself down with all the rest, and owed its status as evidence to the fact that it had been set down in writing. Hardy did naturally take the trouble to explain that it was an extraordinary phenomenon; however, the infant shrub, laden with cherries instead of red currants, that had made its way out of the belly of a lady of Barentin one winter's morning found itself joining company, not too surprisingly, with numerous metaphors from the vegetable kingdom which have been used from time immemorial to symbolize the human body,[7] but in this case with one important difference – here one was not dealing in metaphors but with reality. The fact that it had taken on all the appearance of metaphor and was closely associated with it and based on 'traditional associations between gestation and vegetable production' and with 'the medieval practice of likening the tree to gestation and the female sex'[8] did not seem to disconcert anyone, not even Hardy. And so whilst the family of the President of the Cour des Aides was understandably upset, the social status of the lady who had given birth removed from the phenomenon any possible connotations of the type referred to as 'popular naivety'.

It should also be recognized that this was a field (medicine and childbirth) where the medical records and dossiers abounded in equally stunning events which were never completely rejected by the medical profession on the grounds of their extraordinary character. One thinks in particular of the dossiers received by the members of the Royal Society of Medicine,[9] in which there are references to all kinds of curiosities and strange occurrences which fully accord with the kind of female world which was so influenced by mystery and subject to displays of physical violence. 'I believe in that phenomenon as much as I do in the existence of the sun,' wrote Dr Bousquet in 1785, overwhelmed by a young girl of 14 'whose breasts were producing foreign bodies akin to the seeds and flowers of the umbellar thistle'.[10] His letter to the Royal Society of Medicine was accompanied by a little bag containing these precious golden grains. The case was discussed, naturally, and even though in high places a hoax may have been suspected, there was a perfectly normal discussion about the young girl as there was in so many other cases in which the body had apparently been responsible for producing disorders of an incredible nature. Therefore it is not surprising to find the pens of memorialists flowing with some of these strange phenomena in which the normal existed side by side with the bizarre, particularly where diagrams were concerned or drawings of persons or events. The excesses and aberrations of nature[11] are recorded in books and encyclopedias which feature strange creatures with unusual abnormalities like the '30-year old male monstrosity born in Naples in 1742 with the lower quarters of a male child protruding from somewhere in the gastric region'.

Some texts might have been revised on the grounds of getting to what was real, and then offered back for consumption to a wide and cultured public. Thus credulity could also be a matter for scientific activity; it was certainly the preliminary step (and no doubt indispensable) of any attempt at rational explanation.

Bothered as he was by credulity in all its forms, L.-S. Mercier dedicated several chapters to it in his *Tableaux* as well as in his '*Parallèle de Paris et de Londres*' ('Comparison between London and Paris').[12] His rationalism led him towards a controlled mistrust of religious phenomena, manifestations of which he related critically and with a hint of irony. For him, miracles, cures, king's evils and ghosts were manifestations of the same thing, usually quite ridiculous and more often than not motivated by the need for the extraordinary.

It is quite interesting to spend some time wandering through the maze of his assertions, which are sometimes contradictory. Two of the ideas he proposed are stimulating as far as the present discussion is concerned but he does not take on board either their consequences or their implications, and in fact in the same chapter goes so far as to take up the opposite theses, which were more traditionally held and faithful to his period.

Castigating (albeit gently) the devotion of Parisians to St Genevieve, he describes perfectly the particular forms it took according to social status; for although everyone might believe it, how one in fact manifested that belief was dependent on the position allotted to one in society:

Ordinary folk and common people come shaking their sheets and covers in pursuit of the saint; they come to ask for cures for every kind of disease and fever and to drink filthy water from a fountain alleged to be miraculous. But the worthies from the *parlement* and other sovereign courts ask her for rain during time of drought and the healing and restoration of princes!...Neither reason nor philosophy has found anything to replace these profound and happy little illusions.[13]

Along with this idea that belief was shared differently according to social class[14] comes a doubt, almost a conviction: what, in the end, if the people themselves had precious little belief in all this but simply went along with it all as a spectacle offered to them and which they themselves had appropriated? He puts forward this hypothesis on the basis of a Parisian summer custom which took place each 3 July and which involved the burning of the effigy of a Swiss who, while drunk, had struck the statue of the Virgin with his sword. Blood had immediately issued from the statue and so, each year, reparation was made for this profanity to the sound and accompaniment of drums. Mercier, who found this custom ridiculous, added that this showed that even the most common and regular practices gave at most an equivocal picture of the real belief of a people and that more often than not it was simply a spectacle for the populace and nothing more.

Our most majestic ceremonies have no other basis and it is thus that the Holy Ampulla is still used to anoint our Kings. No one in the assembled throng any longer believes that it descended from on high on the beak of a dove and no one believes any more in the miraculous healing of scrofula.[15]

Just when one is given to understand that Mercier might be dissociating himself from any traditional formulations, the paragraphs or chapters that follow would seem to reveal other aspects apparently in contradiction with previous statements and propositions. On the one hand, there is never any question of analysing the contents of the beliefs of the great, whilst those of lesser men and women make their appearance only to be taken apart and consequently controlled. On the other hand, popular faith and credulity are treated with severity tempered by nostalgia. Mercier claims to envy those who sobbed openly at the feet of St Genevieve, but unfortunately for him his reason prevented him from abandoning himself thus. He realized that such cults and practices were 'adapted to the limits of the intelligence of the herd', which somewhat devalues his approach.

Leaving aside the specific domain of faith in order to describe 'the love of the miraculous', he shows how its victims are the 'feeble' and how reason and credulous fear can be divided in terms of sex with female frailty corresponding to male reason.

To these bold if scarcely innovatory comments is added a slight annoyance at the compulsion to believe anything and everything at all times and on all occasions. Making a comparison between phenomena of belief and 'moral epidemics', Mercier invites the police to crush all such extravagance, thus setting momentarily to one side his usual severity towards them. 'A police which addresses itself to breaking impetuous gusts of this kind and thus extinguishing a public extravagance as one would the start of a fire is a real benefit to government.'[16] This task of destroying prejudice was, according to the author, so noble that as the priests took no responsibility for it, then the police should.

In actual fact – and the developments in the Ernault affair go to prove it – the game played by the police was a complex one. When anything strange occurred, they made a point of being there; but the result of their presence did not always take the form of an obstacle – far from it – even though their repressive activity might be clearly visible.

## When the police moved in with the residents

The initial police reaction to healers, charlatans or any kind of superstitious practice was to oppose it, as edicts and police instructions clearly indicate. One need only open Delamare's *Traité de police*, Book III, section VII, for instance, to see that there was no room left for doubt. Police orders, in the form of a royal edict of 6 July 1682, read as follows:

> Let us ban all superstitious practices in thought, word or deed which either abuse the writings of the Holy Scriptures or the prayers of the Church or indeed say or do those things having nothing to do with natural causes. With regard to those who might be responsible for the spreading of such teaching, together with all such practitioners of it who, having availed themselves of it for whatsoever ends or purpose they see fit, let us see that they are punished in such a way as will be an example.[17]

This was the age of treasure-seekers, discoverers of the philosopher's stone and of magicians and diviners of every sort. It was a bubbling over that was both real and imagined and a possible attempt to hem in a police force who were none too clever. This never-ending problem is recalled in the correspondence of the time as shown in this letter from d'Argenson to Delamare in which he expresses his fears about the extent of possession:

> 7 July 1713. You will be aware that extraordinary happenings of an evil nature should not be made public in Paris where there is a readiness to believe in things that do not exist rather than in those that do and where one usually finds imagination and superstition taking precedence over religion and faith. I beg of you to see to it that those persons who are allegedly possessed be removed as soon as possible from where they are and accommodated somewhere apart; great care should be taken to ensure that all knowledge of their whereabouts is concealed from the public.[18]

Even before the great period of the ecstatics of Saint-Médard, those who were possessed as well as fortune-tellers and other practitioners of the magic arts found themselves being imprisoned. On the margins there might be the odd treasure-seeker convinced that diamonds and great fortunes had been secretly buried by wealthy princes;[19] or elsewhere, poor men whose efforts to grow rich had led them to concoct harmless secrets which allowed men to live to 500 whilst remaining extremely youthful – provided, of course, one took the precaution of drinking every 25 years an elixir guaranteed to 'make one's skin as good as new'.[20] And it was not just those at the top who had to deal with this kind of problem; inspectors and commissioners found themselves dealing with ghosts and phantoms on a day-to-day basis.

> For instance, at one of Lenoir's hearings, there was a leather-worker from the vicinity of the Jardin des Plantes; the man, who was very devout but extremely stupid, was married to a woman whose ugliness and sluttishness were public knowledge. He was tired of having the authorities in his district laugh in his face when he told them about a ghost. He declared that he was not going to leave the Lieutenancy unless he received some assistance. This thing had prevented him from consummating his marriage, or so he said, whereas it was in fact his wife . . .[21]

There were others who took so much advantage of the credulity of others that they were condemned to the galleys for life. Such was the case of the priest Robert Pons,[22] who extorted money from the dying by means of an extensive network of accomplices. His operation was based on the unlikely but unique and ingenious trade in accounts of experiences beyond the grave. Thus we see inmates of the *hôtel-dieu* undertaking in their dying agony, and upon payment of a sum of money, to point out places where there was buried treasure – a fiction invented out of nowhere.

So it was that the police took on board little Madeleine and her family. The type of activity involved in this case is particularly interesting because of its variety and because it corresponds to a function of traditional policing which is little known. As has often been said, the Paris police was not solely an instrument of repression; as well as being an agent of control, there were also elements of dithering and occasionally, incitement.

The calendar of events probably explains it better. Quickly submerged by an agitated crowd and solemnly reproved by the clergy, Chaban, Secretary of State for the Police, demanded that the child's mother should cease receiving people. Inspector Ferrat, who was responsible for carrying out the order, simply reported that the mother, in a letter, had announced to spectators that at the present time the little one had gone off to Versailles. This had failed to stop the regular gathering of crowds, however, and on the evening of 10 May, Madeleine left her house in a sedan chair to go and live for the time being in the Rue de Seine, where her mother immediately opened her doors once again to the public. The authorities, fed up with all this upheaval, threatened the Ernault woman with arrest. She resisted, however, shed a few tears and refused to leave her door shut, 'because if she did that, her daughter would become ill'. Others attempted to reason with her, arguing that she was a very bad example for other unnatural mothers who would then have no hesitation in prostituting their children 'in the sordid hope of profiting from the simplicity of the public'. Nothing of the kind. She calmly replied that the gifts she had received had not even managed to meet the costs of the house and the removal . . .

At no time during these months of May and June did the police adopt a firm position. They were no doubt uncertain about what steps to take and did not wish to upset the Ernault family. The Inspector, the Commissioner and the Lieutenant-General alike only managed to contain the disorder; they never intervened directly at its source nor denied the phenomenon itself. Moreover, by the beginning of July an 'account' of the story was being sold on the streets; and the crowd was even thicker, but this time it was divided – 'the majority of those who came did not think she was pregnant, but believed instead that it was a matter of a foreign body. The doctors and midwives, however, expressed no such doubts.'

In mid-July, the midwife announced that the birth was imminent. A duchess, whose name is not known, asked to be present at the birth as well as Mlle Gossin from the Comédie-Française, who had been to see the young girl quite frequently. Then came a police resolution which was surprising, to say the least. It was a resolution which had not been taken at the top of the hierarchy and was probably not ordered by the Lieutenant-General of Police; it seems to have been the personal initiative of one of the policemen himself, Inspector Gillot. He had been following the affair closely for some time and had been sending him notes every other day. On 3 August 1756, following his report that Jacquotte (the name that had been popularly given to the child) 'was more upset than usual and had had one or two slight pains but nothing further', he wrote, 'I have made the decision to sleep there so as to be in a position to provide you with an exact account of this event.' He reminds one on several occasions of this decision in his letters: '19 August 1756. I am sleeping here every night so that in the event of anything occurring, I can warn Monsieur immediately.'

Apparently no one, not even one of his superiors, commented on the bizarre nature of his decision, let alone the fact that it might be superfluous or even inopportune. Gillot remained at the Ernaults' and was there for quite some time. Perhaps even he himself became somewhat impatient; on 25 August he refers to his own home and makes the note that 'I will continue to sleep here up until the time that Monsieur gives me orders to the contrary.'

Here we have police activity pushed to its upper limit and in some ways faithful to its own perception of its work, that is to be present at the event, infiltrate and become a part of it even to the extent of becoming fully incorporated in it. The aim was the achievement of perfect control which would conform to the idea of order and the image of policing defined as the 'science of the right moment'. In the days of the ecstatics of the cemetery of Saint-Médard, inspectors and clerks made daily notes of their actions and words, as the archives of the Bastille testify. That it was

Gillot's own decision to award himself this task, and thereby attract attention to himself by splashing himself with some of the glory if ever this prodigy actually occurred, is of little importance. He was only able to take it on because his decision conformed with the current modes of police functioning and were in keeping with that particular social utopia from which the police scarcely ever departed.[23] He stayed with the family because he believed the news of the impending birth. By being there both night and day he was participating in the belief, and in some ways giving it life and breath, perhaps even encouraging and reviving it, if it should falter. What followed was to illustrate this even more clearly.

### From rumour to error

The news was prodigious enough in itself. The parents were also determined to broadcast it and the crowd was both curious and receptive. When the police stepped into the whole business this was not particularly unusual. They did it for the most part by maintaining a physical presence, which allowed them to witness events at the same time as maintaining some control over them; and for the rest by consenting to the circulation of the news by means of leaflets and broadsheets, at least up until the time when it became necessary to recognize the mistake. Following this, another pamphlet had to be issued specifically for making a public justification of the error, which was something of a rare event.

From the first complaint registered with the commissioner by the Ernault parents in May 1756 to the imprisonment of the mother in October and her subsequent release six months later, the course of events was indeed tortuous and involved. Rumour became news; certainty gained its authenticity in the written word before being finally abandoned as an error which was then presented to the public in the form of a confession to having been deceived. A strange course indeed, and perhaps what makes it so original is the fact that not only were the police present at every stage but that proceedings were endorsed, justified and authenticated by them from beginning to end – from the credible to the true, and from the true to the erroneous.

The fact that a written version of little Madeleine's unlikely story was in circulation should come as no surprise for, invaded as it was by crime, accidents and major or minor catastrophes, the city was not simply content to pass on these incidents by word of mouth, inflating or deflating the news as it passed from ear to ear: it also carried on the trade in written form.[24]

Newsmongers, duly licensed against the distribution of unsound or libellous material, regularly cried their wares, these 'accounts' of strange, astounding or disturbing stories for which the city served as a theatre. All of these leaflets carried the mention 'With Permission', and were only allowed to circulate if they had in fact been authorized by the police. The ignominious, the unheard of and the desperate were the privileged sources of these stories of a sheet and a day and could be bought for next to nothing on the street corner, all of which helped multiply to infinity the reactions of the citizens to their environment.

The written evidence in support of the adventures of Madeleine/Jacquotte went more or less like this:[25] news of the pregnancy was sold in the streets in June or July 1756; this was followed in August 1756 by another sheet entitled *Details, or Further Explanation of the First Account Concerning the Girl by the Name of Magdeleine-Charlotte-Jacquotte, Daughter of Louis Renaud*[26] *and Magdeleine Laflèche Being Happily Delivered of a Son who has been Named Jean-Louis* . . . This broadsheet was an authorized publication; it gives an account of an event which, as we know, never took place; and Gueulette, commenting on it in 1758 in notes written on the back of the account, shows no sign of surprise or regret for the mistake: 'It appears that this account was intended to have been passed off as having police approval. It was most certainly sold off to bidders in the street where I myself bought it. The pregnancy has proved to be false, however, and the birth, in consequence, extremely false.'[27]

A denial of the whole affair (also in August, it would appear) was published under the title *Justification of the Two Accounts* and it too had received permission to be sold. It explained how the error had managed to creep in and mentions a criticism of the account of the birth which the parents had been careful to distribute. There is some attempt in the criticism to rehabilitate the memory of the young man, who had died in prison broken with grief, and in this justification, mention is made of the fact that the parents had shown no concern for the law. A month later, the mother was imprisoned in La Salpêtrière and only came out six months later on an appeal from her husband who had had responsibility for the children.

One needs to unravel this tangled skein of contradictory information published with the approval of the authorities. If there were credulity, then one is forced to admit that it had nothing more to support it than the wind.

In the absence of the text of the first 'Account' announcing and explaining the unfortunate pregnancy, an examination of the 'Details', or announcement of the happy news of the birth is extremely interesting, particularly as it was false and had to be officially recognized as such.

How was it possible to have had any doubts, when in the first few lines there is the announcement of the baby's birth and baptism and a declaration that the names of the godmother and father would be given. All the details then follow – the length of the labour, the time of birth, the invaluable services of the male midwife who was none other than that of the Dauphine herself and the whole of this extraordinary delivery accomplished by Madeleine after so much exhausting trial and effort.

The whole affair was then developed at length in order to give it more weight and credibility; the midwife was shown to be surrounded by well-recognized and highly competent scientific authorities from such institutions as the Faculty of Medicine and the Academy of Surgeons and by the most illustrious scholars with the approval of the royal family itself. The child-prodigy, thus encompassed and overseen by the great and mighty, became the property of the State: 'It became a duty never to abandon this young girl for a moment and from that point onward, she was regarded as a sacred charge to be held in trust by the State.'

This first part of the account which enlists every means of authentication possible (detailed information, presence of the Faculty of Medicine) also plays on a note of concern for the child which could not fail to go down well with those who bought the text, grabbed by the news, for it was only six years after the abduction of children from off the very same streets of Paris; it must undoubtedly have had a traumatic effect on ears and minds. That Madeleine should be considered a sacred charge entrusted by the State to a lofty medical authority was some proof that children were still at the heart of the social system, even if they were the children of the poorer classes. If one bears in mind that it was the worker or artisan who had lost a son or daughter and who had participated in the revolt of 1750, one can see how the reasoning and logic of this leaflet announcing the birth took into account the prevailing social climate of the Parisian population of 1756. For the news to be well received, not only did it need to contain elements showing the event to be authentic, it also had to be presented in a form which was on the whole reassuring and which would allow the reader to assimilate it in a wider context which was both socially and politically satisfying. One can read from this that the King and the State were reluctant to see off young Madeleine, the tobacconist's daughter, and in a context which was so conciliatory by comparison with 1750, the 'credible' easily became established.

The second part of the account deals with the quite extraordinary aspects of the course of the birth itself and then proceeds to marvel at this utterly exceptional and hitherto unheard-of forcible intrusion into one of the most fragile and vulnerable of human frames. Sets of contradictions – weakness and strength; ordinary and extraordinary; natural and phenomenal – were manipulated and appropriated with no concern for detail or precision.

The whole thing comes to a rather rapid conclusion by proceeding to give the names of the godmother and godfather – as it said it would at the beginning – whilst in fact ensuring that no such names were there on the grounds that permission to give them had not been granted. The presence of the names of 'Monsieur le Comte de —— and Mlle la Marquise de —— who held the child at the baptismal font (although we cannot mention them by name)' was sufficiently logical and authenticating as to remain unperturbed by any actual absence of names which in the end were superfluous to the act of believing. Who would have doubted for one moment the presence of this count and marchioness? Did the blanks representing their names not possess a reality equal to the actual letters of their respective patronyms?

Time went by. Towards the end of September and the beginning of October, some doubts were expressed among the doctors and midwives and attempts were made to protect themselves from public criticism. On 10 October, for instance, they declared unanimously that the child was definitely not pregnant 'but that there were only swellings throughout the body and that all it could be was an accumulation of fluid'.

Now was the time to beat a dignified retreat from the whole of this fable. Doctors were certain that the 'bulk' they had felt had been sufficient to suggest a pregnancy but the police wasted no time in obtaining an order for the detention of the mother and daughter. Meanwhile on the streets they were selling the *Justification of the Two Accounts* which calmly explained why the deception had been possible; the text is exemplary in showing how far it is possible for 'truth' and hearsay to travel down the same road, even at times merging as one.

The title of this pamphlet bears no resemblance to the others; nor is it concerned with detail, narrative, or telling a strange tale. The purpose of the flysheet was contained entirely within its title which was primarily to justify itself. This involved a dual approach, the one being to admit the error and the other to present the argument in such a way as to show that it was impossible not to have been taken in. If the justification was also a form of defence and legitimization and a means of dissociating oneself from blame, then what it said was essentially determined by an attempt to contrive that, and thus the main concern of the argument was to present the evidence in such a way that proof of initial innocence was more important than the formulation of some 'truth' which, though forever elusive, was to triumph in the end.

It was in fact around this difficult theme of the constitution of the truth that the text was composed, and did so in two distinct stages, for it was necessary to show that it was quite normal to publish the announcement of the pregnancy and then of the birth, given the 'truth' of these facts.

How did the pregnancy come to be believed? In this case the process was quite simple. It was all the result, as usual, of that indefinable phenomenon generally referred to as 'talk'. In Paris there was this girl of nine and a half who was seven months pregnant – and so the rumour, by definition, got around. Those who were curious came to have a look and, to quote, their eyes were the surest means of establishing proof of the truth. The medical profession came along too since this supposed pregnancy 'naturally' fell within their field of competence. Thanks to the eyes of the visitors and the confirmation of the pregnancy by medical opinion, the rumours blew all the more swiftly and ever further afield. From then on, the truth was established, which 'gave rise to the first account'. What was in it? Only what was circulating orally – hearsay – in fact, nothing more than the truth, the truth that their eyes had seen. It was all sewn up – talk was truth, thanks to the eyes, to medical authentication and to the publication of the news. The truth was none other than what had been seen and what had been said and truly that was the truth – because they had seen it and said that it was so.

We also know, from evidence of other events of the same sort unconnected with medicine, that for rumour to become truth, there was no need for the stamp of approval from the authorities. In this case the support of the medical declaration was an additional bonus but it was in no way indispensable to the process of elaborating the truth.

It was more difficult, apparently, for the authors of the text to justify the publication of the announcement of the birth. However, a similar kind of machinery was put in place in order to present an argument which hopefully might achieve some semblance of the truth, although it was likely to be a semblance of an altogether different order. In this instance, it was a case of convincing everyone that there was good reason for having been on the outside of the truth.

For part two of the demonstration of proof, one sees the appearance of a person who is named and accused of acting as an agent directly responsible for promoting the 'deception', a surgeon and the 'so-called midwife of Mme la Dauphine'. How could one possibly have believed him? There was nothing haphazard about the way things had been done, for we read in the justification that everything was by 'general agreement'. This 'general agreement' was incontestable by virtue of the fact that it was 'generally agreed'.

In the case of a suspected pregnancy however, there was only one event which would obviously serve as proof, and that was the birth of the child itself, for which, as we know, it was just a matter of waiting... It was announced by a second account which, as it made quite clear, was exactly in keeping with public opinion and thus the very opposite of a lie. The mechanics remained the same – the child was born, yes, well and truly born, because it was the voice of the public that made the announcement.

However, it is not possible to invent a birth, and in the end there could be no mistaking that Madeleine had not had a child and never would have one. The parents issued a note criticizing the account of the delivery but the flysheet confessed to a deception by this surgeon who was full of ambition and had wanted to draw attention to himself. They had been deceived, just as everyone had been deceived – probably more so – and therefore had taken it upon themselves to disabuse the public.

One sees very clearly in this *Justification of the Two Accounts* that it was impossible to separate the 'generally agreed' from aspects of the truth because each was welded to the other so as to construct a process by which, following the birth of the truth from hearsay and rumour, the same rumours once again might become a posteriori the sole means of authentication – except, of course, in exceptionally rare cases where a little girl happened to decide that she was not in fact harbouring a child in her belly.

The mechanics of this spiral (in which truth was based on news and information which themselves ultimately provided the possibility of proving the truth) were not simply the prerogative of the man in the street. When the authorities, whether intellectual, political or judicial, denounced the countless rumours appropriated and sometimes made more dangerous by the people, they were a long way from realizing that their own modes of thinking, interpreting and speaking contained identical forms of apprehending the truth or reality. The story of these three bulletins (two erroneous reports and one justification admitting guilt) is proof of this. The three texts had been approved by the police and were part of the same line of thought. In each case they were written to encourage belief, even though two-thirds of the material was shown to be completely false. In order to gather support they had played on traditional patterns of deference to the written word. The techniques used in the final account, whose job it was to nullify the first two, departed little from the initial approach. In putting an end to the belief they relied on self-defence, which once again meant the integration of the 'truth/generally agreed' equation, the very same as had been responsible for creating the false news about the pregnancy and the birth in the first place. At that level, therefore, there was no difference, although what one was required to believe now was exactly the opposite of what had been believed previously. These accounts, which had received police backing, had alternately encouraged belief and then attempted to establish the truth once evidence of the error had become manifest. Just like the Parisians themselves, they did it by the same means as they had used to lay hold of what was real, namely by availing themselves of the rumours which the affair had provoked.

The Lieutenant-General of Police acted in response to this news–gossip–rumour and generally agreed. He drew up strategies on the basis of the moods of all and sundry plucked from here and there, all over the city, not concerning himself much with their substance or merit or their exact origins. In the Archives of the Bastille, there are reports kept on a daily basis which illustrate this particular way of thinking and acting. What happened was that the Lieutenant-General gave commissions to several officers from various police units, making them responsible for gathering and collating current opinion in the form of what was being said in a number of public places.[28] These officers kept minutely detailed reports on what they had seen and heard and these reports were made exclusively to the Lieutenant-General, on whom they were directly dependent;[29] these were the famous *gazetins de la police secrète*,[30] the form and phraseology of which are as revealing as their content.

Reading these reports, which were so punctiliously kept, one notices immediately that not only was the Lieutenant-General being sustained by rumour (which lent itself admirably to the construction of his policy) but that he was working on material and information (provided by his officers) whose precise source was never exactly known, its extent being scarcely mentioned, let alone its initial author. One might be tempted to think, and with good cause, that if these reports were being produced in roughly the same way from the beginning to the end of the eighteenth century then it must have been in keeping with the wishes of Lieutenant-Generals and appropriate to their ways of working and of getting to know the world around them. The approach used in these written records certainly indicates a system of policing whose function was to take more than a close interest in the slightest whispers passing back and forth between all and sundry, with no effort to cut out the extraneous, to separate the valid from the invalid, the possible from the plausible or the *a fortiori*, or the true from the false. The whole tone is monotonous and the content homogeneous; the same techniques used throughout mean that each item of news received was given equal status. It might be confidential information; a fag-end of gossip or public uproar; an impression or an exact factual account that was either very important or derisory; it might be spread abroad by one person or thousands; it might have sprung from the imagination or result from the urgency of a situation, it made no matter.

In these writings, which ultimately are very monotonous, there is nothing in particular which stands out; everything is atonal for all the information is treated in the same way whether it comes from the court or the street, the army or the royal family. Furthermore, the wording and composition are also a part of this levelling process; it is the impersonal, and endlessly repeated pronoun 'it' (*on*) which is the subject and which is in fact king, throughout these reports, taking precedence over the King himself. Should a rumour be notified, a tale told or an accident occur which provoked some comment, it is the immutable 'it' which without fail calls the tune. Stuck there from the first line till last, 'it' is the producer of black or white without any distinction whatever – 'it is said'; 'it is certain';

'in addition it'; 'it was definitely felt in the neighbourhood that...'; and so on and so forth. On and on roll these texts, based on countless words and rumours which exited from mouths one knows not where. It is very rare to find a more precise subject than this inevitable 'it'; occasionally, in the flow of the pen, one does come across 'a few artisans and particular persons complaining about...'[31] But it is the exception, as are attempts to find the authors of the received information. These amount to no more than, 'These facts were obtained from someone called Soloz who is a hawker of salt; he says that he heard someone speak the words in question';[32] or else, 'This information was received from Sieur Laisné who said that he had heard it from Sieur Abbé le Colan who said that he knew no more about it.'[33] Sometimes the approximations double up on themselves in phrases such as these: 'the majority of people feel that people are not happy' and 'they also said that the public are saying that...'.

If the subjects are effaced, the locations also remain undifferentiated: 'It is being said in the palaces as well as in the various cafés, public esplanades and private houses that...'[34] Reference to the strength or vehemence of the statements are extremely rare and the reports are noticeably lacking in any variety of rhythm or intensity of tone. With some effort it is possible to discern from afar subtle differences between 'they did not hesitate to say that...' and 'they also said it but under their breath'. The impression produced by reading these *gazetins* is that everything had the same effect, namely that what was heard was sovereign, a constituent of the truth and grounds for action that required no further information about the place whence it had originated, the social milieu in which it was circulating, nor the seriousness of which it might be an indicator.

Not only did the police find it desirable to be present in this oral system (police officers infiltrated cafés, streets and esplanades; the inspector slept in with the residents when there were strange goings-on), but the police also turned themselves into an immediate mouthpiece for it, carrying the news to the very top of the hierarchy without in this instance offering the means of assessing it – that was not required. The police were positively inhabited by hearsay and rumour, unable to keep their distance since it was in these that they found their motives for action. At this level of analysis, we can perhaps understand better how ridiculous were their attempts to prove or denounce popular fears and credulity and see to what extent they themselves acted as proprietors, links and relays of the same, thus embodying what they at the same time were denouncing. It is no longer possible to see them as invested with a knowledge which sought to repress credulity and superstition, false information and fraud (even though a part of its activity was based on such assignments). It has to be understood in its complexity; that is, in its primary movement towards fusion with what it was seeking to extirpate in the bosom of the populace and which gave it so much cause for fear and apprehension, namely an immediate attachment to gossip and rumour.

## But the neighbours remained sceptical

Madeleine's story offers the historian something of a chance, for it allows us to discover, with some degree of accuracy, the main actors in the event as well as those around it, either by virtue of giving their consent, or by keeping their distance from it. As we have already examined the respective roles of the doctors and police, let us for the time being single out the reactions of the people in the course of the months of waiting and see whether or not these conform to what was often said of them on these occasions.

Whether or not the parents believed in the pregnancy of their child, it is impossible to tell from the records and notably from those of Inspector Gillot, even though he was living on the premises. There is every likelihood that they did believe it; but what is most important is to see them as they set about presenting this event – seeing what they could make out of it for themselves, finding the best way of promoting Madeleine to the public and doing everything they could to make the spectacle of their pregnant child really important. The father himself openly admitted to having set things up in this way when he requested the release of his wife in February 1757. He confessed to having gained money from it but blamed the initial error on the doctors who had spread the news as far as the court.

The attitude of the parents was a determining factor and the mother, in particular, was responsible for creating misgivings in the immediate neighbourhood. In fact, once they were installed in the Rue de Seine as a result of a police injunction, Mme Ernault gained in confidence – too much so – and in June, when their influence was at its peak, the mother's cravings for making a profit intensified. She began sizing up the crowd and sifting them out, only allowing in 'those who were dressed in a particular way' and refusing the others on the grounds that they did not have permission. Some of the women from the market of the abbey of Saint-Germain-des-Prés who were pushed out of the front door were not fooled by her tactics. They bawled at the woman through the window that, 'if they had had an *écu* to put in her purse or a tippet on their shoulder, they knew very well they wouldn't have needed permission or anything of the kind.' They could also see that the better-off visitors were bringing pretty little gifts with them for Madeleine and her future infant; there were little knick-knacks, a nightdress-case trimmed with muslin and a little Indian silk jacket.

Doubt began to creep in as a result of this social differentiation of her public by the Ernault woman and the doubt was also retriggered by the death of young Denis in prison at Bicêtre, where he had expired in grief. As time went by, the crowds began to thin out but still the doctors were active. The public, however, had done its calculations and by the beginning of August they no longer believed that the birth would happen: 'Once, according to the calculations of the public, she had passed her term, there were no longer any visits to speak of.'

No one (according to the reports of Inspector Gillot) seemed to react to the false account of the termination of Madeleine's confinement, as though the whole affair had already been summed up, leaving just the doctors to grapple with their doubt and a so-called male midwife to wrestle with his ambition. It was the justification of the two accounts in which it was announced that the details of the birth and the delivery had been wrong that provoked a veritable eruption of disorder. While the doctors were awaiting the delivery for 8 September, the mother of the young girl went off to do her shopping at the market of Saint-Germain-des-Prés at 5 o'clock in the evening of 18 August. She was recognized by a baker's wife and was insulted and booed by all the women at the market who ran behind her shouting that 'she ought to be killed because she had caused the death of this innocent boy whom she had accused'.

The violence was so fierce that Commissioner Hubert was obliged to intervene and the market gates were closed while the Guard came to the protection of Mme Ernault, who had been forced to take shelter in a shop selling lingerie and underwear. She had to go out in disguise through a back door in order to avoid the wrath of the crowd and that same evening four women were arrested for leading the breach of the peace. It took some time for calm to return and Gillot notes that there was a furious outcry over the sentencing of the young wine vendor's boy who had died before he had even been executed. A few days later, the Ernault parents published a criticism of the account of the birth and requested prayers for Denis, the wine vendor's boy. However, as soon as the medical declaration was made that the girl was not pregnant, the police put the child and the mother in prison.

It is interesting to note the gaps and time shifts, as between the various occurrences and social groups. The doctors and the police were the slowest to go back on their initial positions – in fact they lingered on until October, two months after the term should have been up. The publications were spread over a short period, from June to August, and once the announcement of the birth had been made, it needed to be denied almost immediately. For its part, the population had its own rhythm as it awaited the arrival of this prodigy which was marked by events proper to itself and out of step with what was going on between medical opinion, the parents and the police.

The neighbours in the district and the women from the market of Saint-Germain-des-Prés were of more or less the same social status as the Ernault parents, who were retailers of salt and tobacco. Because they were on a similar economic level and shared the same way of life, they were very sensitive to all the external signs of wealth or refinement put out by this family who, to boot, had only just settled in the district, having deserted their original *faubourg*. The effects of this distancing were apparent from the time little Madeleine arrived in the Rue de Seine, with the neighbourhood in a state of alert, and more ready and better placed than others to interpret all these new goings-on taking place before their eyes.

The fact that the mother of the child had wanted to divide the curious into two clans, 'the well-heeled' and the rest, aggravated this feeling of strangeness felt in connection with what was taking place. Those people from the district who had found themselves rebuffed (when in actual fact they were tit for tat just the same as *that* family) were not prepared to put up with the initiation of this kind of demarcation by one of their own kind, of the same status and condition as themselves. They experienced this segregation based on money-making as a form of betrayal which obviously brought with it criticism and animosity and then doubt and the search for fraud and deception. Thus it is possible to state that the first breach occurred at this point in contrast with the support one might have thought would have been naturally in evidence. Those who were 'curious' were not blinded by what was happening to the point of accepting it unquestioningly.

In urban milieux, medical science was gradually taking root and in Paris, seat of the Faculté and the Académie, the official medical bodies had considerable importance. A number of edicts, followed up by the prosecution of offenders, had recently outlawed medical charlatanism and those who dealt in wonder drugs and cures. Wherever dubious practice was spotted or the public abused by quacks and the pharmacopoeia of impostors, the police arrested and condemned these tricksters and criminals along with their frightening drugs. There was widespread concern over popular gullibility which created a ready market of willing victims all prepared to buy and swallow dubious pills and potions.

In its turn, the Faculty of Medicine wished to have its knowledge and learning acknowledged and for all forms of religious and medical superstition to be overcome. It was a difficult battle and in the process of establishing their superiority over the hoards of drug dealers and manufacturers, they uncovered vast chasms of ignorance. It was particularly in the field of obstetrics that medical effort was most intense if for no other reason than to diminish the alarming statistics for death in childbirth. Clinical observation and the attraction of anatomical discoveries led the medical profession on and on into making endless observations and palpations for themselves in an attempt to penetrate the mysteries of the womb, the giver of life.

The fact that little Madeleine had been 'visited' (as the phrase went) and observed day after day should really come as no surprise; nor should the attitude of the women in the district. After the nine months were up, they lost interest in the event. According to Officer Gillot, they had 'done their calculations'; familiarity with childbirth and its bodily imprint in their memories kept them close to a calendar from which there was no separating them – neither curiosity nor the ignorance of the medical profession. They knew in their bodies the time for the child to be born, and although they may have been willing to accept the idea that a child might be pregnant they could not wait indefinitely for the infant to be born; their sense of time was of another order.

What was taking place here was an autonomous action in relation to the body of medical knowledge as well as to the affair itself and this autonomy was being built and pieced together bit by bit. The attitude of the Ernault family had forced a distance which had in its turn given rise to doubt; knowledge of oneself and of 'the things of life' such as motherhood and birth had done the rest. The brief movement of revolt came when the time was ripe and it found immediate support in the publication of the justification, which only served to confirm what everyone already knew. Not only had the child not been born, there was no way it could be born as it did not and had never existed. The resulting emotion in the market of Saint-German-des-Prés was typical. It was founded on the basis of the publication of the news-sheet but it released the pent-up anger and doubt that had been contained for some time, revealing an absence of credulity which the printed sheet had just shown was entirely justified and which had arisen as a result of the tying and untying of the bonds between the Ernault family and the district. Here we have the subtle systems of knowledge and sociability which are only revealed by watching an event as it unfolds day after day.

Even though tales of pregnant girls did not exactly run up and down the streets in the eighteenth century, there were many others of a similar kind which did. They may have drawn on other facts involving other value systems or modes of understanding, but they too in their own way conveyed their particular realities, fantasies, illusions, and frauds, and were equally carried along by assent and affirmation here or scepticism there. In general it is these incidents, anecdotes and extravagances that are totally ignored; the broad-swept memory of the historian can find room only for corporate phenomena of vast proportions; all the rest remains outside the memory, stuffed away in the archives, occasionally turning up in the odd bit of marginal research. But crowds come running to see incidents both great and small; it would be interesting to know, for example, whether the ecstatics of Saint-Médard assumed greater importance in the collective memory of the residents of the period than the Ernault affair or the deceit of Abbé Pons in respect of the dead and dying at the *hôtel-dieu*. It might be worth finding out.

Whatever the case may be, a microscopic analysis of the scandal in the Rue Saint-Victor (Madeleine–Jacquotte Ernault had lived with her parents in the Rue Saint-Victor) allows one to see how it was possible to galvanize around it the various social strata in all their complexities and respective comings and goings. When faced with such an event, one is able to see the deployment of a whole array of actions and reactions, some of them common to the whole of the various social classes and others that were decidedly different. The notion that credulousness can be dismissed as being the property of the least favoured of the social groups becomes redundant when one is given the chance to analyse the whole game of interdependence between the various authorities, the circulation of written material and the propagation of rumour. And finally, if one chooses to retain the expression 'the crowds amongst themselves' as a means of defining those times of spontaneous assembly around some street incident or some previously planned event, then one has to keep in mind that these crowds were largely heterogeneous and split between any number of social and cultural divisions. The social commentators of the day, however, could only perceive them as one vast human body animated by a single soul in one single movement, which in their eyes made them all the more impulsive, dangerous and unpredictable. Louis-Sébastien Mercier, making fun of those who had gone along to a certain rendezvous to see a man shut himself up in a bottle, referred to a people who were gullible and naive, who reacted as one and who were incapable of putting a distance between themselves and the objects of their contemplation: 'Such are the people', he said; 'as a body, they do not believe they can be taken in.'[35] And for that, they were required to have no more than one body.

The Ernault affair allows one to discern the potential for autonomy among the different social groups in relation to an external event, certainly as far as the least well-off from the social classes were concerned, who were 'naturally' or traditionally described as being the least wary in the face of the broadcast of news of a more or less extraordinary nature.

At the same time, the episode also exposed the modes of intervention employed by the authorities (principally the police), which contain an ingenious and paradoxical mixture of incitement, control and repression which occurred simultaneously or in a series of ripples depending on the creative possibilities of the wide range of social attitudes. Being themselves nurtured by and party to the same view of the world as those they administered, the police were, oddly enough, strangers to the event rather than an integral part of it; and the control they exercised over it contained as many factors likely to regenerate it as powers to contain it. In certain cases, the police were responsible for stirring up problems as much as for repressing them, for they contained within themselves, like a mirror, the whole tangle of social complexity; but as far as official documentation is concerned, there is not much recognition of this reality.

Such a plurality of attitudes, particularly in this area comprising extraordinary happenings and phenomena which were responsible for drawing the crowds, no doubt stemmed from the fact that after 1750 (a time of great trouble and mistrust between the King and his subjects), rationalism had found itself in contact not only with a certain degree of scientific thinking but also with a sense of the global and the universal in which there was a combination of the rational and the marvellous, allowing one to think the unthinkable. The police found themselves involved at each of these levels (enthusiasm for reason – inclination to doubt – the implications of the marvellous and miraculous) and responded tit for tat with their own ideas of the disorder that was likely to ensue, with no attempt at an assessment that might be any more rational than anyone else's, thus resembling the masses they were responsible for keeping in order.

These same crowds might best be typified by three particular crazes, of which there were many. During the same year as the Ernault affair, on 18 March 1756, the Lieutenant-General of Police was called on by priests and lawyers to put a stop to the practices of a group of people who had been making a mockery of Lent, and celebrating weird nocturnal sabbaths in the quarries of Charenton.[36] It was apparent that there was evil afoot, and in spite of warnings each night became a theatre for excesses that were considered sacrilegious. Some of the girls dressed up as boys and got together in the *cabarets*, engaging in conversation which embarrassed the men; others sang wicked songs and spewed up before the doors of religious establishments. On Ash Wednesday, wearing cassocks and funeral surplices, hordes of young lads with great heads made out of straw gathered in long lines and went hobbling and limping along, spraying evening strollers with calves' hooves soaked in dirty water. Alongside them there were women and girls 'dressed up as though they were pregnant' and laughing and wailing in the light of their torches. Not everyone found it amusing and those responsible were imprisoned on the King's orders, signed by the Lieutenant-General of Police.

In the same period, the discovery of anatomy and its fascination with corpses produced some strange consequences with the result that police kept watch on cemeteries which had become the scene of somewhat unusual nocturnal trafficking. Corpses were selling for as much as 150 *livres* each:

> Each assistant received 10 for each dead body and sometimes they carried off as many as six or eight in one evening without counting small children, as they were able to get more of them in one coffin. When they had furnished Paris with its needs, they then went on to do the outlying areas.[37]

With the mind fixed on these macabre visions and medical progress in general, all levels of society found themselves gripped with the fear of being buried alive, producing a crop of medical literature which tended to be more haunting than reassuring.[38] The fear of remaining alive in the darkness of the tomb gave rise to a number of ingenious devices such as the lugubrious bells which were intended to indicate signs of life to cemetery wardens. It was a fear which affected everyone and rumours spread in all quarters. There is also an echo of it in Hardy's Journal where he tells the tale of one of the procurators of the *parlement*, a M. Trespagne who died one day in January 1772 and was buried shortly afterwards. He was found by one of the beadles who had come to bring another body. 'His coffin was open as though by an effort made with the side of the head, there was blood everywhere and all the evidence that he had gnawed his own arm in desperation.' Such images as this – the dead man devouring himself because he was still alive – were enough to freeze the living with fear, and they occur quite frequently in contemporary writings. There were enough memoirs, reflections and advice published on this subject to make the imagination run riot. There were bolts that had been shot, broken seals, goblets of water tied to the body with a cord, watchmen ready to hear the slightest moan, moving coffins, etc. It is known, for instance, that Mme Necker, terrified by this idea of life beneath the shroud, was to organize her tomb in minute detail and arrange to be buried so that her face could be seen.[39]

There was derision and fear, but there was also enthusiasm for scientific discoveries both true and false. There were as many people who came to watch the flight of air balloons as there were those who tried to get small balloons, usually made from a pig's bladder, off the ground from their bedroom floor. Both men and women shared this new craze and 'the fair sex willingly gave up the important business of its toilette in order to try things out.'[40] Physicists gave private classes or even stood up and lectured the odd number of loafers who were keen to keep up with current trends. Why not turn up in droves to watch the famous man who had chosen to cross the Seine in elastic boots? He was selling them by advance subscription to innocent purchasers who had been taken in. The inventor found himself imprisoned at the police station by the Lieutenant-General of Police and was told that 'he should not amuse himself at the expense of the people of Paris by finding out just how far it was possible to take their credulity'.[41]

# 10

# The Crowds in Turmoil

The one thing about the crowd, and in the towns of the eighteenth century in particular, was that it was a key part of the urban system. It was also an essential component of the monarchical process, which could not dispense with its existence, at the same time as being one of the major pre-occupations of those in government. In short, it was inevitable, necessary and yet extremely risky. In its very existence it displayed a certain quality that was irreconcilable with the planning and protection constantly formulated on its behalf as a group or collectivity held to be naturally hard-working, loyal, submissive and approving of power from above.

Underlying this scheme of things whereby peace and order founded on obedience might prevail, one finds both the conviction and the argument that the crowd, consisting as it did of ordinary people, was a homogeneous whole which needed close watching so as to prevent it going off course and doing itself harm in mindless outbursts of anger.

Poor and wanting in intelligence, occasionally woman and sometimes child, the crowd had to be protected from itself and then brought to order by a simple system of distribution of provisions in the form of work and the means of subsistence. A regularly nourished and appropriately paid crowd would have no difficulty applauding at each royal passing.

Because the thesis held about it was founded on a very narrow representation of its nature and a crude understanding of its mechanisms and peculiarities, it was inevitably proved to be deficient by everyday practice and by the countless reactions and responses of the crowd. But instead of being called into question as a result of this failure, the argument stuck, reinforced and redoubled itself in strictures of stunning inertia in which the gap was dug deeper between the real, both cruel and flippant, and a utopia that had to be maintained at all costs. When the crowd stopped applauding and rioted instead, those in power were gripped with fear and what they had to say was then full of hate; and the fear which was so intense at times provoked much reaction.

Mobs and crowds were dreaded by the police and as a result constant thought was given to the problem, with no shortage of legislation on the subject. But in spite of all that, it would appear that the police and the authorities allowed themselves to be taken by surprise when insubordination and indiscipline erupted right out onto the street. All this gave Paris, particularly in the years following 1750, a rather strange atmosphere in which the fear of an uprising was on everyone's lips and in which precautions were taken. But if emotions did well up, the police became almost hysterical at the consequences the incident might provoke and so adopted attitudes that were more conciliatory than provocative. In the minds of the authorities, an assembled crowd was the potential seed of a howling mob which might be ready for anything, and it was therefore up to the police to see that the situation was not aggravated and the occurrence of a disaster prevented.

The very idea of an uprising engendered a plethora of writings and theses, albeit repetitive, on the subject of a populace given over to a state of animal-like brutality and spurred on by leaders who had emerged from banditry or the lowest depths of the prisons of Bicêtre or Fort-l'Evêque. Whilst this opinion held firm, another fundamental idea cherished by the state and those in power broke down, such that the concept of the crowd as necessary friend, indispensable support and sacred pedestal whose consent and adherence was constantly sought became that of dangerous enemy and the pernicious pole around which everything could be sent reeling. Power thus found itself gripped in a vice, for it had only two ways, both of them certainties, of thinking of the crowd: namely, as fundamentally assenting and approbatory or as all too readily ungrateful and cruel. Everyday reality, however, had the effect of diminishing both these models, which were so firmly anchored in the minds of the elites, to reveal a much more varied and complex landscape which unsettled those in charge. Subsequently, what knowledge the great and important might have had about the masses of the people finally lapsed into uncertainty due to its entrenchment between these two grand and rigid formulations which banked as much on the wisdom of the crowd as on its folly.

And thus when agitation did occur, anxiety became the only element that was clearly identifiable; and in fact, the reality of the street obliged the police to transform their ritual type of analysis. Up to this point they had named the crowd as such, had identified it and characterized it in simple and antagonistic terms, the main concern, in short, being to contain it in a single term – acclamation. Movements, breaches of the peace and riots spoiled the cards in one's hand; the people became 'unnameable' and the whole machine snarled up in the face of definitions that escaped it. The powers that be did the thinking for the crowd, but the crowd was elsewhere, something other and thus in no way could power or authority lay hold of it in its capacity as thinking subject capable of using strategies and personal analyses of the situation. The gap was immense and whatever L.-S. Mercier says ('in general, it has become impossible for a riot to deteriorate into sedition'),[1] the Parisian street was rarely calm. Obviously the stability of the state was not called into question every day, and L.-S. Mercier is right in this respect, but his optimism with regard to the potential of the police, leaves one wondering:

> If the Parisian, who at times has his more effervescent moments, were to mutiny he would soon find himself enclosed in the huge cage he inhabits; he would be denied grain and when there was nothing left in his trough he would soon be reduced to asking for mercy and pardon.

Note, by the way, the inevitable animal metaphors of the cage and the trough. In fact, the reality was very different from that asserted by the chronicler and it was precisely this 'effervescence' that bothered the police. The effervescence was sporadic but continual, occurring in all places and for all reasons, and in the end it set up a kind of tenacious harassment with regard to all forms of authority, or almost. Further, Nicolas Toussaint des Essarts was not mistaken when he noted in his *Dictionnaire universel de police* that 'the examples of mobs, riots and sedition are regrettably only too common in spite of the active vigilance of the police.'[2]

The proceedings of the police commissioners preserve a monthly record of all of these disputes which made the climate increasingly gloomy; there was a riot at the town gates here or defiance of the guard on patrol there; all havoc was let loose at markets because of the high prices; elsewhere there might be serious incidents amongst workers who had decided to strike, or gatherings in the street. One must also add the prison revolts which were more frequent than one might have supposed; and then there were rising tempers outside the *cabarets* when prices went up or when rumours of the stockpiling of grain went around the city.[3] It is impossible to assess the number of these movements for which historiography has no memory and for which the records of legal proceedings allow no exhaustive analysis either.[4] For the time being, it is simply interesting to note their worrying presence, a presence on which statements and opinions about the crowd were based whilst never properly corresponding to the definitions attributed to it. And thus one saw the entrenchment of a severe tension between fear of the people and the need for them, at the same time as the forging of powerfully defined images of popular cruelty and disorder.

Much has been written over a long period on this matter of revolts and uprisings. The end of the nineteenth century saw the birth of a whole body of reflections and sociological works referred to as the science of the crowd,[5] and historians seized on these in order to improve their understanding and analyses. In fact this new science was elaborated outside the field of history without any description of historical movements or analysis of detail. In 1934, G. Lefebvre gave a paper which he entitled 'Foules historiques, foules révolutionnaires'.[6] He reintroduced the historical dimension and studied crowds outside the animal-type classification attributed to them by Le Bon and his famous theories of collective hypnosis and unleashed instinct. G. Lefebvre states that a collective mentality can form within the crowd but that the economic, social and political conditions produce additional phenomena which vary and whose history and activity is appropriate to the context in which they take place.

Later G. Rudé,[7] who dedicated his book to Lefebvre, concentrated on a scientific description of revolutionary crowds on the basis of police archives and rejected the idea that a crowd was somehow a disembodied abstraction personifying *en bloc* either 'Good' (as Michelet had succeeded in doing in his *French Revolution*[8]) or 'Evil' (as Taine, Burke[9] and Le Bon had decided in their respective works).

Since then the theme has been taken up on numerous occasions by historians and sociologists in a succession of approaches to these movements, usually obscured by the ideological ambivalence surrounding them.[10] The crowd is fascinating and terrifying and it unleashes all kinds of agoraphobic stereotypes. Power, moreover, never ceases to solicit it, attempting to appropriate it, whilst itself remaining a stranger.

Like Georges Rudé and E. P. Thompson, one has to consider things in the detail of their history in order to construct other perspectives.

It is from the fine grain of an event that one learns the details which at the same time as they teach or even explain phenomena to us, also throw us off the track and send the observer off into exile – exile from his or her own stereotypes and ready-made definitions or his or her existing knowledge. Whether they are gathered together, disturbed or up in arms, the people are always seen in a reductionist fashion. When, of its own accord, it chooses to escape the destiny assigned to and imposed on it by the wishes of others, it runs the risk of being retranslated indefinitely in traditional terms of savagery and primitivism. If, for example, it refuses to accept the high cost of grain and the price of a pound of bread, it is thrusting aside the economic effort required of it and thus the image of thankless drudgery; at the same time it assumes the appearance and visage it is presented with, of the crowd as wild animal, prepared to butcher and massacre in order to eat. On first reading, this seditious population would appear to have no autonomy and no space which might allow it to live in any other way other than as conditioned by an authoritarian politics and an impulsive instinct.

However, the reality of the emotion at the time of its surfacing and the manner in which individuals become associated with it give another measure to the event, allowing one to come up against forms of social life other than those usually referred to in theses and dissertations. Disruption, anger, strikes and subversion are something other than the unleashing of instincts manipulated by villains and ringleaders. They are types of behaviour motivated by a personal reading of visible events affecting daily life and a discernment of meaning inciting one to action. Unbeknown to its leaders, the people abandon the definitions of themselves and pack our traditional formulations off into exile.

In the course of observing all these traces of insubordination in the police files and by noting the points at which the people rebelled either furtively or *en masse*, one is struck in the end by the ordinariness of these situations. At the end of the day, the uprising is perhaps not, as one might simply believe, either a breakdown or a definitive rupture with the order of things. Popular emotion would seem to be the necessary junction point between an order which is breaking down and a future which is insecure. And in the midst of this disorder, there is order – a greater desire for justice and honour – and the assembled mob would seem to be the gesture giving shape and form to what is lacking and what it is that has to be overcome. The occasional disorder, expressions of anger and the beginnings of revolt follow a logic and rationality which need to be made clear moment by moment at each juncture. Finally, what the assembled people is seeking is the exchange of what it lacks in a tension between its desire to be momentarily undifferentiated and its differences.[11] The force of this union employs all manner of means in which violence and excess certainly have their place and during which there is a struggle against dissolution, in the full knowledge that this will intervene sooner or later in order that the differences might be rearranged and dealt with under a new order.

When seen from a perspective of order as well as against a quite ordinary system, disruption as it was customarily perceived by the police becomes quite a different object. Obviously, for them the order of things was written quite differently and the images that resulted could not possibly be destroyed by events no matter how surprising.

Once popular emotion has been prised out from the traditionally accepted view (disorder, brutishness, impulsive and uncontrollable reflexes), the actual events of the insubordination can be taken one at a time and studied closely for what they are and what they were intended to be. Whether simultaneous or successive, great or small, it is possible to see how they obey their own knowledge and understanding of the real and their own properly constructed plans. In their anger, defiance or emotion the people put together what they consider plausible within the political situation, and on the basis of this 'suppositional reality', its conviction is built and the shape and form of its action determined. Its protest measures and actions are a response to the whole social body and political processes as they are represented, with the effect that such behaviours are both rational and demonstrative.

What is more, reason and demonstration take on something of a mission in which the revolt reveals truth over error in an obstinate desire to have what it has seen and thought made known, showing that at the present time, more than ever before, what was required was the surveillance and transparency of political operations by which it was supposed to be governed.

It was in this sense that time in Paris was marked by workers' strikes and popular insurrections. These were the catalysts for brief alliances which were put into place with such habitual ease as always to catch the authorities off guard. As far as we are concerned they present us with different images of the construction of reality and upset the order of things by their effort to establish more firmly a different set of values.

These are quite specific political moments, caught in a history which needs disengaging from a view which is too retrospective and too mechanical – too reductionist, in fact.

'The dishonesty of the poet is not that he knows nothing of the sorrows of the working man, but that he speaks of what he does not know.'[12]

### Intrigues among the workers

'Plots and cabals positively multiplied in the eighteenth century which, if they did not provoke general uprisings, nevertheless disturbed the peace and shook the world of work almost daily.'[13] The 1760s represented a turning-point in the century when strikes and conspiracies increased at a rate and rhythm that was impressive. There was a general increase in insubordination and the archives of the commissioners contain a plethora of complaints indicating that lack of discipline was pretty soundly established. These conspiracies and cabals were, more often than not, fairly locally based and usually took off from the workshops or the *cabarets* (where business matters were frequently discussed), and ended up by affecting the streets and indeed the whole district but rarely the whole city.[14] Some were short, others were protracted, and after several attempts at re-establishing calm, they usually erupted all over again.

Whatever the reason – problems getting work, the day's prices, freedom to give notice, relationships with one's masters – as far as the police authorities were concerned, striking and conspiring together were insupportable, for they were the ruination of the dream of an impeccable domestic order based on subordination. Worker indiscipline is a key term in the *Dictionnaire de police*, legal treatises, the works of chroniclers and memorialists, and particularly in police orders and instructions. By prohibiting secret societies and brotherhoods, those in power obviously hoped to build a permanent attachment between the worker and his work – and his workshop in particular, that structure which was so necessary to hierarchy and authority. The number of injunctions issued to prevent a journeyman leaving his master before the completion of the task is beyond count. Police rights over the 'deserter' were total, with the effect that being landed in jail on police orders was the prompt and obvious response to any lapse on the part of the employee. Patent letters from 2 January 1749 confirm some previous measures: journeymen, for example, were forbidden to leave their masters unless they had been granted written notice for that express purpose; nor were they allowed 'to assemble together as a body with the intention of conspiring or forming fraternities'. These provisions were confirmed by Louis XVI in 1781 following the re-establishment of the corporations a year after they had been suppressed by Turgot in 1775.

Whatever the timing of the regulations, the important thing was that in Paris the police were responsible for disputes and under the instructions of the Lieutenant-General. Prison was one of the most frequent measures – the chief argument,[15] as one might say; the reality, however, was much less simple.

There were few large general movements but as soon as discontent crept in, or an injustice was perceived, or there were the beginnings of a new lowering of wages, there were stoppages of work, and acts of defiance. Any provocation was met blow for blow.

Almost always everything revolved around the idea of subordination, which was coming to be less and less tolerated; there was no justification for maintaining an individual in a state of dependence which inhibited his own creativity and inventiveness or – quite simply – his freedom. The guild officials complained about these humiliating confrontations in which their authority was called into question without opposition. The vocabulary they used to characterize these movements is contemptuous, describing the workers as crude and vile animals. In 1727 there was a rebellion amongst the packers at the customs and excise and the General Merchants and Traders made a complaint by letter to the Lieutenant-General in the following terms:

The General Merchants do most humbly bring it to your attention that among the dockers who are paid weekly at the offices of the customs where they are responsible for packing the merchandise brought there by traders and other persons, as is their right, the greater part are brutes and drunkards who cause quarrels every day and who are losing respect for the customs' authority and for those whose living depends on it . . . as these aforesaid dockers lack either restraint or consideration and claim that they are answerable to no one, they are asking the merchants for double that to which they should legally be entitled for their efforts and offices . . . we do therefore request the Lieutenant-General of Police to re-establish order.[16]

Examples such as this can be multiplied; they came from all quarters throughout the whole length of the century, emanating from all the trades on all horizons – tradesmen, fabric-makers, enamel workers or journeymen clockmakers, building workers or pinmakers. The mentions made in the records of deliberations kept by the trades guilds are almost monotonous in this respect, as in the following, for instance:

26 March 1756, seen and approved by us, payment in full by the Guild of Merchants and Manufacturers of Cloth dated 16 March 1756 and also containing information refuting the denial by all cloth workers in the said works of stoppages among workers and attempts to conspire over a considerable period and to force workers not wishing to stop work to pay them by the various use of threats, violence and even assault, on the pretext of getting the merchants to increase the rates of pay. If such an undertaking were to continue for much longer – and it is of the utmost importance to put a stop to it quickly, then these gatherings by workers could be the occasion of riots and seditious activities. Cloth merchants are daily exposed to these and to insults and bad behaviour; it is in the interests of the community and the public good to prevent a disorder of this kind and to see that those who find themselves contravening your orders are imprisoned.[17]

In general, the arguing and wrangling began in an almost microscopic way in the workshop before spreading out onto one street or to the entire trade. The atmosphere of rancour and defiance were such that things could turn sour very quickly, as the journeymen knew only too well. When the shout of 'Bacanal!' went up, other workers, on hearing this cry of discontent through their workshop windows, would reply immediately and lose no time in leaving their shops and workshops in order to join them. The very structure of the workshop was normally quite an adequate support in itself and even when the workers had turned against their master, they still felt at home there. For their part, they wanted to be able to come and go as they pleased and to leave their master if they were dissatisfied; but at the same time they treated this place as they saw fit, with a feeling of belonging, which says much about the confused relationships between workshop and master. In this sense, the conflict which set Symphorien Huot, master locksmith, against several journeymen from the Rue de Vaugiraud tells us a good deal.[18] On account of a debt which he had failed to pay, the journeyman, Champagne, took to the streets on 22 April 1755 and stirred up all the other workmen in his district. The following day, they insulted the master and his wife and went on the rampage through the workshop wielding clubs and sticks before being dispersed by the Guard. Champagne was arrested and explained his actions before commissioner of police Crespy. He said that while his master was absent, he had come with his companions to eat at Sieur Huot's workshop. They had waited for him and then had gone into the shop where they had beaten him and called his wife a 'lackey's clown' and a 'bare bum'. Lying in wait like this to beat up the master and his wife was not the result of any particular plan or strategy and they had felt no need to hide; they just did as usual, getting the other journeymen together, waiting quietly at the master's table and then letting rip – setting things to rights in one's own place, as it were. Paradoxically, it was precisely this familiarity between master and journeymen which was the natural support of worker insubordination and it was the microcosm of the workshop that naturally invited it. The master was almost impotent against this indiscipline, which was shaped by the very structures which should have established dependence and submission. This is what made things so difficult for the police and the guilds; for the enemy was at the very interior of the workshop like a worm in the fruit. And thus, as it is plain to see, the domestic structure was being eroded by those very processes which had been responsible for its elaboration.

The job of breaking up or harassing these collective movements by workers was common enough but something which the authorities actually had difficulty achieving. Searching thoroughly through the archives of Commissioner Hugues of Les Halles between 1757 and 1767, one can see such a movement coming to life; it consisted of boys and journeymen cobblers who caused some agitation throughout the whole district in the year 1763,[19] and not only put the commissioner to the test but also a police inspector named Bourgoin who was responsible for cleaning up the atmosphere. He did this by having workers followed and by means of imprisonments by *lettres de cachet*.

There was a whole series of skirmishes between April 1763 and January 1764 revealing the complexity of the demands and the very loose-knit strategy and organization. As usual it was an apparently trivial incident which triggered the conflict. On 9 April 1763, a traditional dispute arose in the workshop of Nicolas Ferry, master cobbler in the Rue Tiquetonne. Harmless it may have appeared, but behind it there lurked a malaise which lost no time in spreading from master to master, in time extending far and wide. At the outset it revolved around the desire of one of the boys to do the work his own way and not according to his master's instructions. This boy had been in the employment of Nicolas Ferry for a fortnight and he had plenty of work in hand. One morning, the master gave him a pair of shoes for which he had to make 'the heels, which he had already cut out and which had been covered in grain leather'. The boy refused point blank as 'he didn't want to make them into shoes but into dancing pumps instead, so he threw his tools into the shop and went out'. The six other journeymen went with him as a result of this incident.

This refusal to obey and the desire to have some rights in the organization of the work and what was being undertaken in the workshop did not remain an isolated incident. A month later, in the Rue des Deux-Ecus, Pierre Guillet found himself faced with the same kind of problem. His three journeymen refused to do the work they were given and threw the plaintiff's plans on the ground. When Guillet made it clear to them that they were departing from the guild statutes, the three journeymen replied that they had taken an oath to cease work and that that was something sacred. An *entente* had been born.

In fact, the cabal was in full swing and the guild officials were torn between anxiety, the desire to repress it and attempts at conciliation. Identical scenes were being reproduced in each workshop in the district; tools were flung on the ground and demands made to do other jobs than those required. Nicolas Ferry was one of the masters who was to be most singled out in this affair for he was responsible for the accounts in the chamber of his guild. The most unruly and rebellious of the workers installed themselves in June in a *cabaret* situated immediately opposite his workshop and harassed him with insults as well as trying to disaffect other journeymen in the street. The job of tracking them down was made the more difficult by the fact that no one knew their names or addresses, only their nicknames inherited from their place of origin: Messin de Metz or Picard, for example. Although hardly known to the authorities, they were well adapted to the social networks of the streets and *cabarets*; they took oaths of unity and held as many meetings as they could in order to keep up the pressure on the masters whose style of command they refused. Their main weapon, as was often the case in cabals of this kind, was irony, name-calling in the street and the cutting comment which went straight to its target. In their efforts to create disaffection among those who wanted to remain at work, the journeymen camped in front of the windows and shouted, 'Are you afraid of going to Bicêtre then, because you will land up there if you don't watch it.' Baiting and satire of this kind were all intended to affect the outcome of this type of disorder and the raillery was indeed effective! That day, in response to the calls, many boys joined in with the schemers. The arms used were defiance, provocation and straight talking – but also threats of violence and the desire to hold up work practically everywhere.

The Lieutenant-General of Police was informed of the affair and whilst the number of complaints by masters against worker indiscipline and insubordination were on the increase, the usual apparatus was discreetly being put into place. An inspector was instructed to follow the rebels, find out their names and addresses and the places where they met. He was in possession of royal orders in the form of *lettres de cachet* permitting immediate imprisonment of suspects. In August, the problems multiplied; work was left unfinished, tools were downed, pass keys to the workshops stolen, boys hardly taken on before they abandoned their aprons, and there were arguments with the authorities and scuffles in the *cabarets* between those who wanted to see the movement spread and those who wanted to work.

At the same time, as often happened during such intrigues, some of the masters sheltered the rebels and lent their support to their movement, as much from fear of seeing their workshops ransacked as from a desire to cock a snook at their guild with which they were not in agreement.[20] These movements of rebellion provide a clear illustration of the existence of groupings and solidarities precisely in those places where one might not always have expected to have found them and, in particular, they reveal an increase in the strength of somewhat threatening individualisms. On 29 August, the guild of masters met to consider 'the maintenance of good order' and the usual recommendations were restated: one should not leave one's master, nor cause disaffection amongst the others or form assemblies.

The text issued as a result of their deliberations was posted up throughout the whole of the district, but it was a complete waste of time. By the end of the day all the notices had disappeared, either torn to shreds or made utterly illegible. It was an undertaking in which there was an intense feeling of solidarity amongst the journeymen. This made it impossible to arrest the one without there being an immediate rallying together of rebels on the street, which is what happened in the Rue Pavée-Saint-Sauveur. A soldier attempted to arrest a journeyman shoemaker who was tearing down a notice, but the Guard was obliged to retreat in the face of an angry crowd.

Emotional reactions of this kind among the workers comprised aspects that were both private and particular. As we have seen already, achieving solidarity was not necessarily a simple process, with some of the masters, for instance, giving their support and approval to the journeymen. Furthermore, some of the minor officials were also contaminated by the prevailing climate with some of them unashamedly leaving the trade altogether and quitting the paternal household or abandoning their charges with nothing more than the odd sarcastic comment. Some of the masters were incensed and filed complaints. The guild system seemed in disarray. At this precise point in the movement (9 September 1763), one observes a definite fragmentation with a realignment of positions adopted and a real dismantling of the original structures which affected both the organization of the trade and even the families of the master craftsman. The domestic structure had been turned upside-down and the police could do nothing about it except lock up the rebels; but the impact of this was hardly effective at moments of sporadic revolt like this when abandonment of responsibilities and seizure of tools followed each other in turn.

In mid-September, legal action was drawn up by several officials who had remained loyal to the guild, one of whom was Nicolas Ferry. They expressed their fears about all those *cabarets* in the district where rebellion was being fomented and attacks plotted by day or night. Some of the masters had been laid low by blows from journeymen who before striking them had shouted together that 'they [the masters] were themselves worthy of the title of assassin and had to be punished'. The metaphors used were still those of common-law justice and the world of delinquency; the 'conscience' of the workers, so often threatened with prison and arrest, was seeking its revenge. If it were a case of prison and assassination, it should be the masters, and not they themselves, who should be concerned. Their subjection had become so intolerable that it was their aim to over-turn the situation and have the masters experience their own state of dependence. It was they, the masters, who had been designated the principal agents of their unjust subordination.

From that point on, when anxiety was at its height and when the masters felt themselves being squeezed in the ever-tightening grip of a vice that showed no signs of weakening, things began to resolve themselves one case at a time. In October, the archives of Commissioner Hugues were full of withdrawals of complaints by the masters or attempts at amicable conciliation. The conflict came to no real conclusion – there were no agreements signed nor new regulations; each workplace attempted to find its own precarious harmony by establishing a *modus vivendi* with the express purpose of keeping at bay the spectre of a too widespread collec-tive revolt.

The master shoemakers of the Rue Tiquetonne seemed rather relieved and although the odd skirmish was reported here and there it was not serious and quickly damped down. However, in complete contrast, a month later, the Rue Coquillère was at boiling-point. The young cobbler boys had come out onto the street and were drawing up plans against their masters. Others did the same and the harassment was daily. And in this case, it was not an economic matter; the issue was the way of life. Confronted by demands of this kind, the masters found themselves defenceless, uncertain and, more often than not, incompetent. In the face of this, the journeymen and boys decided to conduct their own day as they pleased, rejecting any sense of servility. These gatherings, whether momentary, fragmented or even violent, were still the same expressions of a thinking that had been developed as the result of daily experience that had been judged to be unsatisfactory and pernicious.

Whether it was the cutlers,[21] cleaners and polishers,[22] hosiers,[23] locksmiths,[24] masons,[25] or farriers;[26] whether the issue was the right to carry a sword, the rate for the piece of work – whatever the movement, it grew from such momentary periods of association when potential strength could be assessed and strategies drawn up. Of course, these associations were strictly forbidden and always denounced by the guilds to the police, who daily tried to track down their places of assembly, although these usually held strong, whether they were the cellars of *cabarets*, enclosures or secret passages. The archives reveal both a bitter struggle against these illegal meetings and the impossibility of seeing off this mode of association which was an integral part of life in the trades. Large gatherings made things relatively easy for the police, as the assembly of 300 journeymen locksmiths in *cabarets* close to the Arsenal will testify. They were engaged in making banners with canes and batons which they would have preferred to have been swords.[27] The jailing of the suspected ringleaders did not always do anything to alter the problem, for although it might cause groups to change their meeting-places, it did nothing to alter their determination.

In 1731, the officials of the farrier's guild took fright at the extent of the clandestine activities of their journeymen. They dispatched a number of petitions to the Lieutenant-General of Police granting him permission to move in on attempts at collective mobilization within the guild where there was a threat of insurrection and lawbreaking by workers who were determined to safeguard their way of life and means of representation.

For some months now the apprentice farriers had been getting together on Sundays and feast days to arrange horseshoe competitions with each other and to this end they had been invoking some distant custom. Some of them had become so engrossed in this that they had neglected their work, staying away from their masters for as much as three weeks at a time without giving any notice or warning, as well as disaffecting other journeymen whom they had dragged off with them. They found a suitable refuge in the Samaritaine area of the Seine and there 30 or 40 of them, depending on the day, forged their irons and drank, competing and brawling with one another. Imprisoning the leaders was to no avail: they simply got together elsewhere with others.[28] Forming associations, holding meetings, wearing a sword – these were all means of escaping a hierarchical structure which imposed obedience to it without offering any real identity to those who found themselves in submission.

Faced with this kind of activity, masters and police responded blow for blow. But even when the repression was carried out by means of an arrest without a hearing or on orders of the King it was never massive or open and quite often it was necessary to retreat because, after registering their complaints, the masters themselves often came to request the freeing of their journeymen. Alliances of all kinds were formed during these periods of worker insubordination without any kind of uniform rules or regulations. Each movement had its own particular features and produced a history that was autonomous in relation to the others. Few strikes spread to the whole of the city and each time, in the wake of swift and decisive action on the part of the Lieutenant-General, it was fear and anxiety (on the part of the masses as well of those in power) that usually gained the upper hand. Everyone dreamt of having harmonious workshops and for an end to this incessant friction which not only upset family and domestic life but also the precarious economic equilibrium of each artisanal unit. If the rebels were freed, why should they not find their place in this stable hierarchical chain which at all costs had to be the model for society?

This was certainly the course of events during the mutiny of journeymen hosiers in 1724.[29] Having been obliged to suffer a reduction in the price of their merchandise due to royal regulations, the merchant hosiers knew only one method of softening the blow to their own earnings and this was to reduce the piece rate by 5 *sols* per pair of silk stockings and 2 *sols* 6 *deniers* the pair in fine wool. There was an immediate reaction, with many men leaving their masters. They got together, refusing to return while ever their wages remained cut in this way. So that they could hold out and in order to convince the greatest possible number of journeymen hosiers, they decided to raise funds among those who had remained at work by contributing 6 *sols* each per week to help meet the needs of strikers. Michel, who collected the funds, took the precaution of seeking refuge in the Temple cloister in order to be more secure.

The affair went further – the Lieutenant-General summoned Michel and his two accomplices; but it was a woman who came to let him know that no one would be coming to this interview. She stated quite coolly that 'they knew they would not be hanged for refusing to obey these orders.' Women were quite often the mediators in this kind of conflict. They passed on news and information, knew where the men were hiding and were able to move around the city quite easily, assuring the cohesion of the movement as a result of their activities. Loud and outspoken, their tone was often sarcastic and threatening but on this occasion they came to grief. One did not refuse a rendezvous with the Lieutenant of Police with impunity. Having assessed the atmosphere and the potential danger, the journeymen hosiers decided to file a complaint themselves (and thus become players in the negotiations) whilst at the same time humbly excusing themselves for not having been present at the audience. They wrote that 'they had been so unfortunate as to miss the appointment by a moment or two and offered their most humble apologies'. The mobs and illegal assemblies continued to multiply and the agitation escalated whilst the number of journeymen who were 'clubbing in' and keeping a collection going to support those who had stopped work was put at 2,000.

By order of the King and by way of a swift example, indicative of the severity to be expected, Michel was secretly arrested, orders being sent to the bailiff of the Temple. He was quickly dispatched to the prison of Fort l'Evêque where he was interrogated. He denied everything, explaining his own attachment to his master for whom he had been working for the last four years. He said that he knew nothing beyond the odd amount of hearsay. Yes, he had certainly received a small amount of money but provision for this had been made a long time ago for the relief of the sick in the guild community.

This was the usual kind of defence. Whenever an illicit gathering or assembly was discovered by the police, the protagonists defended themselves by saying that they were acting in the name of charity and that it was necessary to take care of the sick and elderly in their community. Among the archives there are outlines of plans for the formation of associations of working men and women and this provision for a common fund for the support of the most vulnerable usually figures prominently. For example, there is the undated proposal for an association of women workers in the lace industry,[30] in which it is stipulated that 'the expenses incurred by illness shall be borne equally in cases where the illness lasts no longer than eight days'.

The defence of the workman Michel resembles that of so many others; however, he took fright and gave the names of his associates at the same time as explaining that they were also people of good faith motivated by charity and setting a good example.

In the margin of this interrogation, the Lieutenant-General had written that it was necessary to arrest the bit players as well because 'the situation was urgent as the rebellion was increasing each day that passed'. Another note states clearly that 'the King wanted everything sewn up with a punishment that would be exemplary', if only to contain the workers from other trades. A month later when the principal agents were all locked up and institutionalized, the merchants set a contrary operation in motion demanding the release from prison of their workers, declaring that they had been sufficiently punished and insisting that they be returned to their work and duty which they were certain they would accomplish with the best will in the world. Following swiftly on this appeal and personal appeals from the prisoners themselves, which made reference to their family responsibilities, came the order for their release.

This constant coming and going between the authorities and those in league, as well as those solidarities instigated between the master and police and then renounced once the repression had begun to take effect, indicate a vision of work experienced as fragmented but where there was also the possibility of experiencing harmony if one succeeded in frightening some of the hotheads. In this context, the workers, journeymen and apprentice-boys played their own part, knowing how to conduct these collective contests in what was above all a bid to place what was on offer against their own vision of themselves, which might involve, for instance, ways of working, the means of achieving freedom from dependence on the master, or the right not to be considered a servant and therefore entitled to carry a sword. In short, how to exist otherwise in a free relationship – the vision of a workshop that did not necessarily cause a breakdown in the obvious solidarities and close relationships of work, but beyond the all too narrow constraints of the master's family. In the face of these strong and arrogant individualisms that were ready to brave prison in order to claim other definitions for themselves than those traditionally assigned them, one can see to what extent the much-repeated theses about the workers were far from the reality. During the short period of time when the trades-guilds were to be suppressed (the time of Turgot's disgrace and the return of the Lieutenant-General of Police who had been in exile for a year), the only thing the elites could dream of was of their reappearance for quite specific political purposes, namely order and tranquillity. In spite of the upheavals, the conspiracies and the increase in conflicts and strikes since 1760, everyone believed that it was the workshop structure that was the guarantee of public security. No one else could have put it better than Lenoir when he said

> that at least the restoration of the guilds and corporations would achieve a political goal as they tend to instil good inner discipline among at least two-thirds of the population of Paris; that he would see to it that they returned, for without them it would be difficult to achieve a general and individual level of security in a capital which set the tone for all the other towns of the Nation. . . . Re-establishing the corporations and guilds of merchants, artisans and workers is to some extent a means of organizing the people and allowing oneself an important means of getting to know them in spirit and of keeping them calm. This would not be at variance with what one is given to understand as the spirit of free trade.[31]

In 1775, Lenoir still believed that the trades' corporations 'organized the people' and kept them quiet; a utopianism which seems all the more surprising since he had been at the head of the police since 1774 and had been perfectly well acquainted with the Parisian climate for some time. The workers, however, were instigators in rejecting this structure and yet knew perfectly well how to make it work to their advantage when need be.

## When the people got steamed up

> Who then are these instruments of public calamity and disaster? They are always those men whose names and addresses one does not know; individuals who seem strangers in the very town which provides them with their means of subsistence; creatures of the moment who disappear with the same ease as they appeared in the first place. In short, they are the sort who stick at nothing, who are without property and who take flight with the speed of lightning.[32]

This kind of police account never varied. It showed an inability to think of popular emotions in any other terms beyond the traditional sketch of the 'stranger come from other parts', faithless and unlawful, and dragging along with him a whole mass of unscrupulous individuals. Confronted by this tumultuous body that was society, the police considered it their function to control the multitude as they saw fit and 'to be its guiding, yet unseen spirit'.

The reality, however, was rather different; for although rioting was always a formidable spectre for the authorities, it was also one of the traditional forms of existence for the population. Serious disturbances which were bloody and threatening affairs for the monarchy were obviously rare and what there were have been well researched. Their mechanisms and the motives underlying them are well known, as is the firmness with which they were repressed. What are less well known are the minor incidents of the street, arising haphazardly for a variety of reasons and provoking a hue and cry which would attract a rowdy mob and a whole host of trouble to which the Guard and the Watch were usually called in as reinforcements. There was no shortage of pretexts or of methods to use in dealing with them. The police would be preoccupied with the disorder whenever it broke out and just as afraid of it as they were active in dispelling it. The commissioners were always on their guard and their reports are imprinted with an anxiety mixed with prudence and caution. They knew that any mismanagement in the event of an incident could produce serious skirmishes. In February 1745,[33] a minor incident which, as chance would have it, Commissioner Le Comte himself happened to be involved in, shows how much the police feared outbursts and 'shady business'. He writes:

> Being yesterday at four in the afternoon on my balcony with five or six other persons, we heard loud cries coming from a house which is

separated from mine only by a dividing wall. A moment later, a young woman appeared at the window and cried 'Help! Help!' When this young woman spotted me, she yelled, 'Monsieur le Commissaire, they're coming into my house to murder me.'

The commissioner immediately sent for the Guard but the ensuing disorder had led to a gathering of a surprising number of young bucks who had come out of the neighbouring cafés all ready for a good set-to. Suitable arrangements needed to be made. He continues:

I bade the Guard enter my study, so as to avoid a full-scale affair and I thought it in my best interests not to allow them out until the trouble-makers had withdrawn. The most troublesome of them all was called Trinquely, who had only recently come out of Fort-l'Evêque and was at the head of a dozen or so rapscallions who had caused a good deal of trouble throughout Paris.

The spirit of revolt could arise from anywhere – workshops, *cabarets* (always spoiling for a fight), and the prisons which had seen no end of trouble during the century (for example, in 1740, 1749, 1763 and 1767, without counting other less serious incidents).[34] Then there were the libertines who held their assemblies in the *faubourgs*, and at the town gates there was a great deal of trafficking and the harassment of farm employees etc.[35] The most serious agitation arose on account of price rises or when the population was concerned about government activities of a dubious nature such as the disappearances of children organized by the police in 1750. Whether great or small, however, public disorder remained a relatively familiar event. When an incident arose no one could possibly know the proportions it might assume an hour or so later, but everyone was able to recognize it when it did happen and to adjust their behaviour towards it accordingly. Only the police saw anything odd about it, and were at pains to devise strategies in which they might remain as invisible as possible. There was quite a wide gap between the often banal appearance of a scuffle and the manner in which the police and the authorities spoke about it, always hovering between caution and severity without quite making up their minds.

Rebellion exists even before it has been incited. It is born of a single movement, and it is above all noise and anger and the cry of those who want justice done, and the panic of those who witness the tumult and become associated with it. The evidence of witnesses and the results of interrogations, although imprecise (for who in fact is likely to admit to the commissioner interrogating him that, yes, he had actually 'rebelled'?), reveal how a revolt developed and progressed both over and above those participating in it but also with their close support. Autonomous, or almost, the disturbance had its own momentum, because it suddenly found itself corresponding to the urgency of a situation whose contours had long been discernible. Undoubtedly what was most striking in these sporadic urban revolts of the eighteenth century was their strength and determination, their suddenness, as well as the manner in which they were experienced as being a normal state of affairs, indeed legitimate.

The riot was the ceaseless link between the possible and the impossible for the very fact that it was based on the particular mode of existence of the inhabitants. As such, it was handed back to the investigators (commissioners and inspectors), as a movement which was inherent to normal activity and participation in the world about, but also as an event that had taken place outside their field of action and responsibility. The kind of a posteriori reconstruction and representation of events by those who had good cause to fear a severe repression is less fallacious than it might at first sight appear. On the contrary, it comes closest to expressing what a street incident in fact was, namely what one actually lived through and what happened to one and what one saw happening. During these periods of anger, the urban structure was the most convincing and effective social actor. The apartment building, the market, the bridge, the crossroads and the commissioner's *hôtel* were not just the right kind of places to serve as collection points and catalysts of rage and frustration, they were also places which positively favoured such feelings, providing a model and lending them strength and authenticity. Emanating from these places in the urban environment, there was a social and collective knowledge which acted as a base for determination and vindication. One found oneself caught up in a riot on the stairs rather in the way that one might gather round a well to draw water. 'There's a riot going on over there,' the residents in a neighbouring street might say on hearing the noise and sounds of emotions whose cause they would instantly recognize; and they would find themselves in the thick of it because they were practitioners of a collective destiny accustomed to reacting to anything which affected their survival. It is not an exaggeration to say that rebellion took on an ordinary appearance, especially when it sought to re-establish an order which was scoffed at by the authorities. It was not a total overthrow of attitudes or practices but a practical and symbolic setting in motion of a thought and an action which could no longer tolerate the injustices observed in its immediate surroundings.

In that, there is more order and reason than one might have normally read into it; but at the same time, violence often became entrenched with more cruelty than if cohesion and conviction had been the long-term companions of its maturation.

A riot is never unconsidered even if it is unpredictable. In its paroxysm of vehement fury, it relies on whatever has already been creating the daily fabric of life; and as a social form with which one was accustomed, it was immediately identifiable and its risks assessed. What is more, the extent of the risk increased the violence and the desire to be a part of it. Even before one had the time to see what was happening, everyone knew what was going to happen and determination grew in relation to that certainty. As it is quite plain to see, it was amidst this whirlwind and mixture of habit and utter eruption that the crowd found its way in, and in so doing totally escaped all reductionist definitions assigned to it by the authorities for, in the midst of this agitation brought on by external events, it lived totally unto itself.

Tumults and rebellions have their own particular vocabulary and a specific catalogue of gestures which seek to find a concordance with the social and political contexts giving rise to them. Once the crowd has made sense of the social and political meanings from what it sees and hears, it adopts forms it considers necessary for claiming its rights and gaining respect for those norms it considers necessary. For a large part of the time, the question is not the renewal of society nor its reinvention on new bases, but to defend oneself, to maintain in the best possible state conditions that are already difficult, and to prevent things getting any worse. The outbreak of the riot can be seen as an ordinary act; it was the revolutionary postures themselves that contained the multitude of hopes and dreams, even when the demands expressed were by no means innovatory.

Revolt is all of this and yet something other. If one attempts to lay hold of it by means of ideological theory or in some sort of cultivation of the 'true life' of the people, it would be to forget that revolt is born out of fatigue, and dreams out of suffering and the clash between thought and the search for meaning. One forgets that it defies our knowledge because our most tenacious desire is to leave everyone in their place whilst at the same time we persist in defining the other as weird, outlandish – a stranger.

The spring of 1750 was very tense as has already been mentioned. The abductions of children and the anxiety felt by each person set off days of rioting between 16 and 23 May.[36] The cause of each incident was either the arrest of a child in the middle of the street by poorly disguised *archers* who were instantly recognizable, or the unwelcome presence of someone who had been recognized and suspected of being part of the band of policemen who had taken away the children. The skirmishes were violent and the Guard was overwhelmed, whilst on each occasion the people tried to carry the guilty men off to the *hôtel* of the police commissioner, a place both familiar and symbolic, where one could reasonably and legitimately have expected there to be order and security.

The Saturday of 23 May proved to be the most agitated and bloody of them all. Labbé, a police officer, was recognized by the crowd and chased into the Rue Saint-Honoré. He was already wounded but with the help of a woman, he dived into one of the apartment buildings on the market-place. When he was eventually turfed out of there, he was assaulted and dragged off to Police Commissioner La Vergée. Then the crowd got hold of him again and this time they whipped him and pelted him with stones. In the evening, his body was put on a ladder and carried to the front of the *hôtel* of the Lieutenant-General of Police, Berryer, where they left it. It was an act of defiance against the supreme authority and against the very person who they knew perfectly well had himself been giving the orders for the abductions.

Berryer took fright and furtively left the house by the back door. Paris was calm the next day and a decree was drawn up by the Lieutenant and the first president of the *parlement* in an attempt to avoid any fresh disorder. An enquiry directed by Severt, a Counsellor at the court, was also set up. The immediate arrest of rioters and suspected police officers then followed but it seemed that the enquiry was only concerned with condemning the rioters and allowing the guilty police officers to go free subject to the payment of a small fine. On 3 August, three young rebels were hanged at the Place de Grève to the angry murmurings of a hostile crowd. The fact that the police had been to blame was no excuse and had made no difference to the illegitimacy of the revolt. The people who had been a part of that revolt now only sought the orderly return of a world that had suddenly gone out of control.

In this affair, the details of each scene and event reveal, beneath the apparent disorder and impulsiveness, behaviour that was organized and logical; and in this respect, the apartment building on the Saint-Honoré market-place had all the advantages of an observatory. In the course of putting together the different accounts by witnesses and the results of the interrogations, one sees the emergence of attitudes and roles which not only proved to be in keeping with a thorough knowledge of the area but also were conducive to the eruption of a riot. The sequence of events which unfolded gives an indication of the internal mechanisms of the revolt, giving it a controlled and regulated appearance, whose every episode one is able to understand.

The dawn of this book saw us encamped in the apartment building by the market square; teeming and porous, vibrant and susceptible, we saw it in the course of its everyday life – hardworking and quite frequently disturbed and agitated. The riot was to shake it significantly but without causing any fundamental alteration to the roles of each occupant. Because of its architecture and the way in which it was inhabited, it found itself called on to be the theatre of one of the most serious incidents of the whole affair. There was one detail not given earlier, and that was that two years previously, on the second floor, Police Inspector Poussot,[37] who was well known to the Parisians, had been living there. He shared a small apartment with a woman of little virtue known as La Maréchale, who was a 'confidante' of the police and who was mixed up in the world of prostitution and always ready to pass on information and observations to the police. The building had retained its memory of having offered shelter to 'those people' and it was not at all happy about that kind of promiscuity.

When Officer Labbé, one of Poussot's men and a spy for some time, was suddenly recognized in a street adjacent to the market as he was looking for refuge, he plunged into this enclosure that was bordered by three buildings and accessible by three doors. One woman, Geneviève Olivier, widow of a master carpet-maker, soon recognized him and knew immediately the danger threatening him. She had also worked for the police and when Poussot had lived in the building she had 'done the cooking' with La Maréchale and today she was still in contact with La Denis, one of the washerwomen in the building who worked for her. Taking Labbé by the arm, she pushed him in the direction of the building and yelled at him to go up to the fifth floor where La Denis lived. With clothes torn and his arm wounded, Labbé was out of breath and exhausted and so he stopped on the fourth floor and hid at another washerwoman's, La Roseau, who got him out of the way. Telling him to take shelter here had been bad advice because today of all days the building had every reason to avail itself of its memory and it did so with cruelty and violence. That spring, policemen were no more than cruel murderers and the occupants of the building wanted nothing to do with them, especially not to give them shelter.

On the market square, a disturbance blew up all at once. Living and working in this area was a population that had been implanted there for 12 or 18 years or more, with its own customs, codes of behaviour, memories and interests. All of those who went about their business there had a variety of jobs which changed according to the days and the seasons. Thomas Lamotte, for example, was a mason but more often than not he was both cleaner and odd-job man, regularly installing himself in the Quinze-Vingts market in the Rue de l'Echelle. Thus, in between jobs, he could 'do the job of putting up the awnings for the fishmongers in the mornings and taking them down in the evenings and, besides that, sweeping up after the market'.[38] On Saturday, 23 May, he said that he had got back from 'doing a trip for the nurses who had come from Saint-Germain-en-Laye' before getting caught up and carried along by the angry crowd. In the case of the cod-sellers, they had other small jobs to help them through the lean days, like selling song sheets in the street or doing the laundry for a few customers during the great seasonal washing periods.

As one works one's way through the stories of personal apprehension and diffidence, and all the usual strategies used to greater or lesser effect to avoid accusation, one can begin to see from the accounts by witnesses how the revolt managed to break out so suddenly in this partially enclosed enclave. Everything happened in a flash. The shouting, the pursuit, the accompanying gestures – all occurred at top speed, but with all the naturalness one might expect from people who were used to this kind of event. When the butchers saw that they were chasing Labbé, they yelled at the women on the market stalls, 'Get my children out of the way, there's going to be all hell let loose!' 'There's a riot on the way!' This was the cry that signalled that the revolt was no longer a threat or a prediction, but a reality. The women passed the message to each other and took a few makeshift precautions to protect their tools and merchandise. One of them rammed two of the long knives that she used for gutting fish into her baskets for fear of being picked up by the police and of not being able to justify having them on her. Another woman told how frightened she had been and how she had been out of breath when she had got back to her lodgings. Strangely enough, in the course of the interrogation, she seemed to come to herself and while explaining her haste to get away she also added, without thinking, that before running away she had gone off to have a drink with her friend the cooper's wife, itself a confession of how accustomed to riots she had become; and although she knew that she had to say how afraid she was, she did not quite know how to do it. Her little stop-over at the innkeeper's showed that she had not been too terrified and that, all in all, there was a desire here to be present at the rebellion.

The women had responded to the protective warnings of the men by acknowledging their advice and acting as safeguards. However, they all remained vague about the details of their behaviour and, in their replies to the police, they said that in the face of all the noise they had calmly carried on with what they were doing and that it had all happened without them – so they said. Their lack of precision and reluctance to speak only thinly veiled their active presence and participation.

In fact, both men and women were to find themselves caught up inside the building, which proceeded to spring to life in a way which corresponded quite logically to its structure and the manner in which it was inhabited. There was nothing fortuitous about what was going on here centre-stage. At the announcement that a police agent was hidden between its walls, the principal tenant of the building, Devaux, master locksmith by trade and resident of a nearby building, quickly got himself over there. In his capacity as main tenant, he was responsible for the building to the proprietor, M. le Marquis de Putange. He was in charge of collecting the rents and for letting and sub-letting as he saw fit; he also filled in the police registers with the names of the occupants and kept an eye on the place, thus exercising a certain amount of authority over everyone. His responsibilities were recognized and respected.

As soon as he got inside the building on the heels of a heated population who were in the process of searching its every nook and cranny, and omitting no alley, passage-way, window or bedroom in their efforts to lay their hands on the policeman, he, by virtue of his own authority, altered the rebels' game. For an hour, Devaux became a leader, taking control of operations, calming things down or stirring them up according to his own strategy. Torn between two different aims, he became the essential pivot of what was about to happen and which took place quite naturally. He was undoubtedly solidly behind the riot but his role and responsibility as master of the premises meant that he could not take too many risks – at least those were his wishes. Thus, above all, he wanted to find Labbé himself and evict him as quickly as possible from his building to avoid anything unpleasant happening which would compromise him beyond doubt in the eyes of the authorities. He made use of his position with confidence and just when all the doors were banging or when the rebels armed with sticks were shouting, 'After the murderer!', and attempting to break down doors and smash in windows, he intervened to calm things down. 'Steady on, my friend, that's not the way to go about it, not so much noise,' he said to three men who wanted to force their way in to La Roseau's rooms and he covered the door to her room with his own body.

In the face of this resolve, things calmed down and then he said, 'We'll go and search everywhere and if he's there, you'll find him.' At that point, he had given his own consent and approval to the chase. In one instant he had become the leader, a role which he was to lose just as easily an hour later, to be replaced by another individual in the course of another scene. Here, in his own building, he was the master and his social function made him undisputed holder of that office. Devaux's determination convinced Roseau's wife that it was indeed better to open her door than to resist and that it would involve less violence for her. Besides she could then testify that she had acted on orders if things turned out badly. Once the door of the room was open, it was child's play to find Labbé and three men dragged him out from under the bed. His face was bloodied and livid. They held him by the arms and someone grabbed him round the neck. The sight of him inflamed their spirits and incited them to violence; out on the stairs they all shouted that they should throw him through the window or 'into the latrines'.[39] Devaux calmly intervened, strictly forbidding any such attempts to get rid of him.

'No, don't throw him down, take him out and get him off our hands so we don't have any trouble here.' That one phrase summed it up – it was absolutely essential that Labbé left the building for which Devaux was responsible unscathed. As for what was going to happen next in the street below, Devaux didn't want to know; but first he took care to go up and give his journeymen instructions not to come out and to get back to work.

Later, at the enquiry, Labbé's colleagues were to latch onto this expression to show that Devaux had cowardly 'delivered' the man who, as a woman was to say, had been treated 'like an *ecce homo*'.[40] The picture was all in place: as far as the colleagues of police officer Labbé were concerned, Devaux had all the appearance of a Pontius Pilate.

Devaux's attitude was certainly suspect enough to warrant the suggested comparison; seeing Geneviève Olivier, who had pointed out the hiding-place to Labbé, made his hackles rise and he subjected her to a violent torrent of verbal abuse, calling her a whore and a Madam so that she also found herself put out on the street at the same time as Labbé. He then went on to turn all the washerwomen in the building against her, seizing them by the arm and shoving them over to the windows overlooking the street, telling them to 'let rip' at her. The washerwomen needed no asking, although they said later that they had been made to do it. 'Kill her, she's one of La Maréchale's band.' 'No more mischief-makers here watching what everyone is up to.' The insults merged one with another whilst Olivier just managed to escape being massacred thanks to two butcher's stallholders who saved her in the nick of time. From the landing, Devaux both stirred things up and controlled them at one and the same time. 'You're all the same kind, all of you, just a bunch of idiots,' he yelled, but suddenly he took fright and stopped in his tracks; one of the washer-women had just been shouting, 'She's a whore who once lived here, M. Devaux says so.' He gave her a kick and shut her up, saying, 'Do you have to go and open your mouth and mention someone's name, you idiot? You mustn't name anyone.' There we have it – the phrase is exemplary; in a world such as this, where everyone knew each other whilst remaining anonymous at the same time, it was essential not to give the police opportunities like this. To mention someone's name in the thick of a riot was a serious danger which flew in the face of all reason. No one must hear any names, no one must say anything out loud and the name of Devaux, master of this building, must certainly not be mentioned. He wanted to keep well out of the way of what was going on whilst neverthe-less exerting some control over things.

Whilst the building was being rapidly evacuated and with Labbé and Geneviève Olivier finally out onto the street and in the hands of the populace, another episode was taking place, this one more bloody. Dragged before the police, abused and mistreated by the women and put out onto the street again by the police commissioner, Labbé was to die. In this sequence, Devaux no longer had any role to play and another figure had taken his place, this time a lackey from one of the great houses who was engaged in talks with the commissioner and who had made himself there and then the intermediary between the riot and the authorities, a role which he had assumed quite spontaneously on account of his knowledge of current practice and good manners, his wearing of a hat which he knew how to doff, and his good plain speaking. One way or another he had gained credibility quite spontaneously.

Behind the panic and general brouhaha, the clamours and the pushing and shoving, it is possible to see order and coherence. The kind of hostility one has observed against the police and their somewhat unscrupulous auxiliaries who, according to the expression used by Devaux, 'watched what everyone was doing', was an attitude that was familiar. Obviously it had not just taken the abduction of its children in 1750 for the population of Paris to feed its animosity and hatred towards the police spies and agents who were scattered everywhere throughout every *cabaret*, concourse and building. The events of 1750 simply gave the people an additional opportunity for showing the highest authorities (notably the Lieutenant-General of Police) that no one was fooled.

Not being taken for a fool was one of the main motive forces shaping popular life, and familiarity with defiance, dispute and even rebellion was one of its consequences. It was an attitude which generated protest, overturned order, made violent proclamations and engendered turbulent activity. It also underpinned the foundations of the riot, that outward and visible side of discontent and determined expression of an order which refused to be flouted. The riot sought first of all to set things to rights, things which it guessed were out of order, unjust or quite simply shameful.

To do this, it proceeded by a series of scenes and gestures, each sequence leading towards its culminating point (usually the massacre of a man presumed responsible for inflicting violence on the population) and possessing its own internal logic.

Anarchy is only what it appears to be. In the midst of the visible disorder, there reigns some sort of organization geared towards a specific goal. In the building on the market place, for example, it was a matter of finding the suspect, Labbé; elsewhere it would be something else. In each place where the rebellion took place, there would seem to be an individual particularly well placed and suited to become for a certain span of time – usually quite short – the one who carried the others along and determined the actions to be undertaken. Crowds are not in fact manipulated by any previously foreseen leader who has spent a considerable amount of time premeditating a succession of acts of violence to be inflicted on the authorities. The men and the women who are in revolt find the very persons they need to make their action effective there on the spot at the precise time they need them. At each stage as the rebellion advances, one man steps quite naturally out of the group to take control of the activities. It is never a mere fluke of a man but an individual whose normal function has destined him to become for a brief moment the privileged, if furtive, leader of events. Afterwards, he falls back into anonymity, merging once again with the crowd to follow, if he so chooses, other episodes and thus other individuals who at that particular moment are more effective than he in the development of the action.

In the midst of the crowd, behaviour differed markedly and it would be impossible to note all the details. Suffice it to say that the traditionally accepted male and female capabilities were put to good use. At the market, the *men* sensed the gravity of the situation and warned the women, who spread the news like a trail of dust. The men's role was clear and quite unequivocal: they provided protection but also incitement, knowing full well that in the event of things going badly, the women would quite ruthlessly assume the violent role for which they had always been known, and particularly in this case as it concerned their children.

It was Devaux's immediate realization of this female role that astutely led him to station the women at the windows of the building. He shoved them over there quite roughly, aware of the effect that they would have and knowing full well that the crowd would yield to their shrieks and yells. It should be stressed that in this case, the women did not position themselves at the window as it says in the song, but rather were put there by a man who was sure of the results, which is hardly the same thing. In any study involving male and female, the manipulation of sexual roles needs to be taken into account.

When there was a chain of violence linked together episode by episode which ineluctably produced a veritable explosion leading to the death of a man, the women were often very closely associated with the most cruel scenes, especially if these happened to take the form of a ritual. Nor was the murder of Labbé any exception to this particular kind of dramatics. Completely spent and beaten half-dead by stones and fists, the wretch begged for mercy and on his knees pleaded for a confessor. Duparc, a seafood seller, denied having been the last one to finish him off, although the evidence of witnesses seems to agree over this. It would seem that she had put all her rage and fury into insulting him and as she chucked a heavy cobblestone at his head, she may even have said, 'Here you are, you rotten swine, here's your confessor.'

Guilty or not guilty, true or false, it does not matter much. The scene, told and retold endlessly in the course of interrogations, shows that when a disturbance reaches a paroxysm, it reconstructs scenes of cruelty which give way to a symbolism that is easy to understand. Violence, blame and imminent expiry mingle together until the advent of blood and death itself. The women played a great part in this cruel disorder, taking on the symbolism with which they were so often associated, and whose virulence perhaps linked up with that place in their guts where the forces of life-creation coexisted in confusion with the impulses leading to death.

This symbolic role was reinforced by the almost total impunity attributed to the women and by the rout of those who were savaged by them. Women who struck an adversary profoundly wounded his honour, and a police officer thus maltreated by women became an object of derision.[41] Derision can sometimes give way to pity as in the case of Labbé, of whom it was to be said that he had been made an *ecce homo*.

Violence is also a spectacle. It is not necessarily an overflowing of hysteria or the irrational behaviour of the crowd, leading to the disappearance of the individual will. Each one has a chance to play his or her own part and thereby take advantage of the exceptional climate allowing the discharge and unaccustomed physical expression of unwonted emotions. In this context, the women had everything to gain. They made themselves visible by placing themselves in the front row of the fighting and by taking on some of the most lethal behaviour.[42] In this way they used their symbolic role to reinforce a social and political role, of which the least one can say is that it was hardly recognized.

In several ways the female ferocity and harshness thus described corresponded with the social and political system of the *Ancien Régime*. Valiant and invulnerable, the woman as mother encountered violence at the very heart of her maternal role; close as she was to blood and death, she was a figure who remained blameless because at heart she was not responsible for her weakness. These two contrasting images bring with them neither worth nor account in professional and political society but in times of revolt, it is sufficient for her to serve as their incarnation in order to occupy a role centre-stage.

Thus by using to her advantage the symbols that normally diminished her, kept her dependent or even condemned her, she appropriated for herself for a certain period of time a primordial and essential function recognized by others.

A riot is an obscure and complicated syntax. For the observer, it offers aspects of both order and excess, conjuring up dreams of victory over the humiliations of which its participants consider themselves to be the object. It is one of the rational forms of utopia – irreversible and perhaps impenetrable. Even so, neither its rules nor its coherence deliver it from what is essentially earnest and pathetic.

# Conclusion

To begin with, there are the archives: documents, fragments and cuttings, taken from the very heart and living tissue of the city. Thanks to these, it becomes possible to see, sometimes obliquely, some of the shapes and moments of popular Parisian life, and it is in this process of reconstitution that the objects of history (personal life, work, crowd) which usually belong to their own specific or different disciplines, find themselves released from their traditional boundaries.

This book follows a course, that taken by men and women as they embark on life's path. We follow them as they move from childhood into the first brushes with seduction; from being a couple to fighting and quarrelling; from work to festivities; from royal spectacle to the attractions of the street with its freaks and curiosities; and from emotion to revolt.

It is a journey which only appears complete. It does indeed cover most of the principal events by which the individual finds himself daily confronted from birth till death; but this is far from being exhaustive and in no way is it the last word on what might be said of popular attitudes and behaviour. In fact, this work has no end – that never was its purpose – and the method employed is ample proof of this.

It has never been my hope or intention one day to produce the definitive work on the popular practices of urban life during the age of the Enlightenment. I have always considered my research as a personal and intellectual journey which authorizes me to uncover, in the course of its development, those particular spaces where it becomes possible to understand in detail the relationships between men and women face to face with each other, with others and with the political life in which they are the principal participants. I have worked as closely as possible with what the archives have to say and with what they conceal, guided both by current questions and by a distrust (which daily becomes more insistent) of dangerous anachronisms which falsify meaning and send history off course. I wanted to give form to what was concrete with the help of each small piece of text, however tenuous. Reading these in the light of so many others, what has struck me most, and is in fact one of the aspects that has been least explored, is that constant adjustment that takes place between intelligence and disorder; and it is in fact this adjustment and entanglement which I have chosen as the focal point for considering some of the intineraries made by the man and woman of the people.

Disorder is not simple and this book does not retrace the history of disorder; with the help of what is apparently a perfectly obvious and traditional plan, it unearths the manner in which some people use their intelligence and sensitivity to live out (often in a state of great tension) their simultaneous desires for encounter and rupture. It traces the shrewdness of their behaviour, the judgement of individuals and collective discernment. It deciphers modes of thought and makes a statement about the real and imagined perceptions underlying acts of submission at times of defiance, resistance and revolt. It assesses professional and sexual roles and attempts to see what is actually being said or denounced beneath the usual rigid, statutory heading of social class.

But let there be no mistake: this pursuit of rules and rationalities is not a means of ignoring hate and anger, violence and cruelty, irony and unreason. It would be impostorous to erase men's fury, and ignorant not to present the situations which produced it, for to fail to take account of deceit and dishonour would be to give way to naive populism. The history of a society is also the history of the clash that exists between its instinct for survival and desire for union and collaboration with its taste for destruction and ashes. The Parisian people of the eighteenth century lived off this clash.

The contours of the population outlined here show it forever on the look-out for what might prove threatening to it and in search of whatever might strengthen it. It was looking for equilibrium at the heart of a fragility by which it was almost totally defined and its behaviour and decisions are indications of its response to a precariousness which permanently threatened its stability.

Not being taken for a fool was one of its passions or rather one of its necessities, and thus the whole of its intelligence was put into not being abused or deceived. From this came its taste for news and gossip; its desire to know and understand; to give things a name; and the speed with which it circulated its information. Behind the effervescence, the bustle and the emotion can be found a seriousness and much understanding. History owes it to itself to seek out and, without attempting to define it, take hold of this fragile life and thus lend it sense and weight.

The archives say something to someone. It is up to that person to say what it is, thereby opening up endless possibilities of analysis. There are no secrets about archives; they simply lay bare a language which the historian feels and experiences and then explores. It is in this sense that a book so written has no end.

# Notes

## Introduction

1  M. Foucault, 'La Vie des hommes infâmes', *Cahiers du chemin*, 29 (January 1977), p. 12.
2  J. Le Goff, 'Les Mentalités, une histoire ambigüe', in *Faire de l'histoire* (Paris, 1974), vol. 3, p. 89.
3  The expression is that of C. Poni.
4  A journey is always punctuated by dialogue; my thanks here go to Michelle Perrot for the warmth of her concern and to Jacques Revel for the keenness of his approach in the course of seminars and work undertaken jointly (in particular with regard to the file on the Parisian uprising of May 1750).

## Chapter 1. Space and Ways of Life

1  Archives Nationales (AN), $X^{2B}$ 1367, June 1750.
2  A. Farge, *Vivre dans la rue à paris au XVIIIᵉ siècle* (Paris, 1979).
3  F. Boudon, A. Chastel, H. Couzy, and F. Hamon, *Système de l'architecture urbaine – le quartier des Halles à Paris* (Paris, 1977).
4  A. Farge, 'Le Bazar de la rue', *Urbi*, 1 (1979), p. xcvii.
5  A. Farge and A. Zysberg, 'Les Théâtres de la violence à Paris au XVIIIᵉ siècle', *Annales ESC*, 5 (1979), pp. 984–1015.
6  A. Williams, *The Police of Paris, 1718–1789* (Baton Rouge, La., 1979).
7  Lenoir, Lieutenant – General of police, 'Mémoires manuscrits', Bibliothèque municipale d'Orléans, MS 1423, fo. 343.
8  [Translator's note. *cabaret*: tavern.]
9  W. Kula, *Measures and Men* (Princeton, 1986).
10  AN, Y 11253, 10 May 1766.
11  AN, Y 11255, 27 May 1768.
12  [Translator's note. *mouches*: police spies/informers.]
13  I am thinking in particular of the *gazetins* (see p. 246) of the secret police and of Inspector Vanneroux's reports on comments overhead in the cafés. Archives de la Bastille, MSS 10155–70.

14  AN, X$^{2B}$ 1367, 16 June 1750.
15  *Encyclopédie méthodique*, vol. IX: *Jurisprudence contenant la police et les municipalités*, by J. Peuchet (Paris, 1789). Peuchet uses the term *soin* (care) in his introduction to the article entitled 'Police'.
16  *hôtel*: offices/administrative headquarters.
17  *Encyclopédie méthodique*, vol. IX, pp. 563ff.
18  *Code pénal ou recueil des principales ordonnances, édits et déclarations, sur les crimes et délits*, 2nd edn based on an *Essai sur l'esprit et les motifs de la procédure criminelle*, Paris, 1760.
19  Archives of the Prefecture of the Paris Police, AB 405. Quartier Saint-Denis. Reports on posters, 23 July 1779 to 19 April 1786.
20  La Pitié: Parisian jail.
21  Correspondence of Commissioner Thierry, 1756–1776, AN, Y 11261.
22  Ibid., Y 11250.
23  Ibid.
24  *canaille*: the mob/riff-raff.
25  Correspondence of Commissioner Thierry. 1756–1776, AN, Y 11243$^{B}$.
26  Ibid.
27  Jean de Mille, *Pratique criminelle*, ed. A. Lebigre (Paris, Les Marmousets, 1983), p. 37.
28  C. Beccaria, *Traité des délits et des peines*, 1764; reprint (Paris, 1979), p. 123.
29  Lenoir, 'Mémoires', MS 1422, fo. 302.
30  J. Pitt-Rivers, and J. G. Peristiany, *Honor and Grace in Anthropology* (Cambridge/New York, 1992).
31  M. Foucault, 'Usage des plaisirs et techniques de soi', *Le Débat*, 27 (November 1983), pp. 46–72.

Chapter 2  Girls for the Marrying

 1  A. Farge and C. Klapisch, *Madame ou Mademoiselle? Itinéraires de la solitude féminine, XVIII$^e$–XX$^e$ s.*, collected texts (Paris, 1984).
 2  L.-S. Mercier, *Tableau de Paris* 12 vols (Amsterdam 1782–1788); vol. 11: *Filles à marier*, p. 55.
 3  Ibid., vol. 11: *Répugnance pour le mariage*, p. 63.
 4  Ibid., *Filles à marier*.
 5  Ibid., vol. 4: *Filles nubiles*, p. 23.
 6  Ibid., *Filles à marier*.
 7  Ibid., vol. 8: *Grisettes*, p. 77.
 8  Ibid., *Filles à marier*.
 9  Ibid., vol. 4: *Portefaix*, p. 17.
10  E. et J. de Goncourt, *La Femme au XVIII$^e$ siècle* (Paris, 1862; repr. Paris, 1982, preface by E. Badinter).
11  Ibid., p. 233.
12  Mercier, *Tableau de Paris* , vol. 3: *Demoiselles*, p. 86.
13  Ibid., vol. 4: *Noces*, p. 38.
14  Ibid., vol. 12: *L'Education campagnarde*, p. 185.

Chapter 3 'Seduced and Abandoned'

1 The years in question are 1775, 1780, 1785 in the National Archives taken from complaints lodged with the Petit Criminel, series Y.
2 A. Farge, 'Histoires de servantes: sentiments de service', *Les Révoltes logiques*, 8–9 (1979), pp. 79–86.
3 AN, Y 9956, Wednesday 7 December 1785.
4 J. Rancière, *Le Philosophe et ses pauvres* (Paris, 1983).
5 AN, Y 9891, July 1780.
6 Ibid., Y 9890, 22 May 1780.
7 Ibid., Y 9896, 28 October 1780.
8 Ibid., Y 9887, 14 March 1780.
9 Ibid., Y 9829, 10 May 1775.
10 Ibid., Y 9831, 29 July 1775.
11 Ibid., Y 9832, 13 April 1775.
12 Ibid., Y 9846, 18 February 1785.
13 Ibid., Y 9832, 3 June 1775.
14 There are in fact two accounts of this tale, including Basile's, in the literature of the fourteenth century which contain this detail. Beauty moreover gives birth while asleep.
15 M. Soriano, *Les Contes de Perrault* (Paris, 1968), ch. 6, p. 130.
16 AN, Y 9832, 3 June 1775.
17 Ibid., Y 9829, 10 May 1775.
18 Ibid., Y 9956, 26 September 1785.
19 Ibid., Y 9893, 17 August 1780.
20 Ibid., Y 9893, 27 October 1780.
21 Ibid., Y 9956, 7 May 1785.
22 Ibid., Y 9890, 22 May 1780.
23 Ibid., Y 9835, 15 August 1775.
24 One might well believe that such comments were common during interrogations in the eighteenth century but this is not in fact the case and this is why attention has been drawn to them here. In contrast, Ménétra's journal contains many such comments, but in this case we are dealing with an autobiography and not a court appearance.

Chapter 4 Concerning Parents and Children

1 A. Farge, and M. Foucault, *Le Désordre des familles. Lettres de cachet des Archives de la Bastille* (Paris, 1982), p. 28.
2 J.-L. Flandrin, *Familles. Parenté, maison, sexualité dans l'ancienne société* (Paris, 1984), p. 182; *Families in Former Times: Kinship, Household and Sexuality* (Cambridge, 1979), p. 17.
3 A. Farge, *Vivre dans la rue à Paris au XVIIIᵉ siècle* (Paris, 1979).
4 The study of the popular revolt of May 1750 might be regarded as further evidence of the important role of the father.
5 Flandrin, *Familles*, p. 122.
6 Farge, *Vivre dans la rue*.
7 A. Farge, and A. Zysberg, 'Les Théâtres de la violence à Paris au XVIIIᵉ siècle', *Annales ESC*, 5 (1979), pp. 984–1015.

8  Farge and Foucault, *Desordre*, p. 25.
9  *petit Savoyard*: little sweep.
10  *lettres de cachet*: King's order; see p. 68.
11  Each commissioner had his own particular way of keeping his archives. One should also add that the registers of abandoned children have not all been preserved in the Y series. For a more comprehensive study one also needs to consult the orphanage archives.
12  Petit/Grand Criminel: Lower and Higher Courts.
13  Nos. $X^{2B}$ 1367 and $X^{2B}$ 1368 in the Archives Nationales and MS 1101–2 in the Joly de Fleury Collection in the Bibliothèque Nationale. Bibliography for this question is as follows: Commander Herlaut, 'Les Enlèvements d'enfants à Paris en 1720 et en 1750', *Revue Historique* 139 (1922), pp. 43–61 and 202–23; J. Nicolas, 'La Rumeur de Paris: rapts d'enfants en 1750', *L'Histoire*, 40 (December 1981); Ch. Romon, 'L'Affaire des "enlèvements d'enfants" dans les archives du Châtelet (1749–1750)', *Revue Historique*, 587 (July–September 1983); A. Farge and J. Revel, 'Les règles de l'émeute. L'Affaire des enlèvements d'enfants en 1750', in *Mouvements populaires et conscience sociale* (Paris, 1985), pp. 635–46.
14  The various autobiographies that have come to light and which offer precious details and insights are obviously in a different class; of these the work of Jamerey Duval comes to mind or more recently that of Jacques-Louis Ménétra, a journeyman glazier of the eighteenth century, in his *Journal de ma vie*, pref. D. Roche (Paris, 1982). Translated as *Journal of My Life* (New York, 1986).
15  Ph. Ariès, *Centuries of Childhood* (Harmondsworth, 1979).
16  D. Roche, *The People of Paris* (Leamington Spa, 1987), p. 240.
17  Ménétra, *Journal*, p. 19.
18  J. Rancière, *Le Philosophe et ses pauvres* (Paris, 1983), pp. 283ff.
19  Kant, I. *The Critique of Judgement* (1790) §2 (Oxford, 1978).
20  G. Gauny, *Le Philosophe plébéien*, preface by J. Rancière (Paris, 1983), pp. 14–15.
21  Epinal: nineteenth-century centre of popular painting.
22  Michelet: French historian (1798–1874) renowned for his lyrical prose.
23  Ariès, *Centuries*; J. Gelis, M. Laget and M. F. Morel, *Entrer dans la vie* (Paris, 1978); C. Fouquet-Kniebiehler, *L'Histoire des mères* (Paris, 1980); E. Badinter, *The Myth of Motherhood* (London, 1981); Flandrin, *Families*.
24  A. Blanchard, *Essay d'exhortation pour les états différents des malades ... On y a joint un examen général sur tous les commandements et sur les péchés de plusieurs états ...* (Paris, 1713), 2 vols.
25  M. Garden, *Lyon et les Lyonnais au XVIII$^e$ siècle*, Paris, 1970.
26  Badinter, *The Myth of Motherhood*.
27  AN, Y 9525, 8 June 1766, 7 o'clock in the evening. Proceedings.
28  Ibid., Y 13700, 27 March 1778. Register of the Guard (1763–1784) begun on 27 July 1763.
29  Ibid., Y 9829, 12 June 1775. Case brought before Commissioner Graville.
30  *archers*: armed guards/police, formerly bowmen; *hôpital*: orphanage/house of correction/workhouse, depending on context.
31  J. Buvat, *Journal de la Régence, 1715–1723*, 2 vols (Paris, 1845), vol. 2, pp. 77ff.
32  AN, U 363. De Lisle Collection. Secret Council of the *Parlement*, 1687 to 1774. 1720 Revolt.

33   Manuscripts of the Bibliothèque Nationale. MS 49328. Emigration to the colonies, 17th–19th century. 1717 survey by de la Boullaye.
34   *syndics*: guild officials and magistrates.
35   AN, X$^{2B}$ 1367, 30 May 1750. Information.
36   Ibid.
37   Ibid.
38   Bibliothèque Nationale, Joly de Fleury Collection, MS 1101, 42nd witness.
39   'Etre à la paille' meant being held in the worst conditions in jail. One simply had a small amount of straw to sleep on and had to pay to have it changed.
40   AN, X$^{2B}$ 1367, 2 June 1750. Information and additional information.
41   Ibid. 29 May 1750. Information.
42   Ibid., 1368, 23 June 1750. Additional information.
43   Ibid. 22 June 1750. Additional information.
44   Ch. Lefaure and J.-P. Moatti, 'Les Ambigüités de l'acceptable', *Culture technique*, 11 (September 1983).
45   This question of child-labour and apprenticeship, and the conflicts engendered, are dealt with elsewhere.
46   Ménétra, *Journal*, p. 295.
47   AN, X$^{2B}$ 1367, 27 May 1750.
48   Ménétra, *Journal*, pp. 21ff.
49   Abbé du Breil de Pontbriand, *Projet d'un établissement déjà commencé pour élever dans la piété les savoyards qui sont dans Paris* (Paris, 1735), pp. 17ff.
50   Bibliothèque Nationale, Joly de Fleury Collection, MS 1101.
51   Farge, *Vivre dans la rue*.
52   Ménétra, *Journal*, p. 34.
53   AN, X$^{2B}$ 1367, 29 May 1750.
54   Bibliothèque Nationale, Joly de Fleury Collection, MS 1101, 25 June 1750, 78th witness.
55   AN, X$^{2B}$ 1367, 2 June 1750. Information.
56   It is worth noting that female participation in the disturbances recurs constantly even where the abduction of children was not involved.
57   AN, X$^{2B}$ 1367, 29 May 1750.
58   Ibid., 1368, 22 June 1750.
59   Farge and Foucault, *Le Désordre des familles*, p. 352.
60   E. J. Barbier, *Chronique de la régence et du régne de Louis XV, 1718–1763*, Coll. 'Histoire de France'.
61   *Parc civil*: magistrates' court.
62   AN, Y 9303. Chambre du Conseil. Records of 22 March 1769 of the hearing at the *parc civil*, by us, Counsellor to the King and Advocate to the Chamber and Parisian Assizes, comprising two dialogues on the 7th and 17th of the said month between ourselves and the child claimed by the Widow Le Brie on the one hand and by Jean Noiseux and his wife on the other.

## Chapter 5   Undesirable Alliances and Times of Disruption

1   J.-L. Flandrin, *Families in Former Times: Kinship, Household and Sexuality* (Cambridge, 1979).
2   Lenoir, 'Mémoires manuscrits', Bibliothèque municipale d'Orléans, MSS 1421–4.

3   Ibid.
4   A. Farge, *Vivre dans la rue à Paris an XVIIIᵉ siècle* (Paris, 1979).
5   Lenoir, 'Mémoires'.
6   Archives de la Bastille, MS 12008, fo. 18 (for the year 1757).
7   Ibid., MS 11011, fos 225–47 (for the year 1728).
8   Ibid., MS 11019, fos 8–12 (for the year 1728).
9   Ibid., MS 11940, fos 331–42 (for the year 1756).
10  Ibid., MS 11017 (for the year 1728).
11  Ibid., MS 11939.
12  Kept in the Bibliothèque de l'Arsenal in the Archives de la Bastille.
13  Archives de la Bastille, MS 11000, fos 225–9 (for the year 1728).
14  Ibid., MS 11010, fos 14–25 (for the year 1728).
15  Ibid., MS 11996 fol. 110–11 (for the year 1758).
16  Lescombat: see p. 203.
17  Archives de la Bastille, MS 11999, fos 145–67 (for the year 1758).
18  Ibid., MS 12087, fos 38–77 (for the year 1758).
19  Ibid., MS 11940, fos 359–70 (for the year 1756).
20  AN, AD III 8. Handwritten commentary by Procurator Gueulette, 1755.
21  This journal was found in the Archives Nationales amongst the police commissioner's archives in the Y stacks, No. 11741.
22  AN, series AD III, and Nos 6,7 and 8 in particular: arrests and rulings on criminals 1191–1789, factums, street broadsheets, posters and engravings in common use: collection put together by the deputy for the King's Procurator at Le Châtelet, Gueulette, c.1766.
23  In this section, all the references come from the text quoted in n. 21: AN, Y 11741.
24  Rather than give references here to the books on court society, attention should be drawn to the amazing *gazetins de la police secrète* which are so revealing about the lives of the libertines: Archives de la Bastille, MS 3532. Anonymous.
25  *mostra*: Ital. show/display.
26  *marivaudage*: farce in the manner of French playwright Marivaux (1688–1763).
27  Bibliothèque de l'Arsenal, MS 3532. Anonymous.

## Chapter 6   In the Workshop

1   Select bibliography on the question: R. de Lespinasse, *Les Métiers et corporations de la ville de Paris*, 4 vols (Paris, 1879–97), coll. 'Histoire générale de Paris'; E. Coornaert, *Les Corporations en France avant 1789* (Paris, 1968); id., *Les Compagnonnages en France du Moyen Age à nos jours* (Paris, 1966); N. T. des Essarts, *Dictionnaire universel de police*, 7 vols (Paris, 1786–9); M. J. Flammermont, 'Mémoires sur les grèves et les coalitions ouvrières à la fin de l'Ancien Régime', *Bulletin des Sciences économiques et sociales* (1894); F. Funck-Brentano, *La Question ouvrière sous l'Ancien Régime d'après les dossiers de prisonniers par lettres de cachet* (Paris, 1903); J. Hayem, 'La Répression des grèves au XVIIIᵉ siècle', in *Mémoires et documents pour servir à l'histoire du commerce et de l'industrie*, (Paris, 1911); S. Kaplan, 'Réflexions

sur la police du monde du travail, 1700–1815', *Revue Historique*, 529 (January–March 1979), pp. 17–78; E. Martin Saint-Léon, *Le Compagnonnage* (Paris, 1901); B. Geremek, *Le Salariat dans l'artisanat parisien au XIIIᵉ–XVᵉ siècles* (The Hague, 1962, 1982); H. Hauser, *Ouvriers du temps passé, XVᵉ–XVIᵉ siècles* (1899; repr. Paris, 1982); N. Z. Davis, 'Women in the crafts in XVIIth century Lyon', *Feminist Studies*, 8 (Spring 1982); J.-L. Ménétra, *Journal de ma vie* pref. D. Roche (Paris, 1982). Translated as *Journal of My Life* (New York, 1986).

2  Delisle, Simon Clicquot de Blervache, *Mémoires sur les corps de métiers*, awarded first prize by the judges of the Academy of Amiens in 1757 (The Hague, 1758).

3  Lamoignon Collection in the Archives of the *Prefecture of the Paris Police*. Of the 823 orders and instructions that appeared between 1730 and 1763 (an average of 3 per month), 477 concern the crafts in particular and 73 relate to trade and commerce, making a total of 550. Cf. also the article by S. Kaplan, (n. 1 above) and see above for the *ordonnances de police*.

4  In the following ways 170 workshop disputes were documented:

• systematic search of the archives of Commissioner Hugues of Les Halles between 1757 and 1767 (AN, Y 10999–11029);
• systematic search year by year of the complaints brought before the Petit Criminel (in the years 1775, 1780, 1785) deposited in the AN, series Y;
• in-depth survey of the archives of the police commissioners Mutel, Delagrave, Lemaire, Delaubeypie, Divot, Joron.

5  Part of this work was undertaken for a paper given to the symposium at Rouen in November 1983 on socialization: 'L'Atelier à Paris au XVIIIᵉ siècle, une structure de sociabilité en conflit avec elle-même et avec les pouvoirs'; this appears in the preparatory papers for the *Actes du Colloque*.

6  AN, Y 14088, 11 November 1761, archives of Commissioner Crespy.

7  Archives de la Bastille, MS 11936, 11 December 1756.

8  Ch. Desmaze, *Les Métiers à Paris d'après les ordonnances du Châtelet avec les sceaux des artisans* (Paris, 1874), which draws upon the *Dictionnaire historique de la France* by Ludovic Lahanne (Paris, 1873).

9  AN, Y 9525, 8 January 1766.

10  AN, X²ᴮ 1367, interrogation of J. Jacquet.

11  M. Sonenscher, 'Journeymen's migrations and workshop organisation in eighteenth-century France', delivered to conference at Cornell University on 'Work in France', April 1983.

12  AN, Y 11002B, 16 July 1761, Commissioner Hugues.

13  Ibid., Y 11004B, 13 February 1763, Commissioner Hugues.

14  Ibid., Y 10004A, 12 July 1763, Commissioner Hugues.

15  Ibid., Y 11006A, 24 February 1765, Commissioner Hugues.

16  Bibliothèque de l'Arsenal, MS 3532, anonymous.

17  Cf. Davis, 'Women in the crafts' (n. 1 above).

18  In Paris, this custom had practically died out although Jeanne Moyon, guilty of snatching children in July 1750, was made to mount and ride an ass. One should add that this took place shortly after the riots over the abduction of children.

19  Very few of the books dealing with the lives of women workers in the eighteenth century have approached this subject. In contrast, a work by Henri Hauser, which is now quite old, devotes an excellent chapter to the work of

women. For more recent work, see R. Darnton, *The Great Cat Massacre, and Other Episodes in French Cultural History* (Harmondsworth, 1985).
20 AN, Y 11001B, 1 November 1760, Commissioner Hugues.
21 Ibid., Y 11006B, 17 July 1765, Commissioner Hugues.
22 Ibid., Y 14078, 1 October 1752, Commissioner Crespy.
23 Bibliothèque historique de la Ville de Paris, MS NA 66. Contract of apprenticeship of 15 July 1776.
24 AN, Y 14078, Saturday 19 August 1752.
25 Ibid., Y 11002B, 1 July 1761, Commissioner Hugues.
26 Ibid., Y 10999, 29 June 1758, Commissioner Hugues.
27 Ibid., 3 February 1758, Commissioner Hugues.
28 Ibid., Y 11005B, 17 December 1764, Commissioner Hugues.
29 Ibid., Y 11167, 2 April 1750, Commissioner Mutel.
30 E. Levasseur, *Histoire des classes ouvrières en France avant 1789* (Paris, 1901).
31 For a more extensive treatment of this subject, see next chapter.
32 AN, Y 11027, 25 January 1785.
33 Ibid., Y 11006A, 22 January 1765, Commissioner Hugues.
34 Ibid., Y 9525, Thursday 30 December 1762, Commissioner Hugues.
35 *mouchards*: police agents/spies.
36 AN, Y 9535, 8 April 1775, Commissioner Roch.

## Chapter 7   At the Workshop Door

1 This chapter draws upon the archives of the aforesaid Commissioner Hugues and those of the *chambre de police*: journeymen pursued by their community between 1753 and 1789 (Y 9523 to 9531) and interrogations in the *chambre de police* between 1748 and 1786; work was also carried out on personal files in the Archives de la Bastille, for 1756, 1763 and 1775, as well as on all the files relating to the question of workers and their corporations.
2 J.-P. Lenoir, 'Mémoires manuscrits', Bibliothèque municipale d'Orléans, MSS 1421–4, fo. 458.
3 Archives de la Bastille, MS 10138, the register into which Inspector Poussot consigned the proceedings sent via him to the Lieutenant-General of Police and also the methods used to carry out the instructions given him by the latter.
4 Ibid., MS 10144, prison register of the Sûreté de Paris in 1762; this was begun 1 November 1762 and continued to 9 January 1765.
5 J.-L. Ménétra, *Journal de ma vie*, Pref. D. Roche (Paris, 1982). Translated as *Journal of My Life* (New York, 1986).
6 Archives de la Bastille, MS 12245, for the year 1765.
7 Ibid., MS 11172. Abbé Belichon was taken to Lazare, where he seems to have succumbed to madness; his family were later to request his release.
8 AN, Y 9525, 16 May 1766, Commissioner Pelletier.
9 Ibid., Y 9529, 18 February 1779.
10 Ibid., Y 9527, 4 May 1772.
11 Archives de la Bastille, MS 11152, the Violette affair, 1731.
12 Ibid., MS 12127, 15 February 1761.
13 Ibid., MSS 12173–99.

14 Lenoir, 'Mémoires', fo. 260.

15 Archives de la Bastille, MS 10230. Surveillance of the Jews.

16 Ibid., MS 12177, 15 July 1763, for the year 1756.

17 AN, Y 9535, 26 November 1778.

18 Archives de la Bastille, MS 10140, Inspector Poussot, district of Les Halles 1738–54, alphabetical register of arrested persons.

19 The source material does not really indicate which inspectors were appointed to the special branches such as the Bureau de la Sûreté or others. As far as Inspector Poussot is concerned, his register is evidence of his own activity in the district, with no apparent specialization in any particular problem or with a specific section or category of the population.

20 A. Williams, *The Police of Paris, 1718–1789* (Baton Rouge, La., 1979), p. 100.

21 Guillauté, 'Mémoire de réformation de la police envoyé au roi' [Memorandum to the King concerning police reorganization] (1749).

22 R. Cheyne, *op. cit.*

23 A. Farge, *Le Vol d'aliments à Paris au XVIIIᵉ siècle* (Paris, 1974); id., *Vivre dans la rue à Paris au XVIII siècle* (Paris, 1979).

24 A. Farge, and A. Zysberg, 'Les Théâtres de la violence à Paris au XVIIIᵉ siècle', *Annales ESC*, 5 (1979), pp. 984–1015.

25 N. Castan, *Les Criminels du Languedoc, les exigences d'ordre et les voies du ressentiment dans une société pré-révolutionnaire (1750–1790)* (Toulouse, 1980), p. 27. Farge, *Le Vol d'aliments*, p. 66.

26 Castan, *Les Criminels du Languedoc*, p. 39.

27 R. Chartier, 'La Monarchie d'argot entre le mythe et l'histoire', *Cahiers Jussieu, 5: Les Marginaux et les exclus dans l'histoire* (10/18, 1979), p. 275.

28 A. Farge, 'Le Mendiant, un marginal? Les résistances aux archers de l'hôpital dans le Paris du XVIIIᵉ siècle', *Cahiers Jussieu*, p. 312.

29 J.-P. Gutton, *Domestiques et serviteurs dans la France de l'Ancien Régime* (Paris, 1981).

30 L.-S. Mercier, *Tableau de Paris*, 12 vols (Amsterdam, 1781–8) vol. 12, 'Gare! Gare!'.

31 G. Picq, M. Pradine, and C. Ungerer, *La Criminalité aux bords de l'eau à Paris au XVIIIᵉ siècle*, p. 26.

32 P. Peveri, *Vol à la tire et répression dans le Paris de l'époque des Lumières (1750–1775)*, Finals thesis, March 1980, pp. 141ff.

33 A. Farge, and M. Foucault, *Le Désordre des familles, lettres de cachet des Archives de la Bastille* (Paris, 1981).

34 Peveri, *Vol à la tire*, p. 76.

35 M. Perrot, 'Délinquance et système pénitentiaire en France au XIXᵉ siècle', *Annales ESC*, 1 (1975), pp. 67–93.

36 Cour des Miracles: rough area of Paris, in medieval times the haunt of beggars and vagabonds.

## Chapter 8 Invitations to the Crowds

1 J. Boutier, A. Dewerpe, and D. Nordman, *Un tour de France royal, le voyage de Charles IX (1564–1566)* (Paris, 1984); C. Jouhaud, *La Fronde des mots* (Paris, 1985), ch. 5: 'Mazarinades et fêtes frondeuses'.

2  N. Delamare, *Traité de la Police*, 4 vols (1705–38), Book II, section VIII, pp. 368ff.

3  Ibid., section X, p. 393.

4  Delamare Collection in the Bibliothèque Nationale, MS frs. 21650, fo. 124, order of procession of ransomed slaves ...

5  L.-S. Mercier, *Tableau de Paris*, 12 vols (Amsterdam, 1782–6), ch. *Population de la Capitale.*

6  S. Hardy, 'Mes loisirs ou journal des événements tels qu'ils parviennent à ma connaissance'. Bibliothèque Nationale, MS frs. 6680–7.

7  Ibid., MS 6681, 5 May 1774.

8  Ibid., 7 May 1774.

9  Ibid., 11 May 1774.

10  Ibid., MS 6684, 25 October 1781.

11  Bernier, *Conférences sur les ordonnances de Louis XIV*, 1719, vol. II, p. 371, quoted by D. Muller, 'Magistrats français et peine de mort', *XVIII$^e$ siècle* (1972), pp. 79–107.

12  L. Marin, *Portrait of the King* (Basingstoke, 1988).

13  Ibid., p. 46.

14  *amende honorable*: public apology/ritual act of penance.

15  A sole reference suffices here: Michel Foucault's book *Surveiller et punir: la naissance de la prison* (Paris, 1974), the opening pages of which are a masterly explanation of this process. Trans. by Alan Sheridan, *Discipline and Punish: the Birth of The Prison* (London, 1977).

16  M. Bée, 'Le Spectacle de l'exécution dans la France d'Ancien Règime'. *Annales ESC*, 4 (1983), p. 843, an article which largely takes up the Foucaldian problematic, but presents it slightly differently.

17  M. Bloch, *Les Rois thaumaturges* (Paris, 1961).

18  P. Rétat, (ed.), *L'Attentat de Damiens. Discours sur l'événement au XVIII$^e$ siècle* (Paris, Lyons, 1979).

19  Jansenist dispute: arising from the controversial ideas of theologian Cornelius Jansen (1585–1638), similar to Calvinist doctrine, most famously championed by Pascal and opposed by the Jesuits.

20  B. Edelman, *La Maison de Kant* (Paris, Payot, 1984), p. 16.

21  Ch. de Montesquieu, *The Spirit of the Laws* (Cambridge, 1989; first published in French, 1748).

22  This treatise was published in the Flammarion 'Champs' collection (Paris, 1979).

23  L.-S. Mercier, *Tableau de Paris*, vol. 3, ch. 278, 'Sentence de mort'.

24  Ibid. But particularly 2 key observers, viz. the deputy procurator to the King at Le Châtelet, Gueulette, who had the strange habit of making handwritten comments in the margins of the printed editions of sentences passed between 1726 and 1766 (AN, AD III); and then S. Hardy, who gives accounts of almost all the executions between 1764 and 1784 (Bibliothèque Nationale, MS frs, 6680–7).

25  Mercier, *Tableau de Paris*, vol. 3, ch. 279, 'Le Bourreau'.

26  Famous poisoner.

27  Mercier, *Tableau de Paris*, vol. 3, ch. 280, 'Place de Grève'.

28  Ibid.

29  Ibid.

30  S. Hardy, Bibliothèque Nationale, MS 6682, 11 May 1775.

31  Ibid., 30 May 1775.

32  A. Poitrineau, 'Des accidents aux homicides: la mort inopinée en Auvergne au XVII<sup>e</sup> et XVIII<sup>e</sup> siècles', in *La France d'Ancien Régime*. Collection of studies in honour of P. Goubert (Toulouse, 1984), pp. 577–86.

33  Mercier, *Tableau de Paris*, vol. 3, ch. 281, 'Servante mal pendue'.

34  Hardy, Journal, BN MS frs. 6682.

35  R. Favre, *La Mort au siècle des Lumières* (Paris, 1978).

36  L.-S. Mercier, *Tableau de Paris*, vol. 3, ch. 279, 'Le Bourreau'.

37  Dufort, comte de Cheverny, *Mémoires sur les règnes de Louis XV et Louis XVI et sur la Rèvolution*, 2 vols (Paris, 1886), vol. 1, p. 191.

38  Ch. Collé, *Journal et mémoires sur les hommes de lettres, les ouvrages dramatiques et les événements les plus mémorables du règne de Louis XV (1748–1772)* (repr. Paris, 1868), 3 vols, vol. 2, p. 86.

39  On this subject see the pages of Philippe Ariès in *The Hour of Our Death* (London, 1981), 'Sade's view of man and nature', pp. 391ff.

40  A. Farge, *Le Miroir des femmes, Textes de la Bibliothèque bleue* (Paris, 1983).

41  Dufort, comte de Cheverny, *Mémoires*, vol. 1, p. 191.

42  Joseph-François Lafitau, *Mœurs des sauvages américains comparés aux mœurs des premiers temps*, 2 vols (Paris, 1724). Extracts published by the magazine *Le Débat*, 8.

43  Hardy, Journal, BN MS 6682.

44  R. Anchel, *Crimes et châtiments au XVIII<sup>e</sup> siècle* (Paris, 1933).

45  Hardy, Journal, MS 6682.

46  Decree issued by the *Parlement* on 19 March 1765. Handwritten comment by Gueulette, AN, AD III, 11.

47  Comment by Gueulette quoted by Anchel, *Crimes*.

48  Hardy, Journal MS 6682, 6 May 1777, Execution of Desrues.

49  AN, AD III, 6.

50  Ibid., 9, decree by the *cour du Parlement*, 30 June 1750.

51  Ibid., 11, decree by the *cour du Parlement*, 19 March 1765.

52  Ibid., decree by the *cour du Parlement*, 11 October 1764.

53  Ibid., 7, decree by the *cour du Parlement*, 7 May 1743.

54  J.-P. Desaive, 'Le Nu hurluberlu', *Ethnologie française*, 6 (1976).

55  Note that in 1779, S. Hardy remarked that the wearing of hose whilst on the wheel had been in practice for 2 years which, as he comments, was 'altogether more decent', MS 6683.

56  M. Foucault, *Discipline and Punish: The Birth of the Prison*, tr. A. Sheridan (London, 1977). Hardy, Journal MS 6681, 18 February 1772.

57  Hardy, Journal, MS 6682, 4 June 1775.

58  Ibid., MS 6683, 7 October 1779.

59  AN, AD III, 8, handwritten comment by Gueulette on the decree of 3 August 1751.

60  Ibid., 7.

61  La Salpêtrière: women's asylum and house of correction.

62  AN, AD III, 6, the La Dupuis affair.

63  Ibid., handwritten comment by Gueulette.

64  Quoted by R. Anchel, *Crimes*.

65  Dale Van Kley, *The Damiens Affair and the unraveling of the Ancient Regime, 1750–1770* (Princeton, NJ, 1984).

66  Moufle d'Angerville, *Vie privée de Louis XV, les principaux événements, particularités et anecdotes de son règne*, 4 vols (Paris, 1785), vol. 4, p. 209.

67  *taille*: tax, particularly hated by the Third Estate, which bore the brunt of it.

68 Ibid., p. 211.
69 AN, Y 15707, report by the *commandant-major* on the events of 30 May 1770.
70 Ibid., general presentation of all the operations carried out on the occasion of the unfortunate incident which occurred on leaving the Place Louis-XV, Rue Royale on Wednesday 30 May 1770, reports of which were produced as a result of proceedings during the months of May, June, August and September of the same year, the minutes of which have remained in the hands of M. Sirebeau, commissioner at Le Châtelet.
71 L.-S. Mercier, *Tableau de Paris* ch. 'Gare! Gare!' et ch. 'Population de la Capitale'.
72 One quite often comes across errors in L.-S. Mercier in particular with regard to dates, as on this occasion where he mistakenly claims that the date of the accident was 28 May whereas it actually occurred on 30 May.
73 Hardy, Journal, BN MS 6680, 4 June 1770.
74 Moufle d'angerville, *Vie privée*, vol. 4, p. 220.
75 AN Y 9769, information prepared by M$^e$ Coquelin, Commissioner, at the request of M. le Procureur du Roi on the subject of the unfortunate incident in the Rue Royale . . .
76 Of the 132 bodies 26, or a fifth of the total, had nothing on them or in their pockets.
77 Notes on 621 objects were found; given that those were in the possession of 106 persons, this in fact represents an average of 5 items per person.
78 Harpagon-style strong-boxes: after Harpagon, miser and central character in Molière's play *Le Misanthrope*.
79 All the quotes regarding the identification of corpses and interrogations of the wounded have been taken from the information file, AN, Y 9769.
80 Hardy, Journal, MS 6680.
81 Mme Campan, *Mémoires sur la vie privée de Marie Antoinette*, 3rd edn (Paris, 1823), vol. 1, ch. 3 pp. 55–6.
82 Extracts kept in AN, Y 15707.
83 AN, Y 11257, Commissioner Thierry's correspondence, 22 June 1770.
84 Moufle d'Angerville, *Vie privée*, vol. 4, p. 220.
85 AN, Y 15707.
86 Hardy, Journal, BN MS 6680.
87 Antoine Gabriel de Sartine, 1729–1801, Lieutenant Criminel at Le Châtelet in 1755, *maître des requêtes* in 1759, Lieutenant of Police of Paris from November 1759 to 9 August 1774, and then Secretary to the Navy until 1780.
88 Bibliothèque de l'Arsenal, *Histoire de France*, Extracts relating to . . . , MS 3724, p. 240.
89 A. Williams, *The Police of Paris, 1718–1789* (Baton Rouge, La., 1979).
90 Bibliothèque Nationale, Joly de Fleury Collection, MS 2541, Accidents of May 1770. Memos by the police officers of Le Châtelet. The City's response.
91 AN, Y 15707, 'Tableau général . . .'

Chapter 9    The Crowds amongst Themselves

1 L.-S. Mercier, *Tableau de Paris*, 12 vols (Amsterdam, 1782–6), ch. 'Mélange des individus'.

2  N. Ledoux, *De l'architecture considérée sous le rapport de l'Art, des Moeurs, et de la Législation*. Comments by Mona Ozouf in an article which appeared in *Annales ESC* (November/December 1966) and reprinted in her book *L'Ecole de la France* (Paris, 1985), p. 295: 'Architecture et urbanisme: l'image de la ville chez Claude-Nicolas Ledoux'.
3  Ozouf, *Ecole de la France*, p. 295.
4  On this point, one simply needs to refer to the extremely enlightening article by J.-M. Goulemot, 'Démons, merveilles et philosophie à l'âge classique', *Annales ESC*, 6 (1980).
5  Among others: R. Darnton, *La Fin des Lumières. Le Mesmérisme et la Révolution* (Paris, 1984; 1st edn 1968); Catherine Laurence Maire, *Les Convulsionnaires de Saint-Médard* (Paris, 1985).
6  AN, AD III 9. Bibliothèque de l'Arsenal. Archives de la Bastille, MS 11933, the Ernault affair.
7  M.-Ch. Pouchelle, *The Body and Surgery in the Middle Ages* (Cambridge, 1985), pp. 160–7.
8  Ibid., p. 281.
9  Files kept at the Archives de l'Académie de médecine. I worked on these for 2 years in collaboration with J. P. Peter, which gave rise to the following article: J. P. Peter, 'Entre femmes et médecins', *Ethnologie francaise*, 3–4 (1976), pp. 341–8.
10  Archives of the Royal Society of Medicine, p. 179.
11  The title of a book with engravings which appeared in Paris in 1775: Regnault, *Les Ecarts de la Nature ou recueil des principales monstruosités* (Paris, 1775).
12  Mercier, *Parallèle de Paris et de Londres*, with notes and comments on this previously unpublished work by Claude Bruneteau and Bernard Cottret (Paris, 1982), ch. 54: 'De l'histoire des revenants à Paris. Et des revenants à Londres', pp. 162–3.
13  Mercier, *Tableau de Paris*, 'L'Eglise de Sainte-Geneviève'.
14  As regards the Carnival he restates the idea of the sharing of social customs: 'the *canaille* laughing in the roads and thoroughfares and the *beau monde* on the velvet benches of the orchestra and amphitheatres'.
15  Mercier, *Tableau de Paris*, ch. 'Le Suisse de la rue aux Ours'.
16  Ibid., ch. 'Miracles'.
17  N. Delamare, *Traité de la Police*, 4 vols (1705–1738), Book III, section VII: 'Magiciens, Sorciers, Devineurs', p. 562.
18  Bibliothèque Nationale, Delamare Collection, MS frs. 21605, fol. 79.
19  Archives de la Bastille, Ravaisson, vol. XVI, 1749 to 1757, p. 144 'Affaire Godefrin', 1753.
20  Ibid., vol. XIV, p. 317, 'Affaire Forcassy'.
21  J. Peuchet, *Mémoires tirés des archives de la police de Paris*, 6 vols in 3 books (Paris, 1838).
22  AN, AD III 9. Decree by the *Cour du Parlement*, 20 December 1758, pp. 98–103 condemning R. Pons to the *amende honorable* and to life in the galleys for having taken advantage of the rituals and prayers of the Church and the gullibility of the common people. Indignant handwritten note by Gueulette that this drunken and degenerate priest had failed to be sentenced to death.
23  Also on this subject, one should recall the previous passage concerning the position of the police in relation to the world of work; they dreamt of the

existence of a long chain of individuals who could be controlled by one man at the top by a series of orders which would be calmly transmitted from one level to the next. This vertical view of society should be seen parallel with the idea of being 'on the spot' even to the extent of living in with the occupant.

24 R. Chartier, 'La Ville acculturante', in *Histoire de la France urbaine*, vol. 3 (Paris, 1981).

25 'Approximately' because the first paper could not be located: that is the first account announcing the child's pregnancy. We only have the sequel to the first account (AN, AD III 9) with handwritten notes and comments by Gueulette and the police 'Justification' which appeared later and which was found in the Archives de la Bastille (AB 11933). Mention is made there of a fourth printed document which was presumably published by the Ernault parents at the end of the affair, but it was not found. One should also make it clear that these 'accounts' are not dated.

26 The file in the Archives de la Bastille (AB 11933) is classified under the name of Renaud as suggested by the occasional reference, but for the most part the file and excerpts from interrogations and the police reports, bear the name of Ernault.

27 AN, AD III 9.

28 Archives de la Bastille, 10155–70. Bulletins of the secret police produced for the Lieutenant-General and several broadsheets containing day-by-day comments from court and town as they went respectively about the esplanades, drawing-rooms and cafés. It is effectively the journal of public opinion.

29 P. Peveri, 'L'Organisation et le fonctionnement de la police parisienne dans le premier quart du XVIIIᵉ siècle: quelques perspectives de recherches', 12 typewritten pages, 1984, produced as part of a seminar researching the history of the police, conducted in Paris by D. Roche.

30 *gazetins de la police secrète*: secret police bulletins.

31 Archives de la Bastille, MS 10155, fo. 131, 10 November 1725.

32 Ibid., MS 10167, fo. 200, 20 September 1740.

33 Ibid., MS 10167.

34 With the exception, however, of one of the registers which was kept by Officer Vanneroux, who was given special responsibility for the surveillance of cafés. One reads: 'At the Caffé de Cotton they were saying, "Well, what do you think of the orders from the Archbishop?" And the reply was . . .', AB 10170, fo. 96; 'at the Caffé de Foix they said that neither the priest of . . .', AB 10170, fo. 97; 'in several of the cafés on the Rue Saint-Honoré the only talk was of bread and meat . . .', AB 10170, fo. 110.

35 Mercier, *Tableau de Paris*, ch. 'Du merveilleux'.

36 Archives de la Bastille, MS 11940, for the year 1756.

37 MS 10269, 3rd Police Bureau of Health, for the year 1752.

38 Dr Pineau, *Mémoires sur le danger des inhumations précipitées et sur la nécessité d'un règlement pour mettre les citoyens à l'abri du malheur d'être enterrés vivants* (Paris, 1776); Carmont, *Mémoire sur le danger d'être enterré vif et sur les moyens de s'en garantir ou de s'en tirer* (Paris, 1787), BN TC⁵⁴11; Thesis by M. Vinshow, *Terrible supplice et cruel désespoir des personnes enterrées vivantes et qui sont présumées mortes* (Paris/London, 1752), BN TC⁵⁴5; Janin, Ch. *Réflexions sur le triste sort des personnes enterrées vivantes* (Paris, 1772).

39 R. Favre, *La Mort au siècle des Lumières* (Paris, 1978).

40  S. Hardy, 'Mes Loisirs, ou journal des événements tels qu'ils parviennent à ma connaissance', BN MS fr. 6684, 16 September 1783.
41  Ibid., 22 December 1783.

## Chapter 10   The Crowds in Turmoil

1   L.-S. Mercier, *Tableau de Paris*, 12 vols (Amsterdam, 1782–6), ch. 'Emeutes'.
2   N. T. des Essarts, *Dictionnaire universel de police*, 7 vols (Paris, 1786–9), vol. 7, S.V. 'Ouvriers'.
3   S. Kaplan, 'Le Complot de famine: histoire d'une rumeur au XVIII$^e$ siècle', in *Cahiers des Annales* (Paris, 1982).
4   These were quite often detailed complaints, occasionally resulting in the immediate imprisonment of one or two persons picked up by the police, There would be no judgement or ruling following the imprisonment and therefore no further traces. Only the great revolts of 1720, 1740, 1750 and 1775 left behind lengthy files which can be found in the Archives Nationales.
      Note, however, that a systematic enquiry undertaken through the efforts of J. Nicolas, professor at the University of Paris VII, will allow the assessment and mapping of these movements throughout the whole of France.
5   H. Taine, *Les Origines de la France contemporaine* (1876–94); G. de Tarde, *La Philosophie pénale* (Paris, 1890); S. Sighele, *La Foule criminelle* (Paris, 1891); G. Le Bon, *The Crowd: a study of the Popular Mind* (Harmondsworth, 1977); G. de Tarde, *L'Opinion et la foule* (1901); S. Freud, *Group Psychology and the Analysis of the Ego*, 1921.
6   Quatrième Semaine internationale de Synthèse, 1932, directed by H. Berr, papers by Bohn, Alphandéry, Lefebvre, Hardy, Dupréel, pub. by Alcan, 1934. This lecture was also published in 1934 in *Annales historiques de la Révolution française*. One can also find it in the book by G. Lefebvre, *Etudes sur la Révolution française* (Paris, 2nd edn, 1963), pp. 371–2.
7   G. Rudé, *The Crowd in the French Revolution*, preface by G. Lefebvre, Oxford Univ. Press, 1959.
8   J. Michelet, *La Révolution française*, 9 vols (Paris, 1868–1900), vol. 1, pp. 377–9. Originally published from 1847 to 1853.
9   E. Burke, *Reflections on the Revolution in France* (London, 1951), pp. 66–9.
10  R. Cobb, *The Police and the People: French Popular Protest, 1789–1820* (Oxford, 1970); E. P. Thompson, 'The Moral Economy of the English Crowd of XVIIIth Century', *Past and Present*, 50 (1971); N. Z. Davis, *Society and Culture in Early Modern France* (Stanford, Calif., 1975); Y. M. Bercé, *History of Peasant Revolts: The Social Origins of Rebellion in Early Modern France*, tr. A. Whitmore (Cambridge, 1990); id., *Croquants et Nu-pieds. Les soulèvements paysans en France du XVI$^e$ au XIX$^e$ siècle* (Paris, 1974); id., *Fête et révolte. Des mentalités populaires du XVI$^e$ au XVIII$^e$ siècle* (Paris, 1976); S. Moscovici, *The Age of the Crowd* (Cambridge, 1985); J. Beauchard, *La Puissance des foules* (Paris, 1985).
11  M. Maffesoli, and A. Pessin, *La Violence fondatrice* (Paris, 1978), pp. 97–120: 'Le désir du collectif'.
12  J. Rancière, *La Nuit des prolétaires, archives du rêve ouvrier* (Paris, 1981), p. 30.
13  S. Kaplan, 'Réflexions sur la police du monde du travail 1700–1815', *Revue Historique*, 529 (January–March 1979), p. 32.

14  In 1708 and 1724, strike also by journeymen hosiers; in 1746 plots by locksmiths and in 1768 action by painters in building industry and in 1785 by building workers, at least according to Kaplan, ibid.

15  J. Hayem, *La Répression des grèves au XVIII$^e$ siècle. Mémoires et documents pour servir à l'histoire du commerce et de l'industrie en France* (Paris, 1911).

16  Bibliothèque de l'Arsenal. Archives de la Bastille, MS 10152, 24 May 1727.

17  AN, Y 9500, 20 March 1756.

18  Ibid., Y 14081, 22 April 1755.

19  Ibid., Y 11004A and Y 11004B, Commissioner Hugues, for the year 1763.

20  On this subject see ch. 6.

21  AN, Y 9533, 1 November 1748.

22  Ibid., Y 13242, 28 December 1755.

23  Archives de la Bastille, MS 10846, for the year 1724.

24  Ibid., MS 11590, for the year 1764.

25  Ibid., MS 12202 and 11261, for the year 1764.

26  Ibid., MS 11132, for the year 1731.

27  Ibid., MS 11590, for the year 1746.

28  Ibid., MS 11132, for the year 1731.

29  Ibid., MS 10846, for the year 1724.

30  Ibid., MS 10321, undated.

31  J.-P. Lenoir, 'Mémoires manuscrits', Bibliothèque municipale d'Orléans, MS 1423, fo. 225 (memoirs, jottings and letters for and against the proposal for the re-establishment of the trades and crafts corporations).

32  N. T. des Essarts, *Dictionnaire universel de police*. vol. 7, S.V. 'Ouvriers'.

33  Archives de la Bastille, MS 10014, Correspondence of the Lieutenant-General of Police for the year 1745–6.

34  1740: prison revolt at Bicêtre, AN, inventory 450. Archives de la Bastille, MS 10167; 1749: revolt by women at La Salpêtrière, ibid. MS 10138; 1763: conspiracy at Bicêtre, ibid. MS 12184.

35  P. Krumnow, 'Les Rébellions populaires contre les employés de la ferme, 1775–1789', 'maîtrise' in history at the University of Paris VII, 1976.

36  A. Farge, and J. Revel, *The Rules of Rebellion: Child Abductions in Paris in 1750*, trans. C. Miéville (Cambridge, 1991).

37  Cf. p. 9.

38  AN X$^{2B}$ 1367, 8 June 1750.

39  Places: commodities. Cf. H. Guerrand, *Histoire des lieux* (Paris, 1985).

40  *ecce homo*: St John 19: 5.

41  Y. M. Bercé,: 'Les Femmes dans les révoltes populaires', in *La femme à l'époque moderne XVI$^e$, XVIII$^e$ siècle*. Discussion papers from 1984 symposium. Issue 9 of the Association of Modern University Historians, PUPS.

42  A. Ehrenberg, 'Les Hooligans ou la passion d'être égal', *Esprit* (August/September 1985), pp. 7–13.

# Glossary

| | |
|---|---|
| *amende honorable* | public apology/formal act of penance |
| *archers* | police/armed guards (formerly bowmen) |
| *cabaret* | tavern |
| *canaille* | the mob/riff-raff (lit. dogs) |
| *chambrelans* | workers plying their trade outside the craft-guild system |
| *faubourgs* | districts outside city limits. Nowadays, suburbs; eighteenth-century connotation, workers' districts |
| Garde française | militia |
| *hôpital* | workhouse/orphanage/house of correction |
| *hôtel* | offices, administrative headquarters (e.g. of police); originally = mansion or grand house (*hôtel particulier*) |
| *hôtel-dieu* | general hospital |
| *hôtel de ville* | town hall |
| *lettre de cachet* | royal order issued under the King's personal seal |
| *misérabilisme* | a tendency to focus on the mean and wretched |
| *monts-de-piété* | charitable institutions, which developed into 'municipal credit' organizations, and eventually into pawnbrokers |
| *mouchards/mouches* | police spies/informers (cf. 'fly on the wall') |
| *nuit blanche* | sleepless night; night before an execution |
| Parc civil | magistrates' court |
| La Salpêtrière | women's prison for prostitutes and vagrants; later developed into a lunatic asylum, then a general hospital |
| *syndic* | guild officials and magistrates |

# Select Bibliography

_____

This book has been written from manuscript sources and the judicial archives of the 18th century, the details of which can be found below. The reading of recent work has obviously contributed to the development of the discussion and titles are therefore given of those which have been most helpful.

## MANUSCRIPT SOURCES

### Archives Nationales

*Series* Y

Châtelet de Paris and provostship of the Ile-de-France.
Chamber of the King's Procurator: adjudication of institutions related to trade, commerce and crafts (9372–95).
Chambre de police: Overall jurisdiction of matters relating to security of Paris.
9397–9492: Records of sentences passed on the basis of reports received, 1750–89.
9499: Records of police instructions and sentences, 1731–89.
9500: Advice by the Lieutenant-General of Police on the security of Paris, 1750–89.
9523–31: Proceedings on the basis of information received in the Chambre de police against journeymen joiners, wigmakers, etc.
9649–10718: Criminal courts:
  • complaints brought before the *Petit Criminel* 9649–10017
  • complaints brought before the *Grand Criminel* 10018–10509
  • 10620–35: Reports by the *guet* (Watch).
10719–17623: Matters dealt with by the Police Commissioner at Le Châtelet; it is impossible to give a detailed list here of all the bundles of papers studied – the references for each particular matter are given in the chapter notes.

## Series X

The *Parlement* of Paris and in particular $X^{2B}$ 1368–9 on the revolt of 1750 and the question of the abduction of children.

# Bibliothèque de l'Arsenal

## Archives de la Bastille

Hundreds and thousands of documents dealing with everyday police business in the eighteenth century are kept under this title; files on prisoners held by order of the King and *lettres de cachet*; the registers of the police inspectors which were kept on a daily basis; archives of the various police bureaux; security reports; actions and proceedings by street patrols; papers issued by the ministry of the Lieutenance générale de Paris.

10001–16: Correspondence of the Lieutenant-General of Paris.

10018: Papers of Lieutenant-General of Police Hérault.

10092–118: Reports by police inspectors and proceedings by the commissioners at Le Châtelet referred to the Lieutenant-General of Police, 1727–75.

10119–28: Security reports and lists of arrests and declarations made in the three departments of the officers responsible for security, 1760–73.

10129–33: Records kept by the commissioners at Le Châtelet of the patrols carried out in the streets of Paris and of visits by inspectors, commissioners and officers to *cabarets*, billiard-halls and other suspect places, 1750–75.

10137: Register in which Inspector Roussel kept the records of proceedings sent from him to the Lieutenant of Police as well as complaints and declarations which had been sent to him along with his own observations concerning the peace and security of Paris, 1746–51.

10140: Register containing the alphabetical table of persons arrested by Poussot, Inspector in the district of Les Halles 1738–54.

10149–54: Cases appearing before the Lieutenant of Police and subsequent decisions by the Lieutenant, 1725–57.

10155–70: Bulletins of the secret police produced for the Lieutenant-General and several broadsheets containing notes made on the day-by-day comments from town, court, esplanades, drawing-rooms and cafés, 1725–81.

10282: Sixth bureau, public safety and security, the Watch and the militia.

10283–93: Surveillance of strangers and foreigners.

10998–11020: Prisoners' files for the year 1728.

11696–734: Prisoners' files for the year 1750.

11660–2: Absconded workers, 1750.

11920–46: Prisoners' files for the year 1756.

12173–99: Prisoners' files for the year 1763.

12441–3: Prisoners' files for the year 1775.

## Manuscripts at the Bibliothèque de l'Arsenal

3244: Book of police discipline and procedures containing details of the necessary steps to be taken in order to conform to the orders of the King, 1 March 1777.

3532: 'Paradox: that young women should either marry or go mad', eighteenth century.

3656: 'Man's superiority over woman', by Bocquel in 1740.

3657: 'New thoughts on women, by a lady at the court', 1728.

3724: Fevret de Fontette Collection, vol. II, fo. 240, 'Lamentation on the subject of the fire in the city of Paris for the marriage of the Dauphin', 1770.
6115: Various items for Feydeau de Marville, Lieutenant-General of Police.


## Bibliothèque Nationale

### French Manuscripts

6680–7: S. Hardy, 'Mes loisirs on journal des événements tels qu'ils parviennent à ma connaissance' (1764–89).
11366–7: Collection of items concerning the *monts-de-piété*.

### Joly de Fleury Collection

1101–2: 1750 revolt.
1249: Hôpital de la Trinité for the apprenticeship of poor children.
1307–8: Begging, 1724–41, 1750–1.
1329–30: Guild police.
1413–14: Police, cleaning of the streets, revolt of 1774, Shrine of Sainte-Geneviève.
2074–7: Subversive talk, procedures taken in Paris and the provinces from 1756 to 1775 to deal with seditious comments and proposals against the King, the *Parlement* and religion.
2414–32: Law and administration.
2541–3: Accidents of May 1770, *Mont-de-Piété*, trade and craft guilds.

### New acquisitions in French

1989: Essay on the poor and begging, eighteenth century.
9328: Emigration to the colonies, seventeenth to nineteenth centuries.


## Archives of the Prefecture of the Paris Police

### Series AA

Royal Prisons, boxes 4–8 (1660–1756).

### Series AB

362–83: King's Orders, 1750–87.
390: September 1750, February 1775, register of memos of police business.
392–3: Names and judgements passed on persons arrested for theft.
396–404: Registers of criminal proceedings, eighteenth century.
405: Reports on posters and further police clarifications, 1779–86, in the district of Saint-Denis, Inspector Santerre.

### Lamoignon Collection

List of edicts and police orders and instructions dated 1184 to 1763.

## Bibliothèque historique de la Ville de Paris

MS 29618: Documents on police organization as it existed in 1789.
MS 29736: General police matters and those arising from the *hôtel de Paris* in the year 1753.
NA 66: Contracts of apprenticeship, eighteenth century.

## Bibliothèque municipale d'Orléans

MSS 1421–4: 'Mémoires manuscrits' of J.-P. Lenoir (1732–1807), Lieutenant-General of Police in Paris between 1775 and 1776, then from 1776 to 1785.

## PRINTED SOURCES: PERIOD DOCUMENTS

### 1 Dictionaries and general encyclopedias

Brillon, P. J., *Dictionnaire des arrêts, ou Jurisprudence universelle des Parlements de France et autres tribunaux*, Paris, 1711.
*Encyclopédie, ou Dictionnaire raisonné des sciences, des arts et des métiers par une société de gens de lettres*, ed. Diderot and d'Alembert, 34 vols, Paris, 1751.
*Encyclopédie méthodique*, 206 vols, Paris, 1787–1825. Police and municipalities. Jurisprudence.
Ferrière, *Dictionnaire de droit et de pratique*, 2 vols, Toulouse, 1779.

### 2 Police treatises

Bielfeld, Baron de, 'Traité de Police', 1762, in a work entitled *Institutions politiques*, 2 vols,
Delamare, N., *Traité de la Police*, 4 vols, 1705–38.
Essarts, N. T. des, *Dictionnaire universel de police*, 7 vols, Paris, 1786–9.
Poix de Freminville, E. de La, *Dictionnaire ou traité de police générale des villes, bourgs, paroisses et seigneuries de la campagne*, Paris, 1758.

### 3 Legal treatises, works by jurists on the police and criminal justice

Beccaria, C., *Discours sur les moyens de prévenir les crimes en France*, Paris, 1781.
Beccaria, C., *Traité des délits et des peines*, Paris, 1773. repr. Paris, 1979.
Brissot de Warville, J. P., *Les Moyens d'adoucir la rigueur des lois*, Châlons-sur-Marne, 1781.
Ciamarelli, *Traité philosophique et politique de la peine de mort*, Mantua, 1789.
Dareau, F., *Traité des injures dans l'ordre judiciaire, ouvrage qui renferme particulièrement la jurisprudence du Petit Criminel*, Paris, 1775.
Dupaty, Ch., *Lettres sur la procédure criminelle de la France, dans lesquelles on montre sa conformité avec celle de l'Inquisition et les abus qui en résultent*, Paris, 1788.
Jousse, D., *Traité de la justice criminelle de France*, Paris, 1771.
Lemaire, J.-Ch., *La Police de Paris en 1770*, pub. 1863 [memoirs of a commissioner written on Sartine's instructions].

Letrosne, M., *Vues sur la justice criminelle*, Orléans, 1771.

Mille, J. de, *Pratique criminelle*, pub. Paris, 1983.

Muyart de vouglans, P. F., *Institutes au droit criminel, ou principes généraux en ces matières*, Paris, 1757.

Risi, P., *Observations sur les matières de jurisprudence criminelle*, Milan, 1768.

Sallé, J., *Traité des fonctions, droits et privilèges des commissaires au Châtelet de Paris*, 2 vols, Paris, 1759.

Vermeil, F. M., *Essai sur les réformes à faire dans notre législation criminelle*, 2 vols, Paris, 1781.

Willebrand, J. P., *Abrégé de la police accompagné de réflexions sur l'accroissement des villes*, Hamburg, 1765.

## 4   Sources relating to Paris

Brice, G., *Description de la ville de Paris et de tout ce qu'elle contient de plus remarquable*, 4 vols, Paris, 1752.

Denis, L., *Itinéraire portatif, ou guide historique et géographique du voyageur dans les environs de Paris*, Paris, 1781.

Dulaure, J. A., *Histoire physique, civile et morale de Paris*, Paris, 1786.

Hurtaut, et Magny, P. N., *Dictionnaire historique de la ville de Paris et de ses environs*, 4 vols, Paris, 1779.

Jèze, *Etat ou tableau de la ville de Paris*, Paris, 1760.

Pujoulx, J. P., *Paris à la fin du XVIIIe siècle*, Paris, 1801.

Thiéry, M. J., *Almanach du voyageur à Paris*, Paris, 1783–5.

## 5   Chronicles, documents, memoirs

Barbier, E. J., *Chroníque de la régence et du règne de Louis XV, 1718–1763*, 8 vols, Paris, 1857.

Boislisle, A. M. de, *Lettres de M. de Marville, lieutenant général de police au ministre Maurepas, 1742–1747*, 3 vols, Paris, 1896–1905.

Larchey, ed. Loredan, *Documents inédits sur le règne de Louis XV, ou le journal des inspecteurs de M. le lieutenant de police de Sartine*, Brussels and Paris, 1863, from partly published MSS 11357–60 in the Bibliothèque Nationale.

Lescure, M. A. de, *Correspondance secrète inédite sur Louis XVI, Marie-Antoinette, la cour et la ville de 1777 à 1792*, 2 vols, Paris, 1866.

Manuel, P., *La Police de Paris dévoilée par l'un des administrateurs de 1789*, 2 vols, Paris, year II [1793–4].

Ménétra, J. L., *Journal de ma vie, compagnon vitrier au XVIIIe siècle*, ed. and pref. D. Roche, Paris, 1982.

Mercier, L.-S., *Tableau de Paris*, 12 vols, Amsterdam, 1782–6.

Mercier, L.-S., *Parallèle de Paris et de Londres*, ed. Cl. Bruneteau and B. Cottret, Paris, 1982.

Peuchet, J., *Mémoires tirés des archives de la police de Paris*, 6 vols, Paris, 1838.

Raunie, E., *Chansonnier historique du XVIIIe siècle*, 10 vols, Paris, 1879–94.

Retif de la Bretonne, N. E., *Les Nuits de Paris*, 2 vols, Paris, 1930.

## More recent works

Ariès, Ph., *Centuries of Childhood*, Harmondsworth, 1979. Paris, 1960.

Aries, Ph., *The Hour of Our Death*, London, 1981.

Bardet, J.-P., *Rouen aux XVIIᵉ et XVIIIᵉ siècles*, 2 vols, Paris, 1983.

Bercé, Y. M., *History of Peasant Revolts: The Social Origins of Rebellion in Early Modern France*, tr. A. Whitmore, Cambridge, 1990.

Bercé, Y. M., *Fête et révolte. Des mentalités populaires du XVIᵉ au XVIIIᵉ siècle*, Paris, Hachette, 1976.

Bollême, G., *La Bible bleue, anthologie d'une littérature 'populaire'*, Paris, 1975.

Camporesi, P., *Bread of Dreams: Food and Fantasy in Early Modern Europe*, Cambridge, 1989.

Castan, N., *Justice et répression en Languedoc à l'époque des Lumières*, Paris, 1980.

Castan, N., *Les Criminels du Languedoc*, Toulouse, University of Toulouse, 1980.

Castan, N., and Castan, Y., *Vivre ensemble, Ordre et désordre en Languedoc, XVIIᵉ–XVIIIᵉ siècle*, Paris, 1981.

Castan, Y., *Honnêteté et relations sociales en Languedoc, 1715–1780*, Paris, 1974.

Chartier, R., 'La Ville dominante et soumise', in *Histoire de la France urbaine*, vol. 2, Paris, 1981.

Chartier, R., Julia, D., and Compère, M. M., *L'Education en France du XVIᵉ au XVIIIᵉ siècle*, Paris, 1976.

Chassaigne, M., *La Lieutenance générale de police de Paris*, Paris, 1906.

Chaunu, P., *La Mort à Paris*, Paris, 1978.

Chesnais, J.-Cl., *L'Histoire de la violence*, Paris, 1981.

Claverie, E., and Lamaison, P., *L'Impossible mariage. Violence et parenté en Gévaudan*, Paris, 1982.

Cobb, R., *The Police and the People: French Popular Protest, 1789–1820*, Oxford, 1970.

Compère, M. M., *Du Collège au lycée, 1500–1850*, Paris, 1985.

Darnton, R., *The Business of Enlightenment: a publishing history of the 'Encyclopedie'*, London, 1979.

Darnton, R., *La Fin des Lumières. Le Mesmérisme et la Révolution*. Paris, 1984; 1st edn. 1968.

Darnton, R., *Bohême littéraire et Révolution, le monde des livres au XVIIIᵉ siècle*, Paris, 1983.

Darnton, R., *The Great Cat Massacre, and Other Episodes in French Cultural History*, Harmondsworth 1985.

Davis, N. Z., *Society and Culture in Early Modern France*, Stanford, Calif., 1975.

Dessertine, D., *Divorcer à Lyon sous la Révolution et l'Empire*, Lyons, 1981.

Delumeau, J., *La Peur en Occident, XIVᵉ–XVIIIᵉ siècle*, Paris, 1978.

Delumeau, J., *Le Péché et la peur*, Paris, 1983.

Duby, G., *The Knight the Lady and the Priest*, London, 1984.

Elias, N., *The Civilizing Process*, Oxford, 1978.

Farge, A., *Vivre dans la rue à Paris au XVIIIᵉ siècle*, Paris, 1979.

Farge, A., *Le Miroir des femmes, textes de la Bibliothèque bleue*, Paris, 1982.

Farge, A., and Foucault M., *Le Désordre des familles. Lettres de cachet à Paris au XVIIIᵉ siècle*, Paris, 1982.

Favre, R., *La Mort au siècle des Lumières*, Lyons, 1978.

Flandrin, J.-L., *Les Amours paysannes*, Paris, 1975.

Flandrin, J.-L., *Families in Former Times*, Cambridge, 1979.

Flandrin, J.-L., English edn: *Families in Former Times: Kinship, Household* and *Sexuality*, trans. Richard Southern, Cambridge, 1979.

Flandrin, J.-L., *Le Sexe et l'Occident*, Paris, 1981.

Foucault, M., *Discipline and Punish: The Birth of the prison*, Sheridan, London, 1977.

Foucault, M., *The History of Sexuality*: vol. II, *Care of the Self*; vol. III, *The Use of Pleasure*, London, 1987.

Garden, M., *Lyon et les Lyonnais au XVIII^e siècle*, Lyons, 1970.

Gélis, J., *History of Childbirth: Fertility, Pregnancy and Birth in Early Modern Europe*, Cambridge, 1991.

Goffman, E., *Forms of Talk*, Oxford, 1981; *The Presentation of Self in Everyday Life*, London, 1969; *Stigma: Notes on the Management of Spoiled Identity*, New Jersey, 1964; *Interaction Ritual: Essays on Face-to-Face Behaviour*, New York, 1967; *Relations in Public: Microstudies of the Public Order*, New York, 1971.

Goubert, J.-P., and Roche, D., *Les Français et l'Ancien Régime*, 2 vols, Paris, 1984.

Ginzburg, C., *The Cheese and the Worms*, London, 1980.

Gutton, J.-P., *La Société et les Pauvres, l'exemple de la généralité de Lyon, XVIII^e siècle*, Paris, 1980.

Hoggart, R., *The Uses of Literacy*, London, 1957.

Hufton, O. H., *The Poor of the Eighteenth Century, 1750–1789*, Oxford, 1974.

Jouhaud, C., *Mazarinades, la Fronde des mots*, Paris, 1985.

Kaplan, S., *Le Complot de famine: Histoire d'une rumeur au XVIII^e siècle*, Paris, Colin, 1982.

Kaplan, S., *Provisioning Paris*, Ithaca, NY, 1984.

Kaplow, J., *Les noms des rois, les pauvres de Paris à la veille de la Révolution*, Paris, 1974.

Lebrun, F., *La Vie conjugale sous l'Ancien Régime*, Paris, 1975.

Le Roy Ladurie, E., *Carnival of Romans*, Harmondsworth, 1981.

Maire, C. L., *Les Convulsionnaires de Saint-Médard, Prophéties, miracles et convulsions à Paris au XVIII^e siècle*, Paris, 1985.

Marin, L., *Portrait of the King*, Basingstoke, 1988.

Mandrou, R., *La France aux XVII^e et XVIII^e siècles*, Paris, 1967.

Martin, H.-J., *Livre, pouvoir et société à Paris au XVIII^e siècle*, Paris, 1969.

Meyer, J., *La France moderne*: vol. III, *Histoire de France*, Paris, 1985.

Moscovici, S., *The Age of the Crowd*, Cambridge, 1985.

Nicolas J., (ed.), *Mouvements populaires et conscience sociale, XVI^e–XIX^e siècle*, Paris, 1985.

Ozouf, M., *Festivals and the French Revolution*, Cambridge, 1988.

Ozouf, M., *L'Ecole de la France*, Paris, 1985.

Perrot, J.-Cl., *Caen au XVIII^e siècle, genèse d'une ville moderne*, Paris, 1975.

Pétonnet, C., *On est tous dans le brouillard. Ethnologie des banlieues*, Paris, 1979.

Poitrineau, A., *Remues d'hommes, migrations montagnardes en France au XVIII^e siècle*, Paris, 1983.

Rancière, J., *La Nuit des prolétaires, archives du rêve ouvrier*, Paris, Fayard, 1981.

Retat P., (ed.), *L'Attentat de Damiens, discours sur l'événement au XVIII^e siècle*, Lyons, 1979.

Roche, D., *The People of Paris*, Leamington Spa, 1987.

Roche, D., Preface to Ménétra, *Journal de ma vie* [see section 5 above].

Rudé, G., *The Crowd in the French Revolution*, Greenwood, 1986.

Sewell, W. H., *Work and Revolution in France*, Cambridge, 1980.

Van Kley, D., *The Damiens Affair and the Unraveling of the Ancient Regime, 1750–1770*, Princeton, NJ, Princeton University Press, 1984.

Williams, A., *The Police of Paris, 1718–1789*, Baton Rouge, Louisiana, 1979.

# Index

Lightning Source UK Ltd.
Milton Keynes UK
04 March 2011

9 780745 612430